THE NORMANS IN THE SOUTH

By the same author

Mount Athos (with Reresby Sitwell)

THE NORMANS IN
THE SOUTH
1016–1130

JOHN JULIUS NORWICH

LONGMANS

LONGMANS, GREEN AND CO LTD
48 Grosvenor Street London W1
*Associated companies, branches and representatives
throughout the world*

© *John Julius Norwich 1967*

First published 1967

*Printed in Great Britain by The Camelot Press Ltd,
London and Southampton*

For Anne

For Anne

CONTENTS

LIST OF ILLUSTRATIONS

Genealogical trees

Maps

No chapter of history more resembles a romance than that which records the sudden rise and brief splendour of the house of Hauteville. In one generation the sons of Tancred passed from the condition of squires in the Norman vale of Cotentin, to kinghood in the richest island of the southern sea. The Norse adventurers became Sultans of an Oriental capital. The sea-robbers assumed together with the sceptre the culture of an Arabian court. The marauders whose armies burned Rome received at papal hands the mitre and dalmatic as symbols of ecclesiastical jurisdiction.

JOHN ADDINGTON SYMONDS,
Sketches in Italy and Greece

INTRODUCTION

In October 1961 my wife and I went on a holiday to Sicily. I think I was vaguely aware that the Normans had ruled there some time in the Middle Ages, but I certainly knew very little else. At any rate I was totally unprepared for what I found. Here were cathedrals, churches and palaces which seemed to combine, without effort or strain, all that was loveliest in the art and architecture of the three leading civilisations of the time—the North European, the Byzantine and the Saracen. Here, in the dead centre of the Mediterranean, was the bridge between North and South, East and West, Latin and Teuton, Christian and Muslim; superb, unanswerable testimony to an age of tolerance and enlightenment on a scale unknown anywhere else in mediaeval Europe and, even in succeeding centuries, seldom equalled. I became very over-excited and longed to know more. The holidays over, I took the only sensible course and made straight for the London Library.

I was in for a sad surprise. A few works, mostly in French or German, of formidable nineteenth-century scholarship and paralysing dullness, lurked on an upper shelf; but for the ordinary English reader, seeking merely a general account of Norman Sicily, there was practically nothing. For a moment I almost wondered whether that most invaluable and trustworthy of all English institutions had let me down at last; at the same time, I knew perfectly well that it hadn't. If the London Library did not possess the sort of book I wanted, it could only be because no such book was in existence. And so it was that I first came face to face with a question which, after five years, still has me baffled: why is it that one of the most extraordinary and fascinating epics of European history between the ages of Julius Caesar and Napoleon should be so little known to the world at large? Even in France any reference to the subject is apt to be greeted by a blank expression and a faintly embarrassed silence; while in England, which after all suffered a similar—though far less exciting—Norman conquest of its own at almost exactly the same time and was later to provide Sicily with several statesmen and even a queen, the general bewilderment seems to be yet greater. M. Ferdinand Chalandon, author of the still definitive work on the period, included in his monumental bibliography of well over six hundred items only one English author, Gibbon; and though in the sixty intervening years this country has produced a number of scholars, magnificently led by Miss Evelyn Jamison, who have hacked out many a clearing and planted their flags in the darker corners of the forest, to this day I know of only two non-specialist works in English which tell even part of the story in any detail: E. Curtis's *Roger of Sicily*, written with a conscientious if somewhat heavy hand shortly before the First World War, and *The Greatest Norman Conquest*—there's a give-away title if you like—by Mr J. Van Wyck Osborne, whose thoughtful scholarship is endlessly sabotaged by the exuberance of his imagination. Both these books, incidentally, were published in New York; both are long out of print; and neither covers the whole period.

The conclusion was inescapable: if I wanted a complete history of Norman Sicily in English for the average reader, I should have to write it myself. And that is how it comes about that I now put forward, gingerly and with much diffidence, the first of two volumes which will together carry the story through from the first day, in 1016, when a party of Norman pilgrims was accosted in the shrine of the Archangel Michael on Monte Gargano, to the last, a hundred and seventy-eight years later, when the brightest crown of the Mediterranean passed to one of the blackest of the German Emperors. The present volume covers the first hundred and fourteen of those years and closes on Christmas Day 1130, when Sicily at last became a kingdom, and Roger II her king. They are the epic years, the years of endeavour and conquest, dominated by the sons and grandsons of Tancred de Hauteville and, above all, by the towering bulk of Robert Guiscard, one of history's few military adventurers of genius to have started from nothing and died undefeated. Thereafter the mood changes; northern harshness softens in the sun; and the clash of steel slowly dies away, giving place to the whisper of fountains in a shaded patio and the ripple of plucked strings. Thus the second volume will tell of the golden age of Norman Sicily, the age of Cefalu, of Monreale and the Palatine Chapel at Palermo; and then, sadly, of its decline and collapse. True, its spirit was to live on for another half-century in Frederick II, *Stupor Mundi*, the greatest of Renaissance princes two hundred years before his time, and in his lovely son Manfred. But Frederick, though a Hauteville on his mother's side and by his upbringing, was also a Hohenstaufen and an Emperor. His is a glorious, tragic story; but it is not ours.

This book makes no claim to original scholarship. Apart from anything else, I am no scholar. Despite eight years of what is still optimistically known as a classical education and a recent agonising refresher course, my Latin remains poor and my Greek worse. Though I have all too often had to struggle through contemporary sources in the original, I have gratefully seized on translations wherever they have been available and duly noted them in the bibliography; and though I have tried to read as widely as possible around the subject so as to fit the story into the general European context, I do not pretend to have unearthed any new material or to have put forward any startlingly original conclusions. The same goes for fieldwork. I think I have visited every site of importance mentioned in this book (many of them in unspeakably adverse weather) but my researches in local libraries and archives have been brief and—except in the Vatican—largely unfruitful. No matter. My purpose was simply, as I have said, to provide ordinary readers with the sort of book I wished I had had on my first visit to Sicily—something that would explain how the Normans got there in the first place, what sort of a country they made of it, and how they managed to imbue it with a culture at once so beautiful and so unique. Pausing now for breath, I only wish that I could do them greater justice.

ACKNOWLEDGEMENTS

Among the many friends in Italy who have helped and advised me with this book, I should like in particular to thank Dr and Mrs Milton Gendel for all their hospitality as well as for much historical expertise; Miss Georgina Masson, whose deep knowledge of mediaeval Italy and many bibliographical suggestions were invaluable; the Duchessa Lante della Rovere for immensely useful research; Dom Angelo Mifsud, O.S.B., archivist of the Badia della Cava, Salerno; Conte Dr Sigmund Fago Golfarelli, head of the Press Department of the Ente Nazionale Italiano per il Turismo; and the late Father Guy Ferrari, whose recent untimely death is a sad blow for the Vatican Library and for all who work there.

In England I am especially grateful to Dr Jonathan Riley-Smith, whose kindness and erudition have saved me from many a nasty slip. Sir Steven Runciman and Mr Sacheverell Sitwell and their publishers, the Clarendon Press and Messrs Gerald Duckworth & Co., Ltd, have kindly allowed me to quote from their work; and I am also indebted to Messrs Routledge and Kegan Paul Ltd and to Messrs Thomas Nelson & Sons Ltd for their permission to reproduce material from Miss E. Dawes's translation of *The Alexiad* and Professor R. W. Southern's translation of Eadmer's *Vita Anselmi*. Professor Nancy Lambton of London University took endless trouble to track down the Iqbal poem which provides the epigraph for Chapter 13. The translation from the original Urdu was made specially for me by her late colleague, Mr G. D. Gaur—a spontaneous gesture to an unknown enquirer for which I fear I did not thank him adequately in his lifetime. My thanks are also due to Mr C. R. Ligota of the Warburg Institute and to several, alas anonymous, members of the staff of the Bibliothèque Nationale in Paris.

But my deepest gratitude goes to my cousin, Mr Rupert

Hart-Davis. No one understands better than he how a book should be written: no one could have given more generously of his time, experience and wisdom. My debt to him is enormous—and is shared, more than they know, by my readers, for if this book is found to be at all readable, it is due in large measure to him. Here is a debt which can be acknowledged, but never repaid.

Virtually every word of what follows has been written in the Reading Room of the London Library; and it only remains for me to echo the words of so many thousand authors before me—that without the Library's inexhaustible resources, supplemented by the patience, sympathy and good humour of every member of its staff, I do not see how my work could ever, possibly, have been done.

London, 1966   J. J. N.

Note: Translations, except where otherwise indicated, are my own.

PART ONE

THE CONQUEST

I

BEGINNINGS

His starrie Holme unbuckl'd shew'd him prime
In manhood where youth ended; by his side
As in a glistering *Zodiac* hung the Sword,
Satan's dire dread, and in his hand the Spear.

Paradise Lost, Book XI

To the traveller, heading eastwards from Foggia to the sea, the gaunt
grey shadow of Monte Gargano looms over the plain like a thunder-
cloud. It is a curious excrescence, this dark limestone mass rising so
unexpectedly from the fields of Apulia and, heedless of the gentle
sweep of the coastline, jutting forty miles or so into the Adriatic—
curious and somehow awesome. For centuries it has been known as
the 'spur' of Italy—not a very good name even from the pictorial
point of view, since it is much too far up the boot and seems to
have been fixed on backwards. It is more like a hard callus,
accidental, unlooked-for and basically unwelcome. Even the landscape, with its thick beech-forests, more Germanic than Italian;
even the climate, raw and torn by winds; even the population,
sombre, black-swathed and old (in contradistinction to anywhere
else in Apulia, where the average age of the urban population, to
all appearances exclusively male, seems to be about seven), bespeak
a strange foreignness. Monte Gargano, to visitors and natives alike,
is different. It does not really belong.

This feeling has always existed among the Apulians, and they
have always reacted to it in the same way. Since the days of remotest
antiquity an aura of holiness has hung over the mountain. Already
in classical times it possessed at least two important shrines, one to
Podaleirius—an ancient warrior-hero of small achievement and less

3

interest—and one to old Calchas, the soothsayer of the *Iliad*, where according to Strabo 'those who consult the oracle sacrifice to his shade a black ram and then sleep in the hide'. With the advent of Christianity these devotions continued, as frequently happened after the minimum of adjustment necessary to keep up with the times; so that by the fifth century, with a thousand years or so of uninterrupted sanctity behind it, the mountain was fully ripe for the miracle which then occurred. On 5 May in the year 493 a local cattle-owner, looking for a fine bull which he had lost, eventually found the animal in a dark cave, deep in the mountain-side. Repeated attempts to entice it out having proved unsuccessful, he at last in despair shot an arrow in its direction. To his astonishment, the arrow halted in mid-course, turned sharply back and embedded itself in his own thigh, where it inflicted an unpleasant flesh-wound. Hastening homeward as best he could, he reported the incident to Laurentius, Bishop of nearby Siponto, who ordered a three-day fast throughout the diocese. On the third day Laurentius himself visited the scene of the miracle. Scarcely had he arrived before the Archangel Michael appeared in full armour, announcing that the cave was henceforth to be a shrine to himself and to all the angels. He then vanished, leaving behind as a sign his great iron spur. When Laurentius returned with a party of followers a few days later, he found that the angels had been busy in his absence; the grotto had been transformed into a chapel, its walls hung with purple; everything was bathed in a soft, warm light. Murmuring praises, the bishop commanded that a church be built upon the rock above the entrance; and four months later, on 29 September, he consecrated it to the Archangel.[1]

In the little town of Monte Sant' Angelo Laurentius's church has long since disappeared, but the Archangel Michael is not forgotten. The entrance to his cave is now proclaimed by an octagonal thirteenth-century bell-tower and a rather ponderous porch built a hundred years ago in the romanesque style. Within, flight after flight of steps lead down into the bowels of the rock. On each side the walls are festooned with votive offerings—crutches, trusses, artificial limbs; eyes, noses, legs, breasts, inexpertly stamped on sheets

[1] The story is told in the Roman Breviary, Proper Office of the Saints for 8 May.

of tin; pictures, genuine peasant primitives, of highway collisions, runaway horses, overturning saucepans and other unpleasant accidents in which the victim owed his salvation to the miraculous intervention of the Archangel; and, most touching of all, fancy dress costumes which have been worn by small children in his honour— once again in gratitude for services rendered—tiny wooden swords, tinfoil wings and biscuit-tin breastplates, accompanied as often as not by a photograph of the wearer, all now gradually decaying against the dark, damp stone. At the bottom, guarded by a magni- ficent pair of Byzantine bronze doors—gift of a rich Amalfitan in 1076—lies the cave itself, in essence much as Laurentius must have left it. The air within it is still loud with the muttered devotions and heavy with the incense of fifteen hundred years, just as it is damp with the moisture that drips remorselessly from the glistening roof of rock and is subsequently dispensed to the faithful in little plastic beakers. The principal altar, ablaze with light and crowned with a glutinously emasculate statue of the Archangel which could not possibly be by Sansovino, takes up one corner; the rest is given over to crumbling columns, to long-abandoned altars in deep recesses, to darkness and to time.

It was not long before Monte Sant' Angelo became one of the great pilgrim shrines of Europe. It was visited by saints, like St Gregory the Great at the end of the sixth century, or like St Francis in the middle of the thirteenth, who set a poor example to the faithful by carving an initial on the altar just inside the entrance; by em- perors, like the Saxon Otto II, who came with his lovely young Byzantine wife, Theophano, in 981, or their mystic, megalomaniac son Otto III who, in an excess of zeal, walked all the way barefoot from Rome; and also perhaps, on a somewhat humbler level in the year 1016, by a band of Norman pilgrims whose conversation with a curiously-dressed stranger in that very cave changed the course of history and led to the foundation of one of the most powerful and magnificent kingdoms of the Middle Ages.

By the beginning of the eleventh century the Normans had virtually completed the process by which, in barely a hundred years, they had transformed themselves from a collection of almost illiterate heathen barbarians into a civilised, if unscrupulous, semi-independent Christian state. It was, even for so energetic and gifted a race, a stupendous achievement. Men were still alive whose fathers could have remembered Rollo, the fair-haired viking who led his long-boats up the Seine and was enfeoffed with most of the eastern half of modern Normandy by the French king Charles the Simple in 911. To be sure, Rollo was not the earliest of the Norman invaders; the first wave had descended from the forests and the fjords over half a century before, and since then the migration had persisted at a fairly steady rate. But it was he who focused the energies and aspirations of his countrymen and set them on the path of amalgamation and identification with their new homeland. Already in 912 a considerable number of them, led by Rollo himself, received Christian baptism. Some indeed, according to Gibbon, received it 'ten or twelve times, for the sake of the white garment usually given at this ceremony', while the fact that 'at the funeral of Rollo, the gifts to monasteries for the repose of his soul were accompanied by a sacrifice of one hundred captives' suggests that in these early years political expediency may have been no less strong a motive for conversion than was spiritual enlightenment, and that Thor and Odin did not give way without a struggle before the feathery on-slaught of the Holy Ghost. But within a generation or two, as Gibbon himself admits, 'the national change was pure and general'. The same was true of language. By 940 the old Norse tongue, while still spoken at Bayeux and on the coast (where the newer immigrants presumably kept it alive), was already forgotten at Rouen; before the end of the century it had died out altogether, leaving hardly a trace behind. One last great institution remained for the Normans to adopt before they could become Frenchmen—an institution that in the years to come was to exert a perennial fascination over them and their descendants and was soon to form the cornerstone of two of the most efficiently run states the world has ever seen. This was the rapidly rising edifice of French law; and they adopted it with open arms.

A pre-occupation with law was a hallmark of most mediaeval societies of the West; but it remains one of the paradoxes of Norman history that it should have persisted so strongly among a race

6

notorious for its lawlessness throughout Europe. Piracy, perjury, robbery, rape, blackmail, murder—such crimes as these were being committed, cheerfully and continually, on every level from the personal to the national, by Norman kings, dukes and barons, long before the Crusades came still further to debase the moral standards of the civilised world. The explanation is that the Normans were above all pragmatists. They saw the law, quite simply, as a magnificent and firmly rooted structure on which a state could be built, and which could be used as a bulwark to strengthen their position in any enterprise they might undertake. As such, it was not their master but their slave, and they sought to uphold it merely because a strong slave is more useful than a weak one. This attitude prevailed among all the Norman rulers, whether in the north or the south. It explains why even the most unscrupulous among them nearly always managed to produce some ingenious legal justification for everything they did; and why the greatest Norman architects of statehood, King Henry II of England and King Roger of Sicily, were to concentrate above all on building up a massive legal system throughout their realms. None of them ever looked upon the law that they created as an abstract ideal; still less did they make the mistake of confusing it with justice.

This pragmatic approach and preoccupation with outward form were also evident in the Norman attitude to religion. They seem to have been genuinely God-fearing—as everybody was in the Middle Ages—and like most people they clung to the simple, selfish mediaeval belief that the primary object of religion was to enable one, after death, to avoid the fires of hell and ascend to heaven as promptly and as painlessly as possible. The smoothness of this journey could, it was generally believed, best be assured by the straightforward means prescribed by the Church—regular attendance at Mass, the requisite amount of fasting, a little penance when necessary, an occasional pilgrimage and, if possible, generous endowments to religious foundations. So long as these formalities were observed, everyday life in the outside world was largely one's own affair and would not be too harshly judged. Similarly, there was no vital need to submit to the dictates of the Church in temporal matters. As we shall see, the genuine religious sentiments of a

Guiscard or a Roger never stopped them fighting tooth and nail against what they considered unwarrantable encroachments by the Papacy, any more than those of Henry Plantagenet prevented his battle with Becket. Excommunication was indeed a severe penalty, not lightly to be incurred; yet incurred it was, often enough, and at least so far as the Normans were concerned it seems to have had little effect on their policy; they were usually able to get it lifted again before long.

Materialistic, quick-witted, adaptable, eclectic, still blessed with the inexhaustible energy of their Viking forebears and a superb self-confidence that was all their own, the early Norman adventurers were admirably equipped for the role they were to play. To these qualities they added two others, not perhaps in themselves particularly praiseworthy, yet qualities without which their great kingdom of the south could never have been born. First or all they were enormously prolific, which meant a continually exploding population. It was this fact more than anything else that had brought the first immigrants from Scandinavia; and two hundred years later it was the same phenomenon that sent swarms of land-hungry younger sons still further south in their quest for *Lebensraum*. Secondly, they were natural wanderers—not just of necessity but by temperament as well. They showed, as an early chronicler noted, little loyalty to any of the countries which at various moments they called their own. The fastnesses of the north, the hills of Normandy, the broad meadows of England, the orange-groves of Sicily, the deserts of Syria, all were in turn forsaken by fearless, footloose young men looking for somewhere else, where the pickings would be better still.

And what better excuse to leave for such a search, what better framework in which to conduct it, than a pilgrimage? It was not surprising, at the dawn of the second millennium, when the world had not after all come to an end as had been predicted, and a wave of relief and gratitude was still sweeping across Europe, that of the thousands who thronged the great pilgrim roads so large a proportion should have been Normans. Their destinations were various; four in particular, however, enjoyed such sanctity that visits to them were sufficient to earn pilgrims total absolution—Rome, Com-

postela, Monte Gargano and, above all the rest, the Holy Land. At
that period the city of Jerusalem had been for some four hundred
years under Muslim domination, but Christian pilgrims were
welcomed—one of their hostels had been founded by Charlemagne
himself—and the undertaking presented no insuperable obstacle to
anyone with time and energy enough; least of all to young Normans,
who looked upon the journey as an adventure and a challenge and
doubtless enjoyed it for its own sake, quite apart from the lasting—
indeed eternal—benefit which it conferred upon their souls. For
them, too, it had a particular appeal; on their return from Palestine
they could disembark at Brindisi or Bari and from there follow the
coast up to the shrine of the Archangel, who was not only the
guardian of all seafarers and thus in any case presumably due for some
expression of gratitude, but who also occupied a special place in their
affections in his capacity as patron of their own great abbey at
Mont-Saint-Michel.

Such appears to have been the course taken by the forty-odd
Norman pilgrims who paid their fateful visit to Monte Sant' Angelo
in 1016—according, at least, to the testimony of a certain William
of Apulia who, at the request of Pope Urban II, produced his
*Historical Poem Concerning the Deeds of the Normans in Sicily, Apulia
and Calabria* just before the close of the eleventh century. William's
account, in elegant Latin hexameters, begins with a description of
how the pilgrims were approached in the cave by a strange figure
dressed 'in the Grecian style' in a long flowing robe and bonnet.
They found him unprepossessing, and his clothes frankly effeminate;
but they listened to his story. His name, it appeared, was Melus,
and he was a noble Lombard from Bari now driven into exile after
leading an unsuccessful insurrection against the Byzantine Empire,
which at that time held most of South Italy in its power. His life
was dedicated to the cause of Lombard independence—which, he
maintained, could easily be achieved; all that was needed was the help
of a few stalwart young Normans like themselves. Against a combined
Lombard-Norman army the Greeks would stand no chance; and
the Lombards would not forget their allies.

It is hard to believe that piety was the dominant emotion in the
hearts of the pilgrims, as they stepped out into the sunlight and gazed

at the wide plain of Apulia lying beckoning at their feet. They cannot at this stage have foreseen how magnificent an epic lay ahead, nor how far-reaching would be its effects; but they cannot either have failed to realise the huge possibilities inherent in the words of Melus. Here was the chance they had been waiting for—a rich fertile land which they were being invited, implored almost, to enter, which offered them boundless opportunities for proving their worth and for making their fortune. Moreover, an operation of the kind proposed could be amply justified on both legal and religious grounds, aiming as it did at the liberation of a subject people from foreign oppression, and at the restoration of the Roman Church throughout South Italy in place of the despised mumbo-jumbo of Constantinople. It would be some years yet before these vague vistas of glory were focused into a clear ambition for conquest, and longer still before this ambition was so dazzlingly fulfilled; meanwhile the important thing was to hack out a firm foothold in the country, and for this the battle-cry of Lombard independence would do as well as any other.

So they told Melus that they would willingly give him the help he needed. At present their numbers were inadequate; in any case they had come to Apulia as pilgrims and were hardly equipped to embark immediately on a campaign. They must therefore return to Normandy, but only for so long as was necessary to make the proper preparations and to recruit companions-in-arms. In the following year they would be back to join their new Lombard friends, and the great enterprise would begin.

The patriotism of Melus was the more understandable since already by this time the Lombards could boast a long and distinguished history in Italy. Starting as just another bunch of semi-barbarian invaders from North Germany, they had settled around the middle of the sixth century in the territory that still bears their name, and had founded there a prosperous kingdom with its capital at Pavia. Meanwhile others of their compatriots had pressed farther south and had set up semi-independent dukedoms at Spoleto and Benevento. For two hundred years all had gone well; but in 774 Charlemagne swept down into Italy and captured Pavia, and the kingdom was at an end. The focus of Lombard civilisation now shifted to the dukedoms, especially to that of Benevento, which soon promoted itself to a principality and—although it was technically under papal suzerainty by virtue of a deed of gift from Charlemagne —continued to maintain the old Lombard traditions untarnished. There, where Trajan's magnificent triumphal arch still stands to mark the junction of the two principal Roman roads of the South, the Via Appia and the Via Trajana, the Lombard aristocracy grew steadily in influence and wealth, and by A.D. 1000 the three great princes of Benevento, Capua and Salerno were among the most powerful rulers in the peninsula, surrounded by courts ablaze with Byzantinesque splendour and endlessly conspiring to achieve their perennial dream—a united and independent Lombard state that would embrace the whole of southern Italy. With this object in view they deliberately did their utmost to obscure their own feudal position, acknowledging the suzerainty now of the Latin Empire of the West, now of the Byzantine Empire of the East (Benevento occasionally also paying lip-service to the claims of the Pope), for ever playing one off against the other. And naturally they never lost an opportunity of encouraging the various groups of Lombard separatists in the territories of their Byzantine neighbour.

The Byzantine Empire, for its part, had had a sad record in Italy. Hardly had the armies of Justinian and his successor driven the Ostrogoths from the peninsula in the sixth century when they found it occupied by their erstwhile Lombard allies. Quick action might yet have saved the situation, but at that moment Constantinople was paralysed by palace intrigues and nothing was done. Meanwhile the Lombards dug themselves in. In 751 they were strong enough to expel the Byzantine Exarch of Ravenna, after which Greek influence was limited to Calabria, the heel of Italy around Otranto, and a few isolated merchant cities on the west coast, of which Naples, Gaeta and Amalfi were the most important. At first these cities were little more than prosperous colonies of the Empire, but as time went on they evolved into hereditary dukedoms, still fundamentally Greek in language and culture, acknowledging Byzantine suzerainty and bound to Constantinople by close ties of friendship and commerce, but for all practical purposes independent.

The advent of Charlemagne and his Franks, though disastrous to the Lombards, brought no corresponding advantages to the Greeks, serving only to introduce a rival claimant to the overlordship of southern Italy; and it was not until the ninth century, when the great dynasty of the Macedonians assumed power in Constantinople, that Basil I and his successor Leo VI the Wise were able to halt the decline and partially to restore Byzantine fortunes. As a result of their efforts the Theme of Langobardia—or, as it was usually called, the Capitanata—consisting of Apulia, Calabria and the Otranto region, was by the year 1000 a powerful and profitable province of the Empire, which in its turn had once again become the greatest single force in the peninsula. Meanwhile it continued to claim suzerainty over all the land south of a line drawn from Terracina in the west to Termoli on the Adriatic, and thus consistently refused to recognise the independence either of the Greek city-states or of the Lombard principalities.

Government of the Capitanata was beset with problems. First of all the whole territory lay wide open to the ravages of Saracen pirates from North Africa, who now dominated the entire western Mediterranean. Already in 846 they had raided Rome and pillaged St Peter's, and little more than twenty years later an uneasy and mutually painful alliance between the Eastern and Western Emperors had been necessary before they could be dislodged from Bari. A monk named Bernard, on a pilgrimage to Jerusalem in 870, wrote of how he had seen thousands of Christian captives being herded on to galleys at Taranto for shipment to Africa as slaves. Thirty years later—by which time, having gained effective control of Sicily, they had vastly improved their own strategic position—the Saracens annihilated Reggio and soon afterwards became so serious a menace that the Byzantine Emperor agreed to pay them an annual sum in protection money. In 953, however, this payment was stopped and the raids became worse than ever. In the last quarter of the tenth century, hardly a year went by without at least one major outrage.

Then there was the Western Empire to be watched. The general relapse that followed the extinction of Charlemagne's family with

the death in 888 of Charles the Fat had afforded a welcome respite
from its south Italian claims; but with the appearance of Otto the
Great in 951 the dispute had flared up again more violently than
ever. Otto had devoted his immense energies to the task of delivering
Italy from the contagion of Greeks and Saracens alike, and for nearly
twenty years the land had been torn by heavy and entirely inconclusive fighting. Peace seemed to have come in 970, when friendship
between the two Empires was theoretically cemented by the marriage
of Otto's son—later Otto II—to the Greek princess Theophano;
but this only gave young Otto the opportunity, on his accession, of
formally claiming the 'restitution' of all Byzantine possessions in
Italy as part of his wife's dowry. His demands were naturally refused,
and the war began again. Then, in 981, Otto descended into Apulia,
his wrath on this occasion principally directed against the Saracens.
In Constantinople the Emperor Basil saw his chance: of the two
evils, Otto represented by far the greater long-term danger. Messengers sped to the Saracen leader and a temporary alliance was
hastily arranged, as a result of which, after certain initial successes,
Otto was soundly defeated near Stilo in Calabria; only an ignominious flight in disguise saved him from capture. He never recovered from the humiliation and died in Rome the following year,
aged twenty-eight.[1] He was succeeded by a child of three and since
then, not surprisingly, the Western Empire had given little trouble;
but vigilance could never be relaxed for long.

Internally too there were grave difficulties. In Calabria and the
heel, government was straightforward enough, since these regions
had suffered relatively little penetration by the Lombards. On the
other hand they had provided a refuge for large numbers of Greek
monks, fleeing in the eighth century from Iconoclast excesses of
Constantinople and in the tenth from the depredations of the Sicilian
Saracens; and the resulting Greek influence, political, religious and
cultural, was still everywhere supreme. Calabria in particular was
to remain, throughout the Renaissance, one of the principal centres
of Greek learning. But in Apulia the situation was more delicate.

---

[1] Otto is the only German Emperor to be buried in Rome. His tomb can still be seen
in the *Grotte Vaticane*—minus its porphyry cover which, having originally been
removed from the Mausoleum of Hadrian, now serves as the font of St Peter's.

The population was for the most part of Italo-Lombard stock and needed careful handling by the Catapan—the local Byzantine governor—who was compelled to allow a considerable degree of freedom. Thus the Lombard system of government was largely retained; Lombard judges and officials administered Lombard law, Greek procedures being prescribed only for cases of assassination (hypothetical) of the Emperor or (less hypothetical) of the Catapan. Latin was recognised as an official language. In most areas church administration was in the hands of Latin bishops appointed by the Pope; only in a few cities where there was a substantial Greek population were Greek bishops to be found.

Such a generous measure of autonomy was unparalleled anywhere else in the Byzantine Empire; yet the Lombards of Apulia were never content to live under Greek rule. They had always maintained a strong sense of nationality—after five hundred years they were still quite unassimilated into the Italian population —and this nationalist flame was for ever being fanned by the great principalities to the north and west. Besides, Byzantine taxation was notoriously heavy and, more serious still, recent years had shown that even with compulsory military service—always an unpopular institution—the Empire was incapable of guaranteeing the security of the Apulian towns, particularly those along the coast, from the Saracens. The Lombard populations of these towns had no choice but to organise their own defence. Standing militias accordingly sprang up, many of them equipped with enough ships to enable them to engage the pirates before they could make a landfall. Inevitably these militias constituted in their turn a serious danger to the Byzantine authorities, but in the circumstances they could hardly be disbanded. They also built up Lombard self-reliance, so that by the end of the tenth century an active and well-armed resistance movement had come into being. There had been a minor revolt in Bari in 987 and another far more serious one a decade later which took three years to stamp out. Meanwhile, an important Byzantine official had been assassinated. Then, in 1009, Melus had taken up arms. With his brother-in-law Dattus and a sizable following he had quickly gained possession of Bari, followed in 1010 by Ascoli and Trani; but in the spring of 1011 the newly-appointed Catapan gathered all available forces to besiege Bari and managed to bribe certain of the Greek inhabitants to open the city gates to his men. On 11 June Bari fell; Melus escaped and fled to Salerno. His wife and children were less fortunate. They were captured and sent as hostages to imprisonment at Constantinople.

High on a hill overlooking the modern *autostrada* that links Naples with Rome, the monastery of Monte Cassino looks, from a distance, much the same as it must have looked a thousand years ago. Its appearance is deceptive; during the desperate fighting of February and March 1944 virtually the entire abbey was reduced, by relentless Allied bombardment, to a pile of rubble, and the existing buildings are almost all post-war reconstructions. But, for all that, the life of the monastery has continued uninterrupted since the year 529 when St Benedict came to that hilltop and built, over the ruins of a pagan temple to Apollo, the huge mother-abbey that was the first of his foundations and the birthplace of the Benedictine Order.

In the history of the Normans in the South, Monte Cassino plays a continuous and vital part. As the greatest of Italian monasteries, it had been one of the chief centres of European learning throughout the Dark Ages. It had preserved for posterity the works of many classical writers which would otherwise have perished, including those of Apuleius and Tacitus; and it had somehow survived, with this precious heritage, a devastating Saracen raid in 881 in the course of which its church and other buildings had been largely destroyed. Now, at the time our story opens, it was entering upon its golden age. In the next two hundred years its power was to increase to the point where the monastery functioned almost as an independent state, in turn defying Franks, Greeks, Lombards, Normans, even on occasion the Pope himself; and twice seeing its own Abbot, always one of the most influential figures in the Latin hierarchy, raised to the throne of St Peter.

During the latter half of the eleventh century there lived at Monte Cassino a monk called Amatus—or, as he is sometimes called, Aimé —who between about 1075 and 1080 composed a history of the Normans in the South. Unlike William of Apulia who, one suspects, was primarily concerned to show off his mastery of Latin versification,

Amatus wrote in uncluttered prose; and he has left a pains-
taking and reasonably accurate account of events of which he was
a contemporary and often, possibly, an eye-witness. Unfortunately his original Latin text has been lost; all we possess is a
translation into an Italianate Old French made in the fourteenth
century and now surviving as an endearingly illustrated manuscript
at the Bibliothèque Nationale in Paris. For scholars, since Amatus
is unquestionably the most reliable source for the subject and period
he covers, this loss must be a sad blow; but for the rest of us it
means that his work, of which no modern English translation
exists, has been delivered from the heartbreaking convolutions of
mediaeval Latin and is not only for the most part comprehensible
but also, with its liveliness, naïveté and unending orthographical
charm, a joy to read.

Amatus tells us another story of Norman pilgrims which it is
tempting to relate to William's. According to his account a similar
group of some forty young Normans, returning in 999 on an
Amalfitan ship from Palestine, called at Salerno where they were
hospitably received by the reigning prince, Gaimar IV.[1] Their stay
was, however, rudely interrupted by Saracen pirates, to whose appalling brutalities the local populace was too frightened to offer
resistance. Disgusted at so craven an attitude, the Normans seized
their arms and descended to the attack. Their example gave new
courage to the Salernitans, many of whom now joined them; and
the Saracens, whom this delayed opposition had taken completely
off their guard, were all slaughtered or put to flight. Such spirit
was rare in the South. The delighted Gaimar at once offered these
paragons of valour rich rewards if they would only remain at his
court, but they refused; after so long an absence they must be
getting back to Normandy. On the other hand they would be quite
ready to discuss the matter with their friends at home, many of
whom would certainly be interested in the idea and whose courage
would be no whit inferior to their own. And so they departed,
accompanied by envoys from Gaimar laden with all those gifts

[1] Gaimar, who reigned in Salerno from 999 to 1027, is sometimes referred to as
Gaimar III. The numbering of Lombard dukes and princes was never properly stan-
dardised and constitutes a hideous pitfall to the unwary.

best calculated to attract intrepid northern adventurers—'lemons, almonds, pickled nuts, fine vestments and iron instruments chased with gold; and thus they tempted them to come to this land that flows with milk and honey and so many beautiful things.'

Now the year 1016, which saw Melus at Monte Sant' Angelo, also saw the only large-scale Saracen attack on Salerno; whereas in 999, the date which Amatus gives to his story, no such raid is known to have occurred. It may therefore be that, even if the story remains true in its essentials, the author has made at this point one of his rare chronological blunders, and that the two pilgrim visits were roughly contemporaneous. If this were so, might it not be that the two parties of pilgrims were one and the same? Could not the meeting with Melus at the shrine, ostensibly so fortuitous, have been deliberately engineered by himself and Gaimar, who had recently given him refuge and was one of the principal clandestine supporters of Lombard separatism? It is possible. On the other hand it is possible too, as a recent historian has cogently argued,[1] that both stories are legendary and that the earliest Norman arrivals were in fact simple refugees from their homeland who were subsequently pressed into the Lombard cause by Pope Benedict VIII as part of his anti-Byzantine policy. We shall never know. But whether the persuader was prince, patriot or Pope, whether the persuaded were fugitives or pilgrims, of one thing we can be sure: the work was well done. By the spring of 1017 the first young Normans were already on their way.

[1] E. Joranson, 'The Inception of the Career of the Normans in Italy'.

2

ARRIVAL

Et en tant estoit cressute la multitude de lo pueple, que li champ ne li arbre non suffisoit a tant de gent de porter lor necessaires dont peussent vivre. . . . Et se partirent ceste gent, et laisserent petite choze pour acquester assez, et non firent secont la costumance de molt qui vont par lo monde, liquel se metent a servir autre; mes simillance de li antique chevalier, et voilloient avoir toute gent en lor subjettion et en lor seignorie. Et pristrent l'arme, et rompirent la ligature de paiz, et firent grant exercit et grant chevalerie.

(And the people had increased so exceedingly that the fields and forests were no longer sufficient to provide for them . . . and so these men departed, forsaking what was meagre in search of what was plentiful. Nor were they content, as are so many who go out into the world, to serve others; but, like the knights of old, they determined that all men should be subject to them, acknowledging them as overlords. And so they took up arms, and broke the bonds of peace, and did great deeds of war and chivalry.)

Amatus, I, 1, 2

It was perhaps just as well that the Lombard leaders had demanded no references from the warriors whose aid they were seeking, and had imposed no criteria but courage. Word of their invitation had spread quickly through the towns and manors of Normandy, and the stories of the delights which the South could offer, the effeteness of its present inhabitants and the rewards which awaited any Norman prepared to make the journey, doubtless lost nothing in the telling. Such stories have always a particular appeal for the more unreliable sections of any population, and it was therefore hardly surprising that the earliest contingents of Norman immigrants into Italy, despite possible outward similarities with Amatus's *antique chevalier*, should have had little enough in common with the knights of Carolingian

legend whose exploits they so raucously sang. They seem to have
been largely composed of knights' and squires' younger sons who,
possessing no patrimony of their own, had little to attach them to
their former homes; but there was also a distinctly less reputable
element of professional fighters, gamblers and adventurers respond-
ing to the call of easy money. These were soon joined by the usual
riff-raff of hangers-on, increasing in numbers as the party rode
southwards through Burgundy and Provence. In the summer of
1017 they crossed the river Garigliano, which marked the southern
frontier of the Papal States, and made direct for Capua. There,
probably by previous arrangement, they found Melus impatiently
awaiting them with a sizable contingent of his own, all eager for
immediate battle.

The best chance of Lombard success clearly lay in attacking the
Byzantines before they had time to assess the new situation and
summon reinforcements; Melus was therefore right to impress
upon his new allies that there was no time to be lost, and to lead
them at once across the frontier into Apulia. As a result, they seem
to have taken the enemy entirely by surprise. By the approach of
winter and the end of the first year's campaign they could already
boast of several significant victories and could well afford to indulge
in their favourite joke about the effeminacy of the Greeks; and by
September 1018 they had driven the Byzantines from the whole
region between the Fortore in the north and Trani in the south. In
October, however, the tide suddenly turned.

On the right bank of the Ofanto river, about four miles from the
Adriatic, a great rock still casts its shadow over the field of Cannae
where, in 216 B.C., the Carthaginian army under Hannibal had inflicted on the Romans one of the bloodiest and most disastrous
defeats in their history. Here it was, twelve hundred and thirty-four
years later, that the Lombard and Norman forces under Melus
suffered a still greater catastrophe at the hands of the imperial
Byzantine army led by the greatest of all the Catapans, Basil
Boioannes. They were from the start hopelessly outnumbered. At
the insistence of Boioannes the Emperor Basil II had sent massive
reinforcements from Constantinople; Amatus writes that the Greeks
swarmed over the battlefield like bees from a hive and that their

lances stood straight and thick as a field of cane. But there was yet another, if only contributory, reason for the defeat: Norman military prowess was already famous in the Byzantine capital and Basil had accordingly stiffened his army with some northern warriors of his own—a detachment of his Varangian Guard, that great Viking regiment which had been sent him, in return for his sister, by Prince Vladimir of Kiev thirty years before. The Lombards fought bravely, but in vain; all but a handful were slaughtered, and with them collapsed Melus's last hopes of Lombard independence in Apulia. He himself managed to escape, and after months of aimless wandering through the duchies and the Papal States finally found refuge at the court of the Western Emperor Henry II at Bamberg. Here he died two years later, a broken and disappointed man. Henry, who as the chief rival of Byzantium for the domination of South Italy had often supported him in the past, gave him a superb funeral and a magnificent tomb in his new cathedral; but neither the skill of the monumental masons nor the hollow title of Duke of Apulia that Henry had conferred upon him shortly before his death could alter the fact that Melus had failed—and, worse still, that in his determination to bring freedom to his people he had unwittingly done the one thing that rendered that freedom for ever unattainable. He had given the Normans a taste of blood.

They too had fought bravely and suffered severe losses at Cannae. Their leader, one Gilbert, had fallen on the field, and it was a sadly depleted force that regrouped itself after the battle and elected his brother Rainulf as his successor. Now that Melus was gone they must fend for themselves, at least until they could find new paymasters. Dispiritedly they rode away into the hills to look for a place in which to entrench themselves—somewhere that would serve them as a permanent headquarters and would provide a rallyingpoint for the new immigrants who were still trickling steadily down from the north. Their first choice of site was unfortunate; during the construction of their stronghold they suffered a defeat far more humiliating than that of Cannae. William of Apulia tells us that they were suddenly beset by a plague of frogs, which appeared in such numbers that they were unable to continue the work. After they had beaten an ignominious retreat before the croaking chorus, they found a second location which fortunately proved more suitable; but even here they did not remain for long. Thanks to the constant stream of new arrivals their numbers were soon greater than they had ever been. Besides, despite the severity of their first defeat, their reputation as fighters was still unequalled; and their services were in demand on all sides.

The great cauldron of South Italy was never altogether off the boil. In a land surrounded and pervaded by the constant clashing of the four greatest powers of the time, torn apart by the warring claims of four races, three religions and an ever-varying number of independent, semi-independent or rebellious states and cities, a strong arm and a sharp sword could never lack employment. Many young Normans gravitated towards Gaimar in Salerno; others turned to his brother-in-law and rival, Prince Pandulf of Capua—'the Wolf of the Abruzzi'—whose energy and ambition were already causing his neighbours serious concern. Yet others preferred Naples, Amalfi or Gaeta. Meanwhile the Catapan Boioannes was consolidating his victory by building a new stronghold to defend his Apulian frontier—the fortress town of Troia at the mouth of the pass leading through the Apennines and out on to the plain. Having no forces available to provide a permanent garrison—the Varangians having by now returned in triumph to Constantinople—he had to look elsewhere; and, since they were after all merely mercenaries and the Catapan knew a good fighter when he saw one, there can have been little surprise when, only a year or so after Cannae, a well-equipped force of Normans rode off to Apulia to defend the lawful dominions of Byzantium against the continued dastardly attacks of Lombard trouble-makers.

Such an atmosphere of shifting loyalties and easy realignments might well have seemed injurious to Norman interests. Surely, it might be thought, if they were aiming to increase their power to the point where they would ultimately dominate the peninsula, the Normans should have remained united and not scattered so aimlessly among the countless factions that sought their aid. But at this early stage thoughts of dominion were still unformulated, nor was there much unity to be preserved. Self-interest was the first consideration; national aspirations came a poor second, if indeed they figured at all. Norman good fortune lay in the fact that the two so often coincided; and, paradoxically, it was their apparent disunity that prepared the way for their ultimate conquest. Had they maintained their cohesion they could not have failed to upset the balance of power in South Italy, since they were still too few to prevail alone yet already too numerous not to strengthen dangerously any faction to whom they might have given their undivided allegiance. By splitting up, constantly changing their alliances and contriving, in all the petty struggles in which they were involved, to emerge almost invariably on the winning side, they were able to prevent any single interest from becoming too powerful; by championing all causes they succeeded in championing none; and by selling their swords not just to the highest but to every bidder, they maintained their freedom of action.

The Normans were not the only people who had to reconsider their position after Cannae. At one stroke Byzantine power had been re-established throughout Apulia, and Byzantine prestige immeasurably increased all over Italy. The effect on the Lombard duchies was, as might have been expected, considerable. Early in 1019 Pandulf of Capua frankly transferred his allegiance to the Greeks, even going so far as to send the keys of his capital to the Emperor Basil. In Salerno Gaimar, while avoiding such expansive gestures, similarly made no secret of where his sympathies now lay. Most surprising of all—at least at first sight—was the attitude of Monte Cassino. The great monastery had always been considered the champion of the Latin cause in South Italy as represented by the Pope and the Western Emperor. As such it had supported Melus and his Lombards and had even offered his brother-in-law Dattus after Cannae the same place of refuge that he had occupied for a while after the earlier Lombard defeat of 1011—a fortified tower which it owned on the banks of the Garigliano. Then, only a few months later, it too declared itself in support of the claims of Constantinople. Only the Prince of Benevento remained loyal.

All this was bad news indeed for the Emperor Henry, and worse news still for the Pope. Benedict VIII, though upright and morally irreproachable,[1] was not a particularly religious figure. Member of a noble family of Tusculum, it seems doubtful that he had even taken holy orders at the time of his election in 1012; and throughout his twelve-year occupancy of the throne of St Peter he showed himself to be primarily a politician and a man of action, dedicated to the close association of the Papacy with the Western Empire and to the deliverance of Italy from all other influences. Thus in 1016 he had personally led an army against the Saracens; while against the Greeks he had given Melus and Dattus all the support he could, twice arranging with the authorities of Monte Cassino for the refuge of the latter in the Garigliano tower. Now he saw all his efforts brought to nothing and a sudden explosion by Byzantine power to a point beyond anything he had seen in his lifetime. The defection of Monte Cassino must have been a particular blow—though perhaps more understandable when he remembered that its abbot, Atenulf, was the brother of Pandulf of Capua and had recently acquired in somewhat mysterious conditions a large estate near Trani in Byzantine Apulia. Most serious of all, however, was the danger of continued Greek expansion. After the completeness of their recent triumph why should the Byzantines be content with the Capitanata? The Balkan wars that had so long occupied the formidable energies of Basil II and earned him the title of *Bulgaroctonus*— the Bulgar-Slayer—were now over; and the Papal States represented a rich prize which he might well believe to be in his grasp. Once Boioannes crossed the Garigliano there would be nothing between him and the gates of Rome itself; and the sinister family of the Crescentii, longtime enemies of the Counts of Tusculum, would know just how to turn such a catastrophe to their advantage. It was a hundred and fifty years since a Pope had journeyed north of the Alps, but after the news of Monte Cassino was brought to him Benedict hesitated no longer. Early in 1020 he set off to discuss the situation with his old friend and ally Henry II at Bamberg.

It is impossible to read about Benedict and Henry without reflecting how much more suitable it would have been if the Pope

---

[1] Irreproachable, that is, according to his lights. He must bear the stigma of having ordered the first official (though, alas, not the last) persecution of the Jews in the history of mediaeval Rome—as the result of a minor earthquake in 1020.

had been the Emperor and the Emperor the Pope. Henry the Holy fully deserved his nickname. Although perhaps hardly worthy of the canonisation he was to receive in the following century—an honour which appears to have been conferred largely in recognition of the dismal chastity in which he lived with his wife Cunégonde of Luxemburg—and although his piety was liberally laced with superstition, he remained a deeply religious man whose two main passions in life were the building of churches and ecclesiastical reform. These spiritual preoccupations did not, however, prevent him from ruling over his unwieldy empire with surprising efficiency. Despite his perpetual interference in church affairs he and Benedict had been friends ever since 1012 when Henry, still only King in Germany,[1] had supported Benedict in the papal election against his Crescentius rival; and their friendship, strengthened when Benedict intervened similarly for Henry and officiated at his and Cunégonde's imperial coronation in 1014, had been further cemented by Henry's religious and Benedict's political views. The horizon as yet showed no prospect of that long and agonising struggle between Empire and Papacy which was so soon to begin and would reach its apogee only with Frederick II more than two centuries later; for the moment the two still worked in harmony. A threat to the one was a threat to the other.

Benedict arrived in Bamberg just before Easter 1020; and after celebrating the feast with great pomp in Henry's new cathedral he and the Emperor at once settled down to business. At the start they had Melus to give them the benefit of his expertise on the South Italian political scene and Byzantine strengths and weaknesses; but a week after the Pope's arrival the 'Duke of Apulia' suddenly expired and the two had to continue alone. For Benedict, always incisive, the necessary course of action was clear: Henry himself must lead a full-scale expeditionary force into Italy. The purpose of this force, which would be joined at a suitable moment by the Pope himself, would not be to oust Byzantium altogether—there would be time for that later—but to show that the Western Empire and the Papacy

---

[1] The title of Emperor could be adopted only after the elected German king had been crowned by the Pope in Rome. Henry was first to call himself King of the Romans when Emperor-elect.

were powers to be reckoned with, ready to defend their rights. It would thus put new heart into any of the smaller cities or petty Lombard barons who might be wavering in their allegiance, while leaving Boioannes in no doubt that any further Greek advances would be made at his peril.

Henry, though sympathetic, was not immediately persuaded. Delicate as the situation was, the Greeks had not in fact moved beyond their own borders; and even though he did not technically recognise those borders, recent Byzantine actions had after all come about only as a result of Lombard insurrection and could hardly be classed as aggressive. The attitude of the Lombard duchies and of Monte Cassino was indeed a cause for anxiety but, as Henry well knew, they all valued their independence far too much to allow themselves to become Byzantine satellites. They alone would certainly not merit an expedition of the size which Benedict was proposing. When the Pope returned to Italy in June, the Emperor had still not finally committed himself.

For a year he hesitated, and for a year all was quiet. Then, in June 1021, Boioannes struck. By previous financial arrangement with Pandulf, a Greek detachment entered Capuan territory and swept down the Garigliano to the tower which Dattus, with a group of Lombard followers and a still faithful band of Normans, had by now made his headquarters and in which—trusting, presumably, in papal protection—he had decided to remain even after the *volte-face* of Capua and Monte Cassino. (Neither at this time nor at any other in his history does Dattus betray signs of marked intelligence.) The tower had originally been built and fortified as a protection against Saracen raiders. For such a purpose it was on the whole adequate, but it could not hold out for long against the well-equipped Greek force. Dattus and his men fought valiantly for two days, but on the third they were compelled to surrender. The Normans were spared but the Lombards were all put to the sword. Dattus himself was taken to Bari where, in chains, he was paraded on a donkey through the streets; then, on the evening of 15 June 1021, he was sewn into a sack together with a cock, a monkey and a snake and cast into the sea.

News of the outrage travelled swiftly to Rome and Bamberg.

Benedict, of whom Dattus had been a personal friend, was scandal-
ised at this new treachery on the part of Pandulf and Abbot Atenulf,
who were known to have received a large reward for handing over
their compatriot—the last man still capable of raising the banner of
Lombard independence and openly committed to driving the Greeks
out of Italy. Moreover, it was the Pope who had advised Dattus to
take refuge in the tower and had arranged with Monte Cassino that
it should be made available for him. The honour of the Papacy had
thus been betrayed, a crime that Benedict could never forgive. His
letters to Henry in Bamberg, by which he had kept up a steady
pressure ever since his return to Italy, now took on a more urgent
note. The fate of Dattus was only the beginning; the success of this
operation would encourage the Greeks to acts of still wilder audacity.
It was imperative to take strong action while time yet remained. Henry
prevaricated no longer. At the Diet of Nijmegen in July 1021 it was
resolved that he should lead his imperial armies into Italy as soon as
possible. The rest of the summer and all autumn were spent in
preparations, and in the following December the immense host
began to march.

The expedition was intended primarily as a show of strength;
and a show of strength it unquestionably was. For the outward
journey it was split up into three separate divisions, the command
of which Henry typically gave to himself and two of his archbishops
—Pilgrim of Cologne and Poppo of Aquileia. The first division,
under Pilgrim, had orders to march down the west side of Italy
through the Papal States to Monte Cassino and Capua, there to arrest
Atenulf and Pandulf in the Emperor's name. It consisted, we are
told—though all such figures must be treated with suspicion—of
twenty thousand men. The second, estimated at eleven thousand,
would be led by Poppo through Lombardy and the Apennines to
the border of Apulia. Here, at a pre-arranged rendezvous, it would
link up with the main body of the army under Henry—more
numerous than the other two divisions put together—which would
have followed the eastern road down the Adriatic coast. The
combined force would then march inland to besiege and eradicate
Troia, that proud new Byzantine stronghold built by Boioannes

and manned by Normans, of which it had been agreed that a public example should be made.

Pilgrim marched straight to Monte Cassino as instructed, but he arrived too late. The Abbot had not underestimated the wrath of Benedict and knew that he could expect no mercy; on hearing of the approach of the imperial army he at once fled to Otranto and there hastily embarked for Constantinople. But retribution overtook him. Shortly before his departure from the monastery a furious St Benedict had appeared to him in a vision to inform him of the heavenly displeasure he had incurred and to remind him about the wages of sin; and indeed, hardly had his ship put out of harbour when a mighty tempest arose. On 30 March 1022 the vessel went down with all hands and Atenulf was drowned with the rest. Meanwhile Pilgrim continued to Capua. Pandulf was not disposed to give in without a struggle and at once called upon the inhabitants to defend the city walls; but he was so much disliked by his subjects that he found himself no longer able to command their loyalty in the face of the Archbishop's troops. Encouraged by certain Normans in his retinue, who also had no love for their erstwhile paymaster and correctly judged where their own advantage lay, a group of citizens stealthily opened the gates to the imperial army. Pilgrim was thus able to enter Capua, there to receive the submission of its fuming Prince.

The original plan now provided for Pilgrim to turn eastwards to rejoin the rest of the army. Before doing so, however, he decided to move on to Salerno where Gaimar, although his behaviour had been a good deal less reprehensible than that of his brother-in-law, still continued openly to profess pro-Byzantine sympathies and was clearly capable of causing trouble in the future if he were not discouraged. But as Pilgrim soon discovered, Salerno was a very different proposition from Capua. Its defences were considerably stronger and much more determinedly manned, for Gaimar was as popular as Pandulf was hated and his Norman guard was undismayed by the archiepiscopal cohorts. The city was besieged for over a month but, although hard pressed, obviously had no intention of surrendering. Meanwhile time was passing and Pilgrim still had a long hard road through the mountains between himself and his

Emperor. At last a truce was called and he agreed to raise the siege in return for an adequate number of hostages. Having thus protected his rear he turned away from Salerno and headed inland.

Henry also had marched swiftly. Despite the unwieldiness of his army and the rigours of the Alpine winter he and Archbishop Poppo, whose journey had been equally uneventful, had joined up as planned by mid-February 1022. Together they then proceeded inland to a point near Benevento where the Pope was awaiting them, and on 3 March Benedict and Henry made their formal entrance into the city. There they stayed for four weeks, resting and catching up with their correspondence—and, presumably, hoping for news of Pilgrim. Meanwhile the army prepared for action. At the end of the month they decided to delay no longer for the Archbishop and set off for Troia.

Boioannes had, as usual, done his work well. To the imperial troops emerging from the mountain passes on to the plain of Apulia, the immense spur on which Troia stands must have looked virtually impregnable; and the town itself, poised over the very edge of the frontier between Byzantine territory and the Duchy of Benevento, distinctly menacing. But the stern determination of the Pope and the pious fortitude of the Emperor set the required example, and on 12 April the siege began. For nearly three months it was to drag on as the weather grew steadily hotter, its grim monotony broken only by the arrival of Pilgrim with the news from Campania, and Pandulf, still seething, in his train. The news of Atenulf's fate left Henry unmoved; he is said to have merely muttered a verse from the seventh psalm[1] and turned away. Pandulf he condemned to death on the spot but owing to the intercession of the Archbishop, who had grown rather fond of his prisoner during their journey through the mountains, he was persuaded to commute the sentence to one of imprisonment beyond the Alps—an exercise of mercy which many people were before long to have cause to regret. The Wolf of the Abruzzi was led away in chains and the siege continued.

Unlike her famous Anatolian namesake, Troia held out to the end. Certain pro-German chroniclers have tried to maintain that Henry eventually managed to take the town by storm; one, the notoriously

[1] *He made a pit, and digged it, and is fallen into the ditch which he made.*

28

unreliable monk Radulph Glaber (the wildness of whose imagination was rivalled only by that of his private life, which gives him a fair claim to have been expelled from more monasteries than any other *littérateur* of the eleventh century), tells a typically far-fetched story of how Henry's heart was melted by the sight of a long procession of all its inhabitants, led by an elderly hermit carrying a cross. But if Troia had in fact surrendered it is inconceivable that some mention of it would not appear in any of the contemporary South Italian records —and scarcely more probable that Boioannes should have immediately afterwards granted the town new privileges as a reward for its fidelity.

So Henry was deprived of his triumph. He could not continue the siege indefinitely. The heat was taking its toll, and malaria, which remained the scourge of Apulia until well into the twentieth century, was rife in his army. At the end of June he decided to give up. The camp was struck, and the Emperor, who was by now in considerable pain from a gall-stone, rode slowly away into the mountains at the head of his huge but dispirited army. It was not the first time that the South Italian summer had conquered the greatest military forces of Europe; nor, as we shall see, was it to be the last. Henry met the Pope, who had preceded him, at Monte Cassino and here they remained for a few days, Benedict occupying himself with the induction of a new abbot and Henry seeking—successfully, we are told—miraculous relief from his stone. Then, after a short visit to Capua, where another Pandulf, Count of Teano, was installed in the palace of his disgraced namesake, Pope and Emperor left via Rome for Pavia, to attend an important council which Benedict had summoned on Church reform. To Henry such a gathering constituted an irresistible temptation, and it was not until August that he left for Germany.

His expedition had been only a very qualified success. Pilgrim admittedly had done his work well; with Pandulf and Atenulf removed from the scene there should be no more difficulties in Capua or Monte Cassino, while the hostages from Salerno and Naples (the latter had offered them of its own accord rather than face the possibility of a siege by the Archbishop's army) were a guarantee against trouble along that part of the coast. The Apulian campaign, on the other hand, had been a fiasco. Troia's stubborn stand had shown up the fundamental impotence of imperial arms in Italy. Some sixty thousand men had been completely unable to subdue a small hill-town which had not even existed four years earlier. To make matters worse, they had been under the personal command of the Emperor, whose own reputation had thus suffered a heavy blow—while that of Boioannes, who had conceived, built, fortified and populated Troia, had acquired proportionately greater lustre. And the Catapan had yet another advantage, of which Henry was all too well aware; being resident in Apulia, he was able continually to maintain and consolidate his position and to seize without delay every opportunity for improving it. The Western Emperor, in contrast, could work only through his feudal vassals who, as had so recently been demonstrated, were apt to remain loyal only so long as it suited them. While he was on the spot in all his splendour, holding courts, dispensing justice and with a generous hand distributing his imperial largesse, these vassals were only too ready to offer their submission and to pay their homage. Once he was gone, the field was left open to malcontents and agitators; laws would be disobeyed, morale undermined, injunctions forgotten; Boioannes would miss no chances; and what then was to prevent the whole painfully rebuilt imperial structure from crumbling again?

For the Byzantines, as they watched the imperial host lumbering away into the mountains, the prevailing sentiment must have been one of relief. Had Henry taken Troia, all Apulia might have lain at his mercy. Following the reverses already sustained in the west, this would have meant the undoing of all that had been achieved in the past four years. Even as things were, there was much to be rebuilt; but thanks to Troia the foundations had remained secure. Greek diplomacy could get to work again. No wonder Boioannes rewarded the Troians so handsomely.

Thus, for the two protagonists, the campaign of 1022 had been inconclusive. Gains and losses seemed evenly balanced and it was hard to see where the advantage lay. Among the minor participants, Capua had suffered disaster, Salerno and Naples had been severely chastened. For one group only had the events of the year been entirely profitable. The Normans, by their stand at Troia, had saved Apulia for the Greeks and had earned the lasting gratitude of Boioannes. In the west, the part they had played in obtaining the submission of Capua was rewarded by Henry's engagement of a substantial Norman force to maintain and support Pandulf of Teano. Further contingents had been placed by the Emperor along the Byzantine frontier and at various places along the coast to guard against Saracen attacks. The Normans had in fact already mastered the art of being on the winning side, cashing in on all victories and somehow avoiding involvement in all defeats. On both sides of the peninsula they had strengthened their position; to both empires they had become indispensable. They were doing very well indeed.

3

ESTABLISHMENT

> the five fair brothers,
> Who attempted the world and shared it with themselves,
> Coming out of Normandy from the fresh, green land
> To this soil of marble and of broken sherds.
>
> Sacheverell Sitwell,
> 'Bohemund, Prince of Antioch'

HENRY the Holy may have had no delusions about the difficulty of maintaining his influence in Italy after his return home, but not even he could have foreseen the speed with which his work would be destroyed. He had tried hard and he must have felt that in the west at least he had left a relatively stable situation. So, in a way, he had; but there was one eventuality for which he had made no provision. The improvement in his health which had followed the miraculous intercession of St Benedict at Monte Cassino proved, alas, as ephemeral as everything else he achieved in Italy. In July 1024 he died. He was buried not far from Melus in Bamberg Cathedral.

Henry left, as might have been expected, no issue; and with him the Saxon house came to an end. He was succeeded by a distant cousin, Conrad II the Salic. Conrad, both in character and outlook, was quite unlike Henry—he was sublimely uninterested, for example, in the affairs of the Church, except when they affected his political decisions—and there was no particular reason why he should have pursued his predecessor's policies; neither, however, was there any excuse for the act of blatant idiocy which he now committed. At the request of Gaimar of Salerno, who sent a smooth-tongued embassy, well laden with presents, to congratulate him on his accession, the new Emperor at once released Pandulf of Capua from his chains and left him free to return to Italy. Pope Benedict would never for a moment have countenanced such folly; but Pope Benedict was dead. He had preceded Henry to the grave by only a few weeks and had been succeeded, with unseemly haste, by his brother Romanus, who had immediately installed himself at the Lateran under the name of John XIX. Corrupt and utterly self-seeking, John had neither the energy nor the interest to remonstrate with Conrad. So it was that the Wolf of the Abruzzi returned to his old habitat and began once again to justify his name.

His first objective was to recover Capua and to avenge himself on all those of his subjects who had so recently betrayed him. For this he needed allies. On arrival in Italy, therefore, he at once sent out appeals for assistance—to Gaimar in Salerno, to the Catapan Boioannes and lastly to Rainulf the Norman, who was called upon to send as many of his compatriots as he could muster. Gaimar, who as Pandulf's brother-in-law had everything to gain from a restoration of the *status quo* in Capua, complied at once and had no difficulty in persuading Rainulf, who recognised another wide-open opportunity for Norman advancement, to do the same. Only the Greeks were disappointing in their response, although they had an admirable excuse. The Emperor Basil was preparing a military expedition of enormous size against the Saracens, who had by now achieved the complete domination of Sicily. By the time he received Pandulf's appeal the bulk of his army—Greeks, Varangians, Vlachs and Turks —had already arrived in Calabria, and Boioannes was even leading an advance-guard across the straits to occupy Messina in the Emperor's name. Pandulf, however, was not particularly worried at the lack of imperial support. Rainulf had now appeared with a gratifyingly large number of Norman cut-throats to stiffen Gaimar's force, and Capua was unlikely to offer serious resistance. Furthermore a small Greek contingent, somehow detached from the Sicilian expeditionary force, had turned up unexpectedly at the last moment and was now awaiting orders. (If Pandulf were to return to power Boioannes would not have wished it to be without some Byzantine assistance.) There was no point in delaying further. Accordingly, in November 1024, the siege of Capua began.

It lasted a good deal longer than Pandulf had expected. The river Volturno provides the city with a superb natural defence on three sides. Thanks to this, to the immensely strong land-walls which covered the fourth side and, doubtless, to the Capuans' determination to postpone for as long as possible the return of their detested lord, they held out for eighteen months and would indeed probably have continued longer but for an unexpected catastrophe. On 15 December 1025, just as he was about to leave Constantinople for Sicily, the Emperor Basil died. His sixty-five-year-old brother Constantine VIII, who succeeded him, was an irresponsible voluptuary who, despite having technically shared the throne for the past half-century, was quite unfitted to pursue Basil's majestic designs. He therefore called off the Sicilian expedition just as it was gathering momentum, and Boioannes was now able to direct the whole weight of his huge army against Capua.

From that moment the defenders had no chance. In May 1026 the Count of Teano decided that the Capuan throne had become too hot for him and accepted Boioannes's offer of safe conduct to Naples in return for his surrender. The gates of the city were opened and almost exactly four years after his disgrace the Wolf was back where, at least in his own view, he belonged. The chroniclers spare us the details of his vengeance on the Capuans, many of whom might well have preferred to maintain their resistance to the end and then go down fighting. As for the Norman garrison, it probably emerged none the worse; the victorious prince owed much to Rainulf, and in any battle in which Normans had fought on both sides it had already become the regular practice for those on the winning side to seek clemency for their less fortunate compatriots.

And yet Pandulf was still not satisfied. Naples, in particular, worried him. Duke Sergius IV, though nominally a vassal of Byzantium, had behaved with remarkable fecklessness at the time of Archbishop Pilgrim's campaign, putting up no resistance of any kind and offering hostages before he was even threatened. He had not lifted a finger to help Pandulf regain his rightful patrimony; and now he was actually giving refuge to the ridiculous Count of Teano. The fact that this refuge had been arranged by Boioannes did nothing to reassure Pandulf; he merely suspected, not without reason, that this was a deliberate move on the part of the Catapan, to whom the continued availability of a rival claimant to the throne of Capua might well prove useful in the future. In any case Sergius was an untrustworthy neighbour and as such must be dealt with. The only obstacle was Boioannes, who was on excellent terms with Sergius and would certainly come to his assistance against Pandulf should the need arise.

Then, in 1027, the Catapan was recalled. For the Eastern Empire this was an error almost as great as Conrad's liberation of Pandulf three years before. As Basil II's right hand in Italy, Boioannes had by a superb combination of diplomatic and military skill restored Byzantine supremacy in the South and raised it to its highest level for three hundred years. Now, with the Emperor and the Catapan both gone, the decline was beginning. It began in the classic tradition, with insubordination allowed to go unpunished.

If Boioannes had been in Italy, or if Basil had been alive, Pandulf would never have dared to attack Naples; but the Capitanata was now without a governor, and in Constantinople the doddering old hedonist Constantine was incapable of seeing further than the Hippodrome. The Wolf—*le fortissime lupe* as Amatus calls him— seized his chance. Some time during the winter of 1027–28 he swept down on Naples and, thanks as usual to treachery from within, took possession of it after the shortest of struggles. Sergius went into hiding and the terrified Count of Teano sought refuge in Rome, where he died soon after.

Pandulf's position must now have appeared almost unassailable. He was master not only of Capua and Naples but also in effect of Salerno, since Gaimar had died in 1027 and his widow, Pandulf's sister, had assumed the regency for her sixteen-year-old son. With neither the Eastern nor the Western Emperors making the slightest effort to stop him—Conrad had actually travelled to Italy for his coronation a few months before and had docilely accepted Pandulf's homage as Prince of Capua—and the Pope equally ineffectual, he could allow his ambitions free rein. He was still only forty-two; given a modicum of luck and whole-hearted Norman support, he should have little difficulty in taking Benevento and the cities along the coast. Then, if the present state of apathy continued to prevail in Constantinople, there would be nothing to prevent his marching into the Capitanata, and the old Lombard dream of a unified South Italian empire would be realised at last.

Such a prospect could not be expected to appeal to Amalfi, Gaeta and their smaller neighbours. They valued their independence and their close commercial and cultural links with Constantinople; they had no particular affection for the Lombards; and, like everybody else, they disliked Pandulf intensely. Meanwhile the citizens of Naples, few of whom had ever wanted the Prince of Capua in the first place, were beginning to suffer from his harshness and rapacity and to plan his overthrow.

The key to the situation lay with Rainulf. Of all the Norman bands that were now disseminated through the peninsula, his was the largest and most influential; and its numbers were constantly being increased as fresh recruits arrived at his invitation from the north. If Pandulf could enlist his support there would be little hope for the rest of southern Italy. Fortunately, however, the sudden rise of Capua was as unwelcome to Rainulf as to anyone else. He was a born politician, one of the very few Normans at this stage to realise the full measure of the stakes for which he was playing, and he saw far enough ahead to understand that Pandulf's continued success might prove disastrous to Norman interests. He had supported the Prince of Capua long enough; the time had now come to change sides. He knew perfectly well how indispensable his support would be to the city-states, and when messengers arrived—as he knew they would—from Sergius of Naples and the Duke of Gaeta with proposals for an alliance, he was in a position to make his own terms.

The negotiations were successful, and led to plans; the plans were successful, and led to action; the action was successful and in 1029, less than two years after his expulsion, Sergius had returned to Naples and the Wolf was back in his Capuan lair, licking his wounds. The Normans had won again. This time, however, they obtained a more lasting reward for their services. Whether it was granted at their insistence or whether Sergius was himself only too anxious to provide for his future security we cannot be sure; but whatever the reason, early in 1030 Rainulf was formally presented with the town and territory of Aversa—receiving, as an additional token of gratitude and respect, the hand in marriage of Sergius's own sister, the widow of the Duke of Gaeta.

It was, for the Normans, the greatest day since their arrival in Italy. After thirteen years they at last had a fief of their own. Henceforth they would no longer be a race of foreign mercenaries or vagabonds. The land they occupied was theirs by right, legally conferred upon them according to the age-old feudal tradition. They were tenants of their own freely-elected leader, one of their own kind yet now himself a member of the South Italian aristocracy, brother-in-law of the Duke of Naples. To a people so conscious of due form and legality, such an advance in status was of inestimable significance. It had little effect at first on their general behaviour; all the old activities continued—the playing of one side against another, the fomentation of discord among the squabbling Greek and Lombard barons, the selling of their swords to any who would buy. But they now had a clear long-term object in view—the acquisition of land for themselves in Italy. Many rootless groups of Normans still roamed the hills and the highways leading a life of freebooting and brigandage; yet more and more of their leaders would, after 1030, set themselves up in fixed and fortified settlements in imitation of Rainulf, and devote their energies to the carving out of a permanent territory of their own. From the moment that the Normans become landowners their whole attitude begins to change —not only towards their neighbours but towards the country itself. Italy is no longer just a battlefield and a bran-tub, no longer a land to be plundered and despoiled; but one to be appropriated, developed and enriched. It is, in fact, their home.

For a while, Rainulf seems to have occupied himself principally with the task of strengthening and consolidating his new fief.[1]

[1] There has long persisted a popular legend, probably originating with the English chronicler Ordericus Vitalis, according to which Aversa took its name from the Latin *Adversa*, i.e. the place of those who were hostile to the other inhabitants of the country. It is, alas, unfounded. The name already exists in records dating from the very first years of the century, before Rainulf and his followers left Normandy. Aversa, though its cathedral still bears traces of Norman work, is now a curiously uninteresting town, chiefly notable for being the birthplace of Cimarosa and for its enormous lunatic asylum.

Aversa lies on the open Campanian plain between Capua and Naples and was thus bound to receive the attentions of Pandulf before long. So indeed it did; but not altogether in the way that had been expected. In 1034 Rainulf's wife, the sister of Duke Sergius, suddenly died. Pandulf had a niece, whose father had recently succeeded to the throne of Amalfi; and her hand he now offered to the sorrowing widower. The promise of such consolation, with all that it involved—alliance with Pandulf and the inevitable ruin of Sergius, his erstwhile brother-in-law and greatest benefactor—was more than Rainulf could resist. He accepted. Sergius had only recently sustained the loss of Sorrento, which at Pandulf's instigation had revolted against him and established itself as an independent city-state under Capuan protection; he now had to suffer the incomparably heavier blow of the defection of Aversa, and with it the loss of the Norman support on which he most depended. On the personal level the shock was equally shattering; the sister he loved was dead, the brother-in-law he respected had betrayed him. There was no justice, no loyalty, no gratitude. He did not care to go on. Broken in spirit, he left Naples and entered a monastery where, shortly afterwards, he died.

This was probably the most treacherous act in Rainulf's life; but if he felt any remorse he certainly did not show it. He had, as always, but one object—the strengthening of his own position—and in the pursuit of this end he flung himself with enthusiasm into his new alliance. Thus there began a period during which the Prince of Capua, supported by the lord of Aversa and the Dukes of Sorrento, Salerno and Amalfi, showed himself to be unquestionably the greatest power in the land. Only a few years before, Rainulf had been devoting all his energies to curbing Pandulf's ambitions, but since his own advancement the situation had been transformed. The strength of Capua, great as it was, now depended entirely on the Norman alliance, and in any case Rainulf was no longer just an ally; he was a potential rival.

For the time being, however, he was prepared to let Pandulf enjoy his glory. And the Prince of Capua was doing so to the full when the first of the sons of Tancred de Hauteville rode down into Italy.

Some eight miles to the north-east of Coutances in Normandy

lies the little village of Hauteville-la-Guichard. Nothing but its
name now remains to connect it with that strange, gifted clan whose
reputation and influence once bestrode the civilised world from
London to Antioch. At the beginning of the last century, however,
the remains of an old castle could still be seen beside a running
stream, and a French historian, Gauttier du Lys d'Arc, writing of a
visit there in 1827, proudly quotes the words of a local peasant who
lived there: '*Chest ichin, mes bons messeus, qu'est né l'incomparable
Tancrède, et Robert Guiscard, qui veut dire prudent; ils ont baillé des
trésors immenses d'or au bienheureux Geoffroy pour bâtir notre cathédrale,
pour remercier Dieu des graces qu'il leur avait faites d'avoir si bien réussi
dans leurs guerres de Sicile et d'Egypte.*'[1]

Tancred himself is fortunate in having had thrust upon him an
immortality which he did little to deserve. There was nothing
incomparable about this petty provincial baron, commander of a
modest group of ten knights in the militia of Duke Robert of
Normandy; indeed, from the little we know of him, he does not
even appear to have been particularly remarkable—unless it was
for his determined and persistent fecundity. Writing towards the
turn of the century Geoffrey Malaterra, a Benedictine monk whose
Historia Sicula is our principal source for the early beginnings
of the Hautevilles, tells us that Tancred's first wife was a certain
Muriella, a lady 'splendid in morals and birth', by whom he had
five sons—William, Drogo, Humphrey, Geoffrey and Serlo. On
her death he married again, for reasons which Malaterra finds it
necessary to explain in some detail:

Since he was not yet old and could not therefore maintain continence but,
being an upright man, found dishonourable intercourse abhorrent, he
took to him a second wife. For, mindful of the apostolic words; *to avoid
fornication, let every man have his own wife*, and further: *but whoremongers and
adulterers God will judge*, he preferred rather to be content with one legitimate wife than to pollute himself with the embraces of concubines.

The eager Tancred now therefore married the lady Fressenda

[1] 'Here it was, good sirs, that the incomparable Tancred was born, and Robert
Guiscard—that is, the crafty one. They gave our blessed Geoffrey great loads of golden
treasure to build our Cathedral, in thanks to God for bringing them such victories in
their wars in Sicily and Egypt.'

'in generosity and morals not inferior to the first', who presented him in swift and apparently effortless succession with seven more sons—Robert, Mauger, another William, Aubrey, Tancred, Humbert and Roger—and at least three daughters. For this formidable brood the family fief was clearly inadequate. Owing, however, to Rainulf's repeated appeals for reinforcements, the opportunities offered to young Normans in South Italy were well known; and in about 1035 the first three of the Hauteville boys decided to seek their fortunes there. Over the Alps they rode, William, Drogo and Humphrey, and made straight for Aversa; and so it was that they soon found themselves members of Rainulf's army in service with the Prince of Capua.

Pandulf was not long to hold the loyalty of the Hautevilles. Within a year or two, as might have been expected, he had antagonised all his allies. They were shocked by his compulsive double-dealing, insulted by his high-handedness, revolted by his cruelty. Even by eleventh-century standards his behaviour was insufferable—most of all towards the Church. He had already cast the Archbishop of Capua into chains and replaced him with his own bastard son; and now he was deliberately intensifying his persecution of Monte Cassino. Ever since the hasty departure and death of his brother he had borne a grudge against the great monastery, over which he had determined to regain control; in particular he hated Atenulf's successor, the Abbot Theobald. Thus, at the first opportunity, he lured Theobald to Capua and flung him into gaol. A new abbot was immediately elected, but Pandulf took no notice; setting up one of his henchmen as 'general administrator', he seized control of all the monastery revenues, expropriated the land and parcelled it out as a reward for those Normans who had served him best. The poor monks were powerless; they could offer no resistance, even when they saw all their precious treasure and plate being carried away to Capua. They were kept half-starved—on the day of the Assumption there was not even any wine to celebrate the Mass— and Amatus, who was probably there at the time, reports that before long most of the brothers had left the monastery in despair, the abbot included—'and those that remained were wretchedly treated'.[1]

---

[1] *et cil qui remainstrent estoient vilanement traitié.*

The standard of revolt was raised by the young Prince of Salerno, Gaimar V,[1] who had now grown to manhood and was determined to assert himself against his uncle's tyranny. He had all the makings of a worthy antagonist. 'This Gaimar', writes Amatus, 'was more courageous than his father, more generous and more courteous; indeed he possessed all the qualities a layman should have—except that he took an excessive delight in women.'[2] This pardonable weakness did not, however, mitigate the anger of young Gaimar when in 1036 he heard that his own niece had been the victim of an attempted rape by the Prince of Capua. For him it was the last straw; but it was also just the sort of excuse he had been waiting for. The other cities and duchies were, for the most part, only too pleased to give him their support; Rainulf switched his allegiance with the effortlessness born of long practice, and within a few weeks the whole land was once again in arms.

Pandulf had been somehow able to retain the loyalties of one or two of his old allies, including that fair-sized contingent of Normans whose support he had purchased with lands from Monte Cassino. The defection to Gaimar of Rainulf and his followers consequently meant that the active forces on both sides were now largely composed of Normans—a fact which explains the somewhat indecisive nature of the fighting which followed. Gaimar would, as he himself knew, ultimately prove the stronger; but he knew also how quickly the pendulum could swing, and with a wisdom beyond his years he realised that no lasting victory could be achieved without imperial ratification. The only problem was—which Empire? In the past fifteen years both the Eastern and the Western had sent armies to assert their power in South Italy; this was perhaps a moment to play one against the other. The Prince of Salerno therefore sent appeals to both Emperors for their intervention and arbitration, justifying his recent actions by a long and detailed rehearsal of his uncle's crimes.

Conrad II, already in North Italy, was well aware of the chaotic

---

[1] Or IV. See p. 16 n.

[2] *Cestui Gamérie estoit plus vaillant que le père et plus libéral et cortois à donner, liquel estoit aorné de toutes les vertus que home sécular doit avoir fors de tant que moult se délictoit de avoir moult de fames.*

situation prevailing in the south, for which, by his thoughtless release of Pandulf twelve years before, he bore the indirect responsibility. During those years, however, Conrad had learned much; he had also built up a reputation for strength and, above all, for justice. He could not ignore Gaimar's appeal—particularly after he heard that a similar one had already been addressed to Constantinople. His own authority must be maintained over his vassals, and the supremacy of the Western Empire over the Eastern in the peninsula must be clearly demonstrated. In the first months of 1038, at the head of his army, he marched down to restore order.

He went straight to Monte Cassino. Several of the fugitive monks had already made their way to his court and laid their complaints before him; but on arrival at the monastery he found the situation even worse than he had feared. Messengers were at once sent to Pandulf ordering him in the Emperor's name to restore all the monastic lands and property that he had filched and, at the same time, to release the countless political prisoners who were languishing in Capuan gaols.

Pandulf was in a hopelessly untenable position. He had no allies of consequence and no means of opposing the Emperor. At first he adopted the tactics of penitence, offering substantial sums of money and his own children as hostages for his future good behaviour. Conrad accepted; but before long Pandulf's son escaped from his custodians and the Wolf reverted to his old form. Trusting to ride out the storm till the Emperor was safely back in Germany, he fled to one of his outlying castles at Sant' Agata dei Goti (its ruins still stand) and barricaded himself in. It was no use. The Emperor, ably assisted by Rainulf and his Normans, dealt with Pandulf's few remaining adherents in a swift mopping-up campaign and then returned to Capua where he solemnly installed Gaimar on the throne, to the plaudits of a populace heavily bribed with Salernitan gold. The game was up—Pandulf had one course only open to him. He fled to his old friends in Constantinople. But even here he was unlucky. On his arrival, to his intense surprise and for reasons which he could not understand, he was immediately clapped into prison.

Conrad returned the same summer to Germany. His expedition

had been short, but entirely successful. He had dealt with Pandulf, restored Monte Cassino to its old prosperity, and demonstrated once again the power and efficacy of imperial justice. Equally important, he had left supreme in South Italy a strong, energetic and remarkably virile young man who respected him and owed him a debt of considerable gratitude. Within a year the Emperor would be dead, aged barely fifty; but he would leave his southern dominions far healthier and more stable than poor Henry, his predecessor, had been able to do.

The real triumph was Gaimar's. While still only at the threshold of manhood he had raised himself to a position higher than ever his father or uncle had attained. In doing so he had incurred no enmities, broken no promises. He had not only the approval, but the active support and friendship of the Emperor of the West. He was generally popular in Italy. He had intelligence and health, and was outstandingly handsome. For him indeed the future seemed to smile.

But the Normans too had cause for satisfaction. Rainulf and his men had ended up as usual on the winning side. They had fought for Gaimar, and they had fought for Conrad. Their losses has been small, their numbers were still increasing. Most important of all, Gaimar had arranged that the Emperor, before leaving Italy, should confirm Rainulf's possession of Aversa by granting him a title of nobility and simultaneously transferring his vassalage from Naples to Salerno. And so it came about that in the summer of 1038 Conrad II formally invested Rainulf the Norman with the lance and gonfalon of the County of Aversa. As the new Count rose from his knees, no one knew better than he did why this investiture had been performed—simply to ensure that he, as sworn vassal to the Prince of Capua and Salerno, would be obliged to defend his suzerain as and when necessary from all his enemies. But at the moment this was of little consequence. The important fact was that Rainulf was now not only a major landowner, a local aristocrat and one of the most powerful military leaders in Italy; he was also a member of the imperial nobility, possessor of rights and a title which could be withdrawn from him only by the Emperor himself. Another vital and essential step had been taken towards his by now clearly-beheld objective—the Norman domination of the South.

As for the three young Hautevilles, their introduction into Italian politics had taught them much. They had seen how tumultuous was the land of their choice, how quickly an intelligent youth could scale the heights of power, how easily a prince could be brought low. They had learnt, too, that in a land of such shifting currents and brittle alliances diplomacy was as important as courage, that a sharp sword was valuable but a sharp mind more valuable still. They had witnessed both the strength of the imperial hand when it was imminent and its ineffectiveness when it was remote. And they had before them the example of a leader who, playing his cards with subtlety and care, had in twenty years achieved wealth, influence and nobility.

These were lessons that they would not forget.

4

SICILY

There's Sicily, for instance,—granted me
And taken back, some years since . . .
Browning, *King Victor and King Charles*

THE Prince of Salerno's appeal for assistance, to which Conrad II had reacted so promptly and effectively in 1038, had met with a disappointing lack of response from Constantinople, whither it had also been addressed. Since the removal of Boioannes in 1027 Greek influence in Italy had steadily declined. Pandulf was not the only one to have taken advantage of the weakness of Constantine VIII. In Apulia the Lombards were again growing restive under a succession of ineffectual Catapans; while the Saracens, who had seen in the death of Basil II the merciful hand of Allah, had redoubled the violence of their attacks and were extending the radius of their operations dangerously near to Constantinople itself.

If only the Bulgar-Slayer had left a son all might have been well. As things were, the problem of the succession was becoming increasingly confused. Constantine died in 1028, leaving no sons either—only three daughters, of whom the eldest, badly disfigured by smallpox, had long ago been packed off to a convent. The other two, Zoë and Theodora, were almost equally ill-favoured, both unmarried and well past their prime. It was typical of Constantine that he did nothing to remedy this situation until he was on his deathbed; he then picked on the elderly Mayor of Constantinople, Romanus Argyrus, and hurriedly married him off to Zoë. Three days later he died, and Romanus and Zoë jointly ascended the throne. Romanus, however, was not to enjoy it for long. He soon fell victim to a disagreeable wasting disease which caused his hair and beard to fall out—a condition ascribed by some to the prodigious quantity of aphrodisiacs he had vainly consumed in the hopes of begetting a son on the fifty-year-old Zoë, and by others to slow poison. The latter is not unlikely; for the Empress having at last awakened to the realisation of the joys she had been missing, was clearly determined to make up for lost time and had taken a lover— a handsome though epileptic young Paphlagonian money-changer called Michael. This youth was in fact the brother of the most powerful eunuch of the court, a certain John the Orphanotrophos, who had become the virtual administrator of the Empire and, being determined that his family should found a dynasty—he himself being regrettably disqualified from doing so—had purposely introduced Michael to Zoë with this end in view. The plot was successful; the Empress fell besottedly in love and soon was making no secret of her eagerness to be rid of her useless husband. On Good Friday 1034 Romanus expired in his bath. That same evening Michael married his elderly mistress and became Emperor.

For the beginning of a new reign, such circumstances were hardly auspicious; but Michael IV, with his brother's help, proved a notable improvement on his predecessor. Before long he started to develop plans for continuing the work begun by Basil II and driving the Saracens from Sicily. Their continual raids were no longer merely an annoyance; they were rapidly becoming a threat to Byzantine security. And it was not only the coastal towns that were suffering from their depredations. The city merchants complained that the high seas were alive with pirates, prices of imports were rising accordingly and foreign trade was beginning to suffer. To all Greeks, Sicily remained part of the Byzantine birthright; it still possessed a considerable Greek population. That it should still be occupied by the heathen was therefore an affront to both national security and national pride. The Arabs must go.

The chances of launching a successful campaign were in some ways more favourable for Michael than they had been for Basil ten years earlier. Civil war had now broken out among the Arab rulers in the island. The Emir of Palermo, al-Akhal, had suddenly found himself confronted with an insurgent army led by his brother Abu Hafs and stiffened by six thousand warriors from Africa under

46

the command of Abdullah, son of the Zirid Caliph of Kairouan; and, in 1035, growing desperate, he appealed to Byzantium for help. Michael agreed—such an opportunity, he knew, might never be repeated. Before he could send more than a token force, news of al-Akhal's assassination removed this useful pretext for a Sicilian landing; but the revolt was now rapidly spreading through Sicily, and the Saracens, more and more hopelessly divided, seemed unlikely to be able to offer much resistance to a concerted Byzantine attack. Moreover, a major pirate raid on the Thracian coast had recently aroused alarm in the capital, which was beginning to feel itself threatened. And so preparations for the expedition continued as before, more slowly—since time now seemed to be on the side of the Greeks—but with all the care and thoroughness of which the Emperor and his sinister, efficient brother were capable. Only the avowed object was changed: there was no longer any question of honouring an alliance. The Greeks were out to reconquer Sicily.

When, therefore, in 1036 Gaimar appealed to Constantinople for military assistance in South Italy, prior commitments in Sicily furnished as valid an excuse as when Pandulf had made a similar appeal a dozen years before. Even without such an excuse, it is far from certain whether Michael would have taken decisive action; Pandulf had been a useful ally to Byzantium in the past and his cause was still by no means hopeless; why should the Eastern Empire bestir itself to eliminate the man who for twenty years had been one of the greatest thorns in the flesh of its western rival? Two years later, however, the situation had changed. Pandulf had been soundly beaten and his position was destroyed, apparently beyond hope of recovery. Gaimar on the other hand was powerful, and he was ambitious. If ever he were to turn against Byzantium, he could make serious trouble in the Capitanata. Besides, the Sicilian plans were taking shape and it was hoped that the Prince of Salerno-Capua and his fellow-rulers, who had suffered as much as anyone from the Arab raids, would make generous contributions in men and money. If Pandulf had had time to reflect a little, his imprisonment on arrival at Constantinople might have come as less of a shock.

The Sicilian expedition sailed in the early summer of 1038. It had been put under the command of the greatest of living Byzantine generals, the gigantic George Maniakes, still glorious from a series of Syrian triumphs six years before. Maniakes was, in character and achievement as in physique, well over life-size—one of those colourful near-geniuses thrown up at intervals through history who seem to have the world at their feet, only to lose it again through some compensatory defect which betrays them in a moment of crisis. The historian Michael Psellus has left us a fearsome description:

I myself saw the man, and marvelled at him; for nature had combined in his person all the qualities necessary for a military commander. He stood to the height of ten feet, so that to look at him men would tilt back their heads as if towards the top of a hill or a high mountain. His countenance was neither gentle nor pleasing, but put one in mind of a tempest; his voice was like thunder and his hands seemed made for tearing down walls or for smashing doors of bronze. He could spring like a lion and his frown was terrible. And every thing else about him was in proportion. Those who saw him for the first time discovered that every description they had heard of him was but an understatement.

The army which this magnificent ogre was to command was as usual heterogeneous. Its strongest element was an impressive Varangian contingent under the almost legendary Norse hero Harald Hardrada, returning from a pilgrimage to Jerusalem; its weakest a body of grumbling Lombards and Italians from Apulia who made no secret of their disgust at having been forced into Byzantine service. In between came the great bulk of Maniakes's force, composed principally of Greeks and Bulgarians. They were transported by a fleet of galleys commanded by a certain Stephen, an erstwhile ship-caulker whose only distinction was to have long ago married the sister of the Orphanotrophos and so to have woken up one morning to find himself the Emperor's brother-in-law—an event which had led to his rapid elevation to several positions of high responsibility, all well beyond his powers to fulfil.[1]

The expedition did not go at once to Sicily but first headed round to Salerno, there to collect a contribution from Gaimar. They found the young prince more than ready to help. The growth of his power

[1] Of Stephen, Psellus writes: 'I saw him after the metamorphosis. . . . It was as if a pygmy wanted to play Hercules and was trying to make himself look like the demi-god. The more such a person tries, the more his appearance belies him—clothed in the lion's skin but weighed down by the club' (tr. E. R. A. Sewter).

Norman Knights. Three eleventh-century chessmen from Southern Italy (Cabinet des Médailles, Paris)

Ystoire de li Normant, by Amatus of Monte Cassino. A page from the manuscript in the Bibliothèque Nationale, Paris had led to an unwontedly peaceful political climate, and the increasing numbers of idle Norman adventurers, bored, predatory and totally unprincipled, looking for trouble and constrained to live off the land, were proving a grave embarrassment to him. He retained, naturally, the Count of Aversa and his more trustworthy followers, who would be indispensable if an emergency should arise; but from the remainder, three hundred of the youngest and most headstrong were given their marching orders for Sicily and, encouraged by promises of large rewards, were embarked together with a number of Italians and Lombards on Stephen's ships. They included, inevitably, the Hautevilles.

The island of Sicily is the largest in the Mediterranean. It has also proved, over the centuries, to be the most unhappy. The stepping-stone between Europe and Africa, the gateway between the East and the West, the link between the Latin world and the Greek, at once a stronghold, observation-point and clearing-house, it has been fought over and occupied in turn by all the great powers that have at various times striven to extend their dominion across the Middle Sea. It has belonged to them all—and yet has properly been part of none; for the number and variety of its conquerors, while preventing the development of any strong national individuality of its own, have endowed it with a kaleidoscopic heritage of experience which can never allow it to become completely assimilated. Even today, despite the beauty of its landscape, the fertility of its fields and the perpetual benediction of its climate, there lingers everywhere some dark, brooding quality—some underlying sorrow of which poverty, Church influence, the Mafia and all the other popular modern scapegoats may be the manifestations but are certainly not the cause. It is the sorrow of long, unhappy experience, of opportunity lost and promise unfulfilled; the sorrow, perhaps, of a beautiful woman who has been raped too often and betrayed too often and is no longer fit for love or marriage. Phoenicians, Greeks, Carthaginians, Romans, Goths, Byzantines, Arabs, Normans, Germans, Spaniards, French —all have left their mark. Today, a century after being received into her Italian home, Sicily is probably less unhappy than she has been for many centuries; but though no longer lost she still seems lonely, seeking always an identity which she can never entirely find.

The Greeks first reached Sicily in the eighth century before Christ. Dislodging the indigenous inhabitants and a few Phoenician trading posts, they introduced the vine and the olive and built up a flourishing colony. This soon became one of the major cultural centres of the civilised world, the home of poets such as Stesichorus of Himera—whom the gods struck blind for composing invectives against Helen of Troy—and philosophers such as the great Empedocles of Acragas, who did much valuable work on the transmigration of souls and, having already served a long and tedious apprenticeship as a shrub, suddenly relinquished his mortal clay for higher things one morning in 440, when another branch of scientific enquiry led him too far into the crater of Mount Etna. But the golden age did not last long. The Peloponnesian War and the famous Athenian expedition brought the island into the thick of European affairs and opened the way to the first inroads by Carthage which, together with various Greek tyrants in individual cities (of whom Dionysius of Syracuse is the most celebrated), maintained its power until the third century B.C. Finally in 241, as a result of the First Punic War which stained the whole island red, Sicily was established as a Roman Province.

During the age of the Republic, the Romans treated Sicily with little respect. That monstrous inferiority complex to which they always gave way when confronted with Greek culture led to further destruction and exploitation on a colossal scale. A few free Greek cities managed to retain their independence, but over much of the island liberty was almost extinguished as the slave-gangs toiled naked in the fields, sowing and harvesting the corn for Rome. From time to time a serious slave revolt or a scandal such as the corrupt governorship of Verres—made notorious by the castigations of Cicero—casts a harsh though fleeting light on the prevailing conditions, but for most of this period Sicily bore her sufferings in silence. With the Empire the situation improved a little; Hadrian, that indefatigable traveller, paid a visit in A.D. 126 and climbed Etna, but at no time was the island considered more than the principal granary of Rome. As such it was taken for granted. No serious attempt was made to impose Roman civilisation, and despite a certain influx of Latin-speaking settlers it remained essentially Greek in language and outlook.

By the middle of the fifth century the Roman Empire in the West was on the threshold of extinction, and more and more of the provinces and colonies were slipping from its grasp. In A.D. 440 Sicily fell to the Vandals, who shortly afterwards passed it by treaty to the Ostrogoths; and for a time the island was ruled by Gothic counts. The Sicilians were treated with consideration, but they always resented their barbarian overlords. They therefore gave an enthusiastic welcome to the 'liberating' forces of the Emperor Justinian in 535. The Goths withdrew without showing any sign of fight except at Panormus—the present Palermo, but then a small port of very secondary importance.[1] Here the local governor attempted a stand; but Belisarius, most brilliant of Justinian's generals, ordered the Byzantine fleet to sail into the harbour, so close inshore that the masts of the ships rose above the town walls. He then had boats full of soldiers hoisted to the yard-arms, whence they were able to shoot down on the defenders. The Goths gave in.

Sicily was once again an imperial province. At one moment, indeed, it almost became a good deal more. In the middle of the seventh century the Byzantine Emperor Constans II, understandably concerned for the future of his western provinces under the whirl-wind surge of Islam, took the immense decision to shift the balance of the Empire westwards and to transfer his capital accordingly. Rome was the obvious choice; but after a depressing twelve-day visit there in 663—he was the first Emperor for nearly three hundred years to set foot in the Mother City—he gave up the idea and settled instead in the infinitely more congenial Greek atmosphere of Syracuse. It is fascinating to speculate how the history of Europe would have been changed if the capital had remained in Sicily; but the palace and court officials never became reconciled to the change, and five years later one of them, in a fit of uncontrollable nostalgia,

[1] Despite its superb geographical position, Palermo became the metropolis only under Saracen occupation. This explains why the city possesses virtually no classical antiquities—temples, theatres, even ruins—on the scale of those to be found elsewhere on the island. Almost the sole exceptions are a beautiful mosaic pavement of Orpheus and the animals and another representing the Four Seasons, now to be seen at the National Museum.

attacked the Emperor in his bath and felled him with the soap-dish. By now the Arabs were directing their main offensive towards Asia Minor and Constantinople itself, and so Constans's son and successor, Constantine IV the Bearded, had no choice but to return at once to the Bosphorus. Sicily was left in peace again.

This peace continued, generally speaking, throughout the eighth century, during which Sicily, like Calabria, became a haven for refugees from that *'calvinisme anticipé'*,[1] the iconoclast movement in Constantinople; but in the ninth it was shattered. The Muslims had waited long enough. They had by now overrun the whole of the North African coast, and had in fact already been harassing the island for some time with sporadic raids. In 827 they saw their chance of achieving permanent occupation: the local Byzantine governor, Euphemius by name, was dismissed from his post after an unseemly elopement with a local nun. His reply was to rise in revolt and pro-claim himself Emperor, appealing to the Arabs for aid. They landed in strength, rapidly entrenched themselves, took little notice of Euphemius (who in any case soon came to a violent end) and three years later stormed Palermo which they made their capital. Subse-quent progress was slow: Messina fell in 843 and Syracuse, after a long and arduous siege during which the defenders were finally reduced to cannibalism, surrendered only in 878. But after this the Byzantines seem to have admitted defeat. A few isolated outposts in the eastern part of the island held out a little longer—the last, Rometta, even into the middle of the tenth century—but on that June day when the banner of the Prophet was raised over Syracuse, Sicily became, to all intents and purposes, a part of the Muslim world.

Once the wars of conquest were over and the country had settled again, life continued pleasantly enough for most of the Christian communities. They were normally allowed to keep their freedom, on payment of an annual tribute which many must have preferred to the military service that had always been compulsory under Byzantine rule; and the Saracens displayed, as nearly always through-out their history, a degree of religious toleration which permitted the churches and monasteries and the long tradition of Hellenistic

[1] Lenormant.

scholarship to flourish as much as ever they had done.[1] In other ways too the island benefited from its conquerors. The Arabs brought with them a whole new system of agriculture based on such innovations as terracing and syphon aqueducts for irrigation. They introduced cotton and papyrus, citrus and date-palm and enough sugar-cane to make possible, within a very few years, a substantial export trade. Under the Byzantines Sicily had never played an important part in European commerce, but with the Saracen conquest it soon became one of the major trading centres of the Mediterranean, with Christian, Muslim and Jewish merchants thronging the bazaars of Palermo.

And yet, among the many blessings conferred upon Sicily by her Arab conquerors, that of stability was conspicuously absent. As the links of loyalty which at first held the Emir of Palermo and his fellow-chieftains to the North African caliphate grew ever more tenuous, the emirs themselves lost their only cohesive force; they became increasingly divided against each other and so the island found itself once again a battleground of warring factions. And it was this steady political decline, culminating in the Zirid invasion under Abdullah referred to above, that in 1038 brought the Greeks —and their Norman allies—to Sicily.

Some time during the late summer the Greek army landed on Sicilian soil. At first they carried all before them. Courageously as the divided Saracens fought, they could do little to stem the tide. Messina fell almost at once and was followed, after heavy fighting, by Rometta, the key fortress that commanded the pass linking Messina with the northern coastal road to Palermo. Of the next stage of the campaign we know little—the chroniclers are silent or

---

[1] Towards the end of the tenth century St Nilus, the famous Calabrian abbot, sent the Emir of Palermo a sum of money with which he hoped to ransom three of his monks, captured by Saracen raiders. He supported his request with a letter to the Emir's chief notary, a Christian, but can hardly have expected as cordial a response as he in fact received. The Emir liberated the monks and returned the ransom under cover of a letter saying that he would have provided the monastery with a grant of immunity from raids, if the Abbot had only requested it. He went on to invite Nilus to settle in Sicily, promising him that he would enjoy there all the honour and veneration that were his due.

impossibly vague.[1] There seems, however, to have been a slow but
steady advance on Syracuse where, in 1040, we find Maniakes and
his troops laying siege to the city. The Muslim garrison resisted
fiercely, and held their assailants long enough to allow Abdullah to
muster a relief force in the mountains behind Syracuse with the
object of swooping down on Maniakes's rear. Word of this plan
reached the Greeks just in time; wheeling round, Maniakes surprised Abdullah's men near Troina and immediately attacked. The
defeat was absolute. The Muslims fled in disorder and the garrison
of Syracuse, realising that they could no longer hope for relief,
surrendered without more ado. The exultant Greek population lost
no time in arranging thanksgiving services, and disinterred from
their hiding-places all their most treasured religious relics to do
greater honour to their glorious liberator; though they cannot have
been best pleased when Maniakes had the body of St Lucia removed
from its coffin and, finding the saint (as Amatus describes her) 'as
whole and sweet-smelling as the first day she was put there', sent
her with his compliments to the Emperor.

It is hard to estimate how much of this early success was due to
the Norman contingent in Maniakes's army. The Norman chroniclers, from whom most of our information comes, stress the valour
of their compatriots to the point where the Greeks often appear to
have had nothing to do but pick up the spoils when the battles were
over. Certainly the Normans fought hard and well; and it was during the siege of Syracuse that William de Hauteville, catching sight of
the redoubtable Emir of the city as he rode out on a sortie, made a
sudden charge, unhorsed him and left him dead on the ground. For
this exploit he was ever afterwards known as *Bras-de-Fer*, the Iron-
Arm; and the glory which he won before the walls of Syracuse was
to serve him in good stead on his return to the mainland.

Yet the main credit for the success of the expedition up to this
point must go to Maniakes. What might have been a disastrous

[1] One of the few clues remaining is the abbey church of S. Maria di Maniace near
Maletto, built on the site of one of Maniakes's victories by the local Greek population
soon after the battle, enlarged and restored by Count Roger I and Countess Adelaide
towards the end of the century. This was the church around which, in about 1170,
Queen Margaret was to found the large and richly-endowed Benedictine abbey of
Maniace, last of the great Norman foundations in Sicily.

defeat by Abdullah's forces was turned to victory by the effectiveness of his intelligence and the speed and energy of his generalship. He himself had suffered negligible losses, except possibly at Rometta, and in less than two years had restored the eastern half of the island to Christian hands.[1] It was a tragedy, not only for him but for the whole Byzantine Empire, that at this of all moments he should have been recalled, in disgrace, to Constantinople.

The demoralisation of the Byzantine forces and their collapse after the victory of Syracuse were so sudden and so complete that one can readily understand the Saracens' contention that Allah had again intervened on their behalf. Everything seemed to go wrong at once. And just as he takes the credit for the victories, so now some at least of the blame must fall on the personality of Maniakes. Superb general as he was, he cannot have been an easy colleague. He had never attempted to hide his contempt of Stephen, and when he heard after Troina that Abdullah had somehow managed to escape by sea through the naval blockade, he forgot himself so far as to lay hands upon the admiral physically. Stephen—for whom, in view of his assailant's size, the experience must have been not only humiliating but also alarming in the extreme—determined on revenge and sent an urgent message to his imperial brother-in-law denouncing Maniakes for treasonable activity. Maniakes was summoned to the capital where, without being given any opportunity to answer to charges made against him, he was cast unceremoniously into prison. His successor, a eunuch called Basil, proved as incapable as was Stephen; the Greeks lost their momentum and their morale; and the retreat began.

Meanwhile the Normans had left in disgust. Once again Maniakes seems to have been at fault. Many an inspired general has proved intolerable off the battlefield, and Maniakes's undoubted propensities towards violence could not fail to lead him into trouble with his men. Soon after the capture of Syracuse a dispute arose over the distribution of spoils, of which the Normans had decided that they

---

[1] The Castello Maniace which now stands on the southernmost tip of the Syracuse peninsula dates only from the thirteenth century. But even though it has no direct historical association with the great George, it remains a magnificent memorial to his name.

were receiving less than their fair share. This claim may have been justified; a Greek city, liberated by a Greek army, clearly provided no opportunity for plunder or pillage and it is doubtful if these self-confessed mercenaries had received much recompense for the best part of two years' campaigning. At all events the Normans persuaded the leader of the Salerno contingent, a Greek-speaking Lombard called Arduin, to remonstrate with Maniakes on their behalf. Amatus's story that Arduin had himself refused to surrender a captured Arab horse to the Commander-in-Chief may or may not be true; if so, the fact must have inflamed the general's wrath still further. What is virtually certain is that Arduin was stripped and beaten for his presumption, and that he, the Normans and their Salternitan comrades left the Greek army forthwith and returned to the mainland, taking the Scandinavian brigade with them.

With the departure of all their best fighting men, followed by that of their only capable general, there was little hope left for the Greeks. But more trouble was to come. For several years dissatisfaction had been growing in Apulia. Young Argyrus, the son of Melus who had recently returned to Italy after years of imprisonment in Constantinople, had inherited all his father's rebellious spirit; and he had little difficulty, particularly after the Greek press-gangs had begun their forcible recruiting for the Sicilian expedition, in working up the Italians and Lombards in Apulia against their Byzantine masters. Already in 1038 several Greek officials had been murdered; in 1039 the situation was near flash-point; and in 1040 Argyrus gave the signal for revolt. The Catapan was assassinated, and all the local militias along the Apulian coast rose up in a mutiny which the local Greek garrisons, themselves seriously depleted, were unable to contain.

5

INSURRECTION

Et lo matin li Normant s'en aloient solachant par li camp, et par li jardin lo
menoit à Vénoze laquelle estoit de près de Melfe, liez et joians sur lor chevaux,
et vont corrant çà et là: et li citadin de la cité virent cil chevalier liquel non
cognoissoient, si s'en merveilloient et orent paour. Et li Normant a une proie
grandissime et sanz nulle brigue la menoient ad Melfe. . . . Et d'iluec s'en vont à
la belle Puille, et celles choses qui lor plaisoit prenoient, et celle qui ne lor plaisoient
leissoient. . . .
   Il firent lor conte Guillerme fil de Tancrède, home vaillantissime en armes et
aorné de toutes bonnes costumes, et beauz et gentil et jovène.

(And in the morning the Normans rode gaily off through the meadows
and gardens towards Venosa, which is not far from Melfi, happy and
joyful on their horses, cavorting hither and thither; and the citizens of the
town saw these unknown knights, and wondered at them and were
afraid. And the Normans returned with immense plunder and brought it
back without trouble to Melfi . . . And from there they set off for lovely
Apulia, and what they liked they took, and what they did not like they
left. . . .

   And William, Tancred's son, they made their Count, a man most
courageous in war, and possessed of all good qualities; handsome, and
noble, and young.)

Amatus, II

BY the time the news of the insurrection reached Constantinople,
the Emperor Michael was obviously dying. His epilepsy now made
it necessary for his throne to be placed so that purple curtains could
be drawn at a moment's notice in the event of a sudden seizure,
while most of his failing energies were taken up with ascetic practices and charities—in particular the asylum for reformed prostitutes
which he had recently founded in the capital. His brother the
Orphanotrophos, however, acted swiftly and appointed an able

young general, Michael Doukeianos, as the new Catapan with instructions to restore order in Apulia at any cost. Doukeianos left at once and, summoning all available men, by the end of 1040 had managed to damp down—though not by any means entirely to extinguish—the flames of revolt. He was a man of energy and imagination and, but for one mistake, he might easily have succeeded in restoring Byzantine fortunes in Italy. By that one mistake he destroyed them for ever.

Soon after his arrival the new Catapan found it necessary to pay a hurried visit to Sicily—presumably to hasten the departure of the remnants of the Greek army, whose help was urgently needed in Apulia. On his return journey—he may have taken ship to Salerno—he met Arduin, who had returned with the Normans to Gaimar's court. From the start the two seem to have been on excellent terms; Arduin spoke perfect Greek; he was an experienced soldier who could call on a large number of Normans to fight with him; and his recent quarrel with the disgraced Maniakes may well have been an additional point in his favour. At all events it was not long before Arduin, a Lombard, accepted the Catapan's offer of the post of *topoterites,* or military commander, of Melfi, one of the principal hill-towns along the Byzantine frontier.

Should Doukeianos have known better? His gullibility certainly proved his undoing, but it must not be too hastily condemned. A strong commander was required for Melfi, and strong commanders were rare among the Greeks in Italy. Arduin could boast an excellent record and had in the past fought well for the Byzantine cause. His departure from Sicily could not possibly be held against him—continued service with Maniakes would have been impossible after what had happened at Syracuse. In language and cultural background he seemed more Greek than the Greeks, and even if he was of Lombard origin, this did not necessarily imply disloyalty; Lombards had often held high positions in the Capitanata. Besides, the need was urgent and Doukeianos could not afford to be too particular. He little knew how hugely he would be betrayed.

Arduin's motives can only be guessed. Ambition certainly played the major part. He was a Lombard; the Lombards were in revolt. Here was an opportunity, and he suddenly found himself with the means to seize it. To command a body of three hundred fearless Norman knights on a victorious campaign must have been an exhilarating experience, and he knew that those same knights, if it was made worth their while, would be ready to leap into action again at his command. His support for the Lombard cause at this moment might therefore tip the scales and make all the difference between the independence and the subjection of his race. Moreover he was still smarting from the treatment he had suffered from Maniakes and was bent on avenging himself on the Greeks. As soon as he reached Melfi, therefore, he began quietly subverting the local populace. Amatus writes in breathless admiration of his technique:

He gave frequent feasts, to which he invited well-born and lowly alike, offering them choice meats; and when they had eaten he would speak to them in gentle words . . . feigning sympathy for the hardships they suffered from their Greek overlords and the insults endured by their womenfolk. . . . Ah, with what wise subtlety did he stir up gentry and people against those who ill-treated them![1]

In March 1041, as soon as he was sure of support within the town, Arduin travelled secretly to Aversa. There, with the covert support of Rainulf, he found his three hundred Norman stalwarts, gathered under twelve chiefs who included William and Drogo de Hauteville. His proposition was simple enough; he would give them Melfi as their headquarters and from there the Lombards and Normans together would drive the Greeks once and for all from South Italy, dividing the conquered territory equally between them. The Normans did not need much persuading, and Arduin's exhortation, if Amatus's account of it is accurate, was nothing short of masterly—working first on their pride, then on their ambition, next arousing their contempt for the enemy and finally appealing directly to their covetousness:

You still occupy this land which was given to you, yet you live in it like mice in the skirting . . . now it is time to reach out with a strong hand, and in this I will be your leader. Follow me; I will go before, you will follow;

---

[1] *Faisoit sovent convit, li gentilhome et li non gentil envitoit a son convit, et lor donoit délicioses viandez; et puiz quant avoient mengié parloit de amicables paroles . . . et feingnoit qu'il estoit dolent de la grevance qu'il souffroient de la seignorie de li Grex, et l'injure qu'il faisoient à lor moilliers et à lor fames. . . . Ha! quel sage soutillesces pour lever la seignorie à li seignor qui lui firent injure, et émut lo puple contre eaux!* [II, 16].

and let me tell you why—because I will lead you against men who are as women, and who live in a rich and spacious land.[1]

The *topoterites* had left his post under cover of darkness, alone; he returned with an army. The inhabitants of Melfi at first hesitated when they saw it; but Arduin's ever-agile tongue persuaded them that this was the means of their deliverance. They opened the gates. It was a momentous decision. From that day Melfi became the spearhead of the revolt. Already heavily fortified by the Greeks and now almost impregnable on its Apennine hill-top, it constituted the perfect mountain stronghold. From it the Norman knights, still highwaymen at heart, could spread out in all directions, raiding and pillaging to their hearts' content; to it they could return with their plunder, confident in its security and in their own immunity from reprisals.[2]

Within days Venosa fell; then Lavello, then Ascoli. The Catapan, bitterly conscious of his own responsibility for what had happened— though he may not yet have realised the full dimensions of the catas- trophe—hastened up from Bari with all the forces he could muster, and on 16 March he sighted the main body of the Norman army, now swelled by large numbers of Lombards, near the banks of the Olivento, a little stream running just below Venosa. Calling a halt, he sent a mesenger across to them, offering them the choice: either they could leave Byzantine territory peaceably and at once, or they must meet his own army in battle on the morrow.

The Normans had heard communications of that sort before, and knew how to deal with them. During the harangue one of the twelve chiefs, Hugh Tuboeuf, had approached the messenger's horse and had been stroking it approvingly; now, as the man finished, he suddenly turned and struck it one mighty blow between the eyes with his bare fist, laying the luckless animal unconscious on the ground. At this, according to Malaterra, the messenger in a paroxysm

---

[1] *Vouz encoire estes en ceste terre qui vouz a été donée et vouz i habitez comme la sorice qui est en lo partus. . . . entre il convient que faille estende vostre main forte et dont je vouz menerai; venez apres moi, et je irai devant et vous apres; et vouz dirai pourquoi je voiz devant, que sachiez que je vouz menerai a homes comme fames, liquel demorent en molt ricche et espaciouse terre* [II, 17].

[2] The hill of Melfi is still crowned by the ruins of its Norman castle. It was, however, largely rebuilt in 1281 and suffered severely in the earthquake of 1851. Little of the original structure now remains.

of fear fainted dead away; but the Normans, having with some difficulty restored him to his senses, gave him a new horse, better than the first, on which they sent him back to the Catapan with the message that they were ready.

The battle was fought the next morning. It ended in a total defeat of the Greeks. Many of them were killed, including nearly all the contingent of Varangians that Doukeianos had brought up from Bari; and a large number were drowned as they tried to cross the swollen waters of the Olivento. The Catapan could only withdraw his battered remnants; more soldiers would have to be found before he met the Normans a second time.

Again the press-gangs scoured the towns and villages of Apulia. They moved quickly and at the beginning of May their work was done. This time it was the river Ofanto that saw the confrontation of the two armies—at Montemaggiore, on that same field of Cannae that Greeks, Lombards and Normans had drenched with their blood twenty-three years before. Though the dispositions were similar, the outcome was radically different from that of 1018. The Normans were again outnumbered, but now it was their turn to sweep their adversaries from the field. Their general was William de Hauteville, the Iron-Arm. He was suffering from a high fever and had not intended to take part in the battle, but as he watched from a nearby hill the temptation suddenly became too great. Jumping from his litter, he charged down the slope into the thick of the fray and led his men to victory.

News of these two consecutive defeats caused grave concern in Constantinople. Doukeianos was transferred to Sicily, where he was given the ungrateful task of salvaging what was left of the expedition; he was succeeded in Apulia by another Boioannes, son of the great Basil. But if there had been any hopes that this young man's ability might match that of his brilliant father, they were soon disappointed. The new Catapan, who had brought no reinforcements with him, rightly decided to avoid pitched battles if he could, and resolved instead to besiege the Normans and the Lombards in Melfi; but they were too quick for him. Streaming from the town before the Greek army had reached it they encamped near by at Monte Siricolo, near Montepeloso. Here, on 3 September 1041, they inflicted their third defeat on the hapless Byzantines and took prisoner the Catapan. Boioannes was handed over to Atenulf, brother of the reigning Prince of Benevento, who had recently been given the titular leadership of the rising. Lashed to his horse, he was paraded in triumph through the streets of the city. Meanwhile the cumulative effect of the three Lombard victories had been to undermine what was left of Byzantine prestige in Apulia; Bari, Monopoli, Giovinazzo, Matera, all declared themselves openly for the insurgents. The revolt was fast gathering momentum.

But now dissension broke out. The Lombards of Apulia were not prepared to be dictated to by Arduin, nor to accept, even as a figurehead, the colourless Atenulf of Benevento, both of whom they rightly suspected of being the unconscious tools of the Normans. In this they were supported by Gaimar, since 1038 the Prince of Capua as well as Salerno, who, being himself by far the most powerful of Lombard princes, deeply resented the choice of Atenulf as leader. A similar split appeared in the Norman ranks. The little colony which had been installed in Troia twenty years before had now, like its counterpart in Aversa, grown in numbers and influence and saw no cause to take orders from a group of freebooting upstarts in Melfi. These Apulian Normans therefore joined with their Lombard neighbours in demanding as their chief young Argyrus, who had after all been the instigator of the revolt and who, as Melus's son, was better qualified by blood for the leadership than was any Beneventan princeling. It was in vain for Arduin and his supporters to point out that they, and not the Apulians, had done all the fighting; the ground was cut from under their feet by Atenulf himself, who was discovered to have sold Boioannes back to the Greeks and to have kept all the ransom money for himself. Their candidate disgraced, the Melfi faction capitulated. In February 1042 Argyrus was formally acclaimed by the Normans and Lombards together in the Church of S. Apollinare at Bari.

This rivalry between Argyrus and Atenulf makes it clear that, whatever the Norman chroniclers may imply, there was still no overt question of a seizure of power by the Normans for themselves; this was still essentially a revolt by Lombards against Byzantines and was generally regarded as such. The possibility of electing a Norman as leader is never suggested, for the Normans are still theoretically mercenaries, fighting for territorial rewards perhaps, but not for political domination. And yet it is not so simple as that. From about 1040 one is conscious of a slow change in the atmosphere. Norman prestige now stems from something deeper than military prowess; Norman views are sought on questions unrelated to strategy and warfare, while they themselves take decisions which affect not only their own position but the future of the peninsula as a whole. Their place in Italy is no longer questioned, and their attitude to the land has something proprietary about it which was not there before. Their future is growing clearer to them all the time, and they seem to be waiting only for a leader who will focus their aspirations and translate them into action.

That leader was not long in coming.

The quarrels among the Normans and the Lombards were as nothing compared to the events which now took place in Constantinople. On 10 December 1041 Michael IV died. The Orphanotrophos was ready. Determined as ever that his own family should continue to occupy the imperial throne, he had already induced Zoë to adopt his nephew—son of the admiral Stephen—as heir-presumptive. This step, however, proved his undoing. Michael V, surnamed Calaphates—the caulker—after his father's early profession, had scarcely assumed power before he banished his uncle, to whom he owed everything, to a distant place of exile. A few weeks later it was the turn of Zoë herself; the old empress's head was shaved and she was unceremoniously packed off to end her days on an island in the Sea of Marmora. The departure of the Orphanotrophos was lamented by no one; but Zoë was an anointed empress of the great Macedonian house, and the news of her exile caused furious rioting throughout the capital. When Michael appeared in the imperial box at the Hippodrome he was pelted with arrows and stones; and within a few hours a mob was marching on the Palace. Zoë was hastily retrieved and displayed on the balcony; but it was too late. The citizens, now backed by the Church and the aristocracy, refused to submit any longer to the misrule of the upstart Paphlagonians. Zoë's younger sister Theodora, whom she had forced to take the veil and who had now for many years led the life of a recluse, was carried protesting from her house to Santa Sophia, where she was acclaimed as Empress; and Michael, who had sought sanctuary in the Monastery of the Studion, was dragged to a public square of the city where, in the presence of his subjects, his eyes were put out. So it was that Zoë and Theodora, cordially detesting one another and both manifestly unfitted to rule, together assumed the supreme executive power of the Byzantine Empire.

This uneasy tandem did not last long. As Michael Psellus, who knew her well, was later to point out, Zoë would have been quite willing to see a stable-boy on the imperial throne rather than let her sister share power with herself; and within two months, though now sixty-four, she flung herself with undiminished eagerness into the arms of her third husband, Constantine Monomachus, an agreeable and attractive roué to whom, as the Emperor Constantine IX, poor Theodora was only too pleased to surrender her share of the throne. Meanwhile the disappearance from the capital of the last of the Orphanotrophos's dreadful family meant the liberation of Maniakes. Restored once again to favour, he was immediately appointed Catapan and sent to redress the ever-worsening situation in Italy. Within a month of Michael V's deposition he had landed at Taranto to find that, with the single exception of Trani, the whole of Apulia north of a line drawn from Taranto to Brindisi had declared for Argyrus.

The horrors of that summer of 1042 were long remembered in Apulia. Maniakes advanced up the coast magnificent in his wrath, burning the towns, massacring their inhabitants—men and women, the aged and the children, monks and nuns alike. Some were strung from the trees, others—including many children—buried alive. Monopoli, Matera, Giovinazzo, or what was left of them, all capitulated, begging for mercy.

At this rate the whole of the Capitanata might have been regained; but once again the Byzantines were betrayed by their own corruption. Constantine Monomachus openly cherished a mistress whose brother, Romanus Skleros, had some time before seduced Maniakes's wife. In consequence a bitter feud had arisen; and when Constantine assumed the throne it was an easy matter for this Skleros to arrange

Monte Sant'Angelo: The cave of the Archangel as it is today

Henry the Holy and the Empress Cunégonde. (Early fourteenth-century
windows from Bad St. Leonard, Austria)

for the Catapan's recall. For the second time in little more than two years Maniakes had fallen victim to palace intrigue; he had no intention of submitting again. This time it was he himself who revolted. Refusing to recognise Constantine, he allowed his army to proclaim him emperor. He seized his successor on his arrival in Italy, stuffed his ears, nose and mouth with dung and tortured him to death; then, leaving the Capitanata to look after itself, he hurriedly crossed the Adriatic—whose storms, according to William of Apulia, he first tried to assuage by human sacrifice. Marching on Thessalonica, he met and defeated an imperial army at Ostrovo in Bulgaria, but fell, mortally wounded, at the moment of victory. His head was carried back to Constantinople and exhibited, impaled on a spear, at the Hippodrome. To a glorious, tempestuous, ill-starred life it was perhaps a not altogether unfitting end.

Meanwhile the Lombards, as usual with Norman support, had fought back, and at the time of Maniakes's second recall were besieging Trani, the one city of northern Apulia which had through-out the hostilities remained unflinchingly loyal to Byzantium. With their enormous wooden siege-engine, the largest that had ever been seen in South Italy and the admiration of all eyes, they were confident that they would soon force the city to capitulate. So, indeed, they would have, but for the bitter and unexpected blow that now struck them. Argyrus, their elected leader, son of the venerated Melus and himself now the living embodiment of Lombard nationalism, went over to the enemy. Before doing so he caused the great siege tower to be burned, and his erstwhile followers had no choice but to retire from Trani, humiliated and bewildered.

Argyrus's defection is hard to explain. That he received heavy bribes from the Greeks is certain; Maniakes's ill-fated successor had brought him letters from Constantine offering him wealth and high rank in return for his allegiance to the Empire. But why were such offers accepted? Argyrus had lived, fought and suffered imprison-ment for his beliefs; his sincerity and integrity had never been questioned, nor had his patriotism. Particularly after the departure of Maniakes Lombard chances of success were excellent, and as elected leader of the revolt he stood to gain far more than even Constantine IX could offer. Perhaps there were other factors of which we know nothing; perhaps, for example, he suddenly perceived that the Normans constituted a greater long-term threat to the Lombard cause than the Greeks. We can only hope so, and be thankful that it was not given to Melus, lying in his over-decorated tomb at Bamberg, to know of his son's dishonour.

The insurgents now found themselves once again without a leader. Of the two Lombards who had first been picked, one had been guilty of sharp practice and the other of arrant treachery, and among their demoralised compatriots no further candidates could be found of sufficient calibre to assume the command. The Normans, moreover, tired of this Lombard double-dealing, had now deter-mined to elect a supreme chief of their own. Since the victories of Syracuse, Montemaggiore and Montepeloso, there was one obvious choice—William Bras-de-Fer; and so, in September 1042, Tancred's eldest son was unanimously proclaimed leader of all the Normans in Apulia with the title of Count.

But counts, in those feudal days, could not exist independently. They could only form part of that continuous chain of vassalage which connected the Emperor, through the princes, the dukes and the lesser baronage, to the humblest of the peasantry. William was therefore obliged to seek a suzerain, and he found one ready to hand. Gaimar of Salerno, who as we have seen was by now only too anxious to associate himself with the insurrection, willingly agreed to William's proposals. At the end of 1042 he rode with Rainulf of Aversa to Melfi, and there he was acclaimed as 'Duke of Apulia and Calabria' by the assembled Normans. Bestowing upon William, as a gage of friendship, the hand in marriage of his niece, the daughter of Duke Guy of Sorrento, Gaimar then shared out among the twelve chiefs all the lands *'acquestées et à acquester'*—not only those territories which had already been conquered, but also all those that might in future fall into their hands. There could have been no more forth-right declaration of intention—the fighting would continue until the last Greek had been driven from the peninsula. Meanwhile the Iron-Arm, confirmed as Count of Apulia under Gaimar's suzerainty with authority to found new baronies as new land was conquered, was allotted Ascoli as his particular fief; his brother Drogo received

Venosa; while Rainulf of Aversa, not one of the twelve but too powerful to be ignored, was granted Siponto and part of Monte Gargano. Melfi itself remained the common property of all the chiefs, their supreme headquarters in Apulia and, as Gibbon puts it, 'the metropolis and citadel of the republic'.

South Italy had suffered a radical change. From now on we hear little more about Lombard nationalism. Gaimar, as Duke of Apulia and Calabria, had a nation of his own which he was resolved to extend at the expense of Greek and Lombard alike; while in 'liberated' Apulia the effective power lay exclusively with the Normans, whose tenure had been legalised at Melfi and who would relinquish their land to no one. They were now entrenched in Apulia even more firmly and widely than in Campania; and they were there to stay.

What, it may be asked, had become of Arduin—he who had brought the Normans to Apulia, installed them in Melfi and who, more than anyone, had been responsible for their success? His bargain with the chiefs at Aversa had been that all conquests should be shared equally between himself and them; but of the original sources only Amatus—without much conviction—suggests that the Normans kept their word. None of the other chroniclers mention Arduin after this time. Perhaps he died, killed in one of the early battles or victim of the fury of Maniakes; perhaps, like Argyrus, he was bought off by the Greeks; or perhaps, as is most likely, the Normans, fearing that his continued presence might create an embarrassment, cast him aside like an old cloak that has served its purpose and is of use no more.

6

THE NEWCOMERS

Cognomen Guiscardus erat, quia calliditatis
Non Cicero tantae fuit, aut versutus Ulysses.

(Guiscard he came to be called; for not cunning Cicero even
Could ever have matched him in craft; nor yet the wily Ulysses.)

William of Apulia, Book II

As the power of Normans increased and news of each succeeding
triumph found its way back to France, so the tide of immigration
swelled; and some time in 1046, a little more than three years after
the dispositions of Melfi, two young men appeared in South Italy
within a few months of each other. Each was, in his own way, to
achieve greatness; each was to found a dynasty; and one was
destined to shake the very foundations of Christendom, to hold one
of the strongest Popes in history within the hollow of his hand, and
to cause the imperial thrones of East and West alike to tremble at
his name. They were Richard, son of Asclettin, later to become
Prince of Capua, and Robert de Hauteville, shortly to win the
surname of Guiscard—the Cunning.[1]

Both started with certain advantages over their fellow-immigrants.
Richard was the nephew of Rainulf of Aversa. His father, Rainulf's
younger brother Asclettin, had been awarded the County of Acerenza at Melfi. His elder brother, also called Asclettin, had been one
of Rainulf's most brilliant lieutenants and, when Rainulf died in
1045, had himself briefly ruled in Aversa until his own death a

---

[1] The name seems first to have been given to Robert by his wife's nephew, Girard of
Buonalbergo. The word itself, in Latin often *Viscardus* and in Old French *Viscart*,
comes from the same root as the German word *Wissen* and our own *Wise*, *Wisdom*.
Gibbon connects it more closely with *Wiseacre*.

few months later. Richard had been brought up in Normandy, but when he reached the peninsula with his impressive following of forty mounted knights he was confident of a glorious future. His hopes were not to be disappointed. Amatus, not perhaps altogether unmindful of the generous endowments which Richard later bestowed on his monastery, has left us a charming description of him:

At this time there arrived Richard, Asclettin's son, well-formed and of fine lordly stature, young, fresh-faced and of radiant beauty, so that all who saw him loved him; and he was followed by many knights and attendants. It was his habit to ride a horse so small that his feet nearly touched the ground.[1]

Robert, on the other hand, travelled alone. Born in 1016, the sixth of Tancred's sons though the eldest by his second marriage, he was unable to afford a suite and could put his trust only in the generosity of his half-brothers. It was unfortunate for him that William Bras-de-Fer should have died just about the time of his arrival, but William was succeeded as Count of Apulia by his brother Drogo, so Robert's future prospects seemed bright enough. In fact, as he would soon learn, his own right arm and the supple intelligence that won him his nickname would prove more effective aids to advancement than any number of family connexions.

The chroniclers of the time left us plenty of descriptions of this extraordinary man, 'a fair, blue-eyed giant, who was perhaps the most gifted soldier and statesman of his age'.[2] The best is by Anna Comnena whose father, Alexius I Comnenus, was afterwards to find himself settled on the imperial throne of Constantinople just in time to defend it against Robert's advancing armies. Anna, it should be remembered, is writing of a time many years later, when the Guiscard was at the summit of his power but no longer young. Her description fascinatingly combines the contempt of one born in the purple for a comparative upstart, the hatred of a loyal daughter for her father's arch-enemy, the admiration

[1] En celui temps vint Ricchart fill de Asclitine, bel de forme et de belle estature de seignor, jovène home et clère face et resplendissant de bellesce, liquel estoit amé de toute persone qui lo véoit; liquel estoit sécute de moult de chevaliers et de pueple. Cestui par industrie chevauchoit un petit cheval, si que petit s'en failloit que li pié ne féroient à terre [II, 43].
[2] Shorter Cambridge Mediaeval History.

69

of any intelligent observer for an unquestionably great man, and an element of that uncomplicated sexual attraction to which Anna remained all her life deeply and unashamedly susceptible:

This Robert was Norman by descent, of insignificant origin, in temper tyrannical, in mind most cunning, brave in action, very clever in attacking the wealth and substance of magnates, most obstinate in achievement, for he did not allow any obstacle to prevent his executing his desire. His stature was so lofty that he surpassed even the tallest, his complexion was ruddy, his hair flaxen, his shoulders were broad, his eyes all but emitted sparks of fire, and in frame he was well-built where nature required breadth, and was neatly and gracefully formed where less width was necessary. So from tip to toe this man was well-proportioned, as I have repeatedly heard many say. Now Homer says of Achilles that when he shouted his voice gave his hearers the impression of a multitude in an uproar, but this man's cry is said to have put thousands to flight. Thus equipped by fortune, physique and character, he was naturally indomitable, and subordinate to nobody in the world. Powerful natures are ever like this, people say, even though they be of somewhat obscure descent.[1]

The two young adventurers found their new home in a state of what was, even by mediaeval Italian standards, unparalleled political confusion. In Apulia the war between the Normans of Melfi—now, despite their technical vassalage to Gaimar, fighting openly for their own self-aggrandisement—and the Byzantines based on Bari had been raging indecisively up and down the coast; it was now spreading to Greek Calabria. The turncoat Argyrus, soon after his defection, had been made Catapan—an appointment which can only be satisfactorily explained if it formed part of his bribe—and for three years had proved as able and energetic a champion of the Greek cause as he had ever been of the Lombard. Byzantine power in Italy was now seriously imperilled and the Greeks were everywhere on the defensive, but it was thanks to Argyrus that the Normans found their advance so costly and so slow. In the west the chaos was greater still. The Emperor Michael, determined to punish Gaimar for his part in the insurrection, had shortly before his own downfall released Pandulf of Capua from prison, and early in 1042 the old Wolf had returned in fury to Italy, thirsting for Gaimar's blood and determined to prove that his fangs were as sharp as ever. He managed

[1] *The Alexiad,* I, 10 (tr. Dawes).

to secure the alliance of certain of his old followers, but neither he nor Gaimar was strong enough to win a clear victory.

In June 1045 Rainulf of Aversa died. He alone had been the architect of Norman expansion in Italy; his foresight had recognised the magnitude of what might be achieved, his political sense and subtlety had guided his more headstrong compatriots towards its realisation. Though he had never hesitated to change sides when Norman interests demanded it, he had remained for nine years loyal to Gaimar and continued so until his death. A few months later, after his successor Asclettin had followed him prematurely to the grave, a brief and ultimately unimportant quarrel over the succession led to a break with the Prince of Salerno and a consequent swing of the Normans of Aversa towards Pandulf; but in 1046 Gaimar invested Drogo de Hauteville as Count of Apulia and gave him his daughter's hand in marriage; Drogo mediated between Aversa and Salerno; and the former harmony was restored.

Allies of Gaimar though they were, the Normans were not, however, prepared—nor even altogether able—to devote their entire energies to the overthrow of Pandulf. They had more important business of their own. For some years many of the largest and most profitable of the castles and estates belonging to Monte Cassino had been in Norman hands, some illegally granted them by Pandulf in return for military support, others freely leased them by the monastery for the protection that it hoped to enjoy in return. In both cases the results had been disastrous. Normans were never desirable neighbours; and the monastery's tenants had everywhere used their holdings as centres for brigandage, from which they would issue forth only to ravage and plunder the surrounding country. For miles round Monte Cassino not a farm, not a vineyard, not a household was safe from their attacks; the land was racked and desolated. At one moment matters reached such a point that the Abbot, having appealed unsuccessfully to the powerless Gaimar, resolved to travel to Germany and lay the matter before the Emperor himself; he would doubtless have done so if he had not been shipwrecked off Ostia. With the return of Pandulf the situation became graver still, and it was more than ever necessary to eliminate these Norman bandits who would be bound to abet the renewed attacks and depredations which the monastery confidently expected from its old enemy.

Now, for the first time, the Normans discovered what it was like to be on the other side of an insurrection. Monks, peasants, towns-folk, villagers, whole neighbourhoods resorted to out-and-out guerrilla warfare. They were desperate and could no longer afford to be scrupulous. Amatus tells how a young Norman baron called Rodolf came one day to the monastery with a band of followers. They entered the church to pray—leaving, as was the custom, their swords outside. No sooner had they done so than the monastery servants seized the pile of weapons and the horses, slammed the church doors shut and began ringing the bells for all they were worth. Assuming that the monastery was being attacked, all the country folk within earshot came hurrying to the rescue, burst open the doors of the basilica and hurled themselves upon the astonished Normans, who had only their short daggers with which to defend themselves. They fought bravely, but had no chance. Soon they surrendered, asking only that out of respect for the house of God their lives should be spared; but their prayers went unheeded. By the time the monks arrived Rodolf was a prisoner and his fifteen Normans lay dead on the church floor. From that day the Normans round Monte Cassino seem to have given less trouble, though we are told that Gaimar was hard put to prevent those of Aversa from rising *en masse* against the monastery to avenge their compatriots.

*   *   *

Una Sunamitis[1]	A Shulamite woman
Nupsit tribus maritis.	Has three husbands.
Rex Henrice,	O King Henry,
Omnipotentis vice,	Regent of the Almighty,
Solve connubium	Dissolve this marriage
Triforme dubium.	Triple and doubtful.

Lines addressed to Henry III by Wiprecht the Hermit

---

[1] *Sunamitis* is an interesting word. It comes from one of the several Vulgate translations of the *Song of Solomon* in which it replaced the more usual version *Sulamitis*. The English text in the 1611 Bible reads: 'Return, return, O Shulamite; return, return, that we may look upon thee' (*Song of Solomon*, vi, 13). The Song of Songs is so patently erotic that it is nowadays hard to believe that the allegorical interpretation—according

Meanwhile in Rome the Papacy had sunk to a level of decadence which was never surpassed—if occasionally equalled—before or since. Three men were circling, as in the closing stage of some grisly game of musical chairs, round the throne of St Peter; no one could tell on whose head the tiara properly belonged. Benedict IX, nephew of Benedict VIII and John XIX, may or may not have been only twelve years old when, after gigantic bribery, he succeeded his uncles in 1033. But he was certainly a wild profligate—his success with women is said to have been such that he was generally suspected of witchcraft—and was so thoroughly despised in Rome that in 1044 the citizens, who had already on one occasion tried to assassinate him at the high altar, hounded him from the city and forced him to abdicate. His place was taken by a creature of the Crescentii, Sylvester III. Less than two months later Benedict managed to evict Sylvester and to return to St Peter's, but he did not stay for long. His debauches were too much even for eleventh-century Rome; he had also set his heart on marriage. He therefore abdicated again, this time in favour of his godfather, John Gratian, who under the name of Gregory VI set himself in all sincerity to restore the self-respect of his office and of the Church. For a time things looked better; but soon Benedict, thwarted of his marriage by the understandable resistance of his intended father-in-law, set himself up once again as Pope; while Gregory, whose election for all his reforming spirit had been deeply stained with simony, had his back to the wall. The Roman clergy, confronted now with three Popes, one at St Peter's, one at the Lateran and a third at S. Maria Maggiore, turned in despair to Henry III, King of Germany, son and successor of the Emperor Conrad.

Henry was twenty-two years old when Conrad died in 1039, but he had been trained for kingship from his infancy and had been King of Germany since the age of eleven. He was a serious, deeply conscientious young man with a clear concept of his responsibilities

to which it describes the relationship between Jehovah and Israel and, by extension, Christ and the Church as represented by a passionate lover and a Shulamite woman— was almost universally accepted from the days of the early fathers until the sixteenth century, when it was vigorously denied by the Anabaptists. In Wiprecht's time it would have been unquestioned.

as a Christian ruler, and he looked upon this undignified wrangling in Rome as an insult to Christendom. Accordingly in the autumn of 1046 he descended into Italy, where, at two separate synods in Sutri and in Rome, all three rival Popes were deposed. In their place he nominated his trusted friend and compatriot Suidger, Bishop of Bamberg, who as Clement II performed the imperial coronation of Henry and his second wife,[1] Agnes of Guienne, on Christmas Day. The new Emperor and the new Pope then continued their southward journey.

The most important point to be settled was the future of Capua. Here, on 3 February 1047, Henry held a conference attended by Gaimar, Pandulf, Drogo de Hauteville and Rainulf II Trincanocte, nephew of the old Rainulf, who had lately in his turn been elected Count of Aversa. The increasing power of Gaimar had for some time been causing the Empire anxiety and it was not altogether a surprise, particularly after substantial sums of money had changed hands, when Henry restored Capua to a triumphant Pandulf. The fury of the Prince of Salerno, who had occupied the principality for nine years, was however also to be expected; and the fighting, which had recently given way to an uneasy truce, flared up again.

The other important result of the Capua meeting can have done little to improve Gaimar's temper. From the imperial point of view his own position and that of the Normans were both highly irregular. His title of 'Duke of Apulia and Calabria' had been conferred upon him by Norman acclamation, and this in its turn was the only authority by which he had invested Drogo and the rest with their titles and fiefs. Neither party, in fact, had any support except the other. It was now for Henry to put the situation on a sound feudal footing. He gave Drogo a full imperial investiture as *Dux et Magister Italiae Comesque Normannorum totius Apuliae et Calabriae*,[2] and at the same time formally confirmed Rainulf in his County of Aversa. Gaimar probably retained his overall suzerainty, though even this is uncertain; but his spurious dukedom was now taken from him, and he never used the title again.

The Emperor now moved on to Benevento, where he received

---

[1] Henry had previously been married to Gunhilda, daughter of King Canute.
[2] Duke and Master of Italy and Count of the Normans of all Apulia and Calabria.

an unpleasant shock. The city closed its gates and refused to admit him. For some years—ever since the replacement of Prince Atenulf by Argyrus at the head of the Lombard insurrection—the Beneventans had been on bad terms with the Normans and with Gaimar; and they seem also to have had a guilty conscience over their extremely ungracious reception a little time before of Henry's mother-in-law, returning from a pilgrimage to Monte Gargano. Henry could not spare the time for a siege; his presence was needed in Germany. Without further fuss he handed the whole duchy over to Drogo and Rainulf, and ordered the always amenable Clement to follow up with a general sentence of excommunication. The two then rode away to the north, leaving the Normans to settle the matter as they saw fit.

In the general turmoil of these years the two newcomers, Robert and Richard, found plenty of employment for their swords. For Robert, however, the first welcome which awaited him at the court of his half-brother was distinctly lukewarm. Drogo was prepared to accept him on equal footing with any other young Norman knight, but he refused to ennoble him or to give him any territory of his own. Available land in Apulia was still scarce and far outstripped by the demand; there must by now have been many Norman captains with long years of Italian campaigning behind them, waiting for promised fiefs which they considered they had richly earned but which, thanks to the dogged resistance of the Byzantines, remained in enemy hands. Drogo's full brother Humphrey had himself had to wait till 1045 before he received his county of Lavello, and even this came to him only on the death of the previous incumbent; to discriminate in favour of Robert, young, inexperienced and untried, would have been to invite rebellion. Furious, Robert rode off for other fields where his qualities might be better appreciated. He fought under various colours in those interminable skirmishes which filled the lives of the petty barons of the day until, some time in 1048, he joined Pandulf of Capua, now despite his sixty-two years once more in full cry against his old enemy Gaimar and, as usual, making life intolerable for all who lived within the increasing radius of his activities.

75

Robert doubtless learned a lot from Pandulf, but their association did not last long. Whether or not Amatus is right in suggesting that they parted after Pandulf broke his promise to give Robert his daughter and a castle we do not know. The point is academic, because in 1049 came the day so long awaited and fervently wished-for throughout Campania. On 19 February Pandulf of Capua died. A French historian[1] writes that: 'Even if we make allowance for exaggeration and legend [in the chronicles of Monte Cassino] . . . it remains true that, of all the many detestable bandits of the eleventh century, Pandulf was one of the vilest.' It is impossible not to agree with him. Only once more in the chronicles does the Wolf of the Abruzzi show his face: another, slightly later writer from Monte Cassino, Leo of Ostia, tells us how, some time after his death, his shade was seen by a certain Pythagoras, page to the Duke of Naples, in a wood. Returning alone after a hunting expedition with his master, Pythagoras encountered two monks 'of extremely reverend appearance' who led him to 'a certain pond, most muddy and horrible of aspect'. Here they found Pandulf 'lately dead, bound with chains of iron and miserably immersed up to the neck in the mud of that same pond. Meanwhile two excessively black spirits, making cords of wild vine-shoots, tied them round his neck and plunged him into the very depths of the pond and pulled him up again.'[2] The image is worthy of Dante, though Leo of Ostia was writing two hundred years before the *Inferno* was thought of. The punishment reserved for Pandulf as he reports it was certainly unpleasant, but it was not undeserved.

Robert returned to Drogo, to find him as adamant as ever about a fief. Drogo, had, however, recently returned from an expedition to Calabria where he had left a number of garrisons to guard the mountain passes. Largely to get him out of the way, he now offered his tempestuous half-brother the command of one of these, at Scribla near Cosenza. Calabria was a desolate land, mountainous, hostile and distinctly uninviting. Until Gaimar and the Iron-Arm first began to open it up in 1044 and built an important castle at Squillace, it had been largely ignored by Normans and Lombards alike. Technically it was still part of the Greek Empire, to which

[1] O. Delarc, *Les Normands en Italie*, p. 185 n.   [2] Leo of Ostia, II, 61.

those of its inhabitants who possessed any political consciousness
—mostly Basilian monks[1] and their disciples—remained theoretically loyal; but Byzantine power was on the wane throughout Italy,
and Calabria, for all its grimness, seemed to offer greater long-term
advantages to an ambitious young man than either Campania or
Apulia. Robert accepted.

Scribla was a hell-hole. Lying deep in the valley of the Crati, hot,
airless and rank with malaria, it offered little prospect of continued
life, let alone of material advancement. Robert soon left it and, with a
picked company of companions-in-arms, set himself up in the time-
honoured Norman tradition of freebooting brigandage on higher,
healthier and more easily defensible ground at S. Marco Argentano.
Even there life was hard. After years of Saracen raids the few towns
in the neighbourhood, mostly grouped together along the coast,
were too well fortified for Robert to attack them. There was no
choice but to live off the land. Scattered farms and monasteries and
the few Byzantine administrative outposts in the area all suffered in
their turn, but so did the Normans. Amatus fancifully compares their
plight with that of the children of Israel in the wilderness, and tells us
that when Robert next saw Drogo he 'confessed his poverty, and what
his lips said his appearance confirmed, for he was exceeding thin'.[2]

Such conditions, however, were an ideal proving-ground for his
wits, and it was during his time at S. Marco that Robert acquired
the sobriquet which he was to keep for the rest of his life. Many
stories are told of his trickery; they redound much to his ingenuity
but little to his credit. Perhaps the most enjoyable, though possibly
apocryphal, of these stories is told by William of Apulia. A certain
hill-top monastery (probably Malvito, near Monte Pareta) was
coveted by the Guiscard for its commanding position, which made
it virtually unassailable. One day a solemn funeral procession was
seen winding its way up the path; the Normans indicated a draped
coffin and asked the Abbot for a requiem mass, in honour of their
dead comrade, to be said in the chapel. Their request was granted.

---

[1] i.e. monks following the Orthodox rite. They take their name from St Basil, the
principal founder of Orthodox monasticism in the fourth century. The Eastern Church
knows no proliferation of monastic orders of the kind familiar in the West.

[2] '*lui dist sa poureté, et cellui dist de sa bouche moustra par la face, quar estoit moult
maigre*' (Amatus, III, 9).

77

Unarmed as was usual on such occasions, they filed into the building and laid the coffin reverently before the altar. The service began. Suddenly the pall was flung back, the corpse leaped to its feet, disclosing the pile of swords on which it had been lying, and the mourners, seizing them, started laying about the astonished monks. The monastery was theirs—though the Apulian is careful to point out that once a Norman garrison had been installed the monks were permitted to continue in residence.

It would be unwise to put too much faith in this report, which crops up in various guises on several other occasions in Norman history. A far better documented story, equally illustrative of Robert's methods and almost certainly true in its essentials, concerns the misfortune which befell a certain Peter, Greek governor of the town of Bisignano near S. Marco. One day the two met for a parley, and Robert, as he approached the appointed place, ordered his escort to halt and rode forward alone. Peter, seeing this, did likewise. As the two drew together Peter leaned a little out of his saddle towards Robert in the customary gesture of salutation. In a flash Robert seized him by the neck and pulled him to the ground. Then, before the Greeks could come to their chief's rescue, he half-carried, half-dragged him back to the waiting Normans, who bore him triumphantly off to S. Marco and later obtained a huge ransom.

Anna Comnena tells another version of this story,[1] but she confuses the names and suggests that Guiscard's victim at this time was in fact his father-in-law. Typically she adds a further gloss of her own. 'When he had once got him in his power, he first pulled out all his teeth, at each tooth demanding a colossal sum of money, and enquired where this money was stored. And he did not stop pulling them until he had taken them all, for both teeth and money gave out simultaneously.'

Although Anna is wrong in referring to Robert's father-in-law in this connexion, the Guiscard certainly contracted his first marriage at about this time. His bride was a certain Alberada, who appears to have been the aunt of an influential Apulian baron, Girard of Buonalbergo—although she can still have been little more than a child at the time, since we find her still alive some seventy years

[1] *Alexiad,* I, xi.

and two husbands later, making an important donation in 1122 to the Benedictine Monastery of La Cava, near Salerno. Her age at her death is unknown; but in the much-restored church of the Abbey of the Santissima Trinità, just outside Venosa, her grave may still be seen.

While Robert was thus forced to live on his courage and his wits, Richard was fast fulfilling his highest ambitions. His initial welcome at Aversa had been chillier, if anything, than Robert's at Melfi; Rainulf II saw in the arrival of his predecessor's brother a threat to his own position and thought only of getting rid of him as quickly as possible. Richard accordingly rode off eastward into the mountains, and after a short period of service with Humphrey de Hauteville joined up with another footloose baron, Sarule of Genzano. With Sarule's help and by methods at once predatory and totally unscrupulous, he soon became powerful enough to challenge Rainulf, who was forced to buy him off with a grant of land previously owned by his brother Asclettin. Next he came to grips with Drogo; but here he was less fortunate, for Drogo captured him and threw him into prison. Richard's career was thus at Drogo's mercy; it was saved only by the death in 1048 of Rainulf, whose infant son Herman needed a regent to govern on his behalf. The first appointment, an undistinguished baron embarrassingly named Bellebouche, having proved unsatisfactory, the choice now fell on Richard. He was still languishing in Drogo's dungeons, but the intervention of Gaimar soon procured his release. According to Amatus, Gaimar then clothed him in silk and brought him to Aversa where, by the will of a joyful people, he was acclaimed Count. To begin with Richard seems to have governed in Herman's name, but within a year or two that name is heard no more. By what seems almost like a tacit agreement, the chroniclers all draw a discreet veil over what happened to the boy. We are left to draw our own conclusions.

7

CIVITATE

*S'el s'aunasse ancor tutta la gente
Che già, in su la fortunata terra
Di Puglia, fu del suo sangue dolente . . .
Con quella che sentio di colpi doglie
Per contrastare a Ruberto Guiscardo. . . .*

(Nay, if there once again together stood
All those, who on Apulia's fateful soil
Bewailed the dark effusion of their blood . . .
With those who felt the body-rending blows
Delivered by the Guiscard's mighty sword. . . .)

Dante, *Inferno*, XXVIII

POPE Clement II lasted less than a year. His body was taken back from Italy to his old see of Bamberg—he is the only Pope to have been buried in Germany—and the odious Benedict IX, who was widely rumoured to have poisoned him, re-established himself for the next eight months at St Peter's. In July 1048 the Emperor Henry's next appointee arrived in Rome. He ruled, under the title of Damasus II, for exactly twenty-three days before expiring at Palestrina. Whether, as some said, the heat had proved too much for him or whether Benedict was simply becoming more expert has never been properly established; but to most of the great churchmen of the time his death made the Papacy seem a less desirable prize than ever, and Henry, called upon to fill the vacancy for the third time in less than two years, was finding the task increasingly difficult. Finally, at a great council held at Worms in December 1048, German and Italian bishops called unanimously for the Emperor's second cousin, a man of tried ability and undoubted saintliness, Bruno, Bishop of Toul.

Bruno's reluctance to accept this invitation was unfeigned, and indeed hardly surprising. He agreed only on condition that his appointment would be spontaneously ratified by the clergy and people of Rome on his arrival, and accordingly set out for the Eternal City in January 1049, dressed as a simple pilgrim. Once there, however, he was immediately acclaimed and consecrated under the name of Leo IX, and for the next six years until his death at fifty-one this tall, red-haired, military-looking Alsatian—he had in fact commanded an army in the field during one of Conrad II's punitive expeditions into Italy—proved himself to be one of the greatest Popes of the middle ages. Like John XXIII in our own day, he did not live to see the culmination of the great work which he began; but though others still greater than he were to carry it forward to a point beyond any he can have dreamed of, it was St Leo IX who first broke the dreadful spell which had for so long paralysed and degraded the Church of Rome, and who laid the foundations for a reformed and resurgent Papacy—foundations on which St Gregory VII and his successors were later so majestically to build.

Scarcely had Leo assumed the papal power when affairs in South Italy thrust themselves on his attention. Nowhere in Christendom was the state of the Church so deplorable. Simony had reached a pitch where the highest ecclesiastical appointments were being trafficked about and put up to auction like so much dead merchandise. The prevailing strictures against marriage were occasionally honoured so far as to stop priests from actually marrying their concubines, but seldom prevented them from raising large families. Church tithes went unpaid and many religious houses considered themselves lucky if they managed to keep the treasures and estates they already possessed. Such was the burden of every despatch that Leo received from the South; and these official reports were confirmed by countless letters of complaint from monks, travellers and even ordinary pilgrims, for whom the journey to Monte Gargano was now an open invitation to assault, robbery and abduction by Norman brigands. The monk Wilbert, Leo's earliest biographer, writes that the Normans, 'welcomed as liberators, soon became oppressors'; to many they were worse than the Saracens, who at least confined themselves to isolated raids, while the Normans kept up an unrelenting pressure on all who were weaker than themselves. Vines were slashed, whole harvests burnt; meanwhile reprisals by the local populace added to the unrest. John, Abbot of Fécamp, who had narrowly escaped with his life after a recent pilgrimage, wrote to Leo at this time: 'Italian hatred of the Normans has now become so great that it is near impossible for a Norman, even if he be a pilgrim, to travel through the cities of Italy without being set upon, abducted, stripped of all he has, beaten and tied with chains—all this if he does not give up the ghost in a foetid prison.'

Such a state of affairs would have amply justified strong action in South Italy; but there were other, political, considerations which made Leo's intervention more necessary still. The Normans were steadily extending their dominion, approaching ever closer to the papal frontiers, and their position had been vastly strengthened when Henry III, two years before, had not only invested them as imperial vassals but had also allowed his anger so to cloud his better judgment as to concede to them the insubordinate Benevento. In doing so he had clearly forgotten—and Pope Clement had been too feckless to remind him—that for some two and a half centuries Benevento had remained, in theory at any rate, papal territory. Though the See of St Peter had never been able to exert full temporal authority over the principality, Leo could not allow it to fall into Norman hands.

No one shared this view more wholeheartedly than the Beneventans themselves. Thanks to the feebleness of their princes, their power and influence had continued to decline since the beginning of the century, and they knew that they could not possibly defend themselves against an all-out attack by the Normans, who already held such key-points on the mountain passes as Bovino and Troia. But to whom could they turn for help? Certainly not to Henry, nor yet to Gaimar, whose own position now entirely depended on the continuation of the Norman alliance; while Byzantium was a spent force in Italy, fighting a rearguard action for its own survival. Their only hope was Rome; and certain Beneventan ambassadors who had come to congratulate Leo on his accession and to request him to lift Clement's excommunication had already hinted that the city might wish, in certain circumstances, to place itself unconditionally under papal protection.

Before reaching any final decisions, however, Leo determined to examine the situation at first hand. For several months in 1049 and again in 1050 we find him travelling through the peninsula, calling at all the principal cities and religious foundations. The ostensible reason for his first visit was a pilgrimage to Monte Gargano, and on his second it was given out that the Pope was travelling on 'Church affairs'; but the greatest authority on the period[1] hints darkly that *'la politique ne fut pas étrangère à ce déplacement de Léon IX'*, and indeed the Pope's true preoccupations must have been an open secret. He found the situation even worse than he feared. It was presumably on the basis of what he saw at this time that he shortly afterwards wrote to the Emperor Constantine complaining of how the Normans, 'with an impiety which exceeds that of pagans, rise up against the Church of God, causing Christians to perish by new and hideous tortures, sparing neither women, children nor the aged, making no distinction between what is sacred and what is profane, despoiling churches, burning them and razing them to the ground'.[2] Strong measures would have to be taken, and taken quickly, against the Normans if anything were to be salvaged of the Church in South Italy and if the Patrimony of Peter itself were to be preserved.

In the winter of 1050-51 Leo travelled to Germany to discuss matters with the Western Emperor, and on his return to Rome in March found awaiting him another delegation from Benevento with the news that the nobles of the city had swept away their erstwhile rulers and had decided to surrender themselves entirely into his hands. It was an offer the Pope had fully expected, and one he could not refuse. A synod in Rome prevented him from leaving immediately but he was in Benevento at the beginning of July, when he found the principality entirely submissive to the Holy See. The next problem was to ensure its protection, and for this purpose Leo invited Drogo and Gaimar to a council. They came at once, and readily gave the Pope all the guarantees he sought—too readily as it

[1] F. Chalandon, *Histoire de la Domination Normande.*
[2] Migne, *M.P.L.*, 143, Col. 777 begins.

turned out. Drogo's authority as Count of Apulia was far from complete, and hardly had he left Benevento to return to Melfi when messengers arrived at Salerno, whither the Pope had continued with Gaimar, to tell of further Norman outrages on Beneventan territory. Leo was furious, and was only slightly pacified by Gaimar's explanations that Drogo was undoubtedly doing his best, but had not yet had a chance of bringing his wilder compatriots under control. Still fuming, he at once dictated a letter to Drogo demanding his further immediate intervention, the speedy restoration of order and whatever reparations might be thought appropriate.

This letter never reached its destination, for the messenger to whom it was entrusted heard news on the way which sent him back at full speed to Salerno. Drogo de Hauteville had been assassinated.

As the Normans' unpopularity grew, so the opposition to them had crystallised into three separate factions—the pro-Byzantines, encouraged and subsidised by Argyrus, who were working for the restoration of Greek power in the peninsula; the Papalists, who would have liked the whole region to follow the recent example of Benevento; and the independents, who saw no reason why the South of Italy should not be left to itself and governed by the old Italo-Lombard aristocracy that could already boast five centuries' experience. Though the pro-Byzantine party must bear the lion's share of suspicion, we shall never know for sure which of these three factions was responsible for Drogo's death. All we can be certain about is that on St Lawrence's Day, 10 August, 1051, the Count of Apulia went to the chapel of his castle at Monte Ilaro (now Montella) to attend a celebratory mass. As he entered the building he was set upon by a certain Risus, who had been lying in wait behind the door, and killed instantly. Risus was presumably not alone, for we are told that several of Drogo's followers perished with him; and since a number of other Norman chiefs throughout Apulia met their deaths on the same day and in similar circumstances we can only conclude that his assassination was part of a vast conspiracy to rid the land once and for all of its oppressors.

If such a conspiracy in fact existed, it was a sad failure. The Normans' hold on the country was not appreciably weakened; they had merely been roused to anger. Moreover, they had lost their leader and, showing little eagerness to elect another, were meanwhile able to take their vengeance free from all control. Drogo had been a moderate man—*sage chevalier*, Amatus calls him—Godfearing and fundamentally honest; and though he may have lacked that last ounce of steel necessary for the full enforcement of his authority, he was well aware of the need for discipline. In spite of the recent events at Benevento, his death therefore marked a further worsening of the situation from Leo's point of view. Drogo had at least been willing to discuss matters reasonably and respectfully and had shown himself amenable if not always effective. Now there was no longer even a spokesman empowered to speak for the Normans as a whole, and the land was declining fast into anarchy. If order and tranquillity were to be restored, it would have to be by force. The Pope had masses said on Ascension Day for Drogo's soul and began to raise an army.

The task proved harder than he had expected. Henry III, though he had been partly responsible for the present situation, was probably still nettled at the Pope's take-over of Benevento; he was also involved in a war with Hungary and various internal problems. He refused all military support. So too did the King of France, who was having quite enough trouble with the Normans at home. Help came, however, from the one quarter whence Leo had least expected it—Constantinople. Argyrus, recently ennobled as a reward for his past services with the empty title of Duke of Italy, Calabria, Sicily and—surprisingly—Paphlagonia, was still his Emperor's principal expert and adviser on Italian policy; and he had recently returned from the capital where he had managed to convince Constantine— in face of furious opposition from the Greek Patriarch—of the necessity of a *rapprochement* with the Latins. The Normans, he argued, were now a far greater menace to Byzantine interests than the Western Emperor, the Lombards or the Pope had ever been, and there was no other way of breaking their power over the peninsula. Argyrus's own Lombard origins may have lent additional feeling to his words; his counsels prevailed and before the year 1051 drew to a close he had reached full agreement with Leo on joint military action.

In Italy itself most of the petty barons of the south and centre answered the Pope's call readily enough. Many had already suffered from Norman raids and were beginning to fear for their own survival, while others simply saw the tide approaching and were anxious to stem it while there was still time. When, however, Leo appealed to Gaimar (whom he had deliberately left till last) he met with a point-blank refusal. It can hardly have surprised him. Drogo had married Gaimar's sister; the Norman-Salernitan alliance had been virtually uninterrupted for fifteen years, to the immeasurable benefit of both sides. If Gaimar were now to desert his allies—and incidentally his vassals—they might well topple his own throne before Leo or anyone else could come to his assistance. Moreover, if things went according to the Pope's plan and the Normans were driven from Italy, there would be nothing to protect the Prince of Salerno from the triumphant Byzantine–Papal alliance; and Gaimar's past record was hardly such as to endear him to the Greeks. He therefore returned to Leo a message, polite but firm, pointing out not only that he could never join any league against the Normans but also that he would find it impossible to stand aside and allow them to be attacked.

The second part of the message came as a blow to the Pope. Though he cannot have expected Gaimar's support, he may well have had hopes for his neutrality. Meanwhile the Prince of Salerno had taken care that his message should be publicised as widely as possible, and news of the position adopted by the mightiest of all the southern rulers was having a dangerously demoralising effect on the Italian and Lombard elements of the army now beginning to assemble. Their despondency was being still further increased by hideous stories, now being spread by Salernitan agents, of the Normans' military prowess, and by warnings of the dire revenge that they would exact, after their inevitable victory, on all those who had dared to take up arms against them.

But there were darker portents than these in the air. Amatus tells us in detail of the many '*signez merveillouz*' which now appeared, both in Salerno and also, apparently, in Jerusalem. A Cyclopean child was born with one eye in the middle of its forehead and with the hoofs and tail of a bull. Another appeared with two heads. A river

—we are not told which—ran red with blood, and an oil lamp in the
Church of St Benedict was found filled with milk. All these things,
Amatus assures us, foretold the death of Gaimar.

And now indeed the Prince of Salerno came in his turn to a
violent end. A pro-Byzantine party had seized power in Amalfi and
had at once risen against the domination of Salerno, refusing to pay
the usual tribute. Somehow the insurgents had managed to secure
the support of part of Gaimar's own family; and so it was that on
2 June 1052 Gaimar V of Salerno was struck down in the harbour
of his capital by his four brothers-in-law, sons of the Count of
Teano, the eldest of whom now proclaimed himself as successor.
Both the principal enemies of Byzantium had thus been murdered
within a year, and although the Greeks do not seem to have been as
directly responsible on this occasion as they do for the death of
Drogo, it is hard to absolve them altogether from guilt.

Of that section of Gaimar's family which had remained loyal, one
member only escaped capture and imprisonment by the insurgents.
This was the prince's brother, Duke Guy of Sorrento, who at once
galloped off to fetch help from his Norman friends. For them the
situation was as serious as it was for Salerno. Gaimar had been their
only ally; if Salerno should fall under Byzantine influence they
would be surrounded and, with Leo in his present mood, probably
doomed as well. Fortunately Guy found them already mobilised
between Melfi and Benevento. Fortunately too he found that, after
nearly a year of chaotic interregnum, they had at last elected a chief
—his own sister's husband, Humphrey de Hauteville. It was typical
of the Normans that before agreeing to help they should have
negotiated with Guy a high price for their assistance; but the
distracted Duke was prepared to agree to anything, and only four
days after Gaimar's death the Norman army was encamped before
the walls of Salerno.

Against the massed Norman force the four brothers of Teano
had no chance at all. Taking Gaimar's young son Gisulf with them,
they barricaded themselves in the citadel; but their own families
had fallen into Norman hands and Guy was therefore able to
negotiate for the return of his nephew, before whom, as legal heir
and successor of Gaimar, he immediately did homage. The Normans

would have preferred to see Guy himself assume the throne of Salerno at such a moment, but they were impressed by his selflessness. They too then declared themselves for Gisulf, who confirmed them in all their existing territorial possessions. It only remained to deal with the rebels, and these within a day or two were forced to capitulate. Gisulf and Guy, showing once again a moral sense rare for their time and position, had promised that their lives should be spared; but as the prisoners left the citadel the Normans, pointing out that they for their part had promised nothing, fell upon them with their swords. They killed not only the four ringleaders but, in grisly reprisal, thirty-six others as well—one for every wound that had been found on Gaimar's body.

Gaimar V of Salerno was the last of the great Lombard princes of South Italy. At the peak of his power his domains extended over the wide territories of Capua, Sorrento, Amalfi and Gaeta, and his suzerainty over the Normans of Aversa and Apulia. His influence was felt through the length and breadth of the peninsula, as he proved when, by the prestige of his name alone, he almost effortlessly sabotaged the military preparations of the Pope of Rome himself. Only sixteen when he came to the throne, having then and throughout his life to contend with the unscrupulous ambitions of Pandulf of Capua on the one hand and the Normans on the other, he proved a match for both, and he did so without once breaking his word or betraying a trust. Up to the day he died his honour and good faith had never once been called in question. He was then forty-one years old. Under his son Gisulf the principality of Salerno was to survive for one more generation, but it never regained its former glory, and in 1075 it lost its independence for ever. The Normans saw to that.

To Leo IX, watching from Benevento, these developments can have afforded little comfort. The murder of Gaimar, much as it must have shocked and revolted him, had momentarily strengthened his position; but in the events which followed, the Normans and Salernitans had given unmistakable proof of how quickly and devastatingly they could act in unison, and the lesson had not been lost on the already apprehensive papal troops. Many of these had discreetly deserted and the remainder, if they were to be persuaded to fight at all, would have to be heavily reinforced. Back went Leo to Germany, to make a second, more urgent appeal to Henry III. His journey was not entirely in vain; while celebrating the Christmas of 1052 with the Emperor at Worms he managed to obtain formal imperial recognition of the papal title to Benevento and certain other South Italian territories. But thanks to the machinations of Leo's old enemy, Bishop Gebhard of Eichstätt, the army which Henry had at last reluctantly put at his disposal was recalled before it reached the frontiers of Italy, and the Pope found himself with no alternative but to do his own recruiting. Fortunately he had with him his chancellor and librarian, Frederick, brother of the Duke of Lorraine; and this warlike priest—later to become Pope Stephen IX —was able to procure a body of some seven hundred trained Swabian infantry which was to prove the mainstay of the army. Around this solid nucleus there quickly gathered a motley and undisciplined collection of mercenaries and adventurers, most of whom had apparently thought it wise to leave Germany—'à la suite', as a French historian[1] puts it, 'de fâcheuses aventures'.

As it decended through Italy in the spring of 1053, the army continued its snowball growth. As Gibbon describes it:

In his long progress from Mantua to Beneventum, a vile and promiscuous multitude of Italians was enlisted under the holy standard: the priest and the robber slept in the same tent; the pikes and crosses were intermingled in the front; and the martial saint repeated the lessons of his youth in the order of march, of encampment, and of combat.[2]

Although few of the new adherents may have been persons of unblemished moral character, Gibbon's description is exaggerated; it is unlikely that the Papal forces were much more tatterdemalion than most of the other armies of the Middle Ages. But by the time that they reached Benevento at the beginning of June they were numerically more than a match for anything the Normans could put into the field, and nearly all the non-Norman barons of South Italy had rallied again to Leo's standard. The Duke of Gaeta, the Counts of Aquino and Teano were there, and Peter, Archbishop of Amalfi; there too were detachments from Rome and the Sabine hills, from Campania and Apulia, from the Marsi, Ancona and

[1] Chalandon.   [2] Gibbon, ch. LVI.

Spoleto, all drawing new courage from each others' presence and, most of all, from that of their solemn, white-robed leader, who had now assumed personal command of the army and was steadily infusing them with his own serene confidence.

Leo had been in contact with Argyrus during the journey south and had arranged to join the Byzantines near Siponto in northern Apulia. Since, however, the main road east from Benevento was dominated by the Norman-held fortresses of Troia and Bovino, he now led his army along a more circuitous northern route, through the valley of the Biferno and thence east behind Monte Gargano. The Normans watched his progress carefully. Their own situation, they now knew, was more serious than at any time since the first of their number had arrived in Italy thirty-six years before. On the results of the fighting that lay ahead depended their whole future in the peninsula; if they lost, there would be no second chance. And victory looked a good deal less certain than it had in 1052. They were outnumbered and without allies; even the Salernitans, who owed their city and probably their lives to Norman valour, had let them down in their hour of need. Ranged against them were not only two armies, the Papal and the Byzantine, but also the entire indigenous population of Apulia, who looked upon them with unconcealed loathing and were determined to do all they could to ensure their destruction. On their side they had only their formidable military reputation; courage, cohesion and discipline; and their own sharp swords.

Richard of Aversa had already joined Humphrey with all the warriors he could muster; Robert Guiscard had arrived from the depths of Calabria with a sizable force of his own; and the combined army which must by now have comprised, apart from certain essential garrisons, virtually the entire adult male Norman population of South Italy, threaded its way through the mountains and down on to the Apulian plain. Its first task was, obviously, to prevent Leo from linking up with the Byzantines. Once reaching Troia, therefore, it turned north and, on 17 June 1053, on the bank of the river Fortore near Civitate, found itself face to face with the papal army.

The story of the battle of Civitate is one of the best-documented chapters in the whole history of the Normans in the South. All the principal chroniclers on the Norman side recount it in detail, and their accounts agree. More surprising is the extent to which these versions are confirmed by German and papal sources—including a letter to the Emperor Constantine from Leo IX himself.[1] Naturally some allowance for personal or political bias has to be made; but in general the different versions resemble each other so closely that we can piece together what is probably a fairly accurate picture of the course of events.

Neither side was eager for immediate battle. The Pope wished to wait for the arrival of the Byzantines, while the Normans, who, for all their unscrupulousness in the affairs in this world, suffered genuine misgivings at the prospect of raising their swords against the Vicar of Christ, still hoped to reach a peaceful settlement. No sooner were they encamped, therefore, than they sent a deputation to Leo, humbly putting their case before him and offering him their homage. William of Apulia adds that they admitted their past wrongs and promised their loyalty and obedience. But it was no use.

The tall, long-haired Teutons jeered at these Normans of shorter stature. . . . They surrounded the Pope and arrogantly addressed him: 'Command the Normans to leave Italy, to lay down their arms here and to return to the land whence they came. If they refuse this, then accept not their peaceful proposals.' The Normans departed, sorrowful that they had failed to make peace, and carried back the haughty replies of the Germans.[2]

And so the following morning, on the little plain that extends before the confluence of the Fortore and its tributary, the Staina, battle began. Pope Leo maintains—and his word cannot be doubted —that the first Norman onslaught was made while negotiations were still in progress; but it must be remembered that he was deliberately playing for time, hoping every moment for the arrival of Argyrus, while the Normans, equally conscious of the approach of the Greek army, were keen for the battle to begin—if begin it must—as soon as possible. They also had another even more urgent reason for haste; they were starving. The local peasantry refused them all provisions, and to deprive them further had already begun to gather in the harvest, even though much of the corn was still green. The

---

[1] Already quoted on p. 83.　　　[2] William of Apulia, II, 80 ff.

Norman soldiers often had nothing with which to sustain themselves but a handful or two of grain, dried before the fire. Their sudden attack may have been the only means of forcing the issue.

It came from the Norman right flank and was led by Richard of Aversa. Facing him were the Italians and Lombards of the Papal army. The Apulian notes that this heterogeneous group was drawn up without any attempt at military order, the soldiers having no idea of how to dispose themselves in war; and Richard went through them like butter. At the first shock of impact, they broke in confusion and without further ado fled from the field, with the Count of Aversa and his men in hot pursuit. Meanwhile, however, Humphrey de Hauteville, who was commanding the centre, had found Leo's Swabians a very different kind of adversary. Successive Norman charges failed utterly to disrupt their ranks, and in the fighting which followed they wielded their two-handed swords with a courage and determination that the Normans had never encountered since they came to Italy.

The left wing of the Norman army had been placed under Robert Guiscard and included the contingent that he had brought with him from Calabria. Their orders were to remain in reserve and then to enter the fray at whatever point their presence seemed most to be required. Here is William of Apulia again, in a translation which, while keeping as closely as possible to the sense of the original, tries to recapture something of his own racy Latin hexameters:

> Then Robert, perceiving his brother enmeshed in a furious struggle,
> Beset by a desperate foe who would never bow down in surrender,
> Called up the troops of his ally Girard, Lord of bright Buonalbergo,
> With those who obeyed him alone, his devoted Calabrian cut-throats,
> And splendid in courage and strength, he flung himself into the
> battle.
> Some were despatched by his lance; there were others whose heads
> were sent spinning
> With a blow of his sword—while even his hands wrought dire mutila-
> tions.
> The lance in his left hand, the sword in his right, ambidextrously
> flashing,
> Turning aside every blow, confounding all those who attacked him,
> Dashed three times from his horse, three times he leaped back to the
> saddle;

Inspired by unquenchable fire in his heart, that would lead him to
                                                            triumph.
Just as the ravening lion, that falls on inferior creatures,
Grows more wildly enraged if he finds his authority challenged,
Rising huge and superb in his wrath and, admitting no quarter,
Tears and devours every beast in his path, as he scatters the others,
So the great Robert dealt death to the Swabian hordes who opposed
                                                            him.
Varied the means he employed; some had feet lopped off at the ankles,
Others were shorn of their hands, or their heads were sliced from their
                                                            shoulders;
Here was a body split open, from the breast to the base of the stomach,
Here was another transfixed through the ribs, though headless already.
Thus the tall bodies, truncated, were equalled in size with the smaller;
Enabling all to behold how the glorious palm of the victor
Goes not to overgrown giants, but to those of more moderate stature.

What, however, eventually decided the day was not so much the
courage of Robert and Humphrey as the arrival of Richard of
Aversa, returned from his murderous pursuit of the Italians and
Lombards. He and his followers now plunged once again into the
fray, and this further addition to the Norman ranks destroyed the
last hopes of the papalists. Even now, however, the German contingents refused to surrender; those same tall, long-haired Teutons,
who had laughed at the stockiness of the Normans and persuaded
the Pope to reject their proposals of peace, fought on and were
killed to the last man.

Standing high on the ramparts of Civitate, Pope Leo had watched
the battle. He had seen half his army put to ignominious flight,
the other half remorselessly butchered. His Byzantine allies had
let him down; had they arrived in time the battle might have
ended very differently, but they would never dare to take on the
Normans alone. And now he had to face yet another humiliation;
for the citizens of the town, anxious to ingratiate themselves with
the Normans, refused his request for asylum and handed him over
to his enemies. But the Normans, though victorious, were not
triumphant. In the past few hours they had been too occupied with
the Swabians to remember their supreme antagonist; now, as they
gazed on the proud, melancholy man standing before them, they
seem to have been genuinely overcome. Falling on their knees,

they implored his forgiveness. Then after two days of solemn obsequies for the dead, who were buried where they lay, they escorted the Pope back to Benevento.

Leo was in an ambiguous position. He was not, in the strictest sense of the word, a prisoner. Contrary to his expectations, he and his retinue were being treated by the Normans with the utmost consideration and courtesy. As Amatus puts it:

The Pope was afraid and the clergy trembled. But the victorious Normans reassured them and offered the Pope safe conduct, and then brought him with all his retinue to Benevento, furnishing him continually with bread and wine and all that he might need.[1]

On the other hand, though he was able to transact day-to-day papal business, he was certainly not a free agent; and it soon became clear to him that the Normans, for all their solicitude, had no intention of allowing him to leave Benevento until an acceptable *modus vivendi* had been established.

The negotiations dragged on for the next nine months. They cannot have been easy. For most of this time Leo seems to have remained intractable. As late as January 1054, in his letter written from Benevento to the Emperor Constantine (of which there will be more to say in the next chapter), he makes it clear that as far as he is concerned the struggle will continue. 'We shall remain faithful to our mission to deliver Christendom, and we shall lay down our arms only when the danger is past,' he writes, and looks forward to the day when, by the Eastern and Western Emperors together, 'this enemy nation will be expelled from the Church of Christ and Christianity will be avenged'. But as the months wore on, his health grew worse; and when Henry, whose arrival with an army he had been confidently awaiting, still showed no signs of coming to his aid, he saw that he had no choice but to make terms. We have no means of telling what was eventually agreed, nor are there any surviving papal bulls to attest formal investitures; but we can safely assume that Leo eventually gave his *de facto* recognition to all the Norman conquests to date, including very probably certain terri-

[1] 'Li pape avoit paour et li clerc trembloient. Et li Normant vinceor lui donnerent sperance et proierent que securement venist lo pape, liquel meneront o tout sa gent jusque a Bonvenic, et lui aministroient continuelment pain et vin et toute choze necessaire'. (III, 38).

tories within the principality of Benevento—though not the city itself, which retained its papal allegiance. Once this agreement had been reached there was no longer any reason to prevent his return to Rome, and he accordingly left on 12 March 1054—with Humphrey, courteous as ever, accompanying him as far as Capua.

For the unhappy Pope, whose five hard years of papacy had been spent in almost continuous travel through Germany and Italy, this was the last journey; and he who had been accustomed to pass many hours of every day in the saddle now made his final entry into Rome on a litter. Worn out by his exertions, disillusioned by the betrayal of his Emperor and cousin, broken by his shattering defeat at Civitate and deeply wounded by the fulminations of Peter Damian and others, who attributed this defeat to the wrath of God against a militarist Pope, he had succumbed during the long months of mental anguish at Benevento to a wasting disease which caused him constant pain.[1] On his arrival at the Lateran, he knew that his end was near. He gave instructions that a grave should be quickly prepared in St Peter's and that his litter should be laid alongside it; and there on 19 April 1054, the date which he himself had predicted, he died surrounded by the clergy and people of Rome. His death was serene and peaceful, but clouded by the consciousness of failure. No Pope had worked harder for the reform of the Church in Italy; few of those who had tried had been more totally unsuccessful in their own lifetime. During those last days he is said to have been granted several heavenly visions; but he could hardly have seen how superbly the work he had begun would be carried on after him, nor how quickly the seeds he had sown would ripen and bear fruit. Least of all could he have suspected that within only thirty years of his death those same Normans, against whom he had staked all and lost, would emerge as the sole friends and preservers of the resurrected Papacy.

Meanwhile for the Normans a new chapter had begun in their

[1] There is no reason to believe the subsequent inevitable rumours that Leo, like his two predecessors, was a victim of slow poison administered at the instigation of Benedict IX. Such rumours had by now become little more than a conditioned reflex after the death of a Pope; the principal proponent of the theory, Cardinal Benno, goes so far as to accuse the incorrigible Benedict of the murders of six Popes within thirteen years.

great Italian adventure. The battle of Civitate had been as decisive for them as that which was to be fought thirteen years later at Hastings would be for their brothers and cousins. Never again would their basic rights in South Italy be questioned; never again would their wholesale eviction from the peninsula be seriously contemplated. They had shown themselves to be something more than just another ingredient in the Italian stewpot, a sparring-partner for Capuans, Neapolitans or a few half-hearted Byzantine provincials. This time, without a friend or ally, they had taken on the Vicar of Christ and with him the best fighters, German and Italian, that he could put into the field. And they had won. Their possessions, already ratified by the Emperor, had now been confirmed by the Pope. Their reputation for invincibility stood at its highest. The attitude of the outside world towards them would now be tinged with a new respect.

All this, and much more besides as yet undreamed of, had been won in a few nightmare hours on the banks of the Fortore. Not many travellers pass that way nowadays; but those who do may still see, a mile or two to the north-west of the modern village of San Paolo di Civitate, the ruins of an old cathedral; and they may still trace the line of the ramparts from which Pope Leo watched the destruction of his army and his hopes. Of the city itself that treated him so basely, nothing remains; it was totally annihilated, as if by some divine if belated retribution, at the beginning of the fifteenth century. But excavations of the site in 1820 revealed, just outside the walls, several huge piles of skeletons. All were male, all bore the marks of dreadful wounds, and a large number were found to be of men well over six feet tall.

8

SCHISM

Upon Michael, neophyte and false Patriarch, brought only by mortal fear
to assume the monkish habit, and now for his abominable crimes notorious; upon Leo, so-called Bishop of Ochrid; upon Constantine, chancellor
of that same Michael, who has publicly trampled the liturgy of the Latins
beneath his feet; and upon all those who follow them in their aforesaid
errors and presumptions, except that they repent, let there be Anathema
Maranatha as upon the Simoniacs, Valesians, Arians, Donatists, Nico-
laitans, Severians, Pneumatomachi, Manichaeans, Nazarenes, as upon all
heretics and finally upon the Devil and all his angels. Amen, Amen, Amen.

> Last paragraph of Humbert's Bull of Excommunication.

DURING his honourable captivity in Benevento Pope Leo had set
himself to learn Greek. His biographer, Wibert, suggests that he
did so because he wished to be able to read the Holy Scriptures in
that language. Such a desire was praiseworthy, and may have been
genuine enough; but it seems likely that his real purpose was to be
at less of a disadvantage in his dealings with Constantinople,
which were growing steadily more complicated.

From the political point of view it was clear to the Pope, to
Argyrus, and through Argyrus to the Emperor Constantine, that the
Papal–Byzantine alliance was essential if the Normans were ever to
be eliminated from Italy. Even after the *débâcle* of Civitate—which
might well have ended differently if the two armies had managed to
join up as planned—it could have done much to check the Norman
advance. Instead, within thirteen months of the battle, it came to an
abrupt and painful conclusion, stained with mutual recriminations
and abuse; so that before the end of the decade the Papacy had
openly and enthusiastically espoused the cause of Norman expansion.

The reason for this immense reversal is not hard to trace; it is to be found in one of the greatest disasters ever to have befallen Christendom—the great schism between the Eastern and Western Churches. Looking back over their past history with all the advantage of hindsight, we can see that this rupture was, sooner or later, inevitable; but the fact that it occurred when it did was largely due to the stresses and strains resulting from the Norman presence in South Italy.

The two Churches had been growing apart for centuries. Their slow estrangement was in essence a reflexion of the old rivalry between Latin and Greek, Rome and Constantinople; and the first and fundamental reason for the schism was in fact the steadily increasing authority of the Roman Pontificate, which led to arrogance on the one side and resentment on the other. The old Greek love of discussion and theological speculation was repugnant, even shocking, to the dogmatic and legalistic minds of Rome; while for the Byzantines, whose Emperor bore the title of *Equal of the Apostles* and for whom matters of dogma could be settled only by the Holy Ghost speaking through an Oecumenical Council, the Pope was merely *primus inter pares* among the Patriarchs, and his claims to supremacy seemed arrogant and unjustified. Already in the ninth century matters had very nearly come to a head; beginning with a purely administrative dispute over the Archbishopric of Syracuse, the quarrel soon spread—first to personalities, when Pope Nicholas I questioned the suitability of the Byzantine Patriarch Photius for his office, and thence to dogma when Photius publicly (and truthfully) claimed that a Roman bishop, Formosus of Porto, was in Bulgaria delivering himself of violent attacks against the Orthodox Church and insisting on the inclusion of the word *Filioque* in the Nicene Creed. This word, by which the Holy Ghost is said to proceed not only from the Father but also from the Son, had for some time been slowly gaining acceptance in the West, where, however, it was generally considered to have little theological importance. The Byzantines, on the other hand, considered it destructive of the whole balance of the Trinity, so carefully formulated by the early Fathers at Nicaea over five centuries before; and they bitterly resented the arrogance of Rome in presuming to amend the word of God as revealed to a Council of the Church. After the death of Pope

Nicholas, thanks to the goodwill of his successors and of Photius himself, friendly relations were outwardly restored; but the problems remained unsolved, the *Filioque* continued to gain adherents in the West, and in Constantinople the Emperor maintained his claim to rule as the Vice-Regent of Christ on earth. It was only a question of time before the quarrel broke out again.

The Papal–Byzantine alliance by which Leo IX and Argyrus set such store had from its inception been violently opposed by Michael Cerularius, Patriarch of Constantinople. An ex-civil servant, more of an administrator than a churchman, he had ordered the blinding of John the Orphanotrophos in prison in 1043; intransigent, ambitious and narrow-minded, he both disliked and distrusted the Latins; above all, he hated the idea of papal supremacy. Although, thanks to the influence of Argyrus, he had been unable to prevent the alliance, he had determined to sabotage it in whatever way he could. His first opportunity came over the question of ritual, when he learned that the Normans, with papal approval, were enforcing Latin customs—in particular the use of unleavened bread for the sacrament—on the Greek churches of South Italy. Immediately he ordered the Latin churches in Constantinople to adopt Greek usages, and when they refused he closed them down. Next, and still more disastrous, he induced the head of the Bulgarian Church, Archbishop Leo of Ochrid, to write to the Orthodox Bishop John of Trani in Apulia a letter violently attacking certain practices of the Western Church which he considered sinful and 'Judaistic'.

This letter, which contained a specific injunction to John that he should pass it on to 'all the bishops of the Franks, to the monks and the people and to the most venerable Pope himself', reached Trani in the summer of 1053—just at the time when the principal Papal Secretary, Humbert of Mourmoutiers, Cardinal of Silva Candida, was passing through Apulia on his way to join Leo in his captivity. John at once handed it to Humbert, who paused only to make a rough Latin translation and, on his arrival at Benevento, laid both documents before the Pope. To Leo, who already felt bitter about the non-appearance of the Byzantine army at the one moment when its presence had been most needed, this gratuitous insult came as the last straw. Furious, he ordered Humbert to draft a detailed reply setting out the arguments for papal supremacy and defending all the Latin usages which had been called in question. Humbert did not mince his words; both Pope and Cardinal were determined to give as good as they got—the very form of address they chose, 'To Michael of Constantinople and Leo of Ochrid, Bishops', was calculated to hit the Patriarch where it would hurt most—and it was perhaps just as well that, before the letter could be despatched, another missive arrived in Benevento, this time bearing at its foot the huge purple scrawl of the Emperor Constantine himself. He had clearly been horrified to learn, rather belatedly, of the patriarchal machinations, and was now doing his utmost to set matters right. His letter is lost, but is unlikely to have contained anything very remarkable; Leo's reply suggests that it simply expressed condolences for Civitate and made vague proposals for a further strengthening of the alliance. Far more surprising was a second letter, accompanying the Emperor's. This, apart from one or two infelicities of phrasing, seemed to radiate good-will and conciliation; it prayed for closer unity between the Churches, and contained no reference whatever to the disputed Latin rites. And it was signed by Michael Cerularius, Patriarch of Constantinople.

Cerularius, having at last been persuaded by the Emperor or—more probably—by Bishop John of Trani how much was at stake, seems, however reluctantly, to have made a genuine effort to heal the breach; and Leo would have been well-advised to overlook being addressed as 'Brother' instead of 'Father' and other similar little pinpricks and let the matter rest. But he was tired and ill; and encouraged by Cardinal Humbert, who throughout the events which were to follow showed himself to be every bit as waspish and bigoted as the Patriarch, he determined to make no concessions. He therefore agreed that papal legates should be sent to Constantinople to thrash the whole question out once and for all, and allowed Humbert to draft two more letters in his name for these legates to deliver. The first of these, to Cerularius, addressed him as 'Archbishop', which was at least one degree politer than before; but it was otherwise quite as aggressive as its predecessor, being concerned less to defend the Latin usages themselves than to attack the Patriarch's presumption in questioning them in the first place. It also reprimanded him

for having pretensions to oecumenical authority—which was probably due to a mistake in the Latin translation of his letter—and
suggested that his election had been uncanonical, an accusation
which was not remotely justified. Leo's second letter was to the
Emperor and was, as we have seen, largely devoted to political
affairs, in particular his determination to continue his war against the
Normans. Nevertheless it carried a sting in its tail; the last paragraph
contained a vehement protest against the Orthodox Patriarch's 'many
and intolerable presumptions . . . in which if, as Heaven forbid, he
persist, he will in no wise retain our peaceful regard'. Perhaps to
soften the effect of this veiled threat, the Pope concluded with a
commendation of the legates whom he would shortly be sending to
Constantinople. He hoped that they would be given every assistance
in their mission, and that they would find the Patriarch suitably
repentant.

Such tactics were a grave miscalculation. If the Pope valued the
Byzantine alliance—and the Byzantines were, after all, the only allies
he had against the Norman menace—it was foolish of him to reject
the opportunity of conciliation with the Orthodox Church; and if
he had been a little better informed about affairs in Constantinople
he would have known that the personal goodwill of the Emperor
would never suffice to override the Patriarch, who was not only a
far stronger character than Constantine—by now a sick man, almost
crippled with paralysis—but who also had the full weight of public
opinion behind him. Finally it was hardly tactful to choose as legates
on this particularly delicate mission Humbert himself, narrow-
minded and rabidly anti-Greek, and two others, Frederick of
Lorraine, the papal chancellor, and Archbishop Peter of Amalfi,
both of whom had fought at Civitate and might be expected to
share Leo's resentment at the Byzantines for letting them down.

This tight-lipped trio set off in the early spring of 1054 and
arrived in Constantinople at the beginning of April. From the outset
things went badly. They called at once on the Patriarch, but took
offence at the manner in which they were received and stomped
unceremoniously from the Palace without any of the customary
civilities, leaving the Pope's letter behind them. Their own anger
was, however, nothing to that of Cerularius when he read this latest

document. It confirmed his worst suspicions. Against his better judgment he had been induced to make a gesture of conciliation, and here it was flung back in his face. Worse was to follow: for the legates, who had since been received by the Emperor with his usual courtesy, had been encouraged by this reception to publish in Greek translation the full text of the Pope's earlier, still undespatched, letter to the Patriarch and Leo of Ochrid, together with a detailed memorandum on the disputed usages.

To the Patriarch this was the final insult. Despite the fact that the earlier letter had been addressed, however disrespectfully, to him, he had not even heard of its existence until now, when it was being angrily discussed all over the city. Meanwhile a closer examination of the second letter—which had at least, after a fashion, been delivered—revealed that the seals on it had been tampered with. Immediately he thought of his old enemy Argyrus. Was it not more than probable that Humbert and his friends had called, on their way to Constantinople, at his Apulian headquarters and shown him the letter? And if he had seen it, might he not even have altered the text? Forgetting, in his anger, that Argyrus's interest was to heal the breach between the two Churches rather than to open it further, Cerularius decided that the so-called legates were not only discourteous; they were dishonest as well. He therefore refused to recognise their legatine authority or to accept from them any further communications.

A state of affairs in which a fully accredited Papal legation, cordially welcomed by the Emperor, remained unrecognised and totally ignored by his Patriarch could not continue for long; and it was lucky for Cerularius that news of Pope Leo's death, which reached Constantinople within a few weeks of the legates' arrival, to some extent solved the problem for him. Humbert and his colleagues had been Leo's personal representatives; his death thus deprived them of all official standing. The Patriarch's grim satisfaction at this development can easily be surmised; it may, however, have been somewhat mitigated by the absence of any corresponding discomfiture on the part of the legates. Seemingly unabashed by this blow to their status, they now became more arrogant than ever.

The publication of the draft reply to Leo of Ochrid's letter had provoked a firm riposte from one Nicetas Stethatus, monk at the monastery of Studium, criticising in particular the Latins' use of unleavened bread, their habit of fasting on Saturdays and their attempts to impose celibacy on their clergy. This document, though outspoken and occasionally clumsy, was couched in polite and respectful language; but it drew from Humbert, instead of a reasoned reply, a torrent of shrill, almost hysterical invective. Ranting on for page after page, describing Stethatus as a 'pestiferous pimp' and a 'disciple of the malignant Mahomet', suggesting that he must have emerged from the theatre or the brothel rather than from a monastery, and finally pronouncing anathema upon him and all who shared in his 'perverse doctrine'—which, however, it made no attempt to refute—this extraordinary diatribe can only have confirmed the average Byzantine in his opinion that the Church of Rome now consisted of little more than a bunch of crude barbarians with whom no agreement could ever be possible.

Cerularius, delighted to see his enemies not only shorn of their authority but making fools of themselves as well, continued to hold his peace. Even when the Emperor, now fearing with good reason for the future of the papal alliance on which he had set his heart, forced the luckless Stethatus to retract and apologise to the legates; even when Humbert went on to raise with Constantine the whole question of the *Filioque*, detestation of which was by now a cornerstone of Byzantine theology, no word issued from the Patriarchal Palace, no sign that the high Orthodox authorities took any cognizance of the undignified wrangle which was now the talk of the city. At last—as Cerularius knew it would—this imperturbability had its effect. Humbert lost the last shreds of his patience. At three o'clock in the afternoon of Saturday, 16 July 1054, in presence of all the clergy assembled for the Eucharist, the three ex-legates of Rome, a cardinal, an archbishop and a papal chancellor, all in their full ecclesiastical regalia, strode into the church of Santa Sophia and up to the High Altar, on which they formally laid their solemn Bull of Excommunication. Then, turning on their heel, they marched from the building, pausing only to shake the dust ceremonially from their feet. Two days later they left for Rome.

Even apart from the fact that the legates were without any papal authority and that the Bull itself was therefore invalid by all the standards of Canon Law, it remains an extraordinary document. Here is Sir Steven Runciman on the subject:

Few important documents have been so full of demonstrable errors. It is indeed extraordinary that a man of Humbert's learning could have penned so lamentable a manifesto. It began by refusing to Cerularius, both personally and as Bishop of Constantinople, the title of Patriarch. It declared that there was nothing to be said against the citizens of the Empire or of Constantinople, but that all those who supported Cerularius were guilty of simony (which, as Humbert well knew, was the dominant vice at the time of his own Church), of encouraging castration (a practice that was also followed at Rome), of insisting on rebaptising Latins (which, at that time, was untrue), of allowing priests to marry (which was incorrect; a married man could become a priest but no one who was already ordained could marry), of baptising women in labour, even if they were dying (a good early Christian practice), of jettisoning the Mosaic Law (which was untrue), of refusing communion to men who had shaved their beards (which again was untrue, though the Greeks disapproved of shaven priests), and, finally, of omitting a clause in the Creed (which was the exact reverse of the truth). After such accusations, complaints about the closing of the Latin churches at Constantinople and of disobedience to the Papacy lost their effect.[1]

In Constantinople, where the narrow-minded arrogance of Humbert and his friends had already made them thoroughly disliked, the news of the excommunication spread quickly. Demonstrations in support of the Patriarch were held throughout the city. They were first directed principally against the Latins, but it was not long before the mob found a new target for its resentment—the Emperor himself, whose evident sympathy for the legates was rightly thought to have encouraged them in their excesses. Luckily for Constantine, he had a scapegoat ready to hand. Argyrus himself was in Italy, as yet unaware of what had happened and still working for the papal alliance; but those of his family who chanced to be in the capital were instantly arrested. This assuaged popular feeling to some extent, but it was only when the Bull had been publicly burnt and the three legates themselves formally anathematised that peace returned to the capital.

[1] *The Eastern Schism.*

Such is the sequence of the events, at Constantinople in the early summer of 1054, which resulted in the lasting separation of the Eastern and the Western Churches. It is a sad, unedifying story because, however inevitable the breach may have been, the events themselves should never, and need never, have occurred. More strength of will on the part of the dying Pope or the senile Emperor, less bigotry on the part of the ambitious Patriarch or the pig-headed Cardinal, and the situation could have been saved. The fatal blow was struck by a disempowered legate of a dead Pope, representing a headless Church—since the new Pontiff had not yet been elected—and using an instrument at once uncanonical and inaccurate. Both the Latin and the Greek excommunications were directed personally at the offending dignitaries rather than at the Churches for which they stood; both could later have been rescinded, and neither was at the time recognised as introducing a permanent schism. Technically indeed they did not do so, since twice in succeeding centuries—in the thirteenth at Lyons and in the fifteenth at Florence —was the Eastern Church compelled, for political reasons, to acknowledge the supremacy of Rome. But though a temporary bandage may cover an open wound it cannot heal it; and, despite even the balm applied by the Oecumenical Council in 1965, the wound which was jointly inflicted on the Christian Church by Cardinal Humbert and Patriarch Cerularius nine centuries ago still bleeds today.

9

CONSOLIDATION

Roger, the youngest of the brothers, whom youth and filial devotion had heretofore kept at home, now followed his brothers to Apulia; and the Guiscard rejoiced greatly at his coming and received him with the honour which was his due. For he was a youth of great beauty, tall of stature and of elegant proportion . . . He remained ever friendly and cheerful. He was gifted also with great strength of body and courage in battle. And by these qualities he soon won the favour of all.

Malaterra, I, 19

In the general exhilaration that followed their victory at Civitate, the Normans little suspected the magnitude of the events in Constantinople for which they had unwittingly provided the spark, nor the fact that in doing so they had probably saved themselves from extinction. They were on the other hand fully aware that the defeat of a massed papal army had added immeasurably to their reputation. Through the towns and villages of the peninsula there were now many who believed them to be genuinely invincible, as a result of some sinister contract with the powers of darkness; while even those who continued to suspect that they might yet succumb to a superior force were compelled to admit that for the moment no such force appeared to exist. This prevailing mood of defeatism offered them an advantage which the Norman leaders were quick to seize; and the records for the next few years tell of an almost unbroken succession of minor victories as one town after another fell, with hardly a struggle, to their attacks. Their principal target was what remained of Byzantine Apulia, where the demoralised Greeks, already deprived of papal support, unsuccessful in their attempted negotiations with Henry III and soon temporarily to lose the leadership of Argyrus, were incapable of prolonged resistance.

By the end of 1055 Oria, Nardo and Lecce had all capitulated, while Robert Guiscard, plunging deep into the heel of Italy, had taken Minervino, Otranto and Gallipoli in one gigantic stride and was building up his power and reputation at such a rate that Count Humphrey, fearing for his own position, hastily despatched him back to his old stamping-ground in Calabria.

By this time Robert had attracted a considerable following, and his second term of occupation of San Marco must have been even more terrifying for the local inhabitants than his first. Fortunately for them he did not stay long. A highly satisfactory expedition against the southern territories of Gisulf of Salerno, during which Cosenza and certain other neighbouring towns fell to the Normans, occupied a few months, and soon after his return to the camp messengers arrived with an urgent summons for him to return to Melfi. Count Humphrey was dying. The two half-brothers had never been close—William of Apulia reports that on one occasion Robert so angered the Count that he found himself cast into a dungeon—but Humphrey seems to have understood that there was no other possible successor and he therefore appointed Robert guardian and protector of his infant son Abelard, and administrator of all his lands during Abelard's minority. Then, in the spring of 1057, he died. He had been a hard, jealous, vengeful man, with a streak of cruelty that had showed itself in the savage tortures inflicted on the murderers of his brother Drogo, and again on certain chiefs who had failed him at Civitate; but even if he lacked Drogo's fundamental goodness of heart and the gay panache of William the Iron-Arm, even if already before his death he was beginning himself to feel outshone by the brilliance of the young Guiscard, he had yet proved himself a strong and courageous leader, fully endowed with all those qualities which had already, in barely twenty years, made the name of Hauteville famous through half Europe.

When he saw Humphrey buried next to William and Drogo in the monastery of the Santissima Trinità at Venosa, Robert can have shed few tears. Geoffrey, his only surviving elder brother in Italy, had failed to achieve any particular distinction; William, Count of the Principate, and Mauger, Count of the Capitanata, two younger brothers recently arrived, were doing well for themselves—especially

William, who had already wrested a castle from the Prince of Salerno at San Nicandro, near Eboli—but neither they nor any other Norman barons could approach the Guiscard in power or prestige. As Humphrey had foreseen, the succession was incontestably his. Even before his election, he had characteristically seized all the lands of his nephew and ward Abelard and had added them to his own extensive possessions; and when, in August 1057, he was formally acclaimed as his brother's successor by the Normans assembled at Melfi, and all Humphrey's personal estates devolved upon him also, he became the greatest landowner and the most powerful figure in all South Italy. It had taken him just eleven years.

But though Robert Guiscard was now supreme, his chief rival, Richard of Aversa, was not far behind. The Normans of Melfi and those of Aversa still retained their separate identities, and Richard had consequently not been a contender for the Apulian succession —he had anyway been fully occupied elsewhere. Young Gisulf of Salerno, despite the efforts of his uncle Guy of Sorrento to restrain him, had almost from the day of his accession determined to oppose the Normans in every way he could. It was a short-sighted policy, since, especially after Civitate (where the Salernitans had been noticeable by their absence), the Lombard princes of South Italy could no longer hope to stem the Norman tide, and the policy of co-operation which had served his father Gaimar in such good stead was now even more vital if an independent Salerno was to be maintained; yet Gisulf quickly drew upon himself the armed hostility of Richard of Aversa and managed to keep his throne only by means of a last-minute alliance with Amalfi; while Richard in the north and Robert and William de Hauteville in the south relentlessly harried his borders, paring away the outlying Salernitan territory bit by bit until he was at last left with little more than the city itself.

The days of Salerno were obviously numbered, but it was not the first of the Lombard principalities to fall to Norman arms. Since 1052 Richard had had his eye on Capua, where the young prince Pandulf, son of the 'Wolf of the Abruzzi', showed little of the military vigour or political sense of his odious father. Once already the Count of Aversa had beaten the Capuans to their knees and forced the wretched inhabitants to pay seven thousand gold bezants to

preserve their liberty; and when in 1057 Pandulf died, Richard
struck again. Within days he had ringed Capua with fortified watchtowers, cutting off the citizens from the fields and farms on which
they depended for subsistence. They defended themselves valiantly;
'the women carried the stones to the men and brought comfort to
their husbands, and the fathers taught their daughters the arts of
war; and so they fought side by side, and comforted each other
together'.[1] But the city was unprepared for a siege and before long
the threat of starvation forced it to sue for peace. This time there
was no question of a ransom; Richard was determined on conquest.
The only concession he would allow was that the keys to the gates
and the citadel should remain technically in Capuan hands—which,
for four more years, they did. Meanwhile Richard the Norman
became Prince of Capua, and the hereditary Lombard rule which had
lasted for more than two centuries was extinguished.

For Salerno the situation now became more desperate than ever;
but Richard was in no hurry to finish it off when easier, quicker
returns seemed to be promised elsewhere. In nearby Gaeta he had
recently arranged for the marriage of his daughter with the son of
the ruling Duke, Atenulf, but the boy had died in the early autumn of
1058, shortly before the wedding ceremony. The occasion should
have been one for condolences from the intended father-in-law;
instead the new Prince of Capua addressed to Duke Atenulf a
demand for the *Morgengab*, by which according to Lombard law
one quarter of the husband's fortune became the property of the
wife after the marriage. In this Richard had not one shred of justification; as its name clearly implied, the *Morgengab* was payable only
on the day following the nuptials, as a mark of their successful and
satisfactory consummation.[2] Atenulf naturally refused. This gave
Richard all the pretext he needed. Among the modest appanages of
Gaeta at this time was the little county of Aquino, a short distance
over the mountains to the north; within a few days this innocent,
unsuspecting town found itself under siege and its outlying farms

---

[1] Amatus, IV, 28.

[2] 'This famous gift, the reward of virginity, might equal the fourth part of the
husband's substance. Some cautious maidens, indeed, were wise enough to stipulate
beforehand a present which they were too sure of not deserving.' (Gibbon, ch. XXXI.)

and villages overrun with Normans, burning and pillaging as they went.

Here was a typical example of Norman methods at their worst: the trumping-up of some legalistic excuse, however shaky; a half-hearted attempt to pin the blame on the intended victim; and then the attack itself, whenever possible with a vastly superior force, pursued without regard for decency or humanity. Such techniques are all too familiar in our own day; what was more characteristic of the people and the time was the fact that while the siege of Aquino was still in progress the Prince of Capua took the opportunity of making his first official visit to Monte Cassino, only a few miles away, and there received a hero's welcome. The monastery, which had always formed part of Capuan territory, had as we have seen suffered long and bitterly from Richard's predecessors; and the last of the Pandulfs, while in most respects but a pale shadow of his father, had continued the old tradition of oppression and persecution with unabated vigour. Any conqueror, even a Norman, who would deliver Monte Cassino from this hated régime could be sure of an enthusiastic reception. Amatus, a probable eye-witness, has left us his own account of the scene:

And afterwards the Prince, with a few of his men, ascended to Monte Cassino to give thanks to St Benedict. He was received with royal pomp; the church was decorated as if for Easter, the lamps were lit, the court-yard was loud with singing and rang with the prince's praise. . . . And the abbot washed his feet with his own hands, and the care and defence of the monastery were entrusted to his keeping. . . . And he vowed that he would never make peace with those who might seek to deprive the Church of its goods.[1]

But there was another, deeper reason for the warmth of the wel-come given to the Prince of Capua. Until the spring of 1058 the monastery had been under the control of Frederick of Lorraine, a veteran of Civitate and of the fateful legation at Constantinople and still rabidly anti-Norman, who had been appointed abbot the previous year and had technically retained this position throughout his eight months' papacy as Pope Stephen IX.[2] On 29 March of

[1] Amatus, IV, 13.
[2] There is some confusion among historians over the numbering of the various Stephens who have occupied the papal throne, depending on whether or not they

that year, however, Pope Stephen died, and the monks elected as their new abbot the thirty-one-year-old Desiderius of Benevento. The career of Desiderius provides an admirable illustration of the doctrine of *noblesse oblige* as it existed in eleventh-century Italy. A member of the ruling dynasty of Benevento, he had seen his father killed by the Normans during one of the skirmishes of 1047 and had thereupon decided to renounce the world. For a Lombard prince this was not easy. Twice before he was twenty-five he escaped to a monastic cell; twice he was tracked down and forcibly returned to Benevento. After his family was expelled from the city in 1050 the situation became a little easier and he fled again, first to the island of Tremiti in the Adriatic and later to the desolation of the Majella, but soon he was recalled once more—this time by Pope Leo IX, who had just taken over Benevento and saw how greatly his hand would be strengthened against the loyalists if the young prince, who had by now been received into the Benedictine Order, were a member of his entourage. Desiderius served Leo well, but life in the Curia failed to attract him and as soon as the Pope died he settled at Monte Cassino, there to resume—he hoped—the contemplative life. For four years he seems to have succeeded, but early in 1058 we find him nominated as member of a new papal legation to Constantinople, from which he was saved by news awaiting him at Bari of the death of Pope Stephen. Thanks to a gift of three horses and a safe-conduct from Robert Guiscard he was able to take the direct route, through Norman territory, back to Monte Cassino; and there, on the day after his arrival, he was installed as abbot.

Always reluctantly, Desiderius was fated to play an important part in state affairs, both ecclesiastical and secular, for the next quarter of a century until his own papacy as Victor III. Soon after Civitate and certainly before any other leading churchman, he brought himself to accept the one unassailable fact of South Italian politics— that the Normans were in Italy to stay, and that opposition to them

recognise a doubtful Stephen II, who was elected to succeed Pope Zachary in 752 but died four days later, before his consecration. For this reason Frederick of Lorraine is sometimes known as Stephen X. Most authors, however, prefer to call him Stephen IX; this is, moreover, the title that appears on the inscription of his tomb as ordained by his brother Godfrey the Bearded—who should have known if anyone did.

was therefore not only futile but self-destructive. Only by maintaining their good-will at all costs could the monastery hope to survive.
Events proved him triumphantly right. Amatus has already told us
of the promise by the Prince of Capua—doubtless the direct result
of Desiderius's reception of him—to protect monastic property,
and within a week or two this promise had been reinforced by
a formal charter confirming the great abbey in all its lands and
possessions.

However well-advised Desiderius may have been in his new policy,
the fact that he should first have made it manifest at a moment when
nearby Aquino was fighting for its life against immense Norman
odds must have appeared somewhat heartless; and it was probably
in an attempt to retain some favour with Aquino that he took
advantage of Richard's presence and generally benevolent mood to
suggest that his demand for the *Morgengab* might be reduced, and
that the Duke Atenulf might be asked for only four thousand *sous*
instead of five thousand—'because he was poor', as Amatus explains.
For once, the Prince of Capua made a concession; and the luckless
Atenulf, after a few more weeks of hopeless resistance during which
Aquino reached starvation-point, was at last compelled furiously
to pay up.

To the population of South Italy the progeny of old Tancred de
Hauteville must have seemed interminable. Already no fewer than
seven of his sons had made their mark in the peninsula, four having risen to the supreme leadership and the remaining three firmly
established in the first rank of the Norman baronage. And still this
remarkable source showed no sign of exhaustion, for there now
appeared on the scene an eighth brother, Roger. He was at this time
some twenty-six years old, but though the youngest of the Hautevilles he was soon to prove himself a match for any; while to the
devotee of the Norman Kingdom in Sicily he is the greatest and most
important of them all.[1]

Like the majority of young Normans on their first arrival in Italy,

---

[1] Roger is sometimes surnamed Bosso; but as the name is neither frequent, necessary
or melodious it can be ignored. It tends also to create confusion with Roger's nephew,
Roger Borsa, whom we shall meet anon.

Melfi

Venosa: ruins of the SS. Trinità

Roger made straight for Melfi; but he cannot have stayed there long, for already in the autumn of 1057 we find him in Calabria with Robert Guiscard, who had returned there as soon as his investiture was over. The new Count of Apulia apparently saw nothing in his former freebooting life that was incompatible with his recently-acquired dignities, and it was to this profitable if precarious existence that he now introduced his young brother. Roger proved an apt pupil. Camped near Cape Vaticano, on the summit of the highest mountain in the district so that the local population should remain ever conscious—and fearful—of his presence, he and his men soon subdued much of western Calabria. Such was his success that when, a few months later, the Guiscard had to return in haste to quell a local rising in Apulia—an emergency that was to become ever more familiar in the years to come—he had no hesitation in leaving Roger in charge; and when this rising, despite his efforts, assumed such dangerous proportions that Melfi itself was captured and Robert's leadership seriously imperilled, it was to Roger in Calabria that he called for help. His brother's arrival proved decisive and the revolt was quashed.

It was a happy partnership, but it did not last. The rupture seems to have been Robert's fault. He had always been famous for his generosity towards his followers; now, in his dealings with his brother, he suddenly began to display a parsimoniousness as inflexible as it was uncharacteristic—until Roger, who had in the first months of their association dutifully forwarded to Robert in Apulia much of the plunder resulting from his first Calabrian campaign, now found himself unable even to pay his own retinue. Such at least is the story given us by Malaterra. His chronicle, which was written some years later at Roger's request, may well be tendentious at this point, but it is not altogether improbable. Could it not, perhaps, indicate a new aspect of the Guiscard's character now appearing for the first time—jealousy of his brother, many years younger and possessed of ambitions and qualities in no way inferior to his own? Was there in fact room in Italy for both of them?

At all events, some time at the beginning of 1058 Roger angrily left Robert Guiscard's service. One of the advantages of his late arrival in the peninsula was that he had plenty of brothers already established to whom he could turn, and he now accepted the invitation of William de Hauteville, Count of the Principate, who in the four years since his arrival in Italy had captured nearly all the territory of Salerno south of the city itself and who had sent Roger a message offering him an equal share of all that he possessed— 'excepting only', as Malaterra is careful to point out, 'his wife and children'. Thus it was that Roger soon found himself ensconced in a castle towering high over the sea at Scalea, an admirable vantage-point from which to make regular inroads, largely for the purposes of horse-stealing and highway robbery, into the Guiscard's territories. It must have been a profitable time; Malaterra tells us of one single *coup*—the ambush of a group of wealthy merchants on their way to Amalfi—with the profits from which, in plunder and ransom money, Roger engaged a hundred more soldiers for his growing army.

But the young man was destined for greater things than a life of brigandage, and looking back at him down the perspectives of history we can see that the decisive turning-point of his life in Italy came in 1058, when Calabria was overtaken by a terrible famine. The Normans had brought the trouble on themselves; their deliberate scorched-earth policy had left, over an immense area, not an olive-tree standing, not a cornfield to harvest.

Even those who had money found nothing to buy, others were forced to sell their own children into slavery. . . . Those who had no wine were reduced to drinking water, which led to widespread dysentery and often an affection of the spleen. Others on the contrary sought to maintain their strength by an excessive consumption of wine, but succeeded only in so increasing the natural heat of the body as to affect the heart, already weakened for want of bread, and thus to produce further internal fermentations. The holy observance of Quadragesima, so strongly upheld by the holy and reverend fathers, was set aside so that there was much eating not only of milk and cheese but even of meat—and that, moreover, by persons who had some pretensions to respectability.

This last sentence of Malaterra suggests that in the early part of the year at any rate the situation may not have been too acute, but the unfortunate Calabrians were soon reduced to more drastic extremities.

They sought to make bread with weed from the rivers, with bark from certain trees, with chestnuts or acorns which were normally kept for pigs; these were first dried, then ground up and mixed with a little millet. Some fell on raw roots, eaten with a sprinkling of salt, but these obstructed the vitals, producing pallor of the face and swelling of the stomach, so that pious mothers preferred to snatch such food away from the very mouths of their children rather than allow it to be eaten.

After months of such conditions, followed by a harvest scarcely less meagre than that of the previous year, the desperate populace rose against its Norman oppressors. The revolt began with local refusals to pay taxes or report for military service, continued with the massacre of the sixty-strong Norman garrison at Nicastro and rapidly spread through Calabria. Robert Guiscard, already over-extended and still actively defending his Apulian possessions, was growing used to local uprisings, but these were usually confined to small groups of discontented nobles. This time, with the whole native population up in arms over a steadily increasing area, the situation was more serious. Clearly he could no longer afford the unnecessary internecine squabbles which not only sapped his strength but, as events in Calabria and elsewhere had made plain, also encouraged insubordination among his subjects. Messengers sped to Roger at Scalea; and this time he could not accuse the Guiscard of any lack of generosity in the terms he offered. If Roger would now settle the Calabrian insurrection, half the affected terri-tory, plus all that remained for future conquest between Squillace and Reggio, would be his. He and Robert would enjoy equal rights and privileges in every city and town.

For the Count of Apulia it was the only possible course. He had bitten off more than he could at present chew. In so wild and mountainous a country, with its inhabitants so restless and its lines of communication so slender, no prince however strong could maintain his domination single-handed. Roger seized his chance. Down the coast he rode, at the head of all the soldiers he could muster. Whether he was able to do anything to alleviate the hard-ships of his future subjects is not recorded; we do not even know whether he tried very hard. Nor do the chroniclers tell us what action he took against the insurgents—but they never mention the Calabrian insurrection again.

While his young brother was settling affairs in the South, Robert Guiscard was thinking—reluctantly, one suspects—about consolidation. His instincts were always towards acquisition rather than the maintenance of what he had already won, and his long-term ambitions were fixed, as ever, on aggrandisement and conquest. But it was clear that he could not hope to extend his dominions any further until his Apulian vassals could be kept in more effective control. The Lombards in particular, though no longer in themselves a danger to his authority, were proving a constant irritant and a brake on his progress. As their political power had waned, their national solidarity seemed if anything to have increased. Feeling—with good reason—that the Normans, their erstwhile allies, had betrayed their trust, they remained sullen and unco-operative and made no effort to hide their resentment.

Some means must therefore be found of reconciling the Lombards, even partially, to their Norman overlords. The traditional method of solving such problems was by a marriage alliance, but here there were difficulties. Only one Lombard family of sufficient prestige and distinction was now left in Italy—the ruling family of Salerno. Prince Gisulf had a sister, Sichelgaita; but unfortunately the Count of Apulia's only child, Bohemund, son of his wife Alberada of Buonalbergo, was still little more than a baby and even by mediaeval standards hardly of marriageable age. Possible combinations were thus limited. Robert Guiscard, however, was never afraid of taking the plunge. He now discovered, with much display of consternation, that his marriage to Alberada fell within the prohibited degrees of kinship. He was therefore legally still a bachelor, and Bohemund a bastard. Why should he himself not marry Sichelgaita, thus uniting the Norman and Lombard ruling families over his great South Italian dominion?[1]

Gisulf does not appear to have been any too keen on the idea. He had always hated the Normans, who had already shorn him of almost all he possessed and whom, according to William of

[1] Both Delarc and Osborne have argued that Robert Guiscard's wedding to Sichelgaita did not take place till 1059, after the Council of Melfi. It is certainly true that Nicholas II strengthened the consanguinity laws in April 1059, and that Robert might therefore have been in a stronger position after that time. If his first marriage was in fact uncanonical, this might explain why Alberada seems to have borne him no ill-will;

Apulia, he and his compatriots considered 'a savage, barbarous and abominable race'.[1] On the other hand Pope Stephen, from whom he had been hoping for active support against them, had just died; and Gisulf desperately needed an ally who would be able to hold Richard of Capua and William de Hauteville in check. If the Guiscard could not control his own brother, then no one could. And so, with reluctance, the Prince of Salerno gave his consent—on condition, however, that William were first brought to heel. Robert asked nothing better. He already bore William a grudge for having led his brother Roger astray and encouraged his escapades from Scalea, and was only too pleased to get his own back. His knights and vassals were by now gathering round him for the marriage festivities, and he at once called upon them all to join him in an immediate punitive thrust to the south. The response was, as usual, virtually unanimous. 'No Norman knight refused to accompany him, except only Richard [of Capua], for the loving harmony which formerly existed between Robert and Richard was a little strained.'[2]

Once William had been put in his place, Gisulf made no further objection to the proposed marriage. Readers, if such there be, of Walter Scott's *Count Robert of Paris* may remember the excessively unpleasant Countess Bremhilde, for whom the new Countess of Apulia served as a model. It is a portrait at once unkind and unfair. Sichelgaita was cast in a Wagnerian mould and must be appreciated as such. In her we come face to face with the closest approximation history has ever dared to produce of a Valkyrie. A woman of immense build and colossal physical strength, she was to prove a perfect wife for Robert, and from the day of their wedding to that of his death she scarcely ever left her husband's side—least of all in battle, one of her favourite occupations. Anna Comnena who, as Gibbon points out, 'admires, with some degree of terror, her masculine virtues', reports that 'when dressed in full armour the

after his death she was to have masses said for the repose of his soul and she was eventually buried near him at Venosa. But it does not explain how, soon after the annulment, she came to marry Robert's nephew Richard, son of Drogo. Moreover Malaterra clearly states that the Salernitan marriage was in 1058, and Amatus bears him out. It looks as though we shall have to accept their opinion.

[1] '*Esse videbantur gens effera, barbara, dira.*'

[2] Amatus, IV, 20.

woman was a fearsome sight',[1] and we shall see how, many years afterwards at Durazzo, she saved a dangerous if not desperate situation by her courage and example. At such moments, charging magnificently into the fray, her long hair streaming from beneath her helmet, deafening the Norman armies with huge shouts of encouragement or imprecation, she must have looked—even if she did not altogether sound—worthy to take her place among the daughters of Wotan; beside Waltraute, or Grimgerda, or even Brünnhilde herself.

But however much he may have gained by his wife's alarming ferocity on campaign, Robert had married Sichelgaita for reasons which were diplomatic rather than military; and in this field the union brought him far more lasting advantage. The Guiscard now acquired in Lombard eyes a prestige well beyond that which even his immense natural abilities could have brought him. As William of Apulia puts it, 'this alliance with so noble a family lent new brilliance to Robert's already celebrated name. Those who had heretofore obeyed him only through compulsion now did so out of respect for the ancient law, remembering that the Lombard race had long been subject to the ancestors of Sichelgaita.'

Robert doubtless intended that his future offspring should also benefit from the strain of Lombard nobility which they would inherit from their mother. That they largely failed to do so was not Sichelgaita's fault. In the course of time she presented him with at least ten children, including three sons; none, however, was to show in any significant degree the qualities that earned for their parents their places in history. The Lombard blood attenuated the Norman, and the only one of Robert's progeny to prove himself a worthy son of his father was young Bohemund—now cast out with his mother Alberada to grow up a disinherited bastard, but later to become the first Frankish prince of Outremer and one of the foremost Crusaders of his time. The Guiscard's heir and successor, for all the Lombard loyalties he believed he could command, was to show throughout his life a weakness and timidity which his father would have despised and from the consequences of which only his uncle Roger, a Norman through and through, was able—in part—to redeem him.

[1] *The Alexiad*, I, 15.

10

RECONCILIATION

The acquisition of the ducal title by Robert Guiscard is a nice and obscure business.

Gibbon, ch. LVI

THE death of Leo IX in April 1054 threw the Church once again into a state of deep confusion. Determined as his reforms had been, they had had little time to take root in the stony ground of Rome; the Pope's enforced absence in Benevento had allowed the old aristocratic families to regroup themselves, and the moment he died the Counts of Tusculum, the Crescentii and the rest were back again at their old intrigues. The party of reform still had strength enough to prevent a snap election—which would almost certainly have brought to power the most open-handed of the reactionary candidates—but their two strongest leaders, Cardinal Humbert and Archdeacon Hildebrand, were both abroad and they needed some higher power to support them if their will was to prevail.

The interregnum lasted a year. At last, after both sides had appealed to Henry III for a decision, the reformers proved triumphant and Henry nominated his own principal counsellor, Gebhard, Bishop of Eichstätt, who was duly enthroned at St Peter's on 13 April 1055, under the title of Pope Victor II. It is hard to believe that any immediate successor of Pope Leo—let alone a politician of Gebhard's ability and experience—coming to power less than two years after Civitate, could have had no interest in the Norman problem; yet this was the case. We have seen him earlier in Germany, doggedly obstructing all Leo's efforts to raise an army;

and subsequent events had apparently produced no change in his views. His mind was fully occupied with Church administration and imperial affairs, and when he came to Rome he was still unprepared to give much detailed consideration to the problems of the South. By the spring of 1056, however, the flood of complaints against new Norman outrages forced him to accept the fact that he had underrated them. Leo had been right; such a state of affairs could not be allowed to continue. In August he travelled back to Germany to confer with Henry—perhaps a little sheepishly—on what action was necessary. The Emperor trusted his old adviser implicitly; if the Pope considered that a campaign was called for, then a campaign there would have to be. But as so often happened when action was planned against the Normans, fate intervened on their behalf. Henry was thirty-nine years old and had known hardly a day's illness in his life. At the end of September he was suddenly struck down by fever, and within a week he was dead.

It was lucky for the Empire that Pope Victor was in Germany at the time. Henry was succeeded as King by his five-year-old son, Henry IV, under the nominal regency of his mother, the Empress Agnes of Guienne; but as none of the advisers round the throne possessed half the Pope's knowledge or understanding of imperial affairs, Victor found himself during the next six months wielding the power not only of the Papacy but of the whole Empire of the West. Now once again there were more immediate problems to be faced than that of the Normans and, doubtless with relief, he banished them from his mind. It was not until the spring of 1057 that he returned to Italy; and before the misfortunes of the South could reclaim his undivided attention, he too fell victim to a fever. On 28 July he died at Arezzo. The escort party returning his body to Germany was ambushed and robbed at Ravenna, and he was hastily buried in Theodoric's Mausoleum, then doing service as a Church.

This time the succession was easier. There was no Emperor to consult, the King of Germany was only six and Archdeacon Hildebrand, by far the most powerful and influential member of the Curia, was in Rome and ready to act swiftly. He it was who had persuaded Henry III to appoint Victor two years before, and he now had no difficulty in imposing on the cardinals his new candidate—Frederick of Lorraine, once Pope Leo's chief lieutenant, at present filling in time as Abbot of Monte Cassino and henceforth to be known as Pope Stephen IX.[1] For the Normans Stephen's election seemed to spell catastrophe. Long ago he had boasted to Leo that he could exterminate them with a hundred knights; they had proved him wrong at Civitate and he had not forgiven them. They knew him, then, to be their implacable enemy; they also knew that his elder brother, Duke Godfrey the Bearded of Lorraine, had recently married the widowed Marchioness Beatrice of Tuscany and had thus assumed the control of the strongest and best-organised power in North Italy; and they cannot have failed to hear the universal rumours of how Pope Stephen was planning to take advantage of Henry IV's minority by transferring the Imperial Crown from the House of Franconia to that of Lorraine. Once Godfrey was Emperor, and the combined imperial and papal force was to march down at full strength into South Italy, they would have little chance of survival. The Pope's first actions after his consecration seemed to confirm their worst fears. Still titular Abbot of Monte Cassino, he sent orders to the monastery that it should at once forward to him all its gold and silver plate, promising later repayment at high interest. (The monks complied, but with such bad grace that Stephen regretfully decided not to accept the plate after all.) Next, as we have seen, he decided to send a new legation to Constantinople with instructions to revive the delicate project of a Byzantine alliance.

In the circumstances it was only to be expected that when Stephen died in his turn after less than eight months on the throne of St Peter some degree of suspicion should have fallen on the Norman leaders. Their motives were certainly strong. But they had little experience of the tortuous intriguing that provided a full-time occupation for so many of the inhabitants of the Eternal City, and it is doutful whether at this stage they possessed the technique or the contacts necessary for a *coup* of such magnitude. In the later years in Sicily they were to show themselves a match for any of their oriental subjects in the slippery arts of antechamber or alcove; for the moment, however, they were still very much men of the North, and poison occupied no place in their usual armoury. More likely

[1] See p. 110, n. 2.

suspects—if indeed there was any foul play at all—were, as usual, the Roman nobles, who much preferred the distant, nebulous authority of the Empire to the prospect of domination by the nearer and considerably more powerful House of Lorraine. But Stephen had long been a sick man, and it is a more probable, if duller, hypothesis that, like most people even in the Middle Ages, he died a natural death. It claimed him in Florence at the end of March 1058; and, as the Pope expired, the Normans breathed again.

The reformist leaders were once again absent from Rome—Humbert in Florence and Hildebrand not yet back from Germany, whither he had gone rather belatedly to announce Pope Stephen's election; and once again the reactionaries saw their chance. Experience over the past few years had taught them that on occasions of this kind everything depended on speed. A *coup d'état* was hastily arranged by a Tusculan-Crescentian alliance, and within a few days John Mincio, Bishop of Velletri, was enthroned as Pope under the inauspicious title of Benedict X. From the point of view of Hildebrand and his friends, the choice could have been a lot worse; the new Pope may have been weak-willed, but Leo IX had made him a cardinal and Stephen had considered him as a possible alternative candidate to himself. They could not, however, accept the manner of his election, which they considered uncanonical and corrupt. Leaving Rome in a body, they met Hildebrand in Tuscany and settled down to decide on a Pope for themselves.

The choice fell on Gerard, Bishop of Florence, an irreproachably sound Burgundian who in December 1058, once he was assured of the support of the Empress Agnes and—equally important—of Duke Godfrey of Lorraine, allowed himself to be consecrated as Pope Nicholas II. He and his cardinals, supported by Duke Godfrey with a small military contingent, then advanced upon Rome, where their partisans, led by a certain baptised Jew named Leo di Benedicto Christiano, opened the gates of Trastevere. Quickly they occupied the Tiber Island, which they made their headquarters. Several days of street-fighting followed, but at last the Lateran was stormed, Benedict barely managing to escape to Galeria.[1]

[1] The city of Galeria was abandoned in 1809, but its ruins may still be seen just off the Viterbo road about twenty miles from Rome.

The reform party had won again, but the cost had been considerable. Benedict X was still at large, and he had retained a loyal
following; many Romans who had been forced to swear allegiance
to Nicholas raised their left hand to do so, pointing out that with
their right they had already taken an oath of fidelity to his rival.
More disturbing still was the knowledge that victory could not
even now have been achieved without the military support provided
by Duke Godfrey. In short, after all the efforts of the past decade,
the Papacy was once again where it had been when Pope Leo
had found it—caught fast between the Roman aristocracy and
the Empire, able sometimes to play one off against the other
but never sufficiently strong to assert its independence of either.
The task of reform could not possibly be accomplished in
such conditions. Somehow the Church must stand on its own
feet.

First came the problem of Benedict. Only thirteen years before, his
odious namesake had demonstrated just how much harm could be
done by a renegade anti-Pope; Benedict X was a far more popular
figure than Benedict IX, and this time there was no Emperor ready
to sweep down into Italy and restore order, as Henry III had done.
Duke Godfrey had returned to Tuscany—though this was perhaps
just as well, since he had recently displayed a curious half-hearted-
ness that had led to suspicions of a secret intrigue with the Romans.
And so the Church took a surprising, fateful step. It called upon
the Normans for aid.

Though he may have taken earlier advice from Abbot Desiderius,
the final decision can only have been Hildebrand's. No other member
of the Curia, not even Nicholas himself, would have had the combination of courage and prestige it demanded. Throughout Italy,
and above all among the churchmen of Rome, the Normans were
still considered—not unreasonably—as a collection of barbarian
bandits, no better than the Saracens who had terrorised the South
before them. For many of the cardinals the thought of an alliance
with such men, whose record of sacrilege and desecration was
notorious and who had dared, only five years before, to take arms
against the Holy Father himself and hold him nine months a captive,
must have seemed more appalling by far than any accommodation

with the Roman nobility, or even with Benedict himself. But this ugly, unprepossessing little Tuscan, of obscure, possibly Jewish origins and a standard of learning and culture well below that of most of his colleagues, knew that he was right. Pope and Cardinals bowed, as nearly always, before his will; and in February 1059 he set off in person for Capua.

Richard of Capua was naturally delighted by Hildebrand's approach, and gave him a warm welcome. A year ago Pope Stephen had seemed to threaten him and his compatriots with extinction; now Stephen's successor had sent his most distinguished cardinal to seek Norman aid. It was a sign, moreover, that his recent reception at Monte Cassino was not, as he had feared, an isolated phenomenon but was indicative of a radical change in papal thinking. Such a change was rich in promise. Instantly he put three hundred men at Hildebrand's disposal, and the cardinal returned hurriedly to Rome with his new escort. By mid-March he and Nicholas were together encamped before Galeria, watching their army lay siege to the town. The Normans, employing their usual tactics, inflicted appalling devastation upon the entire region, burning and pillaging in all directions; the Galerians resisted with great courage, beating back repeated attempts to storm the walls, but at last they were forced to surrender. Benedict was captured, publicly unfrocked, and imprisoned in the church of Sant' Agnese in Rome; and the era of Norman-Papal friendship had begun.

The fate of Benedict X came as a profound shock to the reactionary group in Rome. They had expected neither the degree of resolution and unity of purpose with which the cardinals had opposed his election, nor the vigour with which he had subsequently been swept aside. And now, before they were able to recover, Hildebrand dealt them a second blow, still more paralysing in its long-term effects. The procedure governing papal elections had always been vague; at this time it was based on a settlement, originated by the Emperor Lothair I in 824 and renewed by Otto the Great in the following century, according to which the election was carried out by the entire clergy and nobility of the Roman people, but the new Pontiff was to be consecrated only after he had

taken the oath to the Emperor. Such a decree, loose enough in its
original conception and looser still in its interpretation through well
over two hundred years, was bound to lead to abuses. Apart from
the power which it gave to the Roman aristocracy, it also implied a
measure of dependence on the Empire which, though counter-
balanced by the need for every Emperor to submit to a papal
coronation in Rome, by no means accorded with Hildebrand's
ideas of papal supremacy. Now, with the Romans in disarray, a
child on the throne of Germany and the assurance of armed
Norman support if the need should arise, it could at last be
scrapped.

In April 1059 Pope Nicholas held a synod at the Lateran; and
there, in the presence of a hundred and thirteen bishops and with
Hildebrand as always at his side, he promulgated the decree which,
with one or two later amendments, continues to regulate papal
elections to the present day. For the first time the responsibility for
electing a new Pope was placed squarely on the cardinals, while to
prevent simony the cardinal-bishops were also required to super-
intend the election itself. Only after a Pontiff had been elected was
the assent of the rest of the clergy and people to be sought. Lip-
service was still paid to the imperial connexion by a deliberately
vague stipulation that the electors should have regard for 'the
honour and respect due to Henry, at present king and, it is hoped,
future emperor' and to such of his successors as should personally
have obtained similar rights from the Apostolic See, but the meaning
was plain; in future the Church would run its own affairs and take
orders from no one.

It was a brave decision; and not even Hildebrand would have
dared to take it but for the Normans. To both the Empire and the
nobility of Rome it amounted to a slap in the face, however diplo-
matically delivered, and either side might be expected now or later
to seek the restitution of its former privileges by force of arms. But
Hildebrand's conversations with the Prince of Capua, to say nothing
of recent events at Galeria, had given him—and through him the
Church as a whole—new confidence. With the aid of a mere three
hundred Normans from Capua he had thrown the foremost of
his enemies back in confusion; how much more might not be

accomplished if the entire Norman strength from Apulia and Calabria could also be mobilised behind the papal banners? Such support would enable the Church to shake off once and for all the last shreds of its political dependence, and allow the most far-reaching measures of reform to be enacted without fear of the consequences. Besides, the events of 1054 had produced a climate between Rome and Constantinople in which there was clearly no hope of an early reconciliation in the theological field; the sooner, therefore, that the perverted doctrines of the Greeks could be swept altogether from South Italy, the better. The Normans, having at last established tolerable relations with their Lombard subjects, were at this moment forcing the Byzantines back into a few isolated positions in Apulia —notably Bari—and into the toe of Calabria. Left to themselves they would soon finish the job; then, in all likelihood, they would start on the Sicilian infidels. They were by far the most efficient race on the entire peninsula and, for all their faults, they were at least Latins. Should they not therefore be encouraged rather than opposed?

Richard and Robert, for their part, asked nothing better than an alliance with the Church of Rome. However much they and their countrymen may have victimised individual religious foundations in the past, they had always—even at Civitate—shown respect for the Pope, and had taken arms against him in self-defence only after all attempts at a peaceful settlement had failed. They were not so strong that they did not welcome a guarantee against the threat of a combined onslaught by Empire and Papacy, or an ally against any other enemy—Byzantine, Tuscan or Saracen—with whom they might on occasion be faced. On the other hand they were quite powerful enough to negotiate with the Pope on an equal political footing. Their hopes were therefore high when Nicholas II left Rome in June 1059 with an impressive retinue of cardinals, bishops and clergy and—possibly at Robert Guiscard's invitation—headed south-west towards Melfi.

Slowly and magnificently the papal train passed through Campania. It stopped at Monte Cassino where it was joined by Desiderius, now the Pope's official representative in the South and thus in effect his ambassador to the Normans; it wound its way through the mountains to Benevento, where Nicholas held a synod; to Venosa, where he ostentatiously consecrated the new church of the Santissima Trinità, burial-place of the first three Hautevilles and thus the foremost Norman shrine in Italy; and finally to Melfi, where he arrived towards the end of August and found, waiting at the gates of the town to receive him, a huge assemblage of Norman barons headed by Richard of Capua and Robert Guiscard, hastily returned from Calabrian campaigning to welcome his illustrious guests.

The synod of Melfi which was ostensibly the reason for the Pope's visit has largely been forgotten. Its principal object was to try to reimpose chastity, or at least celibacy, on the South Italian clergy—an undertaking in which, despite the unfrocking of the Bishop of Trani in the presence of over a hundred of his peers, later records show it to have been remarkably unsuccessful. Nicholas's presence proved, however, the occasion of an event of immense historical importance to the Normans and the Papacy alike—their formal reconciliation. It began with the Pope's confirmation of Richard as Prince of Capua, and continued with his ceremonial investiture of Robert, first with the Duchy of Apulia, next with Calabria and finally—though the Guiscard had never yet set foot in the island—with Sicily.

By just what title the Pope so munificently bestowed on the Normans territories which had never before been claimed by him or his predecessors is a matter open to doubt. Where the mainland of Italy was concerned, documentary evidence suggests that he was basing himself on Charlemagne's gift to the Papacy of the Duchy of Benevento two and a half centuries before. The frontiers of this territory were then ill-defined and had since proved elastic; at one moment they could have been said to comprise all the peninsula south of the city itself, though they did not by any means do so in the eleventh century. And it was after all only twelve years before that Henry III, restoring Capua to Pandulf in the presence of Pope Clement, had made it quite clear that he considered the principality an imperial fief. With regard to Sicily Nicholas was on still shakier ground; the island had never been subject to Papal control, and his only authority seems to have been the so-called Donation of

Constantine—a document by which the Emperor Constantine I was held to have conferred upon Pope Sylvester and his successors the temporal dominion over 'Rome and all the provinces, places and cities of Italy and the western regions'. This had long been a favourite weapon used in support of Papal claims; it was not until the fifteenth century that, to much ecclesiastical embarrassment, it was exposed as a forgery, shamelessly concocted in the papal Curia some seven hundred years earlier.[1]

But none of those present in Melfi on that August day was likely to raise embarrassing issues of this sort. In any event Nicholas could afford to be expansive; he was getting so much in return. He was admittedly lending papal support to the most dangerous and potentially disruptive of all the political elements in South Italy; but by investing both its leaders, whose relations were known to be strained, he was carefully keeping this element divided. Furthermore Robert Guiscard and Richard of Capua now swore him an oath which changed, radically and completely, the whole position of the Papacy. By a lucky chance the complete text of Robert's oath— though not, unfortunately, Richard's—has come down to us in the Vatican archives—one of the earliest of such texts still extant. The first part, concerning an annual rent to be paid to Rome of twelve pence of Pavia for each yoke of oxen in his domains, is of relatively little importance; the second, however, is vital:

I, Robert, by the Grace of God and of St Peter Duke of Apulia and of Calabria and, if either aid me, future Duke of Sicily, shall be from this time forth faithful to the Roman Church and to you, Pope Nicholas, my lord. Never shall I be party to a conspiracy or undertaking by which your life might be taken, your body injured or your liberty removed. Nor shall I reveal to any man any secret which you may confide to me, pledging me to keep it, lest this should cause you harm. Everywhere and against all adversaries I shall remain, insofar as it is in my power to be so, the ally of the holy Roman Church, that she may preserve and acquire the revenues and domains of St Peter. I shall afford to you all assistance that may be necessary that you may occupy, in all honour and security, the papal

---

[1] The earliest extant copy of this document is to be found at the Bibliothèque Nationale in Paris (M.S. Latin, No. 2777) and dates from the ninth century. The relevant passage reads: *'quamque Romae urbis et omnes Italiae seu occidentalium regionum provincias loca et civitates'*.

Troina

Cerami: the battlefield

throne in Rome. As for the territories of St Peter, and those of the
Principality [of Benevento], I shall not attempt to invade them nor even
to ravage them [*sic*] without the express permission of yourself or your
successors, clothed with the honours of the blessed Peter. I shall con-
scientiously pay, every year, to the Roman Church the agreed rent for the
territories of St Peter which I do or shall possess. I shall surrender to you
the churches which are at present in my hands, with all their property,
and shall maintain them in their obedience to the holy Roman Church.
Should you or any of your successors depart this life before me I shall,
having taken the advice of the foremost cardinals as of the clergy and
laity of Rome, work to ensure that the Pope shall be elected and installed
according to the honour due to St Peter. I shall faithfully observe, with
regard both to the Roman Church and to yourself, the obligations which
I have just undertaken, and shall do likewise with regard to your successors who will ascend to the honour of the blessed Peter and who will
confirm me in the investiture which you have performed. So help me
God and his Holy Gospels.

The ceremonies over, Nicholas returned to Rome, his retinue
now further increased by a substantial Norman force. Richard, whose
oath was presumably on similar lines, headed for Capua while
Robert hastened back to rejoin his army in Calabria, where it was
besieging the little town of Cariati. All three could be well satisfied
with what they had done.

Others, however, did not share their satisfaction. Gisulf of
Salerno had suffered yet another blow to his power and his pride.
His last hopes of mobilising papal support against the hated Normans
had crumbled, and he could now look forward to nothing but an
unglamorous decline in his dwindling domain, for ever at the mercy
of the Prince of Capua and sustained only by occasional reflected
rays from his brother-in-law Robert Guiscard. The Roman aristocracy retreated into its musty palaces, furious and frightened. The
Byzantines saw that they had lost their last chance of preserving
what was left of their Italian possessions. And in the Western
Empire, shorn of its privileges at Papal elections, faced with a new
alliance as formidable militarily as it was politically, and now, as a
crowning insult, forced to watch in impotent silence while immense
tracts of imperial territory were calmly conferred on Norman
brigands, the reaction to Nicholas's behaviour need not be described.
It was lucky for Italy that Henry IV was still a child; had he been a

few years older, he would never have taken such treatment lying down. As it was, the Pope's name was thenceforth ostentatiously omitted from the intercessions in all the imperial chapels and churches; but we may wonder whether Nicholas—or Hildebrand— greatly cared.

II

INVASION

Italien ohne Sizilien macht gar kein Bild in der Seele: hier ist der Schlüssel zu allem.

(Italy without Sicily cannot be conceived: here is the key to everything.)

Goethe, writing from Palermo
in April 1787. (*Italienische Reise*)

The terms of Robert Guiscard's investiture at Melfi and of his subsequent oath of allegiance to Pope Nicholas left no doubt as to the direction of his future ambitions. Sicily, lying green and fertile a mere three or four miles from the mainland, was not only the obvious target, the natural extension of that great southward sweep of conquest that had brought the Normans down from Aversa to the furthermost tip of Calabria; it was also the lair of the Saracen pirates—recently, thanks to the continual internecine warfare within the island, less audacious and well-equipped than in former times, but still a perennial menace to the coastal towns of the south and west. While Sicily remained in the hands of the heathen, how could the Duke of Apulia ever ensure the security of his newly-ratified dominions? In any case he was now a loyal servant of the Pope, and had not Nicholas himself charged him to purge papal lands of the infidel oppressors? Like most of his compatriots, Robert was fundamentally a religious man; and among other less commendable motives there was certainly a spark of the genuine crusader spirit in his heart as he threaded his way south from Melfi, through Calabria and over the high Aspromonte from which he could gaze down

131

across the straits to Sicily, warm and inviting in the September sun, with only the plume of Etna a snow-white warning on the horizon.

But before the Guiscard could spread out the map of Sicily, he must roll up that of Calabria. One or two towns in the region still remained occupied by Greek garrisons; if these were not quickly eliminated they might create serious problems with his lines of communication and supply once the Sicilian venture was properly under way. He rode straight to Cariati. His men had already been besieging it for many weeks without success, but on Robert's arrival it surrendered almost at once; and before he returned to Apulia for the winter Rossano and Gerace had in their turn capitulated. Now only Reggio remained in Byzantine hands. Early in 1060, after a brief excursion to the south-east during which the Greeks were chased from Taranto and Brindisi, the Guiscard was back with his army beneath its walls. There he was met by Roger, whom he left in charge during his absence and who had foresightedly spent the winter constructing massive siege-engines. It was the first time since the Normans came to Italy that they—as opposed to their Lombard allies—had had recourse to weapons of this kind; but Reggio was the capital of Byzantine Calabria and the Greeks were expected to sell it dearly. So indeed they did. At last, however, they were forced to surrender, and the Duke of Apulia rode in triumphal procession through the city, between the long rows of marble villas and palaces for which it was famous. The garrison, to whom Robert had offered generous terms, fled to a nearby fortress on the rock of Scilla[1] where they held out for a little while longer; but they soon realised that their cause was hopeless and, one moonless summer night, all embarked secretly for Constantinople. On that night Greek political rule in Calabria came to an end. It never returned.

Now at last Robert and Roger were ready for Sicily. The chief obstacles had been overcome. The Greeks had been eliminated from all Italy except the city of Bari, where, though possibly hard to evict, they should prove easy enough to contain; and Bari was in

[1] Opposite the legendary Charybdis, on the Sicilian shore. Chalandon translates Malaterra's *Scillacium* as Squillace, but is surely wrong. To reach Squillace, which is some seventy miles from Reggio even as the crow flies, the Greeks would have had to cross the whole Aspromonte massif, passing through Norman-held territory the whole way.

any case far away. Everywhere else the phrase *Magna Graecia*, so long used to describe Byzantine Italy, could be discounted as a quaint historical expression. The Pope had given the expedition his blessing. The Western Empire was powerless to intervene. Even in Sicily itself conditions seemed relatively favourable. In many areas the local population was still Christian and could be expected to welcome the Normans as liberators, giving them all the help and support they needed. As for the Saracens, they were certainly brave fighters—no one questioned that—but they were by now more divided among themselves than they had ever been and were hardly likely to prove a match for a cohesive and well-disciplined Norman army. The island was at this time being squabbled over by three independent emirs. First there was a certain Ibn-at-Timnah, who controlled much of the south-east, with major garrisons at Catania and Syracuse; then there was Abdullah Ibn Haukal, dominating the north-western corner from his palaces at Trapani and Mazara; finally, between the two, was the Emir Ibn al-Hawas with his seat at Enna.[1] All three princes had by now shaken off their earlier allegiance to the Zirid Caliph of Kairouan, who had himself been dislodged from his capital a year or two previously and was now fighting for his life among the tribal factions of North Africa; and all were at constant loggerheads with each other. It did not look as though the Norman conquest of Sicily would take very long.

In fact, from first to last, it took thirty-one years, longer than most of the Normans concerned had been in Italy—longer indeed than many had been alive. For they had reckoned without Apulia, where Robert Guiscard's by now traditional enemies stubbornly refused to lie down, dividing his energies and—more important— his resources at the one time when he desperately needed all he had for the Sicilian operation. The details of his Apulian campaigns against a new Byzantine army and his own rebellious subjects need not in themselves trouble us very much; their importance lies in the effect which they had on the course of events in Sicily. This was not wholly bad. That the continual necessity of fighting on two fronts

[1] Until 1927 this fortress-city was known as Castrogiovanni, a corruption of the Arabic Kasr Janni. In that year Mussolini restored its original name of Enna, by which it had been known throughout antiquity.

delayed and impeded the Sicilian success, rendering it infinitely more hazardous and expensive than it would otherwise have been, is a point which hardly needs emphasis; the Norman expeditionary force was chronically, sometimes disastrously, undermanned and ill-supplied. And yet, paradoxically, it was the Guiscard's Apulian preoccupations during this period that made Sicily the brilliant and superbly-organised kingdom it later became. As Robert found himself compelled to spend more and more of his time dealing with his enemies on the mainland, so the army in Sicily, nominally under his command, fell increasingly under the control of Roger, until the younger brother could at last assume effective supremacy. This, as we shall see, later led to the division of Robert's domains and so allowed Roger, freed of Apulian responsibilities, to devote to the island the attention it deserved.

Roger must have been well aware that, by the terms of the Melfi investiture, all Sicily when conquered would be held by Robert, and that, whatever his own achievements, he could in theory expect only such rewards as his capricious brother might choose to offer him; yet he must also in some degree have foreseen the future pattern of events, and he probably suspected that his opportunities might prove greater than they at present appeared. Certainly he showed himself from the outset to be every whit as eager and enthusiastic as the Duke of Apulia himself. A few weeks after the capture of Reggio he had made an experimental foray across the straits, landing one night with some fifty or sixty chosen followers near Messina and advancing on the town; but the Saracens had emerged in strength and driven the raiders back to their boats. Meanwhile preparations began for the full-scale invasion.

They were painfully slow. Already Apulia was stirring, and in October 1060 Robert Guiscard was summoned back in all urgency. The Emperor Constantine X Ducas, who had the year before assumed the throne of Constantinople, had despatched a new army to Italy in a final effort to save what was left of his Langobardian Theme. It was not a particularly large force, but it took the Normans by surprise at a moment when the Guiscard was away in Calabria and at first met with little resistance. Even when Robert and his brother, Mauger, appeared with a hastily-assembled army of their own they were not immediately able to check the Greek advance, and by the end of the year much of the east coast had been recaptured and Melfi itself was under siege. By January 1061 the situation was so serious that Roger and the rest of the troops in Calabria were sent for. The Sicilian operation looked like being indefinitely postponed.

But Roger was not put off so easily. By mid-February he was back again in Calabria, just in time to seize a new opportunity which suddenly and unexpectedly presented itself. The feuding which had so long continued between two of the Sicilian emirs, Ibn at-Timnah and Ibn al-Hawas, had now flared up into open warfare. Some time before, in a disastrous attempt to patch up their quarrel, Ibn at-Timnah had married the sister of Ibn al-Hawas, but the latter was now holding her in his eagle's-nest fortress at Enna and refusing to return her to her husband. His reluctance was readily understandable and doubtless shared by the lady herself, since she had recently had an argument with Ibn at-Timnah in the course of which he had called in a drunken fury to his slaves and ordered them to open her veins; fortunately her son, in the nick of time, had summoned the doctors and saved her life. Soon after her flight her husband, probably more anxious to preserve his self-respect than his marriage, had marched on Enna to recover his rightful property; but he had been unable to make any impression on the most impregnable stronghold in all Sicily and had instead suffered an inglorious defeat in the valley below. He and the remnants of his army had then retreated in disorder to Catania, and there his spies soon informed him that Ibn al-Hawas was preparing a punitive force with which he had openly sworn to finish him off once and for all.

Roger was at Mileto when, in the second week of February 1061, Ibn at-Timnah arrived in person to seek his aid and to offer him— according to the Arab historian Ibn al-Athir—no less a prize in return for the liquidation of his enemy than the domination of the whole of Sicily. It was not the sort of proposition that he could possibly ignore. Quickly he assembled a force of a hundred and sixty knights and several hundred foot-soldiers, together with a small fleet under Geoffrey Ridel, one of the Guiscard's most able commanders, and landed a few days later in the extreme north-eastern corner of the island. Previous experience warned him against arousing the garrison of Messina; his plan this time, approved by Ibn at-Timnah who was with him, was to follow the north coast along to Milazzo, making sorties inland wherever they seemed indicated and ravaging as much as possible of Ibn al-Hawas's territory on the way. Then, although none of the chroniclers is entirely explicit on the point, his intention seems to have been to secure the Milazzo promontory as a permanent Norman bridgehead in Sicily which could be used for the landing of stores, reinforcements and, ultimately, the main body of the army.[1] At first all went well. Milazzo was taken and so, with hardly a struggle, was Rometta. The plunder was considerable—it included, apparently, a large quantity of cattle—and, to make sure of getting it safely back to Reggio, the entire army returned to Cape Farò, where the fleet was lying at anchor. Meanwhile, however, the alarm had been raised in Messina. The garrison had hurried up the coast and was now drawn up on the hillside just out of sight of the beach. More cautious this time—for the Norman force was far larger than that which they had so effortlessly repulsed the year before—the Saracens planned to wait until the loading operations were in full swing and then attack when the Normans were divided between the beach and the ships. It was a good idea, and it might well have succeeded; fortunately for the Normans, however, contrary winds made embarkation difficult, and before the work could begin Roger learned of the enemy's presence. His half-brother Serlo—one of the four Hautevilles who had not come to seek his fortune in Italy—had a son of the same name who had recently joined his uncle in Calabria and was already showing unusual promise. This boy Roger now sent to attack the Saracens' flank, enjoining him above all to prevent their possible retreat along the narrow coastal strip leading back to Messina. The plan worked; and the Arabs, instead of taking the invaders by surprise, suddenly found themselves surrounded. Few survived.

Roger hastened to follow up his advantage. With any luck Messina

[1] The Allies used the Cherbourg peninsula in much the same way during the Normandy landings of June 1944.

would have been left almost defenceless. He and his men reached the city the same evening, and at dawn on the following day the attack began. But now it was the Normans' turn to be surprised. Despite their losses the people of Messina, men and women together, leaped to the defence of their city. Roger saw that he had miscalculated. There would be no quick victory after all. Moreover, his tiny army would be easy prey for any relief force which Ibn al-Hawas might send out from the interior. He gave the order to retire. It was, for the Saracens, just the encouragement they needed, and it turned the scale of battle. A few minutes later the Norman retreat had turned to flight, with the Messinans in hot pursuit. Here was disaster; but still worse was to come. The contrary winds of the previous day had been the prelude to a great storm which was tearing at the ships lying at anchor off Farò. Embarkation, which had been difficult before, was now impossible. For three days the Normans waited, huddled on the open beach, blocked by the Saracens from any natural shelter and defending themselves as best they could from their repeated attacks. As Amatus frankly reports, 'What with fear and cold together, they were in a most miserable state.' Finally the sea calmed and they managed to get away, but they had not gone far before they were intercepted by a Saracen fleet from Messina, and the ensuing naval battle continued to the very entrance of Reggio harbour. One Norman ship was lost; the others, battered but still afloat, struggled into port to discharge their exhausted and shivering passengers. The expedition, after so promising a start, had ended in something suspiciously like a fiasco.

The blame lay squarely on the shoulders of Roger. Brave as he was, he had not yet learnt that in the art of war prudence is as valuable a quality as courage. Their successes of the last forty years had been largely due to the fact that the Normans, except occasionally in their mercenary days, had never sought a battle that they could not be reasonably certain of winning; nor, since they still depended largely on immigration for their fighting strength, did they ever unnecessarily risk the lives of their men. Twice in the past year Roger had done both. The fate of the Maniakes expedition in 1040—in which several of the older knights in his entourage had probably participated—should have made it clear enough that the

Saracens, divided or not, would fight hard and bitterly to preserve their island; and this self-evident fact had been further confirmed by Roger himself only a year before. To have launched yet another madcap expedition, carelessly planned and inadequately equipped, at a few days' notice and on behalf of an unbalanced and treacherous Emir, was an act of irresponsible folly whose consequences were entirely deserved.

It is to be hoped that Robert Guiscard spoke seriously to his brother on these lines when he joined Roger in Calabria early the following May. He had brought with him as much of his army as he could spare. The spring campaign in Apulia had been highly successful; Melfi had been relieved, Brindisi and Oria recaptured. A few towns in the heel were still in Byzantine hands, but the bulk of the Greek army had retreated to Bari and was unlikely to contemplate any further offensives for the time being. Six clear months of good campaigning weather lay ahead—time, perhaps, to get a firm grip on Sicily before winter closed in. There were other reasons too—apart from his natural impatience—which made Robert anxious to invade the island as soon as possible. Ibn al-Hawas, fully aware of Norman intentions, was already strengthening Messina with eight hundred knights and a fleet of twenty-four ships, and it was plain that the longer the Normans waited, the tougher would be the resistance that they would eventually have to face. Robert was worried, too, about his Apulian vassals. The Byzantine invasion had kept them busy for the past few months, but now that the Greeks had retreated they were beginning to grow restless again. What they needed was a long-term task to perform, a bold and exciting new programme of conquest that would unite them under his leadership against a common enemy. Roger also was chafing; in no way deterred by his earlier reverses, he had spent the spring preparing and planning the main expedition. If it did not start soon he would be off on his own again.

Within a few days of the Guiscard's arrival at Reggio, the armies were ready to embark. Even by the standards of the time they did not amount to a very sizeable force—perhaps some two thousand all told, with knights and foot-soldiers in roughly equal proportions.

They were in fact considerably fewer than Robert had hoped, but the Apulian situation made it unlikely that he would be able to raise more in the foreseeable future. Given good generalship, they should suffice. After the February *débâcle*, however, one thing was plain. No expedition could succeed without securing its lines of communication with the mainland. This meant control of the straits, which in its turn involved the possession of Messina; not, as Roger at least knew to his cost, an easy proposition, but one to which there was no alternative, especially now that the Saracen fleet had been so drastically reinforced. The best chance lay in surprise.

In the middle of May 1061 the nights were dark and still. The new moon appeared on the twentieth, and it was probably on about the eighteenth at dusk that the Norman spearhead of some two hundred and seventy horsemen under the command of Roger de Hauteville slipped out of the little harbour of S. Maria del Farò in thirteen ships, and landed a few hours later on a deserted beach some five miles south of Messina.[1] Their crossing was comparatively long—some ten miles or so farther than would have been necessary if Robert Guiscard had chosen the shortest distance over the straits —but it proved a wise choice. The Saracens were expecting the invading force, whose arrival they knew to be imminent, to take the most direct route and to land, as Roger had done in February, some way to the north of the city; and their land and sea patrols were ceaselessly sweeping the coastline between Messina and Cape Farò. Such a concentration left the southern entrance to the straits totally without defence; Roger and his men passed across unmolested and before daybreak the fleet was back again in Calabria, ready to take the second wave of troops on board.

The purpose of the advance party was primarily reconnaissance, but Roger was not one to err on the side of caution. Moving off from the beach-head towards Messina soon after dawn, he almost at once came upon a Saracen mule-train, laden with money and supplies

[1] In an interesting article, '"Combined Operations" in Sicily, A.D. 1060–78' D. P. Waley suggests that the Normans had learnt the art of transporting horses across the sea from the Byzantines, and that the experience gained in 1061 proved of value five years later at Hastings, where it is known that Duke William's invasion force included knights from South Italy and Sicily.

for the Messina garrison. It was a providential opportunity. The Saracens were taken entirely by surprise and within a few minutes had been slaughtered to the last man; and hardly had the Normans regrouped themselves before a flurry of white sails off the coast announced the arrival of the next section of the invading army.

Roger now found himself with a force of nearly five hundred men. It was still no larger than that which had fared so disastrously on his previous expedition, but this time he knew that another 1500 under Robert Guiscard were on their way. Furthermore the Saracens of Messina had as yet given no indication that they knew of the Norman landings; there was consequently a good chance of taking them unawares. Messina was only a mile or two distant; the sun had hardly risen. Cautiously the Normans advanced. Outside the city they waited, watching; the ramparts, to which three months before the citizens had so magnificently rallied, were now deserted and quiet. For the second time that morning Providence had aligned herself on the Norman side. What was the use of waiting for Robert? Roger could handle this operation by himself. He attacked.

It was over almost as soon as it had begun. Long before the Duke of Apulia had sailed, with the bulk of his army, over a friendly and tranquil sea to his new domain, the city of Messina was in Norman hands. The Saracens had fallen victims to their own caution. In their anxiety to block the Norman's passage across the straits they had left not only the southern approaches to Messina but even the city itself undefended. The garrison, patrolling the coast to the north, never learnt what had happened until too late; and then, rightly concluding that return meant instant capture, fled to the interior. Those on the ships found themselves in a similar situation; once the port of Messina was in enemy control, to sail south into the narrows was to invite disaster. Turning about, they hastily rounded Cape Farò and headed westward to safety.

On his arrival, the Duke of Apulia rode in triumph through a largely deserted city. There had been the inevitable looting, but relatively little carnage. Malaterra tells in shocked admiration of a young Saracen noble who ran his beloved sister through with his own sword rather than allow her to fall into the lascivious clutches of the infidel; but most of the Muslim population managed to escape, unharmed and without much difficulty, into the hinterland. The Guiscard was only too pleased to see them go. Above all, he must ensure the security of Messina; the last thing he wanted was a large untrustworthy element in the population. There remained, in consequence, only the Christian—largely Greek—minority to extend to him a bewildered and cautious welcome and to arrange at his command a service of thanksgiving in their church. Robert was now more than ever at pains to stress the divinely-appointed nature of his expedition; not only was he in any case convinced of it himself—and the circumstances of the city's capture certainly seemed to argue some degree of celestial favour—but it would clearly have a salutary effect if the local Christians could be persuaded to look at the Norman invasion from a religious point of view.

Robert's next task was to transform Messina into the impregnable bridgehead he needed. For a week without respite, day and night, his army worked on the defences. Walls were rebuilt and extended, ramparts raised, towers fortified, new earthworks dug. When all was ready, a contingent of cavalry was installed as permanent garrison. It entailed a grave depletion of his military strength in the the field, but where Messina was concerned he could afford to take no chances. Meanwhile, quick as always to turn Norman ambitions to his own advantage, there reappeared on the scene the sinister figure of Ibn at-Timnah to ingratiate himself once again into Norman counsels. As soon as Roger's earlier expedition had run into difficulties he had removed himself hastily out of harm's way to his castle at Catania; now, more plausible and subservient than ever, he returned to find a new and ready audience in the Guiscard himself. His proposals were unchanged; if the Normans would help him against Ibn al-Hawas, supreme control over Sicily would be theirs.

Whatever Robert's private feelings may have been about Ibn at-Timnah, he could not afford to dismiss him. This man was, with Ibn al-Hawas, the most powerful of the Sicilian Emirs. Now that Messina was secure, his friendship would give the Normans effective control of all eastern Sicily, with the whole length of vital coastline facing the mainland. He could provide guides, interpreters, weapons, food and all the various forms of expertise which Europeans in Muslim lands so conspicuously lacked. Here, it seemed, was yet another manifestation of divine benevolence—though Robert may well have reflected that in this case the Almighty could scarcely have selected a more unlikely vehicle for His purposes. And so it was that a week or so later, as soon as the defences of Messina had been completed to his satisfaction, the Guiscard led his army forth again, with Roger and Ibn at-Timnah riding at his side, on the next stage of his Sicilian adventure.

From Messina there were two ways of approaching the domains of Ibn al-Hawas. The shortest was to follow the coast southwards to a point near Taormina and then, turning inland, to follow the Alcántara valley round the northern slopes of Etna and on to the central plateau. Ibn at-Timnah preferred, however, to lead his Norman friends by the alternative route, passing through territory which, though theoretically loyal to him, had recently shown signs of falling away and would doubtless benefit from a sight of the Norman army at close quarters. This would have an additional advantage in that it would allow Robert to secure the formal allegiance of Rometta, without which the mountain passes commanding the approach to Messina from the west could never be properly secured.

Rometta was then, as it is today, a superb natural stronghold; in addition it had been heavily fortified by the Saracens. To George Maniakes in 1038 it had proved a formidable obstacle, and might easily have done the same in 1061 to Robert Guiscard: fortunately, however, the governor had remained loyal to Ibn at-Timnah. Now, for the second time in only four months, he greeted the Normans' arrival with every sign of pleasure. Presenting himself without delay at their camp, he knelt at Robert's feet, swore allegiance to him on the Koran and offered him, among a host of other gifts, the keys to the citadel and the town. This was the final link in the defensive chain which the Guiscard had flung round Messina; now at last he could proceed in confidence.

Though irritated as always by the slowness of the infantry—Amatus tells us that he was always galloping on ahead with his horsemen and then having to wait while the foot-soldiers caught up —the Duke managed to maintain a remarkable speed. Two days'

journey from Rometta brought him to Frazzanò, at the foot of the
pass leading up to the so-called *pianura di Maniace*, the plateau on which
the gigantic George and the first of the young Hautevilles had distinguished themselves twenty-one years before. Here Robert drew
his breathless army to a halt. Till now there had been no serious
opposition anywhere along the route; the region through which
they had passed was largely Christian, and the local populations
had welcomed them with real—though, as they were soon to learn,
misplaced—enthusiasm. But once they reached the Simeto river
the Normans would be on hostile territory; and spies were already
bringing in reports of the mighty army which Ibn al-Hawas was
preparing to lead against them from his fortress at Enna. The
advance continued, but now the Guiscard was more wary. At
Centuripe he suffered his first check. His attack on the town met with
heavy resistance and, rather than risk losses he could ill afford, he
raised the siege almost at once, leaving the town untaken. A short
excursion eastwards was more successful; Paternò fell without a
struggle, the Muslims melting away before the Norman advance
'like wax before a fire', as Amatus puts it. And then, since the much-
vaunted Saracen army was still many miles distant and not apparently
over-anxious to show itself, Robert wheeled his troops to the right
and advanced along the valley of the Dittaino, plunging ever
deeper into the enemy's heartland until he pitched his camp among
the watermills immediately beneath the great crag of Enna itself.

Of all the mountain-fortresses of Sicily, Enna was among the
highest and the most forbidding. Two centuries before, the
Saracens themselves had been able to capture it from the Greeks
only by crawling one by one up the main sewer. It could clearly
never be taken by storm, and Robert, conscious of the shortage of
time before winter would force his retreat, was anxious to avoid a
siege. He therefore deliberately trailed his coat, challenging Ibn
al-Hawas on his very threshold to come out and fight and to give
the Normans a taste of that formidable reception he was said to have
prepared. Yet the Saracens still held back, and for four days the
Normans waited in a mood of mounting frustration, laying waste the
surrounding countryside and doing their impatient worst to needle
the Emir into action. On the fifth day they succeded.

It is impossible, as so often in the history of this period, to give any reliable estimate of the numbers involved in the battle that followed. We learn from Malaterra that the Saracen army comprised fifteen thousand; it may be an exaggeration, but there is nothing inherently improbable about it. One thing, at all events, is clear; the Normans were outnumbered many times over. Robert Guiscard had at the start only some two thousand men. He had left a strong garrison at Messina, and possibly others at Rometta and elsewhere. Ibn at-Timnah may have supplemented the Norman army with a few Saracen turncoats, but these are not likely to have been many since they are nowhere mentioned in the chronicles. When Malaterra estimates Robert's strength at about seven hundred he may not, therefore, be very far out.

And yet the battle of Enna was an overwhelming victory for the Normans. Geography, as well as numbers, was against them; they had no strong places into which they could retire for rest or consolidation, no well-stocked magazines of arms or supplies. But courage and, above all, discipline—these they had in plenty, and of a kind which the Saracens had never before encountered. To them they added a new and powerful religious fervour to drive them forward when, newly confessed and shriven and with Robert's huge voice still thundering in their ears, they charged into battle. And so the first major engagement, on Sicilian soil or anywhere else, fought between properly constituted armies of Normans and Saracens ended in rout. Five thousand of Ibn al-Hawas's men managed to reach the safety of their fortress; the remainder, by nightfall, lay dead or dying along the river bank. Norman losses were negligible.

Plunder apart, the results of the victory were largely indirect. Ibn al-Hawas with the rump of his army—and, presumably, Ibn at-Timnah's wife—was safe in his citadel, whence the Normans were as far as ever from dislodging him; and although a siege was ordered even before the Norman wounded had been carried from the field, it was plain to all that to capture such a place would be a long and arduous task. Meanwhile, however, news of the battle was spreading quickly through the valleys, where few of the local chieftains shared their Emir's determination. Before long the first of them had appeared at the Guiscard's camp; and in the weeks that followed they came by the score, heads bowed and arms folded across their chests, their mules piled high with gifts and tribute. Such eagerness to make formal submission was hardly surprising; they were now defenceless while the Normans, true to their old habits during siege warfare, were despatching daily raiding-parties to terrorise and lay waste the countryside as only they knew how. Harvest-time was approaching, but the Muslim farmers could expect little from their burnt-out fields and devastated vineyards. Ibn al-Hawas, peering out during those summer nights from his beleaguered stronghold, must have seen the flames from the neighbouring homesteads blazing even more brightly than the Norman campfires directly below him. The sight may not have caused him much distress; his own losses had been far greater. But he must have suspected that for him and for his people this was the beginning of the end; Sicily would never be the same again.

In the short term, however, time was on the Emir's side. Robert Guiscard could not in his present circumstances undertake a winter campaign; he was already dangerously extended and would need to consolidate his gains before he could safely return to the mainland. After two months of siege in the remorseless Sicilian summer, Enna showed no signs of weakening, but Norman patience was beginning to wear thin. Already Roger, impetuous as always, had grown tired of the inactivity and had galloped off with three hundred men on another of his so-called reconnaissance expeditions, leaving a trail of pillage and devastation all the way to Agrigento and returning with enough plunder to reward the entire army. This doutbless proved a valuable sweetener, but it was by now clear that the siege would soon have to be raised. Some time in July or early August Robert gave the signal and, to the relief of the besiegers almost as much as the besieged, led his men away down the valley whence they had come.

With so small an army at his disposal and so many of his men now bent on returning to their Apulian homes, the Guiscard could not hope to secure any part of Ibn al-Hawas's territory. Farther north, however, in that no-man's-land which, though technically within the domains of Ibn at-Timnah, was never safe for long against the incursions of his rival, the Greek Christian inhabitants implored

him to leave a permanent garrison and easily persuaded some of the
more rootless Norman knights to settle on Sicilian soil. And so, in
the autumn of 1061, there arose a few miles from the north coast,
near the ruins of the classical Aluntium, the first Norman fortress
to be built on the island. Perched among the foothills of the Nébrodi,
and commanding the passes which provided the principal channel
for Saracen attacks, it constituted for the local inhabitants both an
effective defence and an ever-present reminder of Norman strength.
In the following years this isolated stronghold was to grow into a
prosperous little town. Such it remains today; and of Robert
Guiscard's work it still retains not only a ruined castle but also the
name, S. Marco d'Alunzio, which he gave it in memory of that other
S. Marco in Calabria where his career had begun only fifteen short
years before.

Back at Messina, Robert Guiscard was joined by Sichelgaita who,
after a brief tour of inspection of her husbands's new domains,
bore him triumphantly off to Apulia for Christmas. Roger accompanied them as far as Mileto in Calabria, which he had made his
mainland headquarters; but he could not rest. Sicily continued to
beckon. There was still too much work to be done—or rather,
perhaps, too many opportunities to be seized. By early December
he was back in the island with two hundred and fifty of his followers.
After a second tornado-like progress through the Agrigento region
he turned back north again to Troina, a higher and more commanding fortress even than Enna. Fortunately it was populated mainly
by Greeks, who at once opened their gates to Roger's army. Here
he spent Christmas; here, too, he learned to his joy that his old love
from early days in Normandy had arrived in Calabria, where she
was awaiting his return and hoping, as she had always hoped, to
become his wife.

Judith of Evreux was the daughter of a first cousin of William
the Conqueror. When she and Roger had first known each other,
any idea of her marrying the youngest and poorest of the relatively
humble Hautevilles must have been out of the question; but since
then many things had changed. A violent quarrel had broken out
between Duke William and Robert de Grantmesnil, Judith's half-

146

brother and guardian, abbot of the important Norman monastery of St Evroul-sur-Ouche. In consequence Robert had fled, with Judith, her brother and sister and eleven faithful monks, first to Rome, where he tried to seek redress from the Pope, and then on to his countrymen in the south. Robert Guiscard had received them well. Anxious to weaken the hold of the Greek monasteries in Calabria, he was already encouraging the settlement of Latin monks wherever possible, and had at once founded, with a handsome endowment, the abbey of S. Eufemia in Calabria where the celebrated liturgical and musical traditions of St Evroul could be maintained.[1] But Roger also had his plans. By now he had achieved in Italy a degree of power and influence second only to that of the Guiscard himself. Few non-ruling families in Europe would any longer consider him an unworthy bridegroom. The moment he heard of Judith's arrival he hurried to Calabria to meet her, and found her waiting for him at the little town of S. Martino d'Agri. They were married on the spot. Roger then led his bride to Mileto, where the union was officially celebrated—with the assistance, in good St Evroul style, of a large concourse of musicians. It was undoubtedly a love match, and the young couple seem to have been very happy; but their honeymoon was all too short. Roger had serious work to do; early in the new year, 'in no way moved by his wife's tearful entreaties', he left her in Mileto and returned to Sicily.

The year 1062 had started well, but it failed to live up to its early promise. After little more than a month's campaigning during which the town of Petralia was the only gain of any importance, Roger returned to the mainland, determined to settle once and for all a domestic issue which had been worrying him for some time. The Duke of Apulia was back again at his old tricks. Already in 1058 he had undertaken to share his Calabrian conquests equally with his brother; since then, however, disturbed by Roger's increasing influence and fearing for his own position, he had refused to honour his promises. While Roger's attention had been focused on Sicily he had grudgingly accepted the money which Robert offered him

---

[1] S. Eufemia was in its turn the mother-abbey of many Sicilian foundations, including that of S. Agata at Catania, now the Cathedral.

instead of the stipulated territories, but now that he was married the position was different. The *Morgengab* tradition which had proved so useful to the Prince of Capua some years before was universally upheld in Norman Italy, and it was unthinkable that any great baron, least of all a Hauteville, should be unable to enfeoff his wife and her family in a manner befitting their rank and station. Messengers were accordingly despatched to the Duke in Melfi carrying Roger's formal demands, together with a warning that if these were not fully met within forty days, he would be compelled to obtain his rights by force.

Thus, for the second time in four years, the whole momentum of the Norman advance was checked while its two greatest architects squabbled over the spoils. As on the previous occasion, it was less the ambition of the junior brother than the jealousy of the senior that provided the spark; Roger was too much of a Hauteville to prove an easy subordinate, but neither in 1058 nor in 1062 do his demands seem to have been unreasonable. The fault was Robert's. Sure as was his political instinct in most situations, he was apt to lose all sense of proportion whenever he suspected that his own supremacy was being challenged or eroded by his younger brother. On this occasion in particular he could ill afford to antagonise Roger. The Byzantine army was still entrenched at Bari and doubtless preparing new offensives; if Robert hoped to hold it in check while at the same time following up the advantages so far gained in Sicily he must have a lieutenant on whose courage and resourcefulness he could rely. And now the situation became even more serious; for during the forty days set by Roger before the expiry of his ultimatum, word came from Sicily that Ibn at-Timnah, who was meanwhile continuing the spring campaign along the north coast, had been led into an ambush and murdered. His death had had an immediately tonic effect on the morale of his enemies, to the point where the Norman garrisons of Petralia and Troina, fearing for their lives, had deserted their posts in panic and fled back to Messina.

At this moment it would still have been possible for the Duke of Apulia to acknowledge his obligations and settle the argument before it was too late. Instead he marched furiously down into Calabria and besieged Roger in Mileto. The story that follows seems to belong to that ridiculous half-way world which lies between musical comedy and melodrama. It is recorded in fascinating detail by Malaterra and is worth summarising here less for its intrinsic historical importance than for the light which it sheds on the characters of two extraordinary men and on the way in which affairs of state were occasionally conducted nine centuries ago.

One night during the siege of Mileto, Roger stole secretly from the city to seek help from the neighbouring town of Gerace, whither he was shortly afterwards pursued by a furious Guiscard. The inhabitants of Gerace, faithful to Roger, slammed their gates on the Duke as he arrived; later, however, disguising himself under a heavy cowl, he managed to slip in unobserved. Once inside the town, he made his way to the house of a certain Basil, whom he knew to be loyal, and with whom he wanted to discuss ways of re-establishing his authority. Basil and his wife Melita, regardless of the risks they were running, asked their distinguished guest to stay to dinner but, unfortunately for Robert, while they were waiting for their meal he was recognised by a servant, who at once gave the alarm. Within minutes the house was surrounded by an angry crowd. Basil, panicking, fled to the nearest church for asylum, but was caught and struck down by the mob before he reached it; Melita was also captured and suffered an even more terrible fate; she was impaled on a stake and died in agony. Robert, on the other hand, the cause of all the trouble, kept his head. His call for silence was obeyed, and his powers of oratory were equal to the crisis. For his enemies, he declared, he had but a single message; let them not, for their own sakes, get carried away by the pleasure of finding the Duke of Apulia in their power. Today fortune frowned on him, but all that ever came to pass did so by the will of God, and tomorrow their respective positions might easily be reversed. He had come among them freely, of his own accord and without any hostile intent; they, for their part, had sworn fidelity to him and he had never played them false. It would be shameful indeed if a whole city, heedless of its oath, should now hurl itself pointlessly against a single, unarmed man. They should remember, too, that his death would earn them the lasting hostility of the Normans, whose friendship they were at present fortunate enough to enjoy. It would be avenged, implacably and without mercy, by his

149

followers, whose anger would be almost as dreadful as the dishonour which would fall upon themselves and their children for having caused the death of their innocent, beloved and devoted leader.

The people of Gerace cannot have been altogether taken in. For fifteen years the name of Robert Guiscard had been enough to send peasants stumbling from the fields to barricade their homes, monks burrowing under the monastery cellars to bury their treasure and plate; it was a little late for him to start playing the injured lamb. And yet his words had their effect. Slowly, as he spoke, the crowd grew calmer. Perhaps after all it might be better not to take too precipitate a decision. The Duke was moved to a place of safety, and all Gerace deliberated what was to be done.

Robert's followers, waiting outside the walls of the town, soon learnt of the turn events had taken. Only one course was open to them. Choking back their pride they sought out Roger, who was encamped a few miles away, and begged for his help. Roger was now enjoying himself. He knew that he no longer had any cause to fear for his own safety; his brother's life was in his hands and he could make whatever terms he liked. Naturally he could not allow Robert to come to any serious harm. For all their quarrelling, he loved him after a fashion; he respected his genius; above all, he needed him for the Sicilian operation. But he saw no reason not to make the most of the present state of affairs. Riding in full state to Gerace, he summoned all the elders to meet him in an open space outside the gates. They arrived to find him purple with rage. Why, he demanded, had the town not immediately handed his brother over to him? It was he, not they, who had suffered from the Guiscard's duplicity; he only had the right to inflict the punishment such conduct deserved. Let the so-called Duke he delivered up to him at once; otherwise, let the citizens of Gerace bid farewell to their town, and to the farms and vineyards with which it was surrounded, for by morning all would be razed to the ground.

The poor burghers were probably only too pleased to comply. Roger's threats offered them a means of escape from an impossible position. Robert was sent for, and hastily handed over; and all waited breathlessly to see what chastisement had been reserved for him. They were due for a surprise. Roger dropped his mask of anger and strode forward, arms outstretched, to greet his brother; and within a moment the two were embracing each other like Joseph and Benjamin—the phrase is Malaterra's—and weeping tears of joy at their reconciliation. Robert immediately promised full satisfaction of all Roger's territorial demands and, still beaming, the brothers rode off together to Mileto. As subsequent events were to prove, the quarrel was even now not entirely over; once the Duke found himself reunited with his wife and the main body of his army he began to regret his too easy acquiescence, and for a short while the fighting broke out anew; but his heart was no longer in it and before long the two greatest of the Hautevilles were friends again.

The manner in which, after this unlovely wrangle, Calabria was finally divided between Robert and Roger is still not altogether clear. It seems to have been based on a scheme according to which each town and castle was individually divided into two separate areas of influence, being thus prevented from giving active support to either brother against his rival. Such a system suggests that the degree of mutual trust now established between the two still fell some way short of the ideal; in practice it must have been so complicated and cumbersome that we can only wonder that it worked at all. And yet both brothers seem to have found it satisfactory enough. Certainly it must somehow have enabled Roger to bestow upon Judith the *Morgengab* she deserved, and upon her family such estates as befitted their new dignity. For Robert Guiscard it had been an expensive lesson, but he had learnt it well.

For Roger, too, the quarrel with his brother had been expensive. It had cost him several valuable campaigning months which should have been spent in Sicily, and it was not until the high summer of 1062 that he was able to return to the island. This time, no doubt remembering the tears which she had shed when he had left her behind in the spring, he took Judith with him. They landed, with an army of three hundred, in early August and went straight to Troina. Despite the ignominious flight of the Norman garrison after Ibn at-Timnah's assassination, the town had suffered no Saracen attacks in Roger's absence, and if he noticed that the welcome which the

Greek inhabitants now extended to himself and his young wife seemed rather cooler than on his first arrival, he attached no particular importance to the point. Everything seemed peaceable enough. After a week or two spent putting the fortifications in order Roger left Judith in the care of the new garrison and set off on his long-delayed campaign.

This was the moment for which the Greeks of Troina had been waiting. As so many of their compatriots and co-religionists were to find during the early years of Norman domination, their new masters were often worse than the old. They were more demanding than the Saracens, tougher and more unscrupulous in getting what they wanted. Even their Christianity was incomprehensible, crude in its practices, barbaric in its language; and their free and easy ways with the local women were already notorious throughout the island. The Troinans had suffered particularly in this last respect. The hasty departure of their first Norman garrison had seemed to them a deliverance; but now it had been replaced, and by a still larger body of troops than before. They laid their plans carefully; and so soon as Roger and his army were a safe distance away, they struck. Their primary objective was the person of Judith. Once they had her in their power they could hold her hostage until the Normans agreed to withdraw from the town. But they had reckoned without the new garrison, who now fought back with all the courage and determination that their predecessors had lacked. All day long the battle continued, up and down the precipitous streets, while messengers sped to Roger with the alarm.

Roger, who had been besieging Nicosia, returned at full gallop, and arrived to find the situation worse than he had feared. Seeing a chance to rid themselves for ever of their Norman oppressors, several thousand Saracens from the neighbouring country had poured into Troiana and had made common cause with the Greeks. Against such numbers the Normans could not hope to defend the whole town; Roger at once ordered a general retreat to the few streets immediately surrounding the citadel. Barricades were hastily erected, look-outs stationed, outposts manned. This time it was the Normans' turn to be besieged. And so they were, for four months— perhaps the most testing period in the entire history of Norman

Sicily. They had been caught completely by surprise; provisions
were already dangerously low and, worst of all, Sicily was soon in
the grip of the earliest and most merciless winter in living memory.
Troina stands nearly four thousand feet above sea level; the Normans were without warm clothing or blankets, and the area behind
their roughly-improvised fortifications possessed little, short of the
buildings themselves, that could be used as fuel. Somehow morale
remained high; Malaterra reports that despite their hunger, toil and
lack of sleep, the besieged Normans kept up each other's spirits,
'hiding their sorrow and feigning a sort of hilarity in countenance
and speech'. Poor Judith, too, sharing a single woollen cloak with
her husband by day and huddling with him under it by night, put
on as brave a face as she could; and yet 'she had only her own tears
with which to quench her thirst, only sleep to palliate the hunger
that tormented her'. Somehow one feels that, for all her courage,
she was no Sichelgaita.

By the beginning of 1063 Roger knew that he could not hold out
much longer. There was hardly any food left, and his soldiers were
too undernourished to support the cold as stoically as they had at the
outset. Fortunately there were signs that the Saracens who kept the
night watch beyond the barricades were also feeling the strain. These
men had one defence against the cold which was denied to the
Normans—the rough red wine of the region, forbidden by the
Prophet but now temporarily hallowed in Muslim eyes for its calorific properties. It did indeed keep them warm; but, as the Norman
look-outs were quick to report, they were consuming it in larger
and larger quantities with other more dangerous effects. Roger
saw his chance. One January night, with the wind whistling colder
than ever down the narrow streets, he prepared his men for a final
offensive. Waiting till silence descended on the Saracen watch-
posts, he stole silently over the barricades. All was as he had
suspected. The sentries had surrendered to the effects of their
potations, and were sleeping like children. Quickly he beckoned to
his followers. Their footsteps made no sound in the deep snow;
the Greek and Saracen forward positions were taken before their
defenders knew what had happened, and by morning Troina was
once again in Norman hands.

Roger's vengeance was swift. The ringleaders of the insurrection were hanged instantly, and the penalties reserved for their accomplices were probably hardly less severe. Malaterra spares us the details, preferring to tell us instead of the great feast with which the Normans celebrated the end of their ordeal. They had deserved it. In the past four months Roger, Judith and their followers had been subjected to hardships greater than those which any Norman leader had been called upon to face since the first of their number appeared in the South. They had come through magnificently, thanks to their courage, their initiative and, above all, their endurance. But they had seen, too, just how precarious still was their Sicilian foothold.

12

CONQUEST

Dextera Domini fecit virtutem.
Dextera Domini exaltavit me.

(The right hand of God gave me courage.
The right hand of God raised me up.)

> Roger's motto, inscribed on his
> shield after the battle of Cerami

THERE was no denying it; Sicily was proving a more formidable proposition than Roger—or anyone else—had expected. His fundamental problem was the same as it had always been, the chronic shortage of manpower. This was not of overriding importance in pitched battles; the Normans had shown at Enna and elsewhere that, at least in mountainous terrain, their superior discipline and military technique would prove decisive over sheer weight of numbers. But a few hundred men could not be everywhere at once, and the advantages of victory were soon lost if political domination could not be maintained. At present their strength was inadequate to keep effective control even in the north-east. Moreover it was now nearly two years since the start of the Sicilian operation, and the element of surprise, one of the most valuable of all weapons to a numerically inferior army, had long since been forfeited. The Norman presence in Sicily had by now had the inevitable catalytic effect on the Saracens, who, once rid of the baleful influence of Ibn at-Timnah, had set aside their differences in the face of a common enemy. The Zirid Sultan Temim had sent his two sons Ayub and Ali, each at the head of an army, to help their Sicilian brethren stem the Christian tide; while Roger had been fighting for survival at Troina, these two young princes had landed at Palermo and Agrigento respectively and had at once begun preparations for a concerted attack.

Roger still had only three or four hundred men; and it was unlikely that Robert Guiscard, fully occupied with the Byzantines in Apulia, would be able to spare him many more. To make matters worse, he had lost all his horses at Troina—where they had probably provided the staple diet for four months—and he now had to make a hurried journey back to the mainland for replacements. It says much for the thoroughness with which he had crushed the revolt that he should have been willing, once again, to leave Judith in the town during his absence; but she had learnt a lot in the past few months, and Malaterra writes approvingly of the way in which she now assumed command of the defences, making regular daily and nightly rounds of the garrison to ensure that all the soldiers were awake and on the alert. After nine centuries it would perhaps be unchivalrous to suggest that these tours of inspection were prompted more by nervousness than by conscience; but in view of what had happened the last time she was left behind, the poor girl could hardly be blamed for feeling a little uneasy.

Her husband, however, was soon back again, with horses and supplies in abundance—though still with very few men. Throughout the spring of 1063, working out from Troina, he and his young nephew Serlo—already the ablest of his commanders and a Hauteville to his fingertips—engaged the Saracens in a quantity of minor skirmishes from Butera in the south to Caltavuturo in the north. Plunder was good and the store-rooms at Troina began to fill up nicely again, but it was not until midsummer that the Normans were able to get to grips with the main Saracen army, now tempered with the newly-arrived Africans, which had recently left Palermo and was now heading east, under the green banner of the Prophet, towards the Christian strongholds.

Eight miles or so to the west of Troina lies the little town of Cerami, in a fold of the hills above the river that shares its name. Rivers seemed to bring the Normans luck; on the mainland the Olivento, the Ofanto and above all the Fortore had run red with the blood of their enemies, and in Sicily the Dittaino had already witnessed a similar triumph. After the events of the previous winter Roger wished at all costs to avoid another siege; the Cerami, on the other hand, provided an admirable rallying-point for his tiny army, together with plenty of good look-out positions from which he could survey the enemy assembling on the hills opposite. Once again, as at Enna, the Normans were heavily—it seemed hopelessly—outnumbered. The size of the Saracen army is unknown; Malaterra estimates it at 'thirty thousand, not counting the foot-soldiers, whose numbers were infinite'. As usual he exaggerates; but a major force of this kind, gathered from all over Sicily and reinforced with important detachments from North Africa, must certainly have run into thousands. Against them Roger could muster only a hundred knights, with another thirty under Serlo; assuming proportionate numbers of infantry, the Norman army in its entirety cannot have been more than five or six hundred strong.

For three days Normans and Saracens watched each other; on the fourth Malaterra tells us that 'our men, no longer able to tolerate seeing the enemy so close without attacking him, confessed themselves with the utmost piety, made their penances and then, trusting in God's mercy and certain of His help, rode off into battle'. Hearing that the Saracens were already besieging Cerami, Roger quickly despatched Serlo with his thirty knights to hold the town as best he could; and once again his brilliant young nephew proved equal to the task. When Roger arrived with the bulk of the army a short time later he found that the first wave of the attackers had already fled. Cerami was still his.

All this, however, as Roger well knew, was but a preliminary. The enemy was regrouping for the main attack, and the Normans barely had time to draw themselves up in line of battle before the Saracen army charged. Ignoring Serlo on the flank, they directed the whole weight of the onslaught against the centre, where Roger himself was commanding, in one enormous and concerted effort to smash the Norman force by sheer impetus and force of numbers. They nearly succeeded, but somehow the Norman line held. Meanwhile Serlo galloped to his uncle's aid. All day the battle continued, until the mangled, trampled bodies lay thick over the field, Then suddenly, as evening drew on, the Saracens turned in flight, Roger and his men close on their heels. The pursuit led ultimately to the Saracen camp.

Loaded down with booty, the Normans now installed themselves in the tents of the Mahommedans, seizing their camels and all else that they found there. Then, on the morrow, they left to seek out those twenty thousand foot-soldiers who had fled to the mountains for refuge. Many of these they killed, the remainder they took captive and sold as slaves, receiving for each a great price. But after a little time, the contagion which arose from the rotting corpses on the battlefield drove them away and they returned to Troina.[1]

To Roger the battle of Cerami was of vital importance. Now at last Norman mastery of the whole region between Troina and Messina was assured. Though sporadic revolts in isolated areas would still occur, it would never again be seriously contested. Once again a Norman force had inflicted an annihilating defeat on a Saracen army many times its own strength; this time the battle had been greater, its result more significant and decisive, than that of Enna two years before. But the Normans had prevailed for the same reasons as always—by a combination of courage and discipline which was then unknown in the Muslim world, shot through with a religious enthusiasm born of their still growing belief in divine guidance. By now this belief had reached the point where Malaterra is able to record without apparent surprise how, just before the Normans rode into battle at Cerami, their ranks were joined by a fair young knight, mounted on a snow-white stallion and armed *cap-à-pie*, in his hand a lance from which there streamed a white pennant bearing a shining cross. It was not long before he was recognised as St George himself, come to lead the soldiers of Christ to victory; and many later testified to having seen his emblem flying also from the point of Roger's own lance at the height of the battle. In recognition of these signs, Roger ordered a sumptuous present to be sent to Pope Alexander II; and so it was that a week or two after the battle the citizens of Rome stood agape while a procession of four camels—the finest of the Saracens' military stable —shambled slowly through the streets.

Pope Alexander must have been delighted with his present; quite

[1] Malaterra, II, 53.

apart from their exotic character and zoological interest, and more important than either, those camels were a living indication to him that Roger was on his side and that he could probably look to the Hautevilles for support as and when necessary. The Pope was having a trying time. The electoral reforms of Nicholas II had had the very effect that they had been specifically designed to avoid. They made a disputed papal succession inevitable, for how could the Empress-Regent Agnes accept any candidate canonically elected in Rome without giving implicit approval to the new dispensations? Nicholas's death in 1061 thus created a situation even more hopelessly confused than usual. Once again there were two Popes struggling for the possession of St Peter's. Alexander's was the stronger claim, since his election by the Cardinal-Bishops—led, as always, by Hildebrand—had been canonically impeccable. On the other hand his rival, the anti-Pope Honorius II, chosen by Agnes and supported by the Lombard bishops—who, as St Peter Damian uncharitably remarked, were better fitted to pronounce upon the beauty of a woman than the suitability of a Pope—had influential partisans in Rome and plenty of money with which to nourish their enthusiasm; and it was only with the military assistance of Richard of Capua—provided now for the second time at Hildebrand's request—that Alexander had been enabled to take possession of his see. Even then Honorius had not given up. As late as May 1063, after Agnes had been removed and an imperial council had declared for his rival, he had even managed to recapture the Leonine City[1] for a short time—and though he was formally deposed in the following year he was to uphold his claims until the day of his death. Throughout this period Alexander needed all the support he could find. In return for his camels he sent Roger a papal banner to go before him and inspire his army in its future campaigns. More significant still, he proclaimed absolution for all those who joined Robert and Roger in their holy task of delivering a Christian land from the domination of the heathen. Henceforth, not only in the hearts of the Normans but in the eyes of Christendom, the conquest of Sicily was a Crusade.

---

[1] That part of Rome on the right bank of the Tiber, including the Vatican and the Castel Sant' Angelo, which was fortified in the ninth century by Pope Leo IV immediately after the sack of the city by the Saracens.

It is a characteristic of wars that they are apt to last considerably longer than the combatants expect. Roger and his men, slipping across the straits of Messina on that moonless May night in 1061, were neither the first nor the last warriors to embark on their troopships in the probable hope that it would all be over by Christmas. As we have seen, by the Christmas of that year the Normans had secured little more than a bridgehead, while at the end of 1062 such celebrations as the unfortunates in Troina may have permitted themselves can have been anything but festive. In 1063 some progress had been achieved but, as the days began to draw in towards the third autumn since the launching of the expedition, Roger must have been conscious of a growing atmosphere of frustration and disappointment among his countrymen. Admittedly their three seasons in Sicily had won them the control of perhaps a quarter of the island, but even this moderate success had been due to a remarkable early run of luck and to a combination of special circumstances which could never be repeated. If they had not managed to take Messina by surprise there was no reason to suppose that a siege of the city would have been any more successful than their attempts on Enna or Agrigento. Most of their advance had been through largely Christian territory where they had become more accustomed to deputations of welcome than to armed resistance; and they had throughout enjoyed the protection of Ibn at-Timnah, who had been able to guarantee them against attacks from the south and south-east while they advanced towards the centre. By contrast, the unconquered land that lay before them was Muslim through and through. Ibn at-Timnah was dead; his enemy Ibn al-Hawas, despite heavy losses, was still holding out at Enna, and the Saracens were now more united than they had been for a century. As the Normans advanced, their supply-lines would grow steadily longer and more vulnerable, and recent experience had proved that not even the native Christians could be trusted to support them once their backs were turned. Finally, as always, they were pitiably few—a factor which might enhance the glory of their victories but, for practical reasons, augured ill for the future. With their present numbers they might conquer, but they could never control.

When the exhilaration of Cerami had passed, these must have been the gloomy reflections that occupied Roger's mind and led him, among other considerations, to reject outright the next opportunity which was put in his way. It came, suddenly and unexpectedly, from Pisa. Whether the Pisans were merely enraged by the incessant incursions of Sicilian-based Saracen pirates or whether, with their well-known eye to the main chance, they were deliberately trying to associate themselves with the Normans in anticipation of their eventual victory is not known. Pisan contemporary records, however, confirm Malaterra's report that in August 1063 the city sent a fleet to Sicily, where it sought Roger's co-operation in a combined land and sea attack on Palermo. Roger's reply was disappointing. He had other unfinished business and could take on no further commitments. Later, perhaps, something of the kind might be arranged; for the moment the Pisans would have to wait. The Pisan admiral argued with him, but it was in vain; Roger merely repeated that he was not ready, and that he could not risk his men in such conditions. At last, despairing of any help from the Normans, the admiral sailed off in dudgeon to attack Palermo by himself. Without any shore support, the attempt was doomed to failure, and the Pisans were lucky to escape more or less unscathed. According to Malaterra their only prize was the great chain with which the Palermitans had blocked their harbour mouth. This, he tells us, they seized; and then 'believing, like true Pisans, that they had achieved some great matter, they returned forthwith to their homes'.[1]

It cannot have been an easy decision for Roger to take. He had no particular love for the Pisans and may well have resented their intervention; at the same time the offer of a fully-equipped fleet for such an operation must have been tempting for an ambitious and

[1] An inscription in Pisa Cathedral claims that the Pisans did in fact manage to land a small force near the mouth of the Oreto, where they laid waste the villas and gardens in the neighbourhood. It also records the capture of six Saracen ships—five of which, however, they burned. All this may well be true; Malaterra probably had no first-hand knowledge of what took place and anyway tends to minimise their achievements as much as he can. What is certainly false is the passage in the *Chronica Pisana* (Muratori *R.I.S.*, vol. VI, p. 167), according to which the Pisans captured Palermo and returned with so much plunder that they were able to start construction of their Cathedral. This was indeed begun in 1063, but Palermo stood until the Normans captured it nine years later.

impatient leader. But by now he had probably received advance information of the new campaign which Robert Guiscard was already planning for the following year. The situation had recently improved in Apulia; Brindisi, Oria and Taranto were back in Norman hands, and the Duke was once again able to turn his attention towards Sicily. Knowing this, Roger would naturally have been reluctant to risk his own meagre resources for the sake of Pisa; better far to husband them in preparation for a grand new all-Norman offensive with his brother.

And so he bided his time until, early in 1064, Robert appeared in Calabria with an army of some five hundred knights and a thousand-odd foot-soldiers. Roger met him at Cosenza to plan the campaign. This time the strategy would be different; they would waste no more energy on Enna or the interior, but would head straight along the north coast of the island to Palermo itself. Once they had the capital, the rest—even in so decentralised a land as Sicily—would surely follow. As always when Hautevilles were in command, the army moved fast. No opposition was encountered, and only a few days after crossing the straits Robert drew up his troops on what seemed a suitable site for their encampment on one of the hilltops overlooking Palermo. His choice nearly proved disastrous. Forty-six years previously the remnants of the first Norman army to appear in Italy, retreating after Cannae, had been driven from their chosen headquarters by a plague of frogs. It had been a humiliating experience, but not a harmful one. The new natural hazard which awaited them proved to be both.

The tarantula spider had long been the scourge of Southern Italy, and particularly of that region around Taranto which gave it its name; but nowhere can it have been more plentiful or malevolent than on the hill now selected by Robert Guiscard. The bite of this Sicilian variety was fortunately not followed by that wild and hysterical agitation of the body which later became famous as both the principal symptom and the only remedy for its poison—and, in the tarantella, accounted for the only dance in Europe to have been developed for purely medicinal purposes. The consequences as related by Malaterra seem, none the less, to have been unpleasant in the extreme:

This *taranta* is a worm which has the appearance of a spider but possesses a cruel and envenomed sting, such that those whom it attacks are forthwith filled with a most poisonous wind. Their distress increases till they are no longer able to contain this same wind, which comes forth noisily and indelicately from their backsides so that unless a hot compress or some other still more powerful calorific is at once applied, it is said that their very lives are in peril.

It was not an auspicious beginning. The camp was hastily transferred to a more salubrious site, but Norman nerve had clearly been shaken. The impetus was gone. The Conca d'Oro, that huge chain of mountains that enfolds the city of Palermo, provided a superb landward defence. Not a movement by an attacking army could pass unobserved from its fortresses and watchtowers, and even when Robert reached the city walls, he was able to make little impression on them. For three months his sorry siege continued, but to no avail. Saracen shipping continued to pass freely through the harbour mouth, and the Palermitans seemed scarcely even inconvenienced. It was like Enna all over again, only this time there was not even a pitched battle by which the Normans could redeem their pride. And so the Guiscard found himself, for the second time in three years, leading a dispirited army back to Italy, where the situation was again deteriorating and from which he could never be absent for long. Apart from the capture of one insignificant little town (Bugamo, now long since disappeared) he had accomplished nothing; even Agrigento, with which he attempted rather halfheartedly to console himself on the return journey, withstood his attack. He now had to face the fact that in the Muslims of western Sicily he was faced with a stronger and more determined enemy than any that he or his family had yet encountered—Lombard, Frankish or Byzantine. As 1064 drew to a close it began to look as if the Norman advance had at last reached its limit.

For four years, like a ship becalmed, the Norman army in Sicily lay isolated and powerless, all its momentum gone. No pitched battles are recorded, no new conquests, no significant advance. For tales of Norman achievement over this period we must look to Northern Europe, to the beaches of Kent and the field of Hastings;

where the Normans in Sicily were concerned, the years around 1066
were among the dullest in their history.

For Roger it must have been a time of maddening frustration. He
never relaxed his pressure on the enemy; but with an army as
diminutive as his the only possible tactics could be those of attrition,
wearing the Saracens down by constant guerrilla activity and playing
endlessly on their nerves so that they never felt safe from the danger
of sudden raid or ambush. With this end in view he moved his
temporary capital forward to Petralia, a town which he had captured
already in 1062 but which now, its rocky escarpments newly fortified, provided an admirable advance headquarters from which all
the country round Palermo was within easy range. Working out
from here to the north, south and west, he was able to keep the
Saracens on the defensive; but that was all. There was only one
consolation; his opponents were now again hopelessly divided.
Ibn al-Hawas had at first welcomed the arrival of the North African
armies under Ayub and Ali; not long after Cerami, however, he had
grown suspicious of the increasing power of the young princes, and
the consequent dissension had quickly ripened into civil war. Even
though Roger was himself still too weak to inflict any major defeat
on the Saracens, he could at least watch with satisfaction while they
did their utmost to destroy each other.

For Robert Guiscard too these were unprofitable years. He had
stepped ashore in Calabria after the abortive expedition of 1064 only
to find himself faced with a new revolt of his Apulian vassals. This,
the most serious uprising with which he had yet had to contend, was
led by Jocelin, Lord of Molfetta, and three of his own nephews;
the brothers Geoffrey of Conversano and Robert of Montescaglioso
and their cousin Abelard, whom the Guiscard had brazenly robbed of
his inheritance after the death of Abelard's father, Duke Humphrey,
seven years before. These three young men, making common cause
with Byzantium through the agency of Perenos, Duke of Durazzo
—who kept them well supplied with money and equipment from
across the Adriatic—had rebelled in April 1064, soon after the
Guiscard's departure for Sicily, and during the months of his absence
had carried all before them. Robert's return in the late summer
slowed their progress to some extent, but despite his efforts the

revolt continued to spread. In 1066 it was further strengthened by a new contingent of Varangians from Constantinople, and by the end of that year not only Bari but the two other principal Apulian ports of Brindisi and Taranto were firmly in Greek hands.

The year 1067 marked a general stalemate, both in Apulia and Sicily. Then, in 1068, almost simultaneously for Robert and for Roger, came relief. At least where the Guiscard was concerned, it sprang from an unexpected quarter. For some years past the Byzantine Empire had been watching with mounting anxiety the steady westward advance of the Seljuk Turks. In little more than a generation these tribesmen from beyond the Oxus had subdued Persia and Mesopotamia. Baghdad, seat of the Arab Caliphate, had fallen to them in 1055; Armenia and Cilicia had followed; and now they were driving inexorably up through Asia Minor towards Constantinople itself. After the death of Constantine X Ducas in 1067 the Byzantines were left without an Emperor, imperial power having passed to his widow, the Empress Eudoxia; but it was clear that in the face of the Seljuk threat a leader must immediately be found, and so it was that Eudoxia was persuaded into a hasty if reluctant marriage with a certain Romanus Diogenes—so called, according to William of Apulia, because of his forked beard— a Cappadocian commander of long experience and undoubted bravery who, on 1 January 1068, was acclaimed Emperor. With the accession of Romanus and his immediate concentration on a desperate military effort against the Turks, the Greek initiative in Italy was halted; and, deprived from one moment to the next of all outside support, the rebellious vassals lost their nerve. One after another they capitulated, until by mid-February only Geoffrey of Conversano remained. Entrenched in his mountain fortress of Montepeloso he held out for several months, deserted by all his former allies, Greek and Norman alike. Then in June the Guiscard managed to suborn one of Geoffrey's officers, who, tempted by the promise of a fief of his own, secretly opened the gates. Robert's army poured in; Geoffrey, taken by surprise, had no course but surrender; the traitor duly received his fief; and the revolt was over.

The satisfaction which Robert Guiscard must have felt as he saw

the Apulian opposition crumble and his own authority re-established
would have been still greater had he known that, just about the time
that he was besieging Montepeloso, his brother was dealing the
final death-blow to all organised military resistance in Sicily. In the
previous year the Saracen forces had been brought once again under
a unified command. The Zirid troops under Ayub had met the
army of Ibn al-Hawas in a last pitched battle, during which the
redoubtable old Emir had been killed. Ayub had at once laid claim
to the succession and had been formally recognised at Agrigento,
Enna and Palermo. This gave him the degree of authority he needed
to assume command of the entire Saracen forces. No longer hamstrung by internecine disputes, he now determined to take the first
favourable opportunity of drawing the Normans out into an open
conflict of the very kind which, since the defeat at Cerami, he and
his compatriots had always sought to avoid; and so on a summer
morning in 1068 the Norman army, out on one of its regular forays
in the countryside south of Palermo, found its way blocked by a
great Saracen host before the little town of Misilmeri.[1]

Roger must have been surprised at so radical a change in the
enemy's tactics, but he does not seem to have been unduly dis-
concerted. Malaterra has left us a report of the speech which he
made to his troops just before the battle. Smiling, he told them that
they had nothing to fear; this was only the enemy that they had
already beaten several times before. What if the Saracen leader had
changed? Their own God remained constant, and if they put the
same trust in Him as they had in the past He would accord them a
similar victory. It is doubtful whether the Normans even needed
these words of encouragement. Familiarity with Saracen military
methods was fast breeding contempt; they themselves were, after
all, soldiers of God, fulfilling His purpose; and the spoils once
again promised to be excellent. All they awaited was Roger's
signal; when he gave it, they charged.

It was soon over. According to Malaterra, hardly a single Saracen
remained alive to carry the dreadful news back to Palermo. As
things turned out, however, this proved unnecessary. Among the
prizes of battle, and just as intriguing to Roger as the camels seized

[1] Known in Arab times as Menzil el Emir, 'the Emir's village'.

at Cerami, the Normans had carried off several baskets of carrier pigeons. The use of these birds had been well-known in classical antiquity but seems to have died out during the Dark Ages until, like so many other ancient arts and sciences, it was revived by the Saracens. It is unlikely that Roger had ever had any in his possession before, but the idea of using them at once for his own purposes was more than he could resist. He ordered that to the leg of each bird should be attached a scrap of material dipped in Saracen blood; the pigeons were then released, to fly back to Palermo with their macabre message. It was, in its way, the culmination of the psychological warfare that Roger had been carrying on for the past four years; and the effect that it had in the capital seems to have been all that he could have wished. 'The air,' writes Malaterra, 'was loud with the lamentations of women and children, and sorrow was great among them as the Normans rejoiced in their victory.'

The battle of Misilmeri broke the back of Saracen resistance in Sicily. Ayub had staked not only his army but his whole political and military reputation on its outcome, and he had lost. With what remained of his following he fled back to Africa, never to return. He left the island in total confusion, its Muslim population in despair. Their army shattered, their leaders gone, they could no longer hope to withstand Norman pressure. Palermo itself lay only ten miles or so from Misilmeri; they would defend it as best they could, but the truth could no longer be doubted—their capital was doomed. And once it had fallen to the Christians, the few Arab strongholds left remaining in the island would soon follow.

But Roger was not ready for the capital. Its inhabitants could not be expected to submit without a struggle; and his own forces, though adequate for pitched battles in mountainous terrain, were hardly sufficient for a siege. Besides, the capture of Palermo would be tantamount to the subjection of the whole island, and this in its turn would entail problems of control and administration which, with only a few hundred men at his disposal, he could not possibly envisage. There was fortunately no cause to hurry; the Saracens were far too demoralised to regroup themselves quickly. Better to wait, to suspend all further offensive operations until Robert had settled affairs in Apulia. Then the two could tackle the Sicilian problem together and in earnest.

The insurrection quashed, Robert Guiscard had treated his rebellious vassals with surprising clemency. Certain of them had had property confiscated, but a large number—including even Geoffrey of Conversano, who bore as much of the original responsibility as anyone—seem to have escaped scot-free. There was, as always with the Guiscard, a good reason for his attitude; he now needed every ally he could find for a last all-out drive against the Greeks. Current Byzantine preoccupations with the Seljuk menace offered him a magnificent and long-awaited opportunity for stamping out the final vestiges of imperial power from the peninsula, and now that his own internal difficulties had been settled he was free to seize it. His first step was to issue a general appeal to all Normans and Lombards in Italy to join him; the Greeks were deeply entrenched after their five centuries of occupation, and even without reinforcements from Constantinople they would be hard to dislodge. Then, hardly waiting for a response to his call, he marched with his full army to Bari.

Capital of Byzantine Langobardia, headquarters of the Greek army of the peninsula, the largest, richest and best defended of all the Apulian cities, Bari was the only possible target for the Guiscard's great offensive. He was, however, well aware that the successful siege of such a place would involve the greatest single military operation the Normans had undertaken in the fifty years since their arrival in Italy. The old city stands on a narrow promontory, jutting out northwards into the Adriatic; Robert was thus faced with the necessity of combining orthodox siege measures against the massive land walls with an immense naval blockade. Herein, apparently, lay his greatest disadvantage. The Normans had little experience of naval warfare. Such ships as they possessed had been used principally as transports, and even for these they were largely dependent on Greek crews from Calabria. For the Greek populations of Apulia, on the other hand, the sea was an integral part of their existence. Upon it they depended for their prosperity, their food, their defence, their communications, even their language and culture; and in consequence they had become known throughout the Mediterranean for the sureness of their seamanship and the accuracy of their navigation. Bari was well-supplied with ships of all kinds, and Perenos of Durazzo would probably be able to provide more if required. With such overwhelming advantages its inhabitants felt that they had little to fear.

And they showed it. Parading to and fro along the ramparts, brandishing aloft all the richest treasures they and their city could boast, using their gold and silver plate to reflect the sunlight into the eyes of the Normans uncomfortably clustered in the newly-dug ditches below, they mocked at the Guiscard's notorious rapacity, challenging him to come up and help himself to what he saw. But Robert, Malaterra tells us, was fully equal to this sort of thing, shouting gleefully back his thanks to the good citizens for keeping his property for him so carefully, and assuring them that they would not have charge of it much longer.

The Duke of Apulia was frequently thus underestimated, but never for very long. The first surprise for the Bariots came with the sudden appearance off their shores of a Norman fleet. Robert's Sicilian experiences, and in particular the abortive attempt on Palermo four years earlier, had taught him a lot about the value of sea power. Ever since then he had been collecting a navy from up and down the Adriatic coast; and though this had been originally intended for use against Saracens rather than Greeks, he had recently summoned every available vessel to Bari. Even now his sea force was embryonic in comparison with what it was to become a few years later; but it was adequate for his purpose. Drawing the ships into line abreast, and harnessing each one to its neighbours with great iron chains forged specially for the occasion, he formed them into a single, solid barrier encircling the entire promontory on which the city stood. The last ship at each end was moored to a heavily-fortified jetty; it could thus be easily boarded by the land forces who, crossing from ship to ship, could hasten to the relief of any part of the line that might be attacked. Meanwhile the army proper had disposed itself along the walls and was already blocking all approaches from the landward side. To the intense surprise of its citizens, Bari was surrounded. The taunts from the ramparts stopped abruptly. On 5 August 1068 the great siege began.

It was long and costly for both sides. The Greek leader Byzantius soon managed to slip through the Norman lines and, somehow evading his pursuers, to reach Constantinople, where he persuaded the Empress to agree to a relief expedition. (Luckily for him, he arrived after the departure of the Emperor for Asia Minor; Romanus, for whom the Normans seven hundred miles away were of little importance compared with the Seljuk hordes on his doorstep, might have shown less sympathy.) Early in 1069 the Greek ships appeared in the Adriatic. The Normans intercepted them and, after an early reverse, eventually sank twelve supply transports off Monopoli; but their cordon around Bari failed to stand up to a direct attack and several of the relief vessels, including that carrying Byzantius together with the new Catapan and a distinguished military commander, Stephen Pateranos, broke through into the harbour with arms and supplies for the beleaguered city. To the Normans their failure must have been not only humiliating but demoralising too; if they could not maintain their blockade Bari might hold out for ever. But the Duke of Apulia refused to give up. All through 1069 the siege dragged on and, despite the assassination of Byzantius in July, all through 1070 as well. Some time during the autumn Pateranos, growing worried by the threat of famine as well as by an increasingly vocal pro-Norman faction within the city, planned to have the Guiscard murdered in his turn. One evening when Robert was sitting at dinner in the wood-and-wattle hut which he occupied near the foot of the ramparts a hired assassin crept up and hurled a poisoned javelin at him through a chink in the wall; if we are to believe William of Apulia it was only Robert's severe catarrh, which prompted him at that precise moment to duck his head under the table to spit, that saved his life. Thanks to this happy chance he escaped unharmed; but on the following morning the Normans began work on a building of stone, without chinks, where their leader could live safe from any repetitions of the incident.

The winter of 1070–71 was hard for besiegers and besieged alike, both physically and in the toll it took of their morale. The stalemate had continued without remission for two and a half years. The city had been relieved before and might be relieved again; meanwhile, however, food supplies were dangerously low. Pateranos decided on a last appeal. The Turkish threat was, he knew, still grave. On the other hand he himself was not without influence in the capital and there was just a chance that he might now be able to persuade the Emperor Romanus, who had had some success in his recent campaigns, to devote part of his resources to the salvation of Apulia before it was too late. The Norman blockade once again proved inadequate; soon Pateranos was speeding on his way to Constantinople.

Robert Guiscard was equally determined to break the deadlock. His *cordon sanitaire*, however formidable its appearance, had not proved conspicuously successful, while on the landward side his army had failed to make the slightest impression on the city walls. Moreover, his enormous siege-towers were being burnt down with depressing regularity every time they were trundled into position. He had made more progress, to be sure, in the diplomatic field; his chief agent within the city, Argirizzo, was using his regular handsome subventions of Norman money to make free food distributions to the poor, and by this and other means converting most of the non-Greek inhabitants to pro-Norman sympathies; even among the Greeks themselves there was a growing feeling that continued resistance was useless and that the time had now come to negotiate. But such opinions carried no weight with the commanders of the city; the die-hards were still all-powerful, and a further Byzantine relief force, if it were to get through, could restore morale overnight. Robert, too, felt the need of some fresh blood, some injection of imagination and new ideas to restore impetus to his army. He sent for Roger.

Roger arrived from Sicily, bringing what men and ships he could, at the beginning of 1071. His appearance was perfectly timed. The Emperor Romanus, despite his preoccupation with the Seljuks, had been moved by Pateranos's appeal and had ordered that a relief force be immediately prepared at Durazzo, under the command of the Guiscard's arch-enemy Jocelin, the Norman lord of Molfetta, who had been a main instigator of the recent insurrection and had subsequently taken refuge in the imperial dominions, where he had been ennobled with the dukedom of Corinth. Pateranos had meanwhile returned to Bari with the news; he had also instructed the citizens to keep a close watch for the approach of the Byzantine ships and, as soon as they sighted them, to set flares along the walls of the city so that their rescuers might be guided safely and speedily into port. But the promise of relief, after so long a siege, went to the Bariots' heads. As Malaterra reminds us, 'nothing comes quickly enough for those who wait', and that same night, though the horizon remained dark, the air was loud with celebration and the ramparts seemed ablaze with flaming torches. To the besiegers below, such signs could mean only one thing: quickly Roger strengthened the watch on the sea side. Some time passed; then, one night, his lookouts reported the lights of many lanterns, 'shining like stars at the mast-tops'. At once he gave the order to embark, and the Norman ships sailed out to meet the enemy.

Malaterra maintains—though it seems unlikely—that the Greeks mistook the Norman ships for those of their compatriots coming out to welcome them, and were consequently caught off their guard. At all events the sea-battle that followed, though fierce, was one-sided. Even a major disaster which befell the Normans when a hundred and fifty of them, all in their heavy cuirasses, ran to the same side of their ship, capsized it and were drowned, failed to restore Byzantine fortunes. The main force of the attack had been directed on the Greek flagship—recognisable from its double mast-lights— and before long the wretched Jocelin found himself a prisoner on board Roger's own vessel, speeding back to the Norman camp where Robert Guiscard was waiting. Robert, Malaterra goes on,

had been in great fear for Roger's safety . . . and when he heard that the Count was returned safe and victorious, he still could not believe it until he saw him with his own eyes; but then he wept for joy, assuring himself that his brother had suffered no hurt. Roger now clothed Jocelin magni-ficently in the Greek style and offered him captive to the Duke.

The Normans had paid dearly enough for their first great naval victory, but it was decisive and complete. Of the twenty Byzantine ships involved, nine were sunk and not one was able to penetrate into the harbour of Bari. After a few more weeks of increasing despair the commanders within the city saw that they could hold out no longer. Argirizzo and his followers seized one of the principal towers, which, despite the entreaties of that section of the population that feared Norman vengeance more than starvation itself, they delivered up to Robert Guiscard; and on 16 April 1071 the Duke, with Roger at his side, rode triumphantly through the streets of Bari. Much to their surprise, he treated the Bariots well. Peace terms were reasonable and he even restored to the citizens certain lands outside the walls where the Normans had recently been in occupation. But then he could afford to be magnanimous. Since the time of Justinian Bari had been Greek—sometimes capital of a great and prosperous province, sometimes merely the centre of a tiny enclave from which the banners of Byzantium fluttered alone in a turbulent and hostile land; but on that day, the Saturday before Palm Sunday, those banners were struck for the last time.

13

PALERMO

Weep as you will your tears of blood,
O grave of Arabian civilisation.
Once this place was alive with the people of the desert,
And the ocean was a playground for their boats. . . .
O Sicily you are the glory of the ocean. . . .
You were the cradle of this nation's culture,
Whose fire like beauty burnt the world;
Sadi the nightingale of Shiraz wept for the destruction of Baghdad;
Dag shed tears of blood for the ruination of Delhi;
When the heavens destroyed Granada
It was the sorrowing heart of Ibn Badrun who lamented it;
Unhappy Iqbal is fated to write your elegy. . . .
Tell me your pains, I too am immersed in pain,
I am the dust of that caravan of which you were the destination.
Fill the colours in the pictures of the past and show them to me;
Make me sad by telling the tales of past days.

Iqbal, *Bāng-i Dara.* Tr. G. D. Gaur

THE core of the Norman army had now been fighting without interruption for more than three years. They had had no respite between the end of the vassals' rebellion with the capture of Montepeloso and the beginning, at Bari, of the last victorious round against the Byzantines. Now, after one of the hardest sieges of Italian history, and one moreover which led to the elimination of their oldest and stubbornest enemy, they might have expected a chance to rest. If so, they were disappointed. Summer was approaching; and summer, for Robert Guiscard, meant only one thing—the season for campaigning and conquest. South Italy was safe at last, and the Sicilian operation had been hanging fire too long. He had dealt with the Greeks; now it was the Saracens' turn.

One of Robert's greatest gifts as a leader was his ability to infect those under his command with his own energy and enthusiasm. Preparations began at once. They were different, both in scale and in kind, from those he had made for his last Sicilian expedition seven years previously; for in the interval the Normans had become a naval power. A curious aspect of their forebears' transformation, in the preceding century, from Vikings into Frenchmen was the speed with which they had blotted out their Scandinavian maritime traditions. Even in Normandy they seem to have shown little awareness of the potentialities of a strong navy; those who had come to settle in Italy had all arrived on foot or on horseback over the mountains, and for the first fifty years in their new homeland seem never to have taken to the sea except when, as in the short passage across the straits of Messina, it was unavoidable. Suddenly all this was changed. In Sicily Robert and Roger had together learnt that without an effective naval force, raised to the same standards of training and discipline as the army, there could be no further conquests. At Bari they had proved the corollary, that with such a force they could undertake and succeed in ventures hitherto unthinkable. In this knowledge, and the new, broader political outlook which it engendered, was to lie the greatness of the Kingdom of Sicily, so soon now to be established.

After the capture of Bari Robert sent his brother back at once to Sicily, while he himself hurried south along the coast to Otranto. Here his fleet had already begun to assemble—causing, incidentally, widespread alarm across the Adriatic in Durazzo, where Duke Perenos hastily ordered the strengthening of his own maritime defences—and here the Guiscard remained until, in late July, no fewer than fifty-eight fully-equipped ships, manned as usual by Greeks, set sail for Calabria. He did not travel with them; by taking the land route with the army he could settle some minor disaffection at Squillace on the way. But he met them a week or two later at Reggio and from there, in the first days of August 1071, the combined force crossed to Sicily.

Roger was waiting at Messina to discuss plans. The primary Norman objective was naturally a co-ordinated land and sea attack on Palermo, but as a preliminary to this he had an idea of his own in

which he thought his brother might be interested. It involved
Catania. Here was a strategically important harbour, roughly half-
way down the east coast of the island and thus, while Norman
strength was concentrated at Messina, within easy striking distance;
moreover, having recently been the seat of Ibn at-Timnah, it was
still fundamentally well-disposed to the Normans and might consequently be taken easily and cheaply. Roger's plan was simple. He
would go to Catania, where he was sure of a courteous reception,
and would seek permission for certain Norman ships to put in at
the harbour there on their way to Malta. Such a request the Catanians
could hardly refuse. Robert would then arrive with the fleet and
enter without opposition. Once within the harbour, he and his men
would have no difficulty in occupying the city.

It was not perhaps the most honourable of proposals but, as
Roger knew, it was just the kind of idea that appealed to the Guiscard. And it worked perfectly. The Catanians were taken completely
by surprise, realising how they had been tricked only when resistance
was already hopeless. They fought courageously, but after four
days were obliged to surrender. The Normans refortified the city
and, leaving behind a strong garrison to ensure its future obedience,
departed for Palermo. Roger, who was anxious to see Judith at
Troina, travelled by land with the bulk of the army; Robert did not
accompany him. Though as strong and energetic as ever, he was
now in his middle fifties; and the way from Catania to Palermo was
long and arduous, particularly in the full blaze of a Sicilian August.
Memories of his last land approach were still painful. Besides,
someone had to command his new fleet. This time he resolved to
go by sea.

In the middle of the eleventh century Palermo was one of the
greatest commercial and cultural centres of the Muslim world.
Cairo doubtless exceeded it in size; Cordova may have outshone it
in magnificence; but for beauty of situation, perfection of climate
and all the broad range of amenities which together constituted
the characteristic Arab *douceur de vivre*, Palermo was supreme. There
are no detailed descriptions of the city at the time of its capture by
the Normans, but change was slow in the Middle Ages and it must

A battle against the Saracens, as depicted on a Sicilian peasant cart

Mazara Cathedral: Roger I strikes down a Saracen. (Stone-carving of 1584)

have been substantially the same as when it was visited by the Arab geographer Ibn Haukal just a century before. He has left us with a picture of a busy commercial metropolis boasting no less than three hundred mosques—in the largest of which, formerly a Christian church, were said to be preserved the mortal remains of Aristotle, suspended in a casket from the roof—countless markets, exchanges, streets of craftsmen and artisans and one of the first paper-mills in Europe.[1] The whole was surrounded by parks and pleasure-gardens, murmurous with fountains and running streams of the kind that the Muslim world understands so well. We can only guess at the size of its population; but the assiduous Abbé Delarc, basing himself on Ibn-Haukal's assurance that the butchers' guild alone numbered seven thousand members, has calculated that eleventh-century Palermo must have sheltered some quarter of a million inhabitants.

It was about the middle of August when Roger arrived with the bulk of the Norman army outside the capital. He had met with no serious opposition on his way from Catania, and now pitched his camp a mile or two to the east of the city, where the little river Oreto ran down to the sea. It was a district of rich palaces and pleasure-domes, of gardens and orange-groves where the great merchants sought solace from the heat and hubbub of the capital—very different from that verminous hilltop where the Normans had encamped seven years before. Still there was no opposition; Roger and his men simply helped themselves, and Amatus writes delightedly of how they shared out 'the palaces and all that they found outside the city, and gave to the nobles the pleasure-gardens full of fruit and watercourses; while even the knights were royally provided for in what was veritably an earthly paradise'.[2]

The Norman army had, however, little enough time to enjoy their idyllic surroundings. Here was a foretaste of the pleasures that

---

[1] Paper had been invented by the Chinese some time in the fourth century A.D. The technique was learnt by the Arabs after the capture of Samarkand in 707 and was introduced into Spain by the Moors in the first half of the eleventh century. From there it soon spread to Sicily. A deed signed by Roger in 1102 is still extant, and is the oldest dated European paper document yet discovered.

[2] 'Lo palaiz et les chozes qu'il troverent fors de la cité, donnent a li prince li jardin delectoz pleins de frutte et de eaue, et pour soi li chevalier avoient choses royals et paradise terrestre li.' (VI. 16)

awaited them, a material incentive to greater effort; but meanwhile there was work to be done. Robert Guiscard and the fleet were expected almost hourly; a suitable landing-place must be found and made safe for his disembarkation. At the mouth of the Oreto stood a small fortress known as the Castle of Yahya, which served the dual purpose of protecting the eastward approach to Palermo and of barring the river itself to hostile ships. It gave little trouble. The garrison, goaded by Roger's taunts, emerged to fight; within minutes fifteen of its soldiers had been killed and thirty more taken prisoner. The castle, renamed after St John, became a Norman stronghold and was soon afterwards converted by Roger, as a thank-offering for his success, into a church.[1]

The Duke of Apulia soon arrived with his fleet, and gave orders for an immediate attack. As the galleys sailed forward to block the harbour entrance the army, now forming a great arc with Roger on the left advancing north-west and Robert on the right pressing westwards along the coast, moved slowly up towards the bastions of the city. The Palermitans were ready. By now they can have had little if any hope of victory, but they knew that on their resistance depended the whole future of Islam in Sicily. Their fight was not just for Palermo but for the glory of the Prophet; if they were to perish in the attempt, had he not promised them the rewards of Paradise? For years they had been expecting this moment, strengthening their fortifications, walling up all but two or three of the city gates. The Norman vanguard, advancing to the ramparts, were greeted with a deluge of arrows and stones.

And so, a bare four months after the fall of Bari, the Normans found themselves engaged on another siege—this time for the greatest prize of all. It was considerably more eventful than its predecessor; the Saracens were bolder and more adventurous than the Greeks had been, making constant sorties and often deliberately opening one gate or another to entice the besiegers forward into hand-to-hand fighting. But their courage was of little avail. Nor did they have better fortune by sea. Robert Guiscard had abandoned

---

[1] In 1150 it became a leper hospital. The church, now known as S. Giovanni dei Lebbrosi, still stands, with a few traces of the old Saracen fortress remaining in the garden to the east of it.

his old tactics of throwing a permanent barrage of ships across the harbour; the idea had not been much of a success at Bari and would in any case have been impracticable, for topographical reasons, at Palermo. Instead he kept the bulk of his fleet at the mouth of the Oreto, ready for quick action as necessary. It proved to be a wise decision. William of Apulia tell us in his relentless hexameters of how one day—it must have been in the late autumn of 1071—a combined Sicilian and African fleet appeared off Palermo. Robert at once ordered all those under his command, Normans, Calabrians, Bariots and captive Greeks, to take Holy Communion; only then did they set sail to meet the enemy. At first they were hard pressed, and there were moments when it even seemed as though the Muslims, who had tented their ships with great lengths of red felt as a protection against missiles, were about to achieve at sea that victory which on land had always eluded them. Slowly, however, the Normans gained the upper hand, until by the end of the day the surviving remnants of the Saracen fleet were scuttling towards Palermo with all the speed of which their exhausted oarsmen were capable. Just in time the Palermitans ran their great chain— successor to that which the Pisans had carried off eight years before —across the harbour-mouth; but the Guiscard refused to be baulked of his prey. Somehow the Norman ships crashed through, and it was in the port of Palermo itself that their blazing firebrands completed the destruction of the Sicilian navy.

During the Middle Ages the greatest danger to any town under-going a protracted siege was that of famine; and in Palermo famine was now spreading swiftly. The mountains of the Conca d'Oro, which had so often protected the capital in the past, had now become a liability, since they enabled the Norman army—larger than any of its predecessors though still probably less than ten thousand strong—to cover a far greater area than would otherwise have been possible. All the main approaches to the south and east were blocked by Roger's troops, while to the west his mobile patrols were just as effective at intercepting relief supplies as were Robert's pinnaces in the roadstead to the north. In the circumstances the Normans might have been content to wait patiently for the city's inevitable surrender; but they too were pressed. In December messengers arrived with grave news for Robert; once again his vassals had betrayed him. His nephew Abelard, still nursing the old grievance, had taken advantage of the Guiscard's prolonged absence to revolt for the second time, abetted by his younger brother Herman and the lords of Giovinazzo and Trani. Together they had won the support of Richard of Capua, now at the zenith of his power, of Gisulf of Salerno and, quite probably, of the Byzantines. The insurrection, having begun in Apulia, was now rapidly spreading through Calabria also. Robert was faced with a cruel decision; should he return at once, letting Palermo slip once again from his grasp, or should he remain to capture and consolidate, at the possible risk of his Italian domains? He decided to stay in Sicily, but no longer to wait while disease and famine in the besieged city slowly sapped its resistance. He would now have to force the issue.

In the heart of the old city of Palermo lay the district of Al-Qasr —the Fortress—a quarter of crowded markets and *souks*, clustered around the great Friday Mosque and ringed by its own nine-gated wall. Here, at dawn on 5 January 1072, Roger's infantry attacked.[1] The battle that followed was long and bloody. Fighting with all the determination of their despair, the defenders poured out from the gates and hurled themselves against their assailants. At first, by sheer force of numbers and momentum, they put the Norman infantry to rout, but just in time Robert Guiscard flung in his waiting cavalry and with one mighty charge saved the situation. Now it was the Saracens' turn to flee, the Normans hard on their heels. They might have escaped with their lives, but the watchers on the walls, knowing that they could not receive them back into safety without also admitting their pursuers, slammed the gates in their faces. Thus the bravest of Palermo's defenders found themselves trapped between the Norman cavalry and the unyielding bastions of their own city. They went down fighting.

Now seven of the Guiscard's huge siege-ladders were slowly nudged into position. To the Normans below, who had already tried the temper of Saracen steel, they must have seemed to lead to

[1] Al-Qasr covered the area which now lies roughly between the Palazzo Reale and the Quattro Canti, bounded by the Via Porta di Castro on one side and the Via del Celso on the other.

certain death, and there was a general reluctance to take the first step. Finally, inspired by one of Robert's magnificent exhortations, a certain Archifrede began to climb. Two others followed. They reached the top unharmed, but in the ensuing struggle on the battlements their shields were smashed and they could go no farther. Somehow they managed to scramble back down the walls and lived to enjoy their glory, Archifrede at least having carved his name in a little corner of history. But Al-Qasr was still unconquered.

The Guiscard saw that he would have to change his tactics. By now the number of turbaned figures milling on the ramparts above him suggested that elsewhere in the city the defences might be under-manned. Telling Roger to maintain the pressure as strongly as ever, he slipped away with three hundred picked troops towards the north-east. Here, between Al-Qasr and the sea, lay the more modern quarter of Al-Khalesa, the administrative hub of Palermo, composed largely of public buildings—the arsenal and the prison, the *divan* and the government offices, the Emir's palace rising importantly from their midst. This district too was fortified, but less forbiddingly than its neighbours;[1] and, as the Guiscard had foreseen, it was now practically undefended. Up went the ladders and soon the Norman scaling-party, buoyant if a little blood-stained, was within the city and opening the gate to Robert and the rest of his men.[2] Their possession did not go undisputed. The defenders of the Fortress, panic-stricken at the news of their entry and furious at having been tricked, came charging down upon them. Another bitter struggle followed; the Saracens were powerless against the Norman swords, but it was nightfall before their last survivors picked their way back along the narrow corpse-strewn streets to the still defiant shadows of Al-Qasr.

That night the defenders of Palermo knew that they had lost. Some even now wished to continue the fight for the honour of their

---

[1] The walls extended along the sides of the square now formed by the Piazza della Kalsa (still preserving its old Arabic name), the Porta Felice, the church of S. Franceso d'Assisi and the Piazza Magione.

[2] Until a few years ago, the gate through which Robert is said to have entered could still be seen. It lay behind the first altar on the right in the little church of S. Maria della Vittoria, just off the Piazza dello Spasimo. But the Church—for no good reason that I have been able to discover—has now been demolished.

Faith, but counsels of prudence prevailed and early the following morning a delegation of notables called on the Duke of Apulia to discuss terms for the surrender of their city. Once again Robert showed himself generous in victory. There were to be no reprisals, he promised, and no further looting. All Saracen lives and property would be respected. He desired their friendship and asked only their allegiance and an annual tribute, in return for which the Normans would undertake to interfere neither with the practice of the Muslim religion nor with the application of the Islamic law.

Despite the crusading character of the whole Sicilian expedition —which the Guiscard had felt and stressed from its very outset— his toleration and amenability at this moment need cause us no surprise. He had no cause to foster the Saracens' hostility to their new overlords. Besides, he had to be free to return to the mainland as soon as possible and therefore wished to avoid protracted negotiations; Al-Qasr had still not surrendered and was quite capable of making trouble for days, even weeks, to come. In any case he was not naturally vindictive—Geoffrey of Conversano and the whole Greek population of Bari could vouch for that—and the rights which he was now granting to the Muslims were only those which they had always allowed in the past to the Christian communities under their domination. Nevertheless, such toleration was becoming increasingly rare—it was only twenty-seven years later that the soldiers of the First Crusade, entering Jerusalem, massacred every Muslim in the city and burned all the Jews in the great central synagogue—and the Saracens had expected harsher treatment. Great must have been their relief when, after protracting the negotiations for a couple of days so that face might be saved and due decorum preserved, they could give their final acceptance to the Norman terms. Even then, neither they nor Robert Guiscard himself can have understood the full significance of their agreement. For the Saracens of Sicily it marked the end of their political independence, but also the beginning of an age of unprecedented order and peace during which, under a strong but benevolent central government such as they themselves had never been able to achieve, their artistic and scientific gifts would be encouraged and appreciated as never before. For the Normans it became the foundation-stone of their new political philosophy, enabling them to build up a state that for the next hundred years would stand to the world as an example of culture and enlightenment, giving them an understanding and breadth of outlook which was to be the envy of civilised Europe.

On 10 January 1072 the Duke of Apulia made his formal entry into Palermo. He was followed by his brother Roger, his wife Sichelgaita, his brother-in-law Guy of Salerno and then by all the Norman chiefs who had fought with him in the campaign. They rode through the city to the ancient basilica of S. Maria, now hastily reconsecrated after two hundred and forty years' service as a mosque.[1] Here the service of thanksgiving was performed, according to the Greek rite, by the old Archbishop of Palermo—who, says that staunch Latin Malaterra, 'although a timid Greek, had continued to follow the Christian religion as best he could'—and, if we are to believe Amatus, the very angels of heaven added their voices to those of the congregation.

Their greatest objective now at last attained, the Normans had indeed good reason for rejoicing; the more so since news of the fall of Palermo had led to the spontaneous capitulation of several other regions, notably that of Mazara in the south-west. Subjection of the island was not yet complete; independent emirates still struggled on at Trapani and Syracuse, to say nothing of Enna where young Serlo had been conducting a guerrilla campaign for the past six months, harassing the local authorities and successfully preventing any relief expeditions from being sent to Palermo. But henceforth final pacification was only a matter of time. Meanwhile there was the question of feudal tenure to be settled. It created no difficulties. Robert Guiscard, already provisionally invested as Duke of Sicily by Pope Nicholas thirteen years before, claimed general suzerainty over the whole island. He reserved, however, for his own direct tenure only Palermo, half Messina and half of the Val Demone—the mountainous region of the north-east in whose conquest he had himself participated. The rest was to be held

---

[1] Traces of this original basilica still survive in the Chapel of the Incoronata attached to the present Cathedral.

by his tenant-in-chief Roger, now Great Count of Sicily, who would
also keep all that he might personally acquire in the future, as would his
two principal lieutenants, Serlo de Hauteville and Arisgot of Pozzuoli.

Serlo, alas, did not live to claim his fief. Some time during the
summer of 1072 he and a handful of his men were tricked into an
ambush near Nicosia, close by the confluence of the Cerami and the
Salso. Outnumbered many times over by the Saracen cavalry, he
knew that he was doomed; but leaping on to a huge rock, he and
his followers fought magnificently to the end and sold their lives
dearly. Malaterra maintains that those who slew him tore out his
heart and ate it, hoping that his heroism might thus be transferred to
themselves, and that his head was sent as a token of homage to 'the
king in Africa'. When the sad news was brought back to Palermo
Roger, who knew his nephew best and haf fought so often by his
side, was inconsolable; Robert, we are told, 'made a manly show of
hiding his own tears, not wishing to add to his brother's grief'. Serlo
had been the best-loved, as well as the bravest, of all the young
Norman knights. He had no chance to fulfil his bright promise;
and now he faces a far unworthier adversary. As this book goes to
press, a firm of contractors is at work methodically demolishing the
rock on which he died—the *Pietra di Serlone* which, carved with a
great cross, has stood for nine centuries in his memory, rising
stark and sheer from the fields.

It was autumn before Robert Guiscard returned to the mainland.
The most likely explanation is that he had by now learnt through
his agents that the situation in Apulia and Calabria was less serious
than he had previously feared, and that it was not expected to
deteriorate further—a theory which appears more probable still in
the light of the speed with which he was to restore order early the
following year. At all events he stayed in Palermo throughout the
summer of 1072, working with his brother on the construction of
two strong citadels—one in Al-Qasr and the other, smaller, commanding the harbour entrance in Al-Khalesa—and on the establishment of a Norman administration to supplement the already
existing Saracen institutions. At the head of this, as Governor of
Palermo in his name, he appointed one of his principal lieutenants

with the title of Emir. It was the first Sicilian example of that characteristic Norman readiness to adopt local forms and customs, and of that easy eclecticism which was to give their new country so much of its character and strength.

A day or two before his departure the Duke called a meeting of all the Saracen notables. The siege and capture of Palermo had, he explained, been a long and expensive operation, one that had cost him much money and, in particular, a very large number of horses. His hearers took the point. Hastily forestalling the specific demands which they knew would follow, they showered upon him presents of every kind, including all the horses and gold he needed; several, indeed, went even further, sending their sons to join his suite as an earnest of their fidelity and allegiance. And so, as 1072 drew to its close, loaded with the riches of his new dukedom and followed by his victorious army which already comprised most of the races of southern Europe and was now further adorned by the flower of young Saracen manhood, Robert Guiscard rode proudly back to Italy. In a life of uninterrupted achievement this had been his greatest triumph. Since the first half of the ninth century Sicily had been wholly or largely in Muslim hands, constituting the most forward outpost of Islam, from which raiders, pirates and expeditionary forces had maintained an unremitting pressure against the southern bastions of Christendom. The task of subduing them, a task which had baffled the two greatest Empires in the world, separately and in combination, for some two hundred and fifty years, had been left for him to perform; and he had performed it— apart from a few isolated pockets of resistance which would trouble him little and Europe not at all—with a handful of men in barely a decade. His satisfaction must indeed have been great; it would have been greater still had he been able to see into the future and so understand the tremendous historical implications of what he had done. For the Norman conquest of Sicily was, together with the contemporary beginnings of the *Reconquista* in Spain, the first step in the immense Christian reaction against the Muslim-held lands of the southern Mediterranean—that reaction which was one of the hallmarks of the later Middle Ages and which was shortly to develop into the colossal, if ultimately empty, epic of the Crusades.

PART TWO

THE BUILDING OF THE KINGDOM

14

POLARISATION

The Eastern Church has fallen away from the Faith and is now assailed
on every side by infidels. Wherever I turn my eyes . . . I find bishops who
have obtained office irregularly, whose lives and conversation are strangely
at variance with their sacred calling. . . . There are no longer princes who
set God's honour before their own selfish ends . . . and those among whom
I live—Romans, Lombards and Normans—are, as I have often told them,
worse than Jews or pagans.

Letter from Gregory VII to Hugh of Cluny,
22 January 1075

ROBERT GUISCARD never returned to Sicily. His talents were
those of a soldier rather than an administrator, and once a territory
was safely in his hands it seemed to lose its attraction for him. In
point of fact, the island when he left it towards the end of 1072 was
by no means conquered. The Saracen Emirs at Trapani in the west
and Taormina in the east still showed no sign of submission; the
death of Serlo had given new impetus to the resistance in the centre;
while south of a line drawn between Agrigento and Catania the
Normans had scarcely even begun to penetrate. But for Robert such
considerations were of little importance. Palermo was his: he was
now Duke of Sicily in fact as well as in name. It was time to look
to his mainland dominions and, once order there had been restored,
to return to his rightful place on the European stage. Fortunately
Roger seemed content to remain on the island. He could complete
the task of pacification at his leisure. It would keep him occupied.

Roger asked nothing better. Though he lacked the Guiscard's
superb *panache*, he was if anything more intelligent and certainly
far more sensitive than his brother. Sicily had captured his imagination from the start and for ten years had continuously fascinated

him. He had probably fallen under that curious spell with which the Islamic world so frequently beguiles unsuspecting northerners; but there was more to it than that. What Robert had seen merely as a bright new jewel in his crown, a territorial extension of the Italian peninsula inconveniently cut off by a strip of water, Roger recognised as a challenge. Those narrow straits, by protecting the island from the eternal squabbles of South Italy, offered Sicily possibilities of greatness far beyond anything that could be hoped for on the mainland. They also afforded him the chance of escaping, once and for all, from his brother's shadow.

Of all the tasks that lay ahead, the most important was to extend Norman authority throughout the island. This, he knew, would take time. After the Guiscard's departure reliable manpower was shorter than ever; with only a few hundred knights under his command Roger could not hope to do much more than consolidate his past conquests. For the rest, he could only trust in his diplomatic skill to sap the Saracen resistance until it died of inanition or at least grew weak enough for him to deal with by military methods. In other words, the Muslims must whenever possible be persuaded voluntary to accept the new dispensations. They must be treated with tolerance and understanding. And so they were. Norman Douglas, in *Old Calabria*, has monstrously slandered his namesakes by claiming that 'immediately on their occupation of the country they razed to the ground thousands of Arab temples and sanctuaries. Of several hundred in Palermo alone, not a single one was left standing.' Nothing could be more at variance with Roger's policy. Although from the early days of the conquest he did all he could to encourage Italian and Lombard colonisation from the mainland, his Saracen subjects still far outnumbered their Christian neighbours and it would have been folly for him to antagonise them unnecessarily; nor thus could he and his successors ever have created that atmosphere of interracial harmony and mutual respect which so characterised the Kingdom of Sicily in the following century.

Naturally the dictates of security came first. Taxation was high for Christian and Saracen alike, and more efficiently imposed than in former times. Roger also introduced, in an attempt to increase his military strength, an annual period of conscription which was doubtless no more popular than such measures ever are with those directly affected. In the outlying villages and the countryside there were also the inevitable odd cases where local governors victimised in varying degrees the populations under their authority. But for the most part—and certainly in Palermo and the major towns—the Saracens seem to have found little cause for complaint. Such of the mosques as they had originally converted from Christian churches were now reconsecrated, but all others were open, as they had always been, for the prayers of the Faithful. The law of Islam was still dispensed from the local courts. Arabic was declared an official language, on equal footing with Latin, Greek and Norman French. In local government, too, many provincial Emirs were retained at their posts. Others, potential troublemakers, were removed; but frequently the removal took the acceptable form of a bribe, perhaps of a free grant of land, to move to some other region where they would have less of a following. Nowhere on the island did the Normans show any of that brutality which was so unpleasant a feature of their conquest of England during this period. In consequence, the sullen resentment so much in evidence among the Saracens in the early days after the fall of Palermo was gradually overcome as Roger won their confidence; and many of those who had fled to Africa or Spain came back within a year or two to Sicily and resumed their former lives.

His new Christian subjects presented the Count with a different problem. Here he had to contend with a growing feeling of disillusion. The enthusiasm with which the Sicilian Greeks had first welcomed the Normans as liberators of their island from the infidel yoke was now wearing thin. The Frankish knights might emblazon the Cross on their banners, but most of them seemed a good deal more brutish and uncivilised than the Muslims. Besides, they followed the despised Latin liturgy; they crossed themselves with four fingers and from left to right; and, worst of all, their installation in Palermo had led to a hideous influx of Latin priests and monks, who were even appropriating some of the newly-recovered Greek churches for their own use. All over Europe the old antipathy between Greek and Latin, sharpened now by a generation of schism, had been growing steadily worse; in Sicily it was assuming unprecedented and ominous proportions.

Roger was fully aware of the danger. He had not forgotten that fearful winter at Troina ten years before, when the Greeks had made common cause with the Saracens against his army, and he and Judith had nearly died of cold and starvation. It had taught him, as nothing else could have done, that their loyalty was not to be taken for granted. Already he had given them full guarantees that their language, culture and traditions would be respected, but this was clearly not enough. He must now give them material help in the reconstitution of their Church. Apart from the aged Archbishop of Palermo, who after his eviction from the capital had been carrying on to the best of his tremulous ability from the neighbouring village of Santa Ciriaca, the Orthodox hierarchy of Sicily had completely collapsed. Such Basilian[1] monasteries as remained were moribund and penniless.

With his usual perspicacity Roger saw that this was the field in which he might most easily regain Greek support. Funds were put at the disposal of the Orthodox community for the reconstruction of their churches, and before long the Count had personally endowed a new Basilian foundation—the first of the fourteen that he was to establish or restore during the remainder of his life. Staffing of the new houses presented no problem. Life had been growing progressively more difficult for the Greek monks of Calabria, where both Robert Guiscard and the Pope—and Roger himself, in those areas under his control—were anxious to complete the process of Latinisation as quickly as possible. Many of them were doubtless only too pleased to be brought to Sicily, where they were welcomed not only by their co-religionists but also by the Government as a desirable reinforcement of the Christian population. One condition only did Roger make: there could no longer be any question of the Sicilian Greeks considering themselves ecclesiastically subject to the Patriarch in Constantinople, nor of their owing any allegiance to the Byzantine Emperor. Administratively they must be subordinated to the Latin hierarchy which was quickly taking shape in the island. Although the links between Sicily and Constanti-

[1] See p. 77 n.

Serlo's rock

Mazara: ruins of the castle built by Roger I in 1073

nople had in practice long ceased to exist, the acceptance of Roman supremacy must have seemed to many Greeks a bitter pill to swallow; but Roger was careful to sugar it with gifts and privileges —even an occasional special exemption from the jurisdiction of the local bishops[1]—and they soon accepted the inevitable.

And so, from those earliest days in Palermo after Robert Guiscard had left all Norman-held Sicily in his effective control, the Great Count began to lay the foundations of a multiracial and polyglot state in which Norman, Greek and Saracen would, under a firmly-centralised administration, follow their own cultural traditions in freedom and concord. It was, in the circumstances, the only possible policy; but Roger's remarkable success in pursuing it could have been achieved only by a combination of his outstanding administrative gifts with a breadth of vision and eclectic intellectual appreciation rare in the eleventh century. He genuinely admired what he had seen of Muslim civilisation, and particularly Islamic architecture; while his apparent interest in the Greek Church was such that at one period the new Orthodox bishops were seriously discussing the possibility of converting him. Sicily was fortunate, at this crucial point in her history, in having a ruler whose own personal inclinations so closely corresponded with the island's needs.

These inclinations certainly made Roger's task easier than it might otherwise have been, but there were other factors which rendered it infinitely more complicated. One was the constant guerrilla warfare along the borders of Norman territory, a nagging reminder that there could be no peace or any major economic development while a good third of the land remained unsubdued. The other was Robert Guiscard. His powers, formidable as they were, could never quite keep pace with his ambitions; and time and again in the years to come Roger was to find himself obliged to lay aside his work in Sicily and hasten across the straits to his brother's aid.

As we have seen, the Duke of Apulia had been in no hurry to return to the mainland. The revolt of his nephews and their allies

[1] Similar exemptions had long been known in the Orthodox world. The monasteries of Mt Athos, for example, were originally independent of the Patriarch of Constantinople and subject only to the Emperor himself; and that of St Catherine on Mt Sinai was later to be elevated still further to the rank of a separate autocephalous Church.

had proved less dangerous than he had at first believed, and he had never doubted his ability to deal with it. Events proved him right. He rode straight to Melfi, where all the loyal vassals were summoned to meet him; then, as the year 1073 opened, he led his army eastward to the Adriatic coast. Trani fell on 2 February; Corato, Giovinazzo, Bisceglie and Andria followed in swift succession; the rebel leaders Herman and Peter of Trani were captured and imprisoned. In March Robert turned his attention to the little town of Cisternino. At first it seemed disposed to offer rather more serious resistance, but the Guiscard was in a hurry. Cisternino belonged, as he well knew, to his prisoner, Peter of Trani. A great wattle screen was hastily prepared, and the unfortunate Peter lashed to it. Behind this cover the Normans advanced. The defenders could not counter-attack without killing their liege-lord, and Peter himself could only cry out to them to surrender. They obeyed.

With the capture of Cisternino the Apulian rising was effectively at an end. It had been stamped out in less than three months. One hostile garrison still remained in Canosa,[1] where it had been stationed by Richard of Capua some time before; but the town was already short of water when Robert's army arrived, and it surrendered with scarcely a struggle. The Guiscard returned in triumph to Trani, where he again showed that sudden impetuous magnanimity which was one of his most endearing characteristics. It would not have been his way to feel any twinges of remorse for what he had done to Peter of Trani at Cisternino; his actions had had the desired effect, and for him the end always justified the means. But he clearly felt that his miserable prisoner had suffered enough. Excepting only the city of Trani itself, he now restored to him all the lands and castles he had previously confiscated.

Robert's clemency did not however extend to all his other erst-while enemies. With a minor Apulian baron he could afford to be generous, but Richard of Capua presented a more serious long-term threat to his position. For fourteen years, ever since the two chief-tains had together received their papal investitures at Melfi, Richard had been building up his influence in the west. He was now supreme

[1] Canosa di Puglia, between Melfi and Barletta, is not to be confused with Canossa in Tuscany, so soon to win its own memorable place in history.

194

in Campania and even as far north as Rome, where he had made
himself indispensable to Pope Alexander—and to Hildebrand—
during their trial of strength with the anti-Pope Honorius. Since
then, however, he had broken his oath of vassalage and in 1066 had
actually marched on Rome; and though on that occasion he had
been driven back by Tuscan forces he was known still to have his eye
on the Patriciate of the City. Like the Duke of Apulia, he had had his
difficulties in the past with insubordinate vassals; and when, only a
year or two before, he had gone so far as to appeal to his rival for
help in putting down a revolt, Robert had obliged with a detachment
of troops that he could ill afford to spare. More recently still, when
the Guiscard had asked him for a contribution towards the Palermo
expedition, Richard had promised a hundred and fifty knights, but
they had never turned up—instead, they had presumably been sent
to reinforce the Apulian rebels. It seemed a curious way for a
brother-in-law to repay past kindnesses. The Prince of Capua was in
short too strong, too slippery and too dangerous. He would have
to be dealt with.

But the momentum of the past three months could not continue
for ever. While busying himself in Trani with preparations for his
great march against Capua, Robert—whose gigantic frame normally
shrugged off fevers and distempers like so many drops of rain—was
struck down by a grave illness. Hoping that a change of air might
restore him, he had himself carried to Bari; but his condition
steadily worsened. Sichelgaita, as always at his side, could no
longer hope for his life. Hastily she summoned his vassals and as
many Norman knights as she could muster and forced them to
elect, as her husband's successor, her eldest son Roger—nicknamed
Borsa, the purse, from his early-ingrained habit of counting and
recounting his money. He was a weak and hesitant thirteen-year-old
who gave the impression that a childhood spent with Robert and
Sichelgaita had been too much for him. This would indeed have
been understandable enough; but it did not make him a good choice
as future Duke of Apulia, particularly since his elder half-brother
Bohemund—the Guiscard's son by his cast-off wife Alberada of
Buonalbergo—had already distinguished himself in the field and
was clearly the only one of his father's sons to have inherited any

195

of the Hauteville qualities. On the other hand, Bohemund does not seem to have been present at Bari, and Sichelgaita was. Her son, she pointed out, being half a Lombard, would be more acceptable to the Lombard populations of Apulia than any full-blooded Norman; and her personality was not such as to invite contradiction. And so Roger Borsa was elected with only one dissentient voice—that of his cousin Abelard, still nursing his old grievance and claiming that he, as Duke Humphrey's son, was the rightful heir to the dukedom. When the vassals, their duty done, took leave of the mighty leader with whom, in one way or another, they had fought for so long, not all hearts may have been equally heavy; but in each there must have been a consciousness that things could never be the same again—that Apulia itself would in future be a diminished place. And indeed, within a few days of their return to their homes, the news was spreading like wildfire the length and breadth of the peninsula: Robert Guiscard was dead.

Word reached Rome towards the end of April, just as the city was mourning another loss—that of Pope Alexander. This time, at least, there was to be no trouble over the succession: the choice was too obvious. Archdeacon Hildebrand had already wielded effective power in the Curia for some twenty years, during many of which he had been supreme in all but name. When, according to a carefully prearranged plan, the crowd seized him during Alexander's funeral service, carried him to the Church of St Peter in Vinculis and there exultantly acclaimed him Pope, they were doing little more than regularising the existing state of affairs; and the canonical election that followed was the purest formality. Hastily he was ordained a priest—a desirable qualification to the Papacy which seems to have been overlooked during the earlier stages of his career—and was immediately afterwards enthroned as Supreme Pontiff in the name of Gregory VII.

Of the three great Popes of the eleventh century—Leo IX, Gregory VII and Urban II—Gregory was at once the least attractive and the most remarkable. Whereas the other two were aristocrats, secure in the possession of all that noble birth and a first-class education could bestow, he was a Tuscan peasant's son, Lombard by race, whose every word and gesture betrayed his humble origins.[1] They assumed the Papacy almost as of right; he achieved it only after a long and arduous—though increasingly influential—apprenticeship in the Curia, and for no other reason than his immense ability and the power of his will. They were both tall, and of outstandingly distinguished appearance; he was short and swarthy, with a pronounced paunch and a voice so weak that, even making allowance for his heavy regional accent, his Roman colleagues often found it difficult to understand what he said. He had none of Leo's obvious saintliness, nor any of Urban's adroit political instinct or diplomatic flair. He was neither a scholar nor a theologian. And yet there was in his character something so compelling that he almost invariably dominated, automatically and effortlessly, any group of which he found himself a member.

His strength lay, above all, in the singleness of his purpose. Throughout his life he was guided by one overmastering ideal—the subjection of all Christendom, from the Emperors down, to the authority of the Church of Rome. But just as the Church must be supreme upon earth, so too must the Pope be supreme in the Church. He was the judge of all men, himself responsible only to God; his word was not only law, it was the Divine Law. Disobedience to him was therefore something very close to mortal sin. Never before had the concept of ecclesiastical autocracy been carried to such an extreme; never before had it been pursued with such unflinching determination. And yet this very extremism was to prove ultimately self-destructive. Confronted by adversaries of the calibre of Henry IV and Robert Guiscard, as determined as himself but infinitely more flexible, Gregory was to learn to his cost that his persistent refusal to compromise, even when his principles were not directly involved, could only bring about his downfall.

One of the Pope's first official acts on his accession was to write his condolences to Sichelgaita. The letter is not included among his collected correspondence, but the version given by Amatus so

---

[1] Hildebrand, or Hildeprand, was a common Lombard name. His father's name, Bonizo, is an abbreviation of Bonipart, which seven centuries later we find again in the form of Buonaparte. Napoleon was also of Lombard stock. He and Hildebrand had much in common.

precisely expresses what we know of Gregory's thinking that it may well have been based on an authentic text. It runs as follows:

The death of Duke Robert, that dearest son of the Holy Church of Rome, has left the Church in deep and irremediable sorrow. The Cardinals and all the Roman Senate do greatly grieve at his death, seeing themselves thereby brought low. . . . But in order that Your Grace should know of Our goodwill and of the perfect love which we bore your husband, We now request you to inform your son that it is the pleasure of the Holy Church that he should receive at her hands all those things which his father held from the Pope Our Predecessor.

It was, by any standards, a profoundly hypocritical letter. Gregory had no cause to love Robert. The Duke had not lifted a finger to help the Papacy in its recent tribulations, while his brother Geoffrey and Geoffrey's son Robert of Loritello were even now ravaging valuable Church lands in the Abruzzi. On the other hand, the Pope was genuinely anxious that the Guiscard's successor should receive a proper investiture for his lands and titles; the Hautevilles were papal vassals, and he had no intention of allowing them to forget it. Roger Borsa was by all accounts a gentle and pious young man; he should prove a lot more amenable than his tempestuous father. In the circumstances, therefore, it can hardly have been a happy surprise for Pope Gregory when a week or two later he received a reply to his letter, not from a sorrowing widow but from Robert Guiscard himself, now well on his way to complete recovery. He was happy to inform the Pope—and through him, doubtless, the Cardinals and the Senate—that the reports of his death had been without foundation. However, he continued cheerfully, he had been most touched by the kind things the Pope had said about him, and asked nothing more than to be allowed to remain His Holiness's most obedient servant.

Robert must have enjoyed dictating his letter; but he too was anxious for a formal reinvestiture. During his Sicilian campaigns the Pope's blessing had been of little significance except as a means of boosting his army's morale; but now that he was concentrating once again on his Italian possessions—and perhaps already beginning to nurse plans for vast enterprises beyond them—a renewed compact with Gregory could only strengthen his hand. It would have a psychological effect on the more obstreperous of his vassals and, more important still, would make it harder for the Pope to withhold his support if Robert should ask it. And so, through the good offices of Abbot Desiderius of Monte Cassino, an interview was arranged between Gregory and the Guiscard, to take place at Benevento on 10 August 1073.

The occasion proved a total fiasco. Indeed it seems possible that the two never even met. There were, for a start, serious difficulties over protocol. The Pope wished to receive Robert in his Benevento palace; the Duke, on the other hand, who may have had some advance warning of an assassination attempt, refused to set foot within the city and proposed that the meeting should take place outside the walls—a solution which Gregory found inconsonant with his papal dignity. Poor Desiderius must have had a thankless task, shuttling backwards and forwards between these two determined and mutually suspicious characters, arguing and cajoling with each in turn in the relentless heat of a Campanian August; but even if his efforts were successful and Duke and Pontiff were at last brought face to face, their confrontation seems to have done more harm than good. The only result was a complete rupture of relations between them—and a recognition by both parties that alliance was impossible and that alternative arrangements would have to be made.

There is something mysterious about the whole Benevento affair. The recent correspondence between the two parties may not have been notable for its sincerity, but it was outwardly cordial—even fulsome—and it revealed on both sides a genuine desire for discussions. What could have happened to alter the situation so radically? The breakdown cannot be ascribed entirely to the Guiscard's suspicions, nor to Gregory's pride. It may be that the Pope had insisted, as an essential preliminary to any agreement, that Robert put a stop to the continual incursions of his brother and nephew into the Abruzzi, and that the Duke had declared himself unable or unwilling to take the necessary action. Certainly Gregory felt very strongly on the matter: he was soon afterwards to send to the affected area a bishop, notorious for his strong-arm methods, whom he had applauded two years earlier for having deprived a number of rebellious monks of their eyes and tongues. But there is no evidence that the Abruzzi question was even raised at Benevento. All we know is that the Pope, on leaving the city, made straight for Capua; that he there confirmed Prince Richard in all his possessions; and that the two of them forthwith concluded a military alliance against the Duke of Apulia.

Back in Rome in the autumn of 1073, Pope Gregory was worried. Some months earlier, shortly after his accession, he had received a secret and urgent appeal from the new Byzantine Emperor, Michael VII, in Constantinople. The Empire of the East was facing the gravest crisis in its history. Two years before, at the very moment when Robert Guiscard was eliminating, by the capture of Bari, the last vestiges of Greek power in Italy, the Byzantine army under the Emperor Romanus IV Diogenes had suffered total annihilation by the Seljuk Turks near the Armenian town of Mantzikert. The whole of Asia Minor now lay open to the invaders, and from Asia Minor it was but a short leap to the capital itself. Romanus was taken prisoner by the Seljuks; their leader, Alp Arslan, soon gave him back his liberty, but on his return to Constantinople Romanus found that his stepson Michael had replaced him on the imperial throne. After a brief and futile attempt at a restoration, he had surrendered to the new government on receiving guarantees of his personal safety. With his long experience of Constantinople, he should have known better. The guarantees were forgotten; the old ex-Emperor's eyes were put out with red-hot irons, and five weeks later he was dead. Michael himself had played little active part in these events. He was a scholarly recluse with no appetite for political intrigue, content to be led by his chief mentor and minister, the brilliant but odious Michael Psellus.[1] And it may well have been on Psellus' advice that he had written to the Pope imploring him to raise a Crusading army by which Eastern Christendom might finally be delivered from the fearful shadow of the infidel.

Gregory was deeply affected by the appeal. The two Churches

---

[1] The character of Psellus is nicely illustrated by the letter which he wrote at this time to the dying Romanus. Himself the principal author of the old man's downfall, he now congratulated him on the fortunate martyrdom by which, he argued, the Almighty had deprived him of his eyes because He had found him worthy of a higher light.

might be in schism, but he still considered himself responsible
before God for the entire Christian world. Besides, this was a
heaven-sent opportunity to bring the Byzantines back once again
into the Roman fold, and he was determined not to let it pass him
by. On the other hand he could not possibly launch an effective
Crusade in the east while he was under a constant threat at home
from Robert Guiscard and his Normans. They must be eliminated,
once and for all. But how? He had few expectations of his new
alliance with Richard of Capua, which he had concluded largely
to prevent the two Norman leaders from joining forces themselves.
Robert Guiscard was unquestionably the stronger of the two, but it
was plain from their years of intermittent warfare that neither would
ever be able to achieve a decisive victory over the other. The Pope's
only remaining southern ally, Gisulf of Salerno, was an even more
hopeless case. The Normans had already relieved him of nearly all
the territory that had once made his principality the most powerful
in the peninsula; and now, as the winter of 1073 drew near, came
the news of another serious blow to his fortunes: Amalfi had
voluntarily placed herself under the protection of the Duke of
Apulia. It was Gisulf's own fault. He had never forgiven the Amalfitans for the part they had played in the assassination of his father
twenty-one years before. Though never strong enough to capture
the city by force of arms, he had always made life as unpleasant
as he could for its people; and many hair-raising tales were told of
the sufferings endured by such luckless Amalfitan merchants as
from time to time fell into his clutches.[1] When in 1073 Duke Sergius
of Amalfi died, leaving only a child to succeed him, his subjects had
therefore taken the one sensible course open to them. Robert had
naturally accepted their offer. He loathed his brother-in-law Gisulf
and had long had his eye on Salerno—which, but for the family
feelings of Sichelgaita, he would probably have attacked long before.
The possession of Amalfi would make his task much easier when the
moment came.

[1] Amatus speaks of one unfortunate victim whom Gisulf kept in an icy dungeon,
removing first his right eye and then every day one more of his fingers and toes. He adds
that the Empress Agnes—who was now spending much of her time in South Italy—
personally offered a hundred pounds of gold and one of her own fingers in ransom,
but her prayers went unheard.

This new and unexpected success for the Guiscard disturbed Pope Gregory more than ever. At once he set to work to raise an army. As 1074 opened, papal messengers were already speeding north from Rome—to Beatrice of Tuscany and her daughter Matilda, and to Matilda's husband, Godfrey the Hunchback of Lorraine,[1] to Azzo, Marquis of Este and William, Count of Burgundy, who was further instructed to pass the appeal on to Counts Raymond of Toulouse and Amadeus of Savoy. The Pope left them in no doubt of his intentions, nor of the order of priority in which he had determined to carry them out. He was not, as he was careful to emphasise, gathering this great host together simply to shed Christian blood; indeed he hoped that its very existence might prove an adequate deterrent to his enemies. 'Furthermore,' he added, 'we trust that yet further good may emerge in that, once the Normans are subdued, we may continue to Constantinople to the aid of those Christians who, beset by most frequent Saracen attacks, do insistently implore our aid.'

The replies to these letters seem to have been prompt and favourable. By March the Pope was able to announce at the Lenten Synod that his army would assemble the following June at a point near

[1] At this point the family relationships between the House of Tuscany and Lorraine have become rather involved, since Beatrice's stepson was also her son-in-law. Thus the position was as follows:

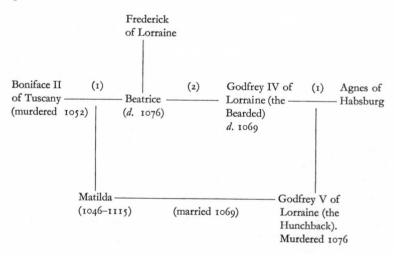

Viterbo, whence it would march against the Duke of Apulia and his followers—whom, for good measure, he now excommunicated. As the weeks went by and more and more troops gathered at the appointed place his spirits began to rise again, until at the beginning of June he felt strong enough to give his enemy one more chance. Peremptory as always, he summoned Robert to meet him at Benevento for a final conference.

Now it was the Guiscard's turn to feel alarm. A generation ago, at Civitate, he and his brothers and Richard of Aversa had successfully routed a papal army, but in those days the Normans were united. This time they were split, the Prince of Capua firmly aligned with the Pope. Robert and his men, fighting without allies, would have to proceed with caution. But perhaps after all there was still a chance of agreement. The reply he returned to Gregory was unctuously humble. His conscience was clear; he had never given the Pope cause for offence or disobeyed him in any way; and he would of course be honoured, anywhere and at any time, to present himself before His Holiness. And so, accompanied by a heavy escort —for he still did not trust Gregory an inch—he rode back to Benevento.

In his long and rampageous career Robert Guiscard had often been astonishingly lucky; but never had Fortune smiled on him more kindly than at this moment. Three days he waited at the gates of the city; the Pope never appeared. Just as all Gregory's plans had been laid and his army stood in readiness for the assault, dissension had broken out in its ranks. Once again the fault lay with Gisulf of Salerno. In recent years the conduct of his ships on the high seas had come dangerously close to piracy. The Amalfitans had probably suffered most, but many Pisan merchantmen had fared little better. When, therefore, the Pisan contingent among the troops provided by the Countess Matilda found themselves face to face with Gisulf in person, they made no secret of their feelings towards him. As soon as Gregory saw what was happening, he hastily packed the Prince of Salerno off to Rome; but it was too late. Sides had been taken up and the whole army was split. Within days it had broken up in confusion.

For the Pope this was disaster—and, where his relations with the

Guiscard were concerned, an intense personal humiliation. Every-thing seemed to conspire against him. The army in which he had put his trust had disintegrated without taking a step into Norman territory; the Crusade which he had as good as promised the Byzan-tine Emperor and on which he had staked his reputation was more remote than ever; the opportunity for reuniting the Churches under his authority was slipping once again from his grasp. Worst of all, he—the Vicar of Christ on earth—had been made to look a fool in front of his enemies. And even this was not the end of his tribula-tions. A party of the Roman aristocracy—disaffected as always—was now actively plotting to get rid of him. He did not know that one of his own cardinals, a member of this group, had recently approached Robert Guiscard and offered him the imperial crown in return for his assistance; or that Robert, seeing that the whole plan was hopelessly unrealistic, had refused to become involved. Even if he had, the knowledge would hardly have given him much conso-lation.

On Christmas Eve 1075 his enemies struck. The Pope was dragged from the altar in the crypt of S. Maria Maggiore when he was saying Mass, and carried off to a secret prison. He was soon found and released by an indignant populace, and had the satisfaction of personally saving his erstwhile captor from being lynched; but not before the world had seen just how shaky were the foundations on which his throne rested.

And now, when he was least ready to sustain it, Gregory received his first intimation of the greatest blow of all—that from which he would never altogether recover. Young Henry IV, King of the Romans and Western Emperor-elect, was preparing to descend into Italy, to dethrone the Pope and to have himself crowned Emperor.

15

EXCOMMUNICATIONS AND
INVESTITURES

Henry, not by usurpation but by God's holy will King, to Hildebrand, not Pope but false monk.

This salutation thou hast deserved, upraiser of strife, thou who art cursed instead of blessed by every order in the Church. . . . The archbishops, bishops and priests thou hast trodden under thy foot like slaves devoid of will. . . . Christ has called us to the Empire but not thee to the Papacy. Thou didst acquire it by craft and fraud; in scorn of thy monastic cowl thou didst obtain by gold favour, by favour arms, and by arms the throne of peace, from which thou hast destroyed peace. . . .

I, Henry, by God's grace King, with all our bishops call on thee: Descend, descend!

Letter from Henry IV to Pope Gregory,
Worms, 24 January 1076

HENRY IV had come to the throne of Germany shortly before his sixth birthday. He was now twenty-five. He had not made a particularly auspicious start to his reign; his mother, the Empress-Regent Agnes, had been totally unable to control him, and after a wild boyhood and a deeply disreputable adolescence he had acquired, by the time he assumed power at the age of sixteen, a reputation for viciousness and profligacy which augured ill for the future. This reputation he was at last beginning to live down, but throughout his unhappy life he remained hot-tempered, passionate and intensely autocratic. Thus as he grew to manhood he became ever more resentful of the increasing arrogance of the Roman Church and, in particular, of those reformist measures by which it was seeking to cast off the last vestiges of imperial control. Henry had been too young to oppose Nicholas II's decree regulating papal elections, but he was determined that this separatist trend should go no further. Even before the elevation of Hildebrand to the Papacy it was plain that a clash between Church and Empire was inevitable. It was not long in coming.

The scene was Milan. Nowhere in Italy did the spirit of ecclesiastical independence from the dictates of Rome burn more brightly than in this old capital of the North, where an individual liturgical tradition had been jealously preserved since the days of St Ambrose seven centuries before; nowhere were the new Roman reforms, especially those relating to simony and clerical celibacy, more bitterly resented by the diehards. On the other hand the government of the city was now dominated by a radical left-wing party known as the Patarines, who, partly through genuine religious fervour and partly through hatred of the wealth and privilege that the Church had so long enjoyed, had become fanatical supporters of reform. Such a situation would have been explosive enough without imperial intervention; but in 1072, during a dispute over the vacant archbishopric of Milan, Henry had aggravated matters by giving formal investiture to the anti-reform candidate while fully aware that Alexander II had already approved the canonical election of a Patarine. Here was an act of open defiance that the Church could not ignore; and at his Lenten Synod of 1075 Hildebrand—now Pope Gregory VII—categorically condemned all ecclesiastical investitures by laymen, on pain of anathema. Henry, furious, immediately invested two more German bishops with Italian sees and added for good measure a further Archbishop of Milan, although his former nominee was still alive. Refusing a papal summons to Rome to answer for his actions, he then called a general council of all the German bishops and, at Worms on 24 January 1076 formally deposed Gregory from the Papacy.

The King had long been eager to come to Rome for his imperial coronation, but his quarrel with successive Popes over investitures had prevented him. After the Council of Worms, however, he saw that his journey could no longer be postponed. Gregory had not reacted to his deposition with the savagery that was already rumoured,[1] but he was clearly not going to accept it lying down. If

---

[1] Writing at a time when castration and mutilation were commonplaces in Constantinople, Anna Comnena harps on the subject with morbid fascination. 'He vented

therefore the Council were not to be held up to ridicule, he would have to be removed by force and a successor installed. The need was for a swift, smooth military operation; and while it was being prepared, steps must be taken to deprive the Pope as far as possible of local Italian support. North of Rome this would be difficult; the formidable Countess Matilda of Tuscany was a devout champion of the Church, her loyalty to Gregory unwavering. To the South, however, the prospects looked more hopeful. The Duke of Apulia in particular seemed to have no great love for the Pope. He might well overlook his feudal responsibilities if it were made worth his while to do so. Once he and his men could be persuaded to participate in a combined attack on Rome, Gregory would not stand a chance.

The importance which Henry attached to the Guiscard's friendship can be judged from his choice of ambassadors—Gregory, Bishop of Vercelli, one of his staunchest supporters against papal claims, and Eberhard, his Chancellor for Italy. They reached Robert, probably at Melfi, early in 1076 and formally offered him an imperial investiture of all his possessions; they may even have mentioned the possibility of a royal crown. But the Duke was unimpressed. His own position was for the moment secure—more so than it had been for a considerable time. He now enjoyed complete freedom of action throughout his domains, and he saw no reason to jeopardise this by giving Henry further excuses to meddle in South Italian politics. His reply was firm, if a trifle sanctimonious. God had given him his conquests; they had been won from the Greeks and Saracens, and dearly paid for in Norman blood. For what little land he possessed that had ever been imperial, he would consent to be the Emperor's vassal, 'saving always his duty to the Church'—a proviso

his rage on Henry's ambassadors; first he tortured them inhumanly, then clipped their hair with scissors . . . and finally committed a most indecent outrage upon them, which transcended even the insolence of barbarians, and so sent them away. My womanly and princely dignity forbids my naming the outrage inflicted on them, for it was not only unworthy of a high priest, but of anyone who bears the name of a Christian. I abhor this barbarian's idea, and still more the deed, and I should have defiled both my pen and my paper had I described it explicitly. But as a display of barbaric insolence, and a proof that time in its flow produces men with shameless morals, ripe for any wickedness, this will alone suffice if I say that I could not bear to disclose or relate even the tiniest word about what he did. And this was the work of a high priest. Oh, justice!' (*The Alexiad*, Bk I, 13, tr. Dawes).

which, as he well knew, would make his allegiance valueless from Henry's point of view. The rest he would continue to hold, as he had always held it, from the Almighty.

It is hard to believe that the ambassadors took the Guiscard's protestations of loyalty to the Church at their face value, but they returned laden with gifts and well pleased by their reception. Even if Robert was not prepared to compromise his own position to oblige King Henry, the last thing he wanted was to antagonise him at such a moment. The stage was being set for the direct confrontation of the two most powerful figures of Western Europe. Its outcome was still impossible to predict, but one thing was certain— the ensuing upheaval would create opportunities for Norman advancement which must not be missed. Hurriedly the Guiscard sent a message to Richard of Capua. Their constant skirmishing had always been indecisive and ineffectual; it was unworthy of them both. All Normans must stand together if they were to profit by the coming crisis. Could not the two leaders now meet to discuss an end to the hostilities between them?

On his way to Capua, the messenger encountered one of Richard's men, bound for Melfi with a similar proposal. A conference was arranged—probably on neutral ground at Monte Cassino, since we know that Abbot Desiderius was present as mediator. He was tired of seeing his monastery lands used as a perpetual battleground, and had long worked for such a reconciliation.[1] In fact the interview gave him little trouble—far less than those nightmare days with Guiscard and the Pope at Benevento three years before. Neither side had made any significant conquests at the expense of the other and both were genuinely anxious to reach an understanding, so the terms were simple enough. Each leader agreed to return what he had won and revert to former frontiers. Once this had been arranged, there was no obstacle to a treaty of alliance.

Meanwhile Pope Gregory had acted with his usual vigour. At his Lenten Synod of February 1076 he deposed all the rebellious

---

[1] Chalandon believes (I, 243) that Desiderius was acting on the Pope's instructions. This seems unlikely. Gregory would not have been pleased to see the Normans reunited at such a moment; nor would he have encouraged leading members of his hierarchy to negotiate with excommunicates.

bishops and thundered out his sentence of excommunication on King Henry himself. The effect in Germany was cataclysmic. No reigning monarch had incurred the ban of the Church since Theodosius the Great seven centuries before. It had brought that Emperor to his knees and it now threatened to do the same for Henry. The purely spiritual aspect did not worry him unduly—that problem could always easily be solved by a well-timed repentance—but the political consequences were serious indeed. In theory the ban not only absolved all the King's subjects from their allegiance to the Crown, but it also rendered them in their turn excommunicate if they had any dealings with him or showed him obedience. If it were strictly observed, therefore, Henry's government would disintegrate and he would be unable to continue any longer on the throne. Suddenly he found himself isolated. He had badly overplayed his hand.

The Pope's grim satisfaction can well be imagined as he watched his adversary struggling to retain the loyalties of those around him; but it must have been tempered by the news reaching Rome from the South. With Robert and Richard now once more a united force, his own position in Italy was gravely endangered. There was still a chance that Henry might extricate himself from his present difficulties and march on the Eternal City, and if this were to occur it was essential that the Norman army should be firmly aligned on the papal side. The situation was, however, complicated by the uncomfortable fact that the Duke of Apulia also lay under sentence of excommunication. Gregory's highly developed sense of his own prestige would never allow him to make the first move towards lifting it, but he could at least arrange for a few hints to be dropped. Already in March 1076 we find him writing to the Bishop of Acerenza, instructing him to give absolution to Count Roger and his men before their return to Sicily and adding—what was probably the real point of the letter—that if Roger were to raise the subject of his brother's position he should be reminded that the doors of the Church were always open to the truly repentant, Robert included. The Pope was ready 'to receive him with a father's love . . . to loose him from the bonds of excommunication and to number him once again among his divine sheep'.

But as spring came to South Italy, and with it the fine campaigning weather, such consoling reflections as these were far from Robert's mind. King Henry would clearly have to delay his journey until he could restore his position among his own vassals; meanwhile the Norman army was once more united and it seemed a pity not to take full advantage of the fact. The time had come for the Duke of Apulia and the Prince of Capua to turn their combined attention towards Salerno, where Prince Gisulf was growing daily more insufferable. Knowledge of his powerlessness against his detested brother-in-law had only increased his tendency to arrogance and bluster. His behaviour had alienated his allies one by one; and his few remaining friends—including Abbot Desiderius and even the Pope, who had no wish to see his last South Italian supporter swallowed up—had vainly begged him, in his own interest, to show a little moderation. Eventually Sichelgaita herself, knowing that Robert's patience could not be much longer restrained, made a final attempt to bring her brother to his senses; but Amatus— admittedly a biased reporter where Gisulf is concerned—writes that the Prince merely flew into one of his rages and warned his sister that she would soon find herself in widow's weeds.

It was his last chance, and he had thrown it away. In the early summer of 1076 Norman tents sprang up before the walls of the city and a Norman fleet drew up in line across the harbour-mouth. The siege of Salerno had begun.

Gisulf's position was hopeless from the outset. In mediaeval siege warfare the besieged normally put their faith in one or more of three possibilities. They might be saved by a relief force despatched by a foreign ally; they might hold out until such moment as the besiegers were forced, through shortage of food or time, to give up the attempt and take themselves off elsewhere; or they might themselves stage a break-out and defeat the enemy in pitched battle. But at Salerno in 1076 there was no chance of any of these. All the other Lombard states of South Italy had already been absorbed by the Normans, and Gisulf had long ago alienated his Italian neighbours. Only the Pope retained some sympathy for him; but the Pope had no army, and even if he had he would not have dreamed of setting himself up against the Normans at such a moment. The second possibility was equally remote, since the surrounding land was rich and fertile—besides, the Norman army was being contin- uously revictualled by its own fleet. Finally, there was no hope of a successful *sortie*. The besieging force contained not only the most experienced and highly-trained Norman troops in the whole penin- sula; it also comprised important contingents of Apulian and Cala- brian Greeks and of Saracens from Sicily—the latter henceforth to form an integral part of the Guiscard's army in all his operations. Faced with such a host, the Salernitan soldiery was overwhelmingly outnumbered; and before long it was also starving.

For years Gisulf had been one of the most hated figures in South Italy; but it was only now, in the last disastrous year of his power, that he revealed the full blackness of his character. Foreseeing the Norman attack some time in advance, he had ordered every inhabit- ant of Salerno to lay in a two-year stock of provisions, on pain of expulsion from the city. It was not an oustandingly sagacious move —anyone could have seen that if Gisulf were to persist in his rabid anti-Norman policy, such an attack was inevitable—but it should at least have spared Salerno any problems about food once the siege had begun. Instead, soon after the enemy had taken up their posi- tions under the walls, the Prince seized one-third of every house- hold's supply for his own granaries. Later, finding even this in- sufficient, he sent his men round the city requisitioning what little remained. The result was famine. At first, Amatus tells us, the citizens ate their horses, dogs and cats; but soon these too were gone. As winter approached, the death-rate steadily increased. Gisulf opened his granary, but his motives seem to have been mercenary rather than humanitarian, since—once again according to Amatus— measures of wheat bought for three bezants were soon being offered for resale at forty-four. Emaciated corpses lay where they had fallen in the streets, 'but the Prince did not spare them so much as a glance, passing cheerfully by just as if he were not to blame.' Few people complained, for it was universally known that complaints were punished by blinding or by one or more of Gisulf's favourite forms of amputation. If his people were to die anyway, it was better to do so quietly.

In such conditions prolonged resistance was impossible. Salerno held out for some six months. Then, on 13 December 1076 through treason from within, the gates of the city were opened. The under-nourished garrison, probably only too pleased to see an end to its sufferings, capitulated without a fight; and the last of the great Lombard principalities of South Italy was no more. Gisulf and one of his brothers, who had clearly had no difficulty in keeping up their own strength, retreated with a few followers to the citadel—whose ruins, inaccurately known as the Castello Normanno, still dominate the city from the north-western heights. There they held out till May 1077, but at last they too had to submit.

Robert was not prepared to negotiate terms. He had decided that henceforth Salerno should be his capital. Here was the greatest and most populous Italian city south of Rome, a proud principality for two hundred years and seat of Europe's most renowned school of medicine for longer still. He would restore its ancient glory and usher in a new period of power and magnificence, to be symbolised by the superb cathedral which he was even now planning to build. He therefore demanded, quite simply, the territorial possessions *in toto* of the Prince of Salerno and of his two brothers, Landulf and Gaimar—and one thing more besides. Among Salerno's most treasured relics was one of St Matthew's teeth, a holy if unattractive object which the Duke of Apulia had long coveted and which he knew Gisulf to have kept with him in the citadel. This too he now ordered the Prince to surrender; but the desiccated fang which Gisulf, faithless to the last, now forwarded to his conqueror, reverently wrapped in a silken cloth, was the former property not of the Evangelist but of a recently-deceased Jew of the city. It was a clumsy deception. Robert at once sent for a priest who had been familiar with the original relic and who now unhesitatingly pro-claimed his new acquisition as spurious. A message was returned to Gisulf forthwith: if the genuine tooth were not despatched by the following day, every one of his own would be forfeit. There were no more prevarications. We can only hope, as we shuffle through the cathedral treasuries of Europe, that all the other relics presented for our veneration have been as scrupulously authenti-cated.

When Gisulf left Salerno he rode straight to Capua. Robert

Guiscard had treated him with his usual generosity, giving him not only his freedom but also money, horses and pack-animals with which to make the best of it; but the Prince's temper was not so easily assuaged. He now hoped to undermine the Norman unity that had been his undoing by sowing new dissension between the two leaders. He was disappointed. Richard of Capua in no way resented the fact that Salerno had passed into the domains of the Duke of Apulia; this had been understood from the beginning. Richard was not even particularly interested in Salerno. What he wanted was Naples—the one city, tightly wedged between his territories and Robert Guiscard's, that had somehow managed to maintain its independence. Robert had promised, in return for his assistance against Gisulf, to help him besiege it; and the Apulian fleet had indeed already arrived off the coast and started the usual blockade. The Prince of Capua was, in short, well satisfied with the alliance, and he gave his visitor short shrift. Gisulf had no alternative but to continue his journey north-west to his last remaining friend, the Pope.

Gregory VII was still away in Tuscany, where he had achieved the greatest—indeed almost the only—triumph of his unhappy pontificate. His sentence of excommunication against Henry had been more successful than even he had dared to hope. The German princes, meeting at Tribur in October 1076, had agreed to give their King a year and a day from the date of his sentence in which to obtain papal absolution. They had already called a diet at Augsburg for the following February. If by the 22nd of that month the ban had not been lifted, they would formally renounce their allegiance and elect another King in his place. Henry could only bow to their decision. From his point of view it might have been worse. It called, quite simply, for his own abject self-abasement before the Pope. If this was to be the price of his kingdom, he was ready to pay it. Fortunately there was still one alpine pass—the Mont-Cenis—unblocked by snow. Crossing it in the depth of winter with his wife and baby son, he hastened through Lombardy and at last found the Pope at the fortress of Canossa, where he was staying as guest of his friend the Countess Matilda pending the arrival of an escort to conduct him to Augsburg. For three days the King waited as a humble penitent for an audience, while Gregory—perhaps uncertain of what to do for the best but doubtless savouring every instant of his adversary's discomfiture—refused him admission. Finally the Pope saw that he had no alternative but to relent and to give Henry the absolution he needed.

The story of Canossa, usually enlivened by an oleaginous illustration of the King, barefoot and dressed in sackcloth, shivering in the snow before the locked doors of the castle, has always been a favourite with the writers of children's history books, where it is apt to appear as an improving object-lesson in the vanity of temporal ambition. In fact Gregory's triumph was empty and ephemeral, and Henry knew it. His humiliation had nothing to do with repentance. It was a cold-blooded political manœuvre which was necessary to secure his crown, and he had no intention of keeping his promises after they had served their purpose. The Pope, too, can have had few delusions about the King's sincerity. Had his Christian conscience permitted him to withhold absolution he would doubtless have been only too happy to do so. As it was, he had won an unquestionable moral victory; but of what use was a victory after which the vanquished returned unabashed to his kingdom, there to launch a bloody civil war against his still rebellious vassals, while the victor remained cooped up in a Tuscan castle, blocked from Germany by the savage hostility of the Lombard cities and powerless to intervene? His triumph had been sweet enough while it lasted, but he found the aftertaste singularly unpleasant.

Not until September did the Pope return to Rome. As usual, bad news awaited him. First there was Gisulf, to tell him of the fall of Salerno. Next came grave reports from Naples, where Richard's army and Robert's navy were mercilessly maintaining their siege. More serious still was the situation to the east, where two Norman armies, under the Guiscard's nephew Robert of Loritello and Richard's son Jordan, were pressing ever deeper into the Church lands of the Abruzzi. But the worst shock of all was still to come. On 19 December the Duke of Apulia attacked Benevento. The Pope was outraged. Technically, the town had been papal territory since the days of Charlemagne, whose gift had been confirmed when the Beneventans had ousted their worthless rulers and voluntarily

placed themselves under the protection of Gregory's old master Leo
IX twenty-seven years before. Since then it had become the principal
bastion of the Papacy in South Italy, with its own papal palace
where he himself had held court. This unprovoked attack was far
worse than a renewed declaration of war; it was a gratuitous
insult to the throne of St Peter itself.

And even that was not everything. Besides showing his contempt
for the Papacy Robert Guiscard, by laying siege to Benevento, was
holding the Pope's own sentence of excommunication up to ridicule.
That same sentence that had brought Henry IV, heir to the Roman
Empire of the West, cringing to Canossa less than a year before had
been directed against this upstart Norman brigand with no adverse
effect whatever. If anything, it seemed to have acted on him like a
tonic. Certainly the populations of Salerno, Naples, the Abruzzi—
for Robert of Loritello and his followers had all been implicitly
included in the ban—and now Benevento itself would be revising
their earlier opinions about the power and authority of the Church.
And they would be right. The Pope had no army, and apparently
no prestige either. There was only one thing he could do. Perhaps
the Guiscard and his odious compatriots had not heard him the first
time. On 3 March 1078 he excommunicated them again.

In normal conditions the new sentence would probably have
passed as unheeded as its predecessor, but the Pope had timed it
better than he knew. A few days after its official publication in Capua,
Prince Richard fell ill; a month later, after an eleventh-hour reconciliation with the Church, he was dead; and the whole pattern of
South Italian politics was changed overnight. Richard, like Robert
Guiscard, had been a vassal of the Pope, and his son Jordan saw at
once that there could be no question of succeeding to his father's
throne while he remained under sentence of excommunication.
Hastily calling off both the siege of Naples and his own operations
in the Abruzzi, he hastened to Rome to make his peace with his
suzerain and to assure him of his undying fidelity.

Robert Guiscard was not by nature a sentimental man, but the
news of his brother-in-law's death cannot have left him entirely
unmoved. The two had arrived from Normandy at the same time

over thirty years before, and their rise to power had been rapid. For as long as many of their subjects could remember they had together dominated the two great Norman communities of the South, building up the early settlements at Aversa and Melfi into the rich and powerful states they had now become. Like all good Norman barons, they had been at war for most of the time; but they had fought side by side as often as face to face, and if on occasion promises had been broken or friendship betrayed, that was all in the game—an integral part of life as they knew it. Neither bore any lasting grudge; each had a healthy respect for the capacities of the other; and for the past two years they had worked in a happy, easy partnership that was proving highly profitable to them both. The Guiscard was now sixty-two; for him Richard's death must have meant the passing of an era.

He himself felt his ambitions and energies undiminished; and plans for conquests more daring and far-flung than any he had yet undertaken were already beginning to crystallise in his mind. But he saw that for the moment he would have to draw in his horns. Young Jordan, by his ridiculous decision to go and grovel in Rome just as they were all doing so well, had destroyed the whole momentum of the Norman advance and made himself a willing tool of the Pope. What was to prevent Gregory from forcing him to march his army, now once more unemployed, to the relief of Benevento? It was not worth the risk. Robert gave his own troops the order to withdraw. Benevento would have to wait.

His fears were justified. At last the Pope had found an ally—and, what was more, an ally with an army—and he was determined to make full use of him. Barely three months after Richard's death, we find Gregory staying at Capua. He can have had no difficulty in imposing his formidable will on the young Prince, alone, inexperienced and pitifully conscious of his exposed position against an angry and predatory Duke of Apulia. Nor had the Pope yet performed that all-important investiture. Jordan may not have liked the proposals which Gregory now put to him, but he was poorly placed to argue.

Fortunately for them both, Robert Guiscard had bitterly antagonised all his principal vassals earlier in the year, when he had forced

216

them to meet the cost of the elaborate celebrations which had attended the wedding of one of his daughters to Hugh, son of the Marquis Azzo of Este. Such exactions were a recognised obligation of vassals in the feudal societies of the North; but to the Norman barons in Apulia, many of whom remembered the Guiscard's beginnings and considered him to be no whit superior in birth or breeding to themselves, his demands had seemed unpardonable arrogance. They paid up because they had no choice; but when Jordan, certainly at the Pope's instigation and probably at his expense, allowed himself to become the focus for a new revolt against the Duke of Apulia, they were ready to answer his call.

The revolt was well-organised and widespread, beginning in the autumn of 1078 simultaneously at several points in Calabria and Apulia and extending rapidly through all Robert Guiscard's mainland dominions. There is no need to trace it in detail. Rebellion was endemic in South Italy; Robert was never secure enough to prevent it altogether, never so weak that he could not deal with it effectively when it came. For this reason one insurrection tended to be very like another. Even the ring-leaders—men such as Abelard, Geoffrey of Conversano or Peter of Trani—changed little, thanks largely to Robert's lack of vindictiveness, between one outbreak and the next. On this occasion nine months sufficed for the Guiscard to reassert his authority to the point where he was able to bring Jordan—through that eternal mediator Desiderius—to a separate peace. Jordan had in fact taken suprisingly little active part in the rebellion he had launched; it may be that his heart was never really in it and that he soon regretted his easy submission to papal pressure. Robert was now able to concentrate on Apulia where, after a whirlwind campaign through the winter of 1078–79, not the least remarkable feature of which was the successful siege of Trani by Sichelgaita while her husband was occupied with Taranto, he soon mopped up the remaining rebels. By the following summer the task of pacification was complete.

Away in Rome, Pope Gregory had watched his hopes crumble. Ill fortune continued to dog him. He, who had devoted his entire life to the service of God, had in the seven years of his pontificate been blocked at every turn by the forces of iniquity. The renewed excommunication which he had hurled at Henry IV, now a very different figure from the grovelling penitent of Canossa, was proving a good deal less effective than the first. His threatened descent into Italy to claim the Imperial Crown could not, it seemed, be very much longer postponed. Once again the Papacy was in grave danger; and once again—since Jordan was clearly a broken reed—the key to the situation appeared to lie with Robert Guiscard. He, like Henry, was a double-excommunicate—except that in his case both sentences were running concurrently—but the fact had not prevented him from reimposing his authority wherever it had been called in question. He was now more firmly entrenched than ever. When, in the past, the Pope had considered trying to regain his allegiance, pride and his old fear of losing face had always held him back. He could not afford such scruples now. If he did not come to terms with the Duke of Apulia—and quickly—Henry IV would do so on his own account and Gregory would soon find himself a Pope without a throne. Already in March 1080 we find his tone softening slightly towards the Normans; at the Lenten Synod of that year he issued a further warning to all 'invaders and pillagers' of Church lands, but this time added a conciliatory note: that if any of these had just cause for complaint against the inhabitants of the territories concerned, they should lay the case before the local governors; and that if justice was still denied them they might themselves take steps to recover what was rightfully theirs—'not in a thieving manner, but in a spirit befitting a Christian'.

The Pope, for once, was trimming his sails. Some time during the spring he instructed Desiderius to begin serious negotiations with Robert Guiscard. They were successful; and on 29 June 1080 at Ceprano, the Duke of Apulia at last knelt before Gregory VII and swore his fealty for all those lands that he had previously held from Popes Nicholas and Alexander. The more recently—and questionably—acquired territories of Amalfi, Salerno and the March of Fermo were left in suspense for the time being, but this was not a point to worry Robert unduly: it was enough for him that Gregory should have implied, in the words of his investiture, his effective *de facto* recognition of the new conquests. The legal technicalities could be settled later. Meanwhile the meeting at Ceprano had been another diplomatic victory for the Guiscard, and both parties were well aware of the fact. Gregory must at last have understood how ill-advised he had been to stand on his dignity at Benevento seven years before, while his own position was still comparatively strong. But it was too late now for self-recriminations of that kind. He needed Robert's support, and he must pay the price demanded. It was his only hope if he were to survive the oncoming storm.

And indeed, as the Duke of Apulia laid his huge hands between those of his Pope and thunderously pledged his loyalty and allegiance, the clouds were gathering faster than either of them knew. Four days earlier, in the little town of Brixen—now Bressanone—just south of the Brenner Pass, Henry IV had presided over a great council of his German and Lombard bishops. There, by common consent, Gregory VII had once again been deposed; and Archbishop Guibert of Ravenna, under the title of Clement III, had been proclaimed Pope in his stead.

16

AGAINST BYZANTIUM

O wisest and most learned of all men. . . . Those who have conversed with you and know you well speak highly of your intelligence and of the piety which you show not only in your religious faith but in the management of all your affairs. You are reputed to be a man of great prudence and at the same time a lover of action, with a spirit at once simple and lively. Thus, both in your character and your habits, do I recognise myself in you; and so I offer you the cup of friendship. . . .

The Emperor Michael VII to
Robert Guiscard

To Robert Guiscard, riding south from Ceprano to his new capital at Salerno during those July days of 1080, life must have looked as rich and radiant as the countryside around him. All his domains were tranquil, all his enemies subdued. His Apulian and Calabrian vassals were licking their wounds. After their last outbreak he had dealt with them rather more harshly than usual; he expected no more trouble for the moment from that quarter. The Pope and the Prince of Capua were likewise on their best behaviour. Admittedly King Henry might soon be making his long-threatened appearance in Rome; but Robert was not afraid of King Henry, who by his very existence was already serving a most useful purpose in keeping the Pope in order. Anyway the Duke's recent oath to Gregory did not oblige him to sit around twiddling his thumbs and waiting for a German army that might never come. He had more important things to do; and at sixty-four he could not afford to waste time.

He had long dreamed—and over the past two years his dreams had gradually ripened into plans—of a great concerted Norman attack on the Byzantine Empire. The Greeks were his oldest and most persistent enemies. He had ousted them from Italy, but even now they had not given up the struggle. Any of his Apulian vassals contemplating revolt could always count on sympathy and support from Constantinople, while the Byzantine province of Illyria just across the Adriatic was the recognised gathering-place for all Norman and Lombard exiles from Italy—his incorrigible nephew Abelard now among them. This alone in Robert's eyes would more than justify a punitive campaign—but his real reasons lay deeper.

Virtually all the Duke's mainland possessions had been conquered from the Greeks, and were thus impregnated with the heady fragrance of Byzantine civilisation. As a result of this the Normans had suddenly found themselves surrounded by the language and religion, the art and architecture and all the other outward mani-festations of a culture more sophisticated and insistently pervasive than any other then known to Europe. Always acutely susceptible to foreign influences, they had not been slow to respond. In Apulia, where the population in general was overwhelmingly Lombard, both impact and response were less; but in Calabria, where the dominant cultural flavour had always been Greek, the Norman overlords had preserved nearly all the old administrative forms and customs and had generally been far more inclined to adopt Byzantine ways than to impose their own. After his investiture by Pope Nicholas with the Duchy of Calabria, Robert Guiscard had gone still further in this direction, deliberately presenting himself to his new subjects as successor to the Basileus, slavishly copying the imperial insignia on his own seals and even wearing, on formal occasions, careful models of the Emperor's own robes of state. It has not been unusual for peoples finding themselves in close proximity to the Greeks to develop, on the cultural level, a marked inferiority complex; it happened to the Romans and, later, to most of the Slavs; the Turks have not recovered from it to this day; and the Normans, even the invincible, confident Normans, were no exception. They knew only one remedy—conquest.

In the last decade Byzantium herself had sunk deeper and deeper into chaos. Around her frontiers her enemies—Hungarians and Russians to the North and West, Seljuk Turks to the South and East—maintained a relentless pressure; while, at her very heart, a succession of incompetent rulers and corrupt officials had brought her to the brink of political and economic collapse. Her ancient glory remained, but her greatness was gone. Never in her seven and a half centuries of history had her condition been more desperate than in the summer of 1080. Robert Guiscard, by a fortunate coincidence, had never been stronger. Constantinople lay, apparently powerless, before him. His army was in need of employment; so too was his fleet. Its novelty still fascinated him, but he was tired of using it for those interminable blockades. The time had come to cast it in a more active role and to find out just how much it could really do. Thirty-five years earlier he had arrived in Italy, the sixth son of an obscure and impoverished Norman knight. The throne of the Eastern Empire would make a fitting end to his career.

Events in Constantinople during the last few years had provided him, if not with an adequate reason for intervention, at least with an excuse. When, in the early summer of 1073, the Emperor Michael had appealed to the Pope for aid against the infidel, he had not thought it necessary to add that he was already in correspondence with the Duke of Apulia. He had in fact written Robert a letter some months before, couched in a style which, if typically Byzantine in all its verbose convolutions, is at least refreshingly devoid of false modesty. Other princes, the Emperor explained, counted themselves sufficiently honoured if they merely received occasional assurances of his peaceful intentions towards them; but the Duke, whom he knew to be similarly endowed with deep religious faith, must not be surprised to find himself singled out for a greater token of imperial regard. What better token could there be than a military alliance, sealed by a loving marriage? He therefore proposed that Robert, after a seemly pause for self-congratulation, should forthwith take upon himself all the enviable duties of an ally of the Empire—defending its frontiers, protecting its vassals and battling ceaselessly with its enemies. In return, one of his daughters would be received with all honour at Constantinople and given to the Emperor's own brother as his bride.

The Guiscard must on the whole have been gratified to receive the letter. Despite its tone, which he probably found more amusing than offensive, it was a further testimonial to his growing reputation. Even with Byzantium in its present plight, imperial marriages of the kind that Michael was now proposing were not carelessly undertaken. On the other hand, he cordially disliked the Greeks— he always had—and he saw no reason to involve himself with them unnecessarily. He therefore sent no reply. The Emperor, clearly astonished at such a display of indifference, tried again. This time his manner was a good deal less patronising; he even resorted to flattery, and actually went so far as to compare the Duke of Apulia with himself. There followed a prolonged encomium of his brother who was, it appeared, outstanding in his wisdom and virtue and 'so handsome, if one must talk of such qualities, that he might be a statue of the Empire itself', born in the purple and thus in every respect an ideal bridegroom for one—the most beautiful, he was now careful to specify—of Robert's daughters.

As a letter it was even more entertaining than its predecessor; but still the Guiscard refused to answer. Only when a third missive arrived towards the end of 1074 did he begin to show interest. Michael had meanwhile improved his proposal. He now suggested his young son Constantine as the Duke's prospective son-in-law, and went on to offer Robert no less than forty-four high Byzantine honours for distribution among his family and friends, carrying with them a total annual grant of two hundred pounds in gold. Robert hesitated no longer. The imperial succession was always a tricky business in Constantinople; there was however no doubt that the son, born in the purple,[1] of the ruling Emperor had a better chance than most, and the opportunity of seeing his own daughter on the throne of Byzantium was not one that he was prepared to miss. The offer of the honours, which would effectively put all his principal lieutenants in receipt of open bribes from Constantinople, was probably less welcome; but it was a risk worth taking. He accepted Michael's proposal, and shortly afterwards the unhappy bride-to-be was bundled off to Constantinople, there to pursue her studies in the imperial *gynoecoeum* until her fiancé should be of marriageable age. Anna Comnena, writing some years later, rather bitchily suggests[2] that young Helena—she had been re-baptised

---

[1] i.e. Born to an Emperor during his reign. To be born in the purple (*porphyrogenitus*) was a far greater distinction than that of primogeniture.
[2] *Alexiad*, I, 12.

with the Greek name on being received into the Orthodox Church soon after her arrival—proved to be considerably less well-favoured than the Emperor had hoped, and that her intended husband was as terrified of the thought of marriage to her 'as a baby is of a bogeyman'. Anna was herself subsequently betrothed to Constantine, with whom she was to fall passionately in love; she can therefore hardly be considered an impartial judge. But we are left, none the less, with an uncomfortable suspicion that Helena had inherited the fearsome build of her parents.

For the next few years Robert Guiscard, busy in Italy, could give little serious thought to Byzantine affairs. Then, in 1078, Michael VII was in his turn overthrown. More fortunate than his predecessor, he was allowed to retire unharmed to a monastery—a welcome translation from his point of view, since the cloister suited his bookish temperament far better than the palace had ever done; within a few years, through sheer ability, he rose to become Archbishop of Ephesus. His dethronement, however, put paid to the Norman alliance, and the unfortunate Helena found herself immured in a convent of her own with which she was, in all probability, rather less well pleased. Her father heard the news with mixed feelings. His immediate hopes of an imperial son-in-law had been dashed; on the other hand his daughter's former position and subsequent treatment gave him an admirable pretext for intervention. Unfortunately Jordan's revolt had broken out before he could take any effective steps; but by the summer of 1080, with order once again restored in his own dominions, he was able to begin preparations in earnest. As it happened, he had lost nothing by the delay. In Constantinople the situation was going from bad to worse. Michael's successor, the elderly general Nicephorus Botaneiates, had failed miserably to halt the decline, and the whole Empire was now in a turmoil of civil war, with the various provincial military commanders in desperate competition for supreme control. Meanwhile the Turks, by playing one off against the other, were rapidly building up their own position, and had recently established the so-called Sultanate of Rum, embracing nearly the whole of Asia Minor. In such conditions it looked as though a well-planned Norman offensive would have excellent chances of success.

He collected all, under age and over age, from all over Lombardy and Apulia, and pressed them into his service. There you could see children and boys and pitiable old men who had never, even in their dreams, seen a weapon; but were now clad in breastplates, carrying shields and drawing their bows most unskilfully and clumsily, and usually falling on their faces when ordered to march. . . . This behaviour of Robert's was a counterpart of Herod's madness, or even worse; for the latter only vented his rage on babes, whilst Robert did so against boys and old men.[1]

Thus Anna Comnena describes the Guiscard's preparations for the campaign; and all through the autumn and winter the work went on. The fleet was refitted, the army increased in numbers—though not as drastically as Anna suggests—and provided with new weapons and equipment. Pope Gregory, obviously remembering his humiliating failure to answer Michael's appeal seven years before, gave it his blessing and sent instructions to all the South Italian bishops to assist the enterprise in whatever way they could. In a mighty effort to stir up enthusiasm among his Greek subjects, Robert had even managed to produce a disreputable and transparently bogus Orthodox monk, who appeared in Salerno at the height of the preparations and gave himself out to be none other than the Emperor Michael in person, escaped from his monastery and trusting in his gallant Norman allies to replace him on his rightful throne. Nobody believed him much; but the Guiscard, professing to be entirely convinced by his claims, persisted in treating him with exaggerated deference throughout the months that followed.

Then, in December, Robert decided to send an ambassador to Constantinople. A certain Count Radulf was accordingly despatched, with instructions to demand satisfaction from Botaneiates for the treatment accorded to the Lady Helena and, if possible, to win the adherence of the large number of Normans who were at that time in the imperial service. His mission was not a success. Whilst in the city he fell under the spell of the most brilliant of all the young Byzantine generals and the one outstanding politician of his generation—Alexius Comnenus, at that time Grand Domestic and Commander of the Armies of the West; and at some point on his homeward journey he heard the news that he had probably been

[1] *The Alexiad*, I, 14 (tr. Dawes).

expecting: Alexius had forced the unhappy old Botaneiates to abdicate, packed him off uncomplaining¹ to a monastery, and on Easter Day 1081 had himself been crowned Emperor.

Radulf found his master at Brindisi. The Guiscard was not in a good temper. Understandably fearful lest he be left defenceless against King Henry, Pope Gregory was repenting of his former attitude and making difficulties again. He had already persuaded Robert to leave him a few troops and was now trying to stop the whole enterprise. Robert had put his foot down. He felt himself in a fairly strong position. The Pope knew that he had recently received a suggestion from Henry, similar to that made by Michael a few years before, for a marriage alliance between Henry's son Conrad and another of the Guiscard's daughters; he would not risk driving his vassal into the enemy camp by a further excommunication. Neither, however, would he take no for an answer; and Robert was still being pestered to draw back just at the time when he needed all his energy and concentration for the coming campaign.

Radulf's report was not calculated to improve matters. Now that the usurper Botaneiates had himself been overthrown there was, he pointed out, no longer any reason for the expedition. The new Emperor, Alexius, had been a good friend of Michael and had in fact long served as guardian to young Constantine, to whom he had even offered a share in his government. Alexius himself wanted nothing but friendship with the Normans; as for the Lady Helena, she would be as safe with him as if she were back in Salerno. Moreover, Radulf went on, it was his duty to inform his master that he had with his own eyes seen the ex-Emperor in his monastery; he thus had proof positive that the pretender to the throne whom Robert kept at his side and by whose claims he set so much store was in fact a cheat and an impostor. Robert had only to send him packing and make overtures of peace and friendship to Alexius. Then Helena might still marry Constantine or, alternatively, return to the bosom of her family; much bloodshed might be averted; and the army and navy could disperse to their homes.

¹ Some time afterwards Botaneiates was asked by an old acquaintance whether he minded the change in his fortunes. He replied: 'Abstinence from meat is the only thing that bothers me: for the rest I care very little.' (*The Alexiad*, III, 1.)

Robert Guiscard was famous for the violence of his rages; and
his fury with the ingenuous Radulf was fearful to behold. No news
could conceivably have been more unwelcome to him. The last
thing he wanted now was peace with Constantinople. His superbly
equipped expeditionary force was lying at Brindisi and Otranto
ready to sail; the grandest prize in Europe lay within his grasp. He
was no longer remotely interested in the imperial marriage, which,
even it it were to take place, would no longer be so imperial anyway.
Still less did he want his daughter back in Italy—he had six others,
and she was serving a much more useful purpose where she was.
So far as he was concerned the disreputable pretender was still
Michael—though it was a pity that he was not a better actor—and
Michael was still the legitimate Emperor. The only important thing
now was to embark before Alexius cut the ground from under his
feet by returning Helena to him or—worse still—King Henry's
appearance in Rome made his departure impossible. Fortunately he
had already despatched his eldest son Bohemund with an advance
party across the Adriatic. The sooner he could join them the better.

Bohemund was now twenty-seven. He was cast in his father's
mould, with broad shoulders surmounting an immense barrel-chest,
a fresh complexion and thick fair hair which he kept close-cropped,
after the fashion of the younger generation of his compatriots. The
most striking thing about him, however, was his enormous height,
which a slight stoop did nothing to conceal. It was another inheritance from his father: Normans and Greeks were inclined to be
stocky, and when Robert was not around Bohemund seemed to
tower above all the other knights and their associates. Of his early
life we know little. He had been a child of four when the Guiscard
had cast off his mother Alberada, but she had brought him up as
everything that a Norman knight should be, and he had fought
loyally and courageously—if without any conspicuous successes—
for his father during the 1079 insurrection. Now that he had been
given his first independent command, he was resolved to show his
true worth. He had already captured the port of Valona, immediately
opposite the heel of Apulia where the straits of Otranto are at their
narrowest, whose sheltered bay would provide a superb natural
bridgehead for the main body of the fleet when it arrived. From

there he had headed south to Corfu; but a preliminary attack on the island had shown him that the local garrison would be more than a match for his small force, and he had wisely withdrawn to Butrinto where he was now awaiting his father's arrival.

The great fleet sailed in the second half of May 1081. It carried, apart from the ships' crews, about thirteen hundred Norman knights supported by a large body of Saracens, some rather dubious Greeks and an unknown quantity of heterogeneous foot-soldiers who must certainly have numbered several thousand. At Valona it was joined by a few Ragusan vessels—the Ragusans, like so many other Balkan peoples, were always glad of the opportunity for a crack at the Byzantines—and then moved slowly down the coast to Corfu where the garrison, seeing now that resistance was useless, surrendered almost at once. Having thus assured his bridgehead, and with it the free passage of reinforcements from Italy, the Guiscard could begin fighting in earnest. His first target was Durazzo—the old Roman Dyrrachium—capital and chief port of Illyria, from which the eight-hundred-year-old Via Egnatia ran east across the Balkan peninsula, through Macedonia and Thrace to Constantinople itself.

But soon it became clear that progress was not going to be so easy. Heading northward round the Acroceraunian promontory—respectfully avoided by the ancients as the seat from which Jupiter Fulminans was wont to launch his thunderbolts—the Norman fleet was overtaken by one of those sudden tempests to which the Eastern Mediterranean is so dramatically subject in the summer months. Several of the vessels were lost, and no sooner had the battered remainder hove to, a few days later, in the roadstead off Durazzo than they saw, looming on the northern horizon, a long and menacing line of high-masted ships. By their curious rig, half-way between the Greek and the Italian, they were all too easily identifiable as Venetians. Their city was not only technically part of the Byzantine Empire, it also had important commercial links with Constantinople; and to protect both these and their manifold other trading interests the Venetians had appointed themselves keepers of the peace throughout the Adriatic and beyond. It was lucky for the Greeks that they had, for the Byzantine navy had been allowed to deteriorate to an even more dangerous degree than the army and no longer possessed any means of itself enforcing imperial authority. That was why Alexius, hearing of the Apulian landings on his coast, had sent the Doge an urgent appeal which he knew would not go unheeded. The Venetians had arrived only just in time, but under the pretext of negotiations they managed to obtain from the Normans a short period of grace during which they prepared for the coming battle. Then, under cover of darkness, they bore down upon the Apulian fleet.

The Guiscard's men fought with courage and determination, but their inexperience of naval warfare betrayed them. The Venetians had taken advantage of the preliminary truce to adopt the old Byzantine trick, used by Belisarius at Palermo five and a half centuries before, of hoisting manned dinghies to the mastheads, from which their soldiers could shoot down on to the enemy below; they had also apparently learned the old Byzantine secret of Greek fire, since Malaterra writes of how 'they blew that fire, which is called Greek and is not extinguished by water, through submerged pipes, and thus cunningly burned one of our ships under the very waves of the sea'. Faced with such tactics, the Normans found themselves at a hopeless disadvantage. After a long battle which cost them dear in ships and men, their line was shattered and the Venetians were able to beat their way to safety in the harbour of Durazzo.

But it took more than this to discourage the Duke of Apulia, who now settled down to besiege the city. The Emperor had put George Palaeologus, his own brother-in-law and one of the bravest of his generals, in personal command of the garrison with instructions to keep the Guiscard occupied while he himself raised an army against the invaders; and the garrison, knowing that relief was on the way, fought stoutly. All summer long the siege continued, enlivened by frequent sorties by the defenders—in one of which Palaeologus fought magnificently throughout a sweltering day with an arrow-head embedded in his skull. Then, on 15 October, the Byzantine army appeared, the Emperor Alexius himself riding at its head.

Alexius Comnenus came of an old and distinguished Byzantine family which had already produced one Emperor—his uncle, Isaac I—and was proud of its long military traditions. When, in his thirty-

third year, he so brilliantly manœuvred his own way to the throne, he
already had well over a decade's experience in the field, fighting in
Epirus and Thrace as well as nearer his home in Asia Minor. In
particular he had gained a useful foretaste of his enemy's methods.
Among the raffish crowd of Normans who had drifted into Byzantine
service at that time was an extraordinary adventurer called Roussel
of Bailleul. Roussel's military record was not unblemished, since
already in 1071 at Mantzikert, seeing that the Greek position was
hopeless, he had refused to lead his men into battle; but he had
somehow charmed his way back into imperial favour—seasoned
soldiers were hard to find—and had soon afterwards been sent
by the Emperor Michael to lead a mixed force of Norman and
Frankish cavalry against Turkish marauders in Anatolia. Once deep
in enemy-held territory he had again betrayed his trust and, with his
three hundred loyal followers, set up a self-declared independent
Norman state on the South Italian pattern. It had not lasted long—
the Emperor easily persuaded the Seljuks themselves to liquidate it,
in return for the formal cession of territories they already held—
but Roussel had managed to escape, and Alexius had been sent to
hunt him down. He had found him in Amasea, where the outlaw
had cheerfully set himself up as governor and had so endeared himself to the local population that they agreed to his removal only on
being told, untruthfully, by Alexius that he had been blinded. A
period of imprisonment at Constantinople had followed, but in 1077,
with the army of Botaneiates marching on the capital, the desperate
Michael had given his captive one more chance; and Roussel, now
reinvested with a new regiment, had inflicted a crushing defeat on
the rebels before turning traitor for the third time and declaring for
the usurper.

On their way from Amasea to Constantinople Alexius had in his
turn fallen victim to Roussel's fascination; and later, when the
Norman was starving in prison, he had even secretly brought him
food. But he had also learnt never to underestimate Norman
intelligence, cunning or military skill. Roussel had probably often
spoken to him of Robert Guiscard, in whose army he had formerly
served; and from the day when the spies first warned him of Robert's
intentions Alexius had known that it would take all the Empire's

remaining strength to survive the expected onslaught. He had worked hard and fast to raise an adequate defence force, and as far as numbers were concerned he had been remarkably successful. But too many of his followers were insufficiently trained or of doubtful loyalty, and it cannot have been with any great feelings of confidence that he led them through the tortuous Macedonian passes and out on to the plain before Durazzo.

The first problem was one of strategy. Should the Byzantine army attempt to besiege the Normans in their own camp, or should they draw them out into a pitched battle? Certain of his advisers favoured the former course, but Alexius decided to fight. Winter would soon be approaching and he simply could not trust his men through a protracted siege. On 18 October, three days after his arrival, he attacked. By this time Robert Guiscard had moved a little to the north of the city and had drawn up his own battle-line, stretching inward from the coast and facing towards Durazzo. He himself had assumed command of the centre, with Sichelgaita, fully armed and mailed, beside him and Bohemund on his left, inland, flank.

As was the invariable rule when the Emperor took the field in person, his imperial Varangian bodyguard was present in strength. At this time it consisted largely of Englishmen, Anglo-Saxons who had left their country in disgust after Hastings and taken service with Byzantium. Many of them had been waiting fifteen years for the chance of avenging themselves on the detested Normans, and they attacked with all the strength and vigour of which they were capable. They fought on foot, since the huge two-handed axes that were their principal weapon were far too heavy to be wielded from the saddle. Swinging these round their heads and then slamming them at horses and riders alike, they struck terror in the hearts of the Apulian knights, few of whom had ever come across a line of foot-soldiers who did not at once break in the face of a charge of cavalry. The horses too soon began to panic, and before long the Norman right had turned in confusion, many galloping straight into the sea to escape what seemed to them certain massacre.

But now, if contemporary reports are to be believed, the day was saved by Sichelgaita. The story is perhaps best told in the words of Anna Comnena:

Directly Gaita, Robert's wife (who was riding at his side and was a second Pallas, if not an Athene) saw these soldiers running away, she looked fiercely after them and in a very powerful voice called out to them in her own language an equivalent to Homer's words 'How far will ye flee? Stand, and quit you like men!' And when she saw that they continued to run, she grasped a long spear and at full gallop rushed after the fugitives; and on seeing this they recovered themselves and returned to the fight.[1]

Now, too, Bohemund's left flank had wheeled to the rescue, with a detachment of cross-bowmen against whom the Varangians, unable to approach within axe-range, found themselves defenceless. Having advanced too far beyond the main body of the Greek army, they were unable to retire to safety and could only fight where they stood. At last the few exhausted Englishmen remaining alive turned and sought refuge in a nearby chapel of the Archangel Michael; but the Apulians immediately set it on fire—they were a long way now from Monte Gargano—and the last of the Varangians perished in the flames.

Meanwhile, in the centre, the Emperor was still fighting bravely; but the cream of the Byzantine army had been destroyed at Mantzikert, and the motley collection of barbarian mercenaries on whom he now had to rely possessed, as he had feared, neither the discipline nor the devotion to prevail against the Normans of Apulia. A sortie from Durazzo under George Palaeologus had failed to save the situation, and to make matters worse Alexius suddenly saw that he had been betrayed by his vassal, the Serbian King Constantine Bodin of Zeta, and by a whole regiment of Turkish auxiliaries of whom he had had high hopes. His last chance of victory was gone; his army was everywhere in full retreat. He turned from the field. Cut off from his men, weak from exhaustion and loss of blood and in considerable pain from a wound on his forehead, he rode slowly and without escort back over the mountains to Ochrid, where he might recover and regroup what he could of his shattered forces.

After this victory the fall of Durazzo could only be a question of time; but despite the fact that the city was now without a governor —George Palaeologus having been unable to re-enter it quickly enough after his sortie—it somehow held out for another four

[1] *The Alexiad*, IV, 6 (tr. Dawes).

months. Not till 21 February 1082 were the Apulians able to burst
open the gates, and then only through the treachery of a Venetian
resident who, according to Malaterra, demanded as his reward the
hand of one of Robert's nieces in marriage. But, from Durazzo on,
the tempo of conquest quickened; the local populations, aware of
their Emperor's defeat and the absence of any nearby imperial army
to which they could look for relief or salvation—many of them felt
no particular loyalty to Byzantium in any case—offered no resistance
to the advancing Normans; and within a few weeks the whole of
Illyria was in the Guiscard's hands. He then marched east to Kastoria,
which also surrendered instantly. It was the most important town
he had taken since leaving Durazzo; its capitulation seemed a good
augury for the future—and a still better one when the garrison, to
whose charge it had been personally consigned by the Emperor,
was found to consist of three hundred more of the Varangian
Guard. If not even the crack troops of the Empire were any longer
prepared to oppose the Norman advance, then surely Constantinople
was as good as won.

But the following April, while Robert Guiscard was still at
Kastoria, messengers reached him from Italy. All over the peninsula,
they reported, Alexius's agents had been busy. Once again Apulia
and Calabria were up in arms, and much of Campania as well. They
also brought a letter from Pope Gregory. Henry was at his gates.
The Duke's presence was urgently required at Rome.

17

FROM ROME TO VENOSA

Remember therefore the holy Roman Church your Mother, who loves
you above all other Princes and has singled you out for her special trust.
Remember, for her you have sworn an oath; and in what you have sworn
—that which, even had you not done so, would still be your Christian
duty to perform—you will not fail. For you are not unaware of how much
strife has been stirred up against the Church by Henry, the so-called king,
and of how urgently she needs your aid. Wherefore act now; for just as
the son will desire to fight against iniquity, so will the Church his Mother
be grateful for his devotion and succour.

We hesitate to place on this letter our leaden seal, lest it fall into the
hands of our enemies and they turn it to fraudulent use.

Gregory VII's letter to Robert Guiscard, 1082

ROBERT GUISCARD had launched his Byzantine expedition only
just in time. Within a week of his departure from Otranto in 1081
Henry IV had appeared on the outskirts of Rome, the new anti-
Pope Clement in his train. Fortunately for Gregory, he had underestimated the degree of resistance that he would encounter and had
brought very few troops with him; so that when, somewhat to his
surprise, he found that the Romans intended to remain loyal to their
own Pontiff, he had had no option but to retire into Lombardy. The
following spring, however, he made a second attempt; and although
it too was to end in failure, by this time the mood in South Italy had
changed. Henry's continued successes in Germany, where he had
now eliminated virtually all serious opposition, and in Lombardy
where he personified the most militant forces of separatism and
reaction, had increased his prestige everywhere; and with Robert
Guiscard already far away and—if the reports were to be believed—
advancing steadily in the opposite direction, there was a growing

feeling among Normans, Italians and Lombards alike that their future lay with the Western Empire. Jordan of Capua was among the first to transfer his allegiance; shrugging off the inevitable excommunication, he now swore fealty to Henry and received from him in return a formal investiture of his principality; and most of the minor Campanian barons followed suit. So, even, did Abbot Desiderius of Monte Cassino who, as the years wore on, was beginning to show an alarming deterioration of moral fibre that boded ill for the future. Away in Apulia poor Roger Borsa, to whom the Guiscard had entrusted the care of his mainland dominions during his absence, was powerless to reassert his father's authority—particularly since Abelard and Herman and their ever-restless friends, many of whom had taken advantage of the changed circumstances to return from exile, were now once again in full revolt.

When, in April 1082—less than a year after his departure—all this news reached the Duke of Apulia at Kastoria, he saw that he had no time to lose. Leaving the command of the expedition to Bohemund, and swearing by the soul of his father Tancred to remain unbathed and unshaven until he could return to Greece, he hurried back with a small escort to the coast where his ships were waiting and crossed at once to Otranto; from there, pausing only to collect what troops he could from Roger Borsa, he made for Rome. He arrived to find the immediate danger past; Henry had withdrawn again from the city—this time to Tuscany, there to ravage the estates of the Pope's staunchest ally, the Countess Matilda. Though he had left his anti-Pope Clement at Tivoli with a regiment of Germans, Clement would give no serious trouble while his protector was away. The Guiscard was able to return to Apulia and put his own house in order.

But Rome was not to be left in peace for long. At the beginning of 1083 Henry reappeared with a larger army than on either of the previous occasions and settled down in earnest to besiege the Leonine City.[1] It was his third attempt, and it was successful. The defenders had grown tired of these annual attacks, and their loyalty had been dangerously undermined by Byzantine bribes, distributed both directly by Alexius's agents within the city and indirectly

[1] See p. 159 n.

by Henry's. Through the spring and early summer they held out, but on 2 June a mixed party of Milanese and Saxons scaled the walls, overcame the guards and finally took possession of one of the towers. Within an hour or two Henry's soldiers had swept into the city and were fighting a furious battle in and around St Peter's. Pope Gregory, however, had been too quick for them. He had no intention of surrendering. Hurrying to the Castel Sant' Angelo, he barricaded himself in and prepared for a new siege.

It would have been easy now for Henry to proceed to his imperial coronation, which anti-Pope Clement would have been only too happy to perform; but he still held only the Leonine City, on the right bank of the Tiber. The rest of Rome remained faithful to Gregory, and he knew that such a ceremony would never be generally accepted while the true Pope remained alive and in the capital. Could not the Romans themselves, who surely stood to gain everything from a reconciliation, somehow mediate between himself and the Pope and so bring about a compromise? It was their duty to try, he told them; and try they did. But again Henry had underestimated. Gregory was not to be moved an inch. Utterly convinced of the justice of his cause and consequently of divine support, he seems to have been equally certain that, sooner or later, he would prevail. If Henry wanted his coronation, he must remember—and observe— the oath he had sworn at Canossa. A general synod would be called the following November and would doubtless discuss the matter further. Meanwhile there was nothing more to be said. Silently, with patience and dignity, he settled down in his stronghold to wait for the Duke of Apulia to come to his relief.

The Guiscard, however, showed no immediate sign of doing so. It was not altogether his fault. Throughout the autumn and winter of 1082 and the first half of 1083 he had been fully occupied with the rebels in Apulia; it was only on 10 June—a week after the imperial troops had entered the Leonine City—that he had recaptured the last stronghold, Canosa, from his nephew Herman and so brought the insurrection to an end. The campaign had been harder than he had expected—Byzantine money had obviously had a lot to do with it—and if he had not been able to appeal to his brother Roger to bring much-needed reinforcements over from Sicily, it would have continued a great deal longer than it did. As soon as it was safe for them to leave Apulia he and Roger had in fact set off in the direction of Rome for a short preliminary campaign against Jordan of Capua; but at this moment the Great Count was urgently recalled to Sicily with his men by a sudden emergency, and Robert, knowing that he had not the necessary forces to take on Henry single-handed, retired to prepare a major expedition for the following year. From his point of view there was plenty of time. His oath, sworn at Ceprano, bound him to render assistance to the Pope—and Popes apart, his own position in Italy would be seriously threatened if Henry, once crowned Emperor and supported by an obedient Clement III, were allowed to have his own way in South Italy. But Henry was at present back in Tuscany, wasting his energies in vain attempts to subdue the Countess Matilda; and his army, Robert knew, was small and not particularly efficient. In six months or so it should be possible for the Duke to get together a new army of his own which he could lead against the King of the Romans without any fear as to the outcome. Then at his leisure he could deliver the Pope—and, perhaps, name his own conditions. Meanwhile Gregory would just have to wait. Safely ensconced in the Castel Sant' Angelo, he seemed to be in no immediate danger. A few months' more discomfort—and even a little more humiliation—would do him no harm.

The projected synod was duly held in November. It proved a farce. The King had sworn that he would not prevent any of the hierarchy faithful to Gregory from attending; but as the appointed day drew near he saw that the Pope on his side had no intention of admitting any of those imperialist bishops whom he had excommunicated and that, in consequence, to keep the oath would be simply to play into his hands. Henry never allowed his promises to interfere with his policies. All Gregory's most fervent supporters, including the Archbishop of Lyons and the Bishops of Como and Lucca, found themselves barred from Rome; and a papal legate, the Cardinal-Bishop Odo of Ostia, was actually imprisoned. In vain did the furious Pope hurl fresh excommunications and anathemas from behind the walls of his fortress; Henry took no notice. The Synod ended, and such few bishops as had managed to attend dispersed to their sees; a ludicrous suggestion by some of the Roman nobles for a compromise, by which Gregory would not actually perform Henry's coronation but would pass him down the imperial diadem on a stick from the battlements of Sant' Angelo, met with the contempt it deserved. The stalemate continued.

And still Robert Guiscard failed to appear.

At the first approach of spring in the year 1084 Henry decided to force the issue. He would never be able to bring his inflexible adversary to terms as long as the Pope could look forward to eventual relief by Robert Guiscard. If, on the other hand, he could take the Normans by surprise while they were still unready for him, he might be able to prevent their ever reaching Rome. That should make Gregory much more amenable. Early in March, leaving only a small garrison in the Leonine City, he accordingly set off for Apulia with his army. He had not gone very far before he was overtaken by messengers from the capital. The Romans, it appeared, had at last grown tired of the struggle and had sent to tell him that they would offer no more resistance; their city was his for the taking.

To surrender at that precise moment to the imperial forces was an act of utter folly; and it sealed the fate, not only of Pope Gregory, but of Rome itself. Had Henry been allowed to continue his advance against the Duke of Apulia, he would either have been beaten by an overwhelmingly superior force or, more likely, would have retreated hastily to the North. In either event the Normans would have subsequently made short work of the German garrison remaining in Rome and would have entered the city as deliverers rather than as conquerors. By changing sides at a time when they knew that the most powerful ruler in Italy, if not in Europe, was preparing to march, the people of Rome made disaster inevitable. They were to pay dearly for their mistake, but they had only themselves to blame.

Hurrying back with all the speed his army could muster, Henry entered Rome in triumph on 21 March and—accompanied by his wife, the long-suffering Queen Bertha of Turin, and his anti-Pope Clement—took up residence in the Lateran. Three days later, on Palm Sunday, Pope Gregory was formally deposed by the Lombard

238

bishops, and Clement consecrated as his successor; and on Easter Day, 31 March, Henry and Bertha were crowned with the imperial crown in St Peter's. For Gregory the situation was now desperate. Parts of Rome still remained loyal to him—the Coelian and the Palatine, for example, both held by his nephew Rusticus, and the Tiber Island, burial-place of St Bartholomew, which remained in the faithful hands of the Pierleoni. The Capitol itself was also holding out. But all these strongholds were already under attack; unless help came quickly they would not last long. Where was Robert Guiscard? A group of the Pope's most trusted cardinals was sent south to find him at all costs and pass on his suzerain's last appeal.

When Robert heard of the Romans' surrender he needed no further persuading. His own future as well as the Pope's was at stake. Those long months of delay, however, had not been wasted, and it was with a formidable army—William of Apulia's estimate of six thousand horse and thirty thousand foot-soldiers may not be far out—that he set off for the capital at the beginning of May. Ahead of him, to give the Pope courage, he sent Abbot Desiderius; and at last, on 24 May 1084, he rode up the Via Latina and, roughly on the site of the present Piazza di Porta Capena, pitched his camp beneath the walls of Rome.

Henry had not waited for him. Desiderius—sitting, as always, firmly on the fence—had no sooner informed the Pope of Robert's impending arrival than he had gone straight to the Emperor with the same message; and his description of the size and strength of the Guiscard's new army had been more than enough to make up Henry's mind. Summoning a council of the leading citizens of Rome, he explained to them that his presence was urgently required in Lombardy. He would of course be back as soon as circumstances permitted; meanwhile, he trusted them to fight gallantly against all attackers and so to prove themselves worthy subjects of the Empire which bore their name. Then, three days before the Duke of Apulia appeared at the gates of the city, he fled with his wife and the greater part of his army, the terrified anti-Pope scurrying behind.

The Romans, already deeply regretting their change of heart two months before, were left in an impossible position. Having first traduced their Pope to the Emperor, they in their turn had found themselves betrayed. And now the presence of the Norman army on their very threshold seemed to paralyse them. It was clearly useless to try to withstand such an army, particularly with Gregory's supporters still so numerous within the city; at the same time, as if possessing some ghastly foreknowledge of what lay ahead, they could not bring themselves to open the gates. For three more days the Duke of Apulia waited in his camp, uncertain perhaps whether Henry's flight was genuine, and meanwhile laying careful plans with the Pope's representatives. Then, on the night of 27 May, under cover of darkness, he silently moved his army round to the north of the city. At dawn he attacked, and within minutes the first of his shock-troops had burst through the Flaminian Gate. They met with a stiff resistance: the whole area of the Campus Martius—that quarter lying immediately across the river from the Castel Sant' Angelo—became a blazing holocaust. But it was not long before the Normans had beaten the defenders back over the bridge, released the Pope from his fortress and borne him back in triumph through the smoking ruins to the Lateran.

For Robert Guiscard that day marked the pinnacle of his glory and his power. The year 1084 had already seen the two greatest potentates of Europe, the Emperors of the East and of the West, fleeing at his approach; it now saw him extend a gracious—if slightly bloodstained—hand to one of the most redoubtable Popes of the Middle Ages and raise him up once again to his rightful throne. At the High Mass of thanksgiving held to celebrate Gregory's deliverance, the mind of both Duke and Pontiff must have gone back to that distant day in 1053 when, on the plain of Civitate, the Hautevilles and their followers had defended against the forces of the Roman Church their right to remain in Italy. Thirty-one years later they had collected several more excommunications, but they had also saved Rome more than once. Not for the first time, the Pope must have been glad that their defence had proved so effective.

But his triumph was short-lived. Although Rome was already but a poor despoiled shadow of what it had once been, it yet remained richer and more populous than any other city in the centre or south of the peninsula, and to the Guiscard's men it offered possibilities of plunder on a scale such as few of them had ever

Cassino, then on to Benevento—where news awaited them that
Clement III had taken advantage of Gregory's departure to reoccupy
St Peter's—and so, finally, to Salerno. There the Pope was settled in
a palace befitting his dignity; and there, on 25 May 1085, he died.
He was buried in the south-east apse of the new cathedral—built,
according to the inscription which runs to this day across the
façade, by 'Duke Robert, greatest of conquerors, with his own
money'—which the Pope had consecrated only a few weeks before
and where his tomb may still be seen.

In spite of the discredit which he had unwittingly brought upon
the Papacy in his last years, the body of his achievement was greater
than he knew. He had gone a long way towards establishing papal
supremacy over the hierarchy of the Church—the practice of lay
investitures was rapidly losing ground and was to die out altogether
in the following century—and even if he had not won a similar
victory over the Empire, he had at least asserted his claims in such
a way that they could never again be ignored. The Church had shown
her teeth; future Emperors would defy her at their peril. And yet,
although he never relinquished his plans to return to Rome at the
head of an army and to regain his throne, Gregory died if not a
broken, at least a disappointed, disillusioned man; and his last
words—'I have loved righteousness and hated iniquity, therefore
I die in exile'—were a bitter valediction.

The previous autumn, with a new fleet of a hundred and fifty
ships, the Duke of Apulia had returned to Greece. Bereft of his
leadership, the Norman expeditionary force had suffered near-
disaster. For a year Bohemund had managed to maintain the
momentum and, after two important victories at Yanina and Arta,
had pressed the Byzantines back until all Macedonia and much of
Thessaly lay under his control; but in the spring of 1083 Alexius
outsmarted him at Larissa and turned the tide. Dispirited, homesick,
its pay long overdue and now still further demoralised by the
immense rewards which Alexius was offering to all deserters, the
Norman army fell away. Bohemund was forced to return to Italy
to raise more money, and his principal lieutenants surrendered as
soon as his back was turned; next, a Venetian fleet recaptured

Durazzo and Corfu; and by the year's end Norman-held territory was once again confined to one or two offshore islands and a short strip of the coast.

The arrival of Robert, accompanied by all three of his sons, Bohemund, Roger Borsa and Guy, and bearing money, supplies and substantial reinforcements, put new heart into the broken remnants of his army. Although now sixty-eight, he seems to have been in no way cast down at the prospect of waging his campaign all over again from the beginning, and immediately settled down to plan the recapture of Corfu. Bad weather delayed his ships at Butrinto until November, and when at last they were able to cross the straits they were set upon by a combined Greek and Venetian fleet and soundly beaten in pitched battle twice in three days. So severe were the Norman losses that the Venetians sent their pinnaces flying homeward to announce the victory. Now, however, it was their turn to pay the price for underestimating the Guiscard. After the preceding encounters, few of Robert's ships were in condition to sail at all, let alone to venture a third battle; but, seeing the pinnaces disappear over the horizon and realising that this was his opportunity of taking the enemy by surprise, he quickly summoned every vessel he possessed that was still afloat, and flung this battered fleet forward in one more onslaught. He had calculated it perfectly. Not only were the Venetians unprepared and depleted, but the heavier galleys, according to Anna Comnena, had been emptied of ballast and provisions and were consequently so high in the water that when, in the heat of the battle, their entire complements of soldiers and crew dashed to the same side of the deck, many of them capsized. (Anna assesses the Venetian dead at thirteen thousand and dwells—perhaps with more morbid pleasure than strict historical accuracy—on the mutilations inflicted by the Guiscard on his 2500 prisoners.) Corfu fell; and it was a generally happier and more hopeful army that settled down in its winter quarters on the mainland to repair the ships and make ready for the following year's campaign.[1]

[1] Anna goes on to describe a fourth battle in which she maintains that the Venetians got their revenge, but there is nothing in Venetian records to substantiate her story; and Dandolo's *Chronicon Venetum* (Muratori, *R.I.S.,* vol. XII) states that the Doge was deposed as a result of the Corfu catastrophe. It looks as though the Princess is guilty of a particularly unscrupulous piece of wishful thinking.

But in the course of the winter a new enemy appeared—one more deadly than the Venetians and the Byzantines together, and one which was destined to bring to an end not only the expedition but what Chalandon calls 'the first, heroic, period of the history of the Normans of Italy'. It was a raging epidemic, probably typhoid, and it struck without mercy. Even when it did not kill, it left its victims in a state of utter exhaustion from which they needed many weeks to recover, and by spring five hundred knights were dead and a large proportion of Robert's army effectively incapacitated. Yet even now the Guiscard remained cheerful and confident. Of his immediate family only Bohemund had succumbed—in conformity with that strange tendency of epidemics to attack the apparently strongest—and had been sent back to Bari to recuperate; and in the early summer, determined to get his men once again on the move, he despatched Roger Borsa with an advance force to occupy Cephalonia.

A few weeks later the Guiscard himself set out to join his son; but now, as he sailed southward, he felt the dreaded sickness upon him. By the time his ship reached Cape Ather, the northernmost tip of the island, he was desperately ill. There was no time to sail down the coast to where his son was waiting; the vessel put in at the first safe anchorage, a little sheltered bay still called, in his memory, by the name of Phiscardo. Here, six days later, on 17 July 1085, he died, his faithful Sichelgaita at his side. He had outlived Pope Gregory by less than two months.

Anna Comnena tells a curious story of how, as Robert lay dying, he looked over the sea to Ithaca and learned from a local inhabitant of a ruined town on the island, which had once been known as Jerusalem; and of how he suddenly remembered the words of a soothsayer who years before had prophesied that: 'As far as Ather you shall bring all countries under your sway, but from there you shall depart for Jerusalem and pay your debt to nature.' The story is presumably apocryphal,[1] but it is of a certain interest in relation to what is certainly the most surprising of all the Guiscard's achievements—his subsequent reputation in legend as a Crusader. The several biblical place-names in north-western Greece—Anna also

---

[1] Holinshed tells a very similar story of the death of Henry IV of England in 1413.

mentions the little harbour of Jericho, formerly Orikos, which Robert had captured during his first Balkan campaign—would naturally have been seized upon, and subsequently misinterpreted, by the minstrels and *jongleurs* who were soon to sing of his exploits; and it has been convincingly demonstrated how various incidents in his Byzantine expedition at last found their way into the *Chanson de Roland*.[1] Robert was indeed a perfect example of the *chevalier sans peur*; but even his most enthusiastic admirers would have been hard put to describe him as *sans reproche*, and it comes as something of a surprise to find him numbered among the stainless paladins of legend. But even this is not all.

> *Poscia trasse Guglielmo, e Rinoardo*
> *E il duca Gottifredi la mia vista*
> *Per quella croce, e Roberto Guiscardo.*[2]

The old ruffian had, specifically reserved for him though still two centuries away in the future, a crown sublimer still—the ultimate accolade of a place in Dante's Paradise.

Despite the claims of his glorious new cathedral at Salerno, Robert Guiscard had always wished to be buried with his brothers in the Abbey Church of the Santissima Trinità at Venosa; his body was therefore packed in salt and a ship made ready to return it, with Sichelgaita and Roger Borsa, to Italy. But the turbulence which had so characterised Robert's life did not, even in his death, desert him. On its way across the Adriatic the vessel, overtaken by a sudden tempest, almost foundered off Otranto and the coffin was swept overboard. It was eventually retrieved, but prolonged contract with the sea water had not improved its contents. In the condition in which it was found, the corpse could clearly travel no farther. The heart and entrails were removed, reverently jarred, and left at

---

[1] See the fascinating article by H. Gregoire and R. de Keyser in *Byzantion*, vol. XIV, 1939.

[2] Thereafter William and Rainouart, and then
Duke Godfrey to the Cross compelled mine eye;
Last, Robert Guiscard flashed across my ken.
Dante, *Paradiso*, XVIII, 46–48,
tr. G. Bickersteth.

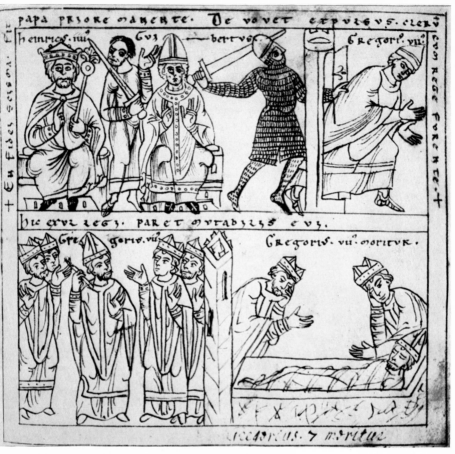

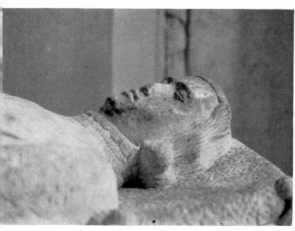

Henry IV and the Anti-Pope Clement III watch while Gregory VII escapes from Rome and dies at Salerno.
(Chronicle of Otto of Freising, 1156, University of Jena)

Salerno Cathedral:
Tomb of Roger Borsa

Sant'Angelo in Formis, near Capua. Desiderius's church, built about 1075

before experienced. They were making the best of it; and the whole
capital was now given over to scenes of rapine and pillage in which
the several brigades of Sicilian Saracens were not conspicuous for
their restraint. To the Romans these Saracens were the forces of
Antichrist. Refractory children were still silenced with gruesome
tales of the outrages of the infidel—of their hideous habits and
unspeakable appetites, and of those lightning raids when they
would sweep down like falcons out of a clear sky, giving no quarter,
selling women and girls—and boys too—by their thousands into
slavery; raids which culminated in that dreaful day when, in 846,
their galleys had sailed up the Tiber, sacked the Borgo and wrenched
the silver plate from the very doors of St Peter's itself. But even then
their depredations had been confined to the right bank of the river;
this time no district was safe, and the Christians were no better than
the Saracens. On the third day, with bestiality and bloodshed still
continuing unabated, the people of Rome could bear it no longer:
suddenly, in desperation, the whole city rose against its oppressors.
Robert Guiscard, for once taken by surprise, found himself surrounded. He was saved in the nick of time by Roger Borsa who, in
a rare burst of activity, smashed his way through the crowds with a
thousand men-at-arms to his father's rescue—but not before the
Normans, fighting for their lives, had set fire to the city.

Here, for Rome, was disaster—disaster unparalleled in its history
since the barbarian invasions six centuries before. Churches, palaces,
ancient temples came crashing down before the advancing flames.
The Capitol and the Palatine were gutted; in the whole area between
the Colosseum and the Lateran hardly a single building escaped the
inferno. Many of the inhabitants perished in their dwellings; others,
fleeing for their lives, were cut down by the Normans as they ran,
or else were captured and sold into slavery. When at last the smoke
cleared away and such Roman leaders as remained alive had
prostrated themselves before the Guiscard, a naked sword roped
round their necks in token of surrender, their city lay empty, a
picture of desolation and despair.

And what thoughts now, one wonders, must have occupied the
mind of Pope Gregory as he surveyed the blackened ruins around
him, the streets impassable with piles of fallen masonry, the corpses

already putrefying in the heat of a Roman June? He had won his battle—after a fashion—but at what a price? The heroic Popes of the past had saved their city from the invaders—Leo I from Attila's Huns, his own namesake Gregory the Great from the conquering Lombards; he, though in many ways greater than either, had delivered it up to destruction. And yet neither in his own letters nor in the chronicles of the time is there any suggestion of remorse for the evil he had brought upon Rome. His conscience seems to have been astonishingly clear. As he saw it, he had been fighting for a principle; it was a great principle and a vital one, and thanks to his own strength and courage it had been upheld. The present sufferings of his people were simply the inevitable retribution which by their faithlessness they had brought upon themselves. God's will had been done.

So, with that sublime arrogance which was one of his chief and most unattractive characteristics, must Gregory have reasoned. But for him too there was to be retribution. The Roman populace, who had acclaimed him with such enthusiasm eleven years before and had endured the hardships of siege and civil war on his behalf, now saw him—and not without good reason—as the cause of all their misery and loss; and they were hungry for revenge. Only the presence of Robert Guiscard and his army prevented them from tearing their once-adored Pope limb from limb. But Robert had no desire to stay in Rome longer than was absolutely necessary; apart from the danger of further outbreaks, he was anxious to resume his Byzantine campaign. During his ill-starred pontificate Gregory had been called upon to suffer many humiliations; but the greatest of all, he now saw, had been saved till the last. When the Normans left Rome, he would have to leave with them. And so he made ready to depart, and a few days later accompanied his deliverer on a brief and largely inconclusive expedition against the anti-Pope Clement, who had dug himself in at Tivoli. They returned on 28 June; and at the beginning of July, escorted by Robert Guiscard and the mighty host of Normans and Saracens that had been at once his salvation and his undoing, he turned his back on Rome for the last time—the proudest of pontiffs, now little better than a fugitive from the city that hated him. Southward they rode, first to Monte

Otranto; the remainder, embalmed in the nick of time, then proceeded on its last journey.

Venosa, says Gibbon, is 'a place more illustrious for the birth of Horace than for the burial of the Norman heroes'. Whether we agree with him or not, we have to admit that the little town nowadays contains more to interest the classical scholar than the mediaevalist. Of the abbey buildings of the SS. Trinità there is little left save a wall or two and a few sad and broken colonnades. The church—transformed by Robert's brother, Drogo, while still Count of Venosa, from a modest Lombard basilica into an edifice worthy to serve as the family shrine of the Hautevilles—still stands, together with the wall of another which Drogo began and Robert continued but neither lived to finish. Unfortunately, however, Baedeker's comment in 1883 that 'it has recently undergone restoration in questionable taste' is all too true; not much remains to tell us of how it must have looked when Pope Nicholas consecrated it in 1058 or when one Hauteville after another was laid to rest in its shade. The vaguely classicising and obviously refurbished tomb of Robert's first wife Alberada, with its self-effacing epitaph to the effect that if anyone is looking for her son Bohemund they will find his tomb at Canosa, is plain enough, somewhat awkwardly set in the north aisle; and we may even with an effort persuade ourselves to accept Norman Douglas's suggestion that one of the poor patches of fresco left on the walls is in fact a portrait of Sichelgaita. But the Guiscard himself is even less worthily commemorated. His original tomb has long since disappeared; only its epitaph, preserved by William of Malmesbury, has come down to us.[1] Gone, too, are the tombs of William, Drogo and Humphrey. Some time in the sixteenth century the remains of all four brothers were united in one simple monument

---

[1] *Hic terror mundi Guiscardus; hic expulit urbe*
Quem Ligures regem, Roma, Lemannus habent.
Parthus, Arabs, Macedumque phalanx non texit Alexin,
At fuga; sed Venetum nec fuga nec pelagus.

(Here lies the Guiscard, terror of the world; by his hand, he whom the Germans, the Ligurians and even Rome itself called King was driven from the City. From his wrath neither the Parthians not the Arabs, nor even the forces of Macedon, could save Alexius, whose only hope lay in flight; while for Venice, neither flight nor the protection of the ocean were of any avail.)

which may yet be seen. It carries no inscription. The only clue to its contents is a line from William of Apulia, still legible in the fresco on the wall above: '*Urbs Venusina nitet tantis decorata sepulchris.*'[1]

Now Robert, as rumour insisted and many said, was a most exceptional leader, quick-witted, good-looking, courteous in conversation, ready too in repartee, loud-voiced, easily accessible, very tall in stature, his hair always close-cut, long-bearded, always anxious to maintain the ancient customs of his race. He preserved the perfect comeliness of his countenance and figure until the end, and of these he was very proud, as his appearance was considered worthy of kingship; he showed respect to all his subordinates, more especially to those who were well-disposed towards him. On the other hand he was very thrifty and fond of money, very business-like and greedy of gain and, in addition to all this, most ambitious; and since he was a slave to these desires, he has incurred the serious censure of mankind.[2]

Such are the flowers which, in Gibbon's phrase, 'the joyful Anna Comnena scatters over the grave of an enemy'. Her description is probably accurate enough as far as it goes, but Anna is too chauvinistic and tendentious an observer to recognise the measure of the Guiscard's greatness. A man who began his career as a penniless brigand and horse-thief and who ended it with both Emperors simultanteously on the run and the greatest of mediaeval Popes in his power deserves a mightier tribute than this. Robert had found South Italy a confusion of races and religions, of principalities, duchies and petty baronies, all of them endlessly, pointlessly at loggerheads; he left it welded together into a single state. He has been taken to task[3] for failing to provide any form of administration to check the power of the Norman barons on the one hand and the Lombard nationalists on the other, and it is true that his talents lay more in the direction of war than of civil government; but the persistent rebelliousness of his vassals—a characteristic which was to endure as long as Norman domination itself—increases rather than diminishes the immensity of his achievement. He began with one advantage only: the supremacy, among the Norman barons of

[1] 'The city of Venosa shines with the glory of such sepulchres.'
[2] Tr. Dawes.
[3] E. Jamison, 'The Norman Administration of Apulia and Capua', *Papers of the British School at Rome*, VI, 1913.

Apulia, of his three brothers before him. For the rest he had to rely solely on his natural gifts—his faultless generalship allied with a superb diplomatic sense; his toughness and resolution in war, his mercy and generosity in peace; his genuine piety on the one hand, which he somehow managed to keep above and apart from his brilliant handling of successive Popes, and, on the other, that easy tolerance and eclecticism which often kept him on better terms with his Italian, Greek, Lombard and even his Saracen subjects than with his Norman vassals. He also possessed, to an extraordinary degree, those two qualities of temperament which, perhaps more than any others, are indispensable to political greatness—the superb self-confidence that melts away doubts and difficulties and allows ambition to keep pace with imagination, and the inexhaustible energy that never failed until, in his seventieth year, death overtook him. As for his personal valour, the most revealing proof is given by William of Malmesbury, who tells of how Duke William of Normandy—the Conqueror—used to screw up his own courage by reminding himself of the Guiscard's; and indeed in their achievements the two greatest Normans of their time had more than a little in common. But in their characters there was one all-important, fundamental difference. The Conqueror, whatever his other qualities, remained throughout his life mean, gloomy and austere. Robert, by contrast, never lost that streak of cheerful irresponsibility with which he began. He was that rarest of combinations, a genius and an extrovert; and, as the chronicles close on his life, they leave us with the picture of a gigantic blond buccaneer who not only carved out for himself the most extraordinary career of the Middle Ages but who also, quite shamelessly, enjoyed it.

With Robert Guiscard dead and Bohemund, its only other able commander, convalescing in Apulia, the Byzantine expedition was at an end. At Sichelgaita's insistence, Roger Borsa had once again been designated by his father as successor to the Dukedom, and had apathetically been recognised as such by what was left of the army; but he had never had much stomach for this—or indeed for any other —campaign, and he certainly had no intention of continuing it now. Neither did he like the idea of leaving Bohemund, even in his present state of health, to his own devices in Italy, where he would be bound to take advantage of his half-brother's absence and make a bid for power. Leaving his men to find their way home as best they could, he therefore returned at once with his mother to take formal possession of his new dominions; while the once-mighty army, hopelessly demoralised by the Guiscard's death and heartily sick of the Balkans in any case, followed in a general *sauve-qui-peut* as discreditable as it was undignified.

Roger Borsa's fears were not ill-founded. Bohemund, as we shall see, did indeed contest his right of succession and, even after being bought off with the best part of southern Apulia, was to remain a painful thorn in his half-brother's flesh for another ten years until he sailed away to win richer prizes still—and, incidentally, immortality—on the First Crusade. After he was gone, other rebellions followed, both Norman and Lombard; and though the anaemic young Duke somehow managed to retain his throne throughout his miserable life, the decline of the Duchy of Apulia which began with the Guiscard's death was to continue uninterruptedly until and even beyond that day in 1111 when his son followed him to the grave. So, mercifully, the spotlight shifts back to Sicily; but before we follow it we must briefly take leave of two other characters who now fade from our story.

First Sichelgaita. History has dealt harshly with her. Her ferocity on the battlefield—a quality which in national heroines like Boadicea or Joan of Arc evokes the rapturous applause of historians—has earned her more ridicule than approbation; while the contemporary Anglo-Norman chroniclers—Ordericus Vitalis, William of Malmesbury and the rest—almost unanimously accuse her of poisoning her husband and Bohemund as well. This ludicrous theory, for which they offer not a shred of evidence, must presumably have its roots in her persistent championing of her own son, Roger Borsa, in preference to the full-blooded Norman Bohemund, as her husband's successor—an attitude which, though it proved to be in the ultimate interests both of Norman Sicily and of Bohemund himself, was finally to destroy the Duchy of Apulia as a separate state. In fact, while her influence on Robert Guiscard was always considerable, she seems to have remained utterly devoted to him throughout the quarter-century and more of their married life; and the poisoning story, like the countless similar rumours that so frequently attended the deaths of mediaeval princes, can be dismissed as nonsense. Sichelgaita was to survive another five years, largely devoted to helping her son to preserve his tottering throne against Bohemund's machinations. She died in 1090 in her native city, and was buried at Monte Cassino.

Finally we must spare a parting thought for her daughter Helena, left disconsolate in a Byzantine convent, serving first as an unwilling pretext for her father's ambitions and later as a pathetic hostage whom he had not the faintest desire to redeem. If we are to believe Ordericus Vitalis—and there is no particular reason why we should —she was joined at some stage by a sister, and the two princesses lived for almost twenty years in the imperial palace at Constantinople, where 'their office was, every morning, when the Emperor had risen from his bed and was washing his hands, to present him with a towel, and, holding an ivory comb, to dress the Emperor's beard'. This assertion has been rejected by a later commentator as 'indelicate and improbable', and indeed it is. A safer, sadder guess would be that the poor girl was left—an unwanted bird in an inadequately gilded cage—to the mercies of some grisly abbess until her father was dead and her mother forgotten. Then and only then did Alexius return her, as he should have done on his accession, to what remained of her family. By then her chances of finding a husband were slim, and there is no record of her ever having married. Eventually she settled down at Roger's Sicilian court. He was the only one of the Hautevilles to have shown her any real sympathy; and though she cannot have cherished any very warm feelings for his Greek subjects, to her uncle her knowledge of their language and customs must have been invaluable. Perhaps this was some consolation to her; but for one who might have been an Empress it was a poor substitute.

18

VICTORS AND VANQUISHED

O Sea! You conceal beyond your further shores a veritable Paradise. In
my own country I knew only joy, never misfortune.
There, in the dawn of my life, I saw the sun in his glory. Now, in exile
and in tears, I witness his decline. . . .
O that I could embark on the crescent moon, fly to the shores of Sicily
and there crush myself against the breast of the sun!

Ibn Hamdis, refugee from Syracuse
after its capture by the Normans

A T the moment that death came to Robert Guiscard on the island of
Cephalonia, his brother Roger was laying siege to Syracuse. In the
thirteen years that had elapsed since the capture of Palermo he had
maintained his pressure on the Saracen resistance until it was now
confined to the centre and south-east of the island; but it had been a
hard struggle, against odds that varied only between the dispropor-
tionate and the overwhelming. There were few pitched battles; this
was a war of sudden sorties and ambuscades, in which a handful of
knights would sweep down from some mountain citadel on to an unsuspecting town, ravage it, annihilate the garrison and disappear once
again into their fastness. It was a war, too, which offered immense
opportunities for deeds of individual daring, a war which is still
fought along the sides of Sicilian peasant carts and, amid the clatter-
ing of tin armour and the thudding of turbaned heads, in the traditional puppet-shows of Palermo.

Gradually the enemy was pushed back. The year 1077 saw the
collapse of the last two Saracen strongholds in the west. The siege
of Trapani was brought to an abrupt end when Roger's bastard son
Jordan led a surprise raid on the grassy promontory where the

defenders grazed their sheep and cattle, and at one stroke deprived them of their principal food supply; the neighbouring stronghold of Erice, on the other hand, perched up on its dizzy pinnacle a mile or two to the east, surrendered only after the unsportsmanlike intervention of St Julian, who suddenly appeared with a pack of voracious hounds and released them upon the infidels.[1] Two years later, in August 1079, Taormina followed. The Emir had long considered his position to be impregnable, but on finding it ringed with no fewer than twenty-two Norman fortresses supported by a naval blockade, he saw that continued resistance was in vain. His surrender was followed by the capitulation of the whole Etna massif, and by the end of 1079 all Sicily north of the Agrigento-Catania line, save only the still indomitable Enna, had accepted the Normans as its overlords.

But now the advance was halted again. Minor revolts among the Saracens of Giato[2] and Cinisi accounted for the rest of 1079 and much of 1080, and in 1081 Roger was needed elsewhere. He was never allowed to forget that however heavily occupied he might be in Sicily he was still, first and foremost, his brother's vassal. If Robert Guiscard called for his assistance on the mainland it was his duty to obey. There was, admittedly, something further to be considered, beyond the narrow issue of feudal obligation: the Count knew perfectly well that he depended on Robert's Italian dominions for his own lines of communication and supply, and that should there occur a catastrophe in Apulia or—worse still—in Calabria, his position in Sicily might well become untenable. All the same, it must have been galling to sacrifice, time after time, a hard-won initiative to answer the Guiscard's call. He had already lost the best part of a year that way in 1075—during which his son-in-law Hugh of Jersey had been killed and his army soundly defeated in a battle undertaken, in defiance of Roger's strict instructions, against

---

[1] For eight and a half centuries from that day the place was known as Monte San Giuliano; only in 1934, with Mussolini's attempt to revive the old imperial past, did it revert to its earlier name. Throughout this period it was noted not only for the steepness of its precipices but also for the beauty of its women. 'They are said to be the loveliest of the whole island—may Allah deliver them into the hands of the Faithful!' notes Ibn Jubair piously.

[2] Now S. Giuseppe Iato.

the Emir of Syracuse—and now, in the spring of 1081, the summons came again. Robert, about to launch his ill-fated expedition against the Byzantine Empire and understandably doubtful about Roger Borsa's reliability in moments of stress, needed his brother in Italy during his absence. Roger cannot have had much enthusiasm for the prospect; responsible now for all three dukedoms—for he himself had even fewer delusions about his nephew—he must have recognised that with the Guiscard's best troops away in Greece he would be hopelessly over-extended in the event of serious trouble.

And the next few weeks proved him right. Almost at once the Count found himself faced with two simultaneous emergencies. One was at Gerace, in Calabria, where a Norman baron had allied himself with the local Greek population and raised the standard of revolt; the other arose in Sicily where Bernavert,[1] Emir of Syracuse, managed to regain possession of Catania. Roger was still occupied at Gerace; without waiting for his return, his son Jordan with two other leaders, Robert de Sourval and Elias Cartomi—the latter almost certainly a converted Saracen—led a force of a hundred and sixty knights against Bernavert and recaptured the city. Thus, when the Count was at last able to return to the island, all was quiet again; but he knew that next time he might not be so lucky.

That winter saw a further strengthening of the fortifications of Messina—which Roger rightly considered the key to Sicily. Then, with the coming of spring in 1082, the same considerations that brought Robert Guiscard hurrying back from Kastoria led him once again to summon his brother to his aid. Leaving Sicily in Jordan's charge, the Count set off at once. This time he knew that his presence was essential, for the Guiscard was faced with one of the most desperate crises of his career. The story of that crisis has already been told. It was more than a year before Roger returned to Sicily, and even then he would probably not have done so for a lesser cause than that which, in the summer of 1083, so urgently called him home. Jordan, his own son—he who had shown such initiative

---

[1] This version—Malaterra's—of the Emir's name is obviously corrupt, but the Saracen sources tell us nothing. The most likely guess is that his name was really Ibn al-Wardi; but Amari, the greatest authority on the Saracens in Sicily, remains unconvinced. See his *Storia dei Musulmani di Sicilia*, vol. III, p. 149 n.

at Trapani and such courage only two years before at Catania—had allied himself with a few discontented knights and rebelled against his father's authority. Already he had taken possession of Mistretta and of S. Marco d'Alunzio, the first Norman castle ever to be built on Sicilian soil; and he was now marching on Troina, where his father's treasure was stored.

Roger sped back to Sicily. His arrival seemed to stop the rebels in their tracks; and he soon saw that the danger was no longer one of a quickly spreading revolt, but rather that Jordan and his friends, out of sheer despair, might take refuge among the Muslims. And so, once order had been restored, he pretended to shrug off the whole matter. The ringleaders, beguiled into thinking that a free pardon would be theirs for the asking, gave themselves up. Only then did the Count reveal his determination. His son's twelve principal accomplices were condemned to be blinded, while Jordan himself languished for several days in hourly expectation of a similar fate. At last he received his father's pardon, and thenceforth served him loyally until his death. Never again in Sicily was Count Roger's authority questioned.

When, in 1081, Jordan had recaptured Catania, he had unfortunately failed to lay his hands on Bernavert himself, who had escaped back to his stronghold at Syracuse. Since then the Emir had lain low; but suddenly, in the summer of 1084—just about the time that Robert Guiscard was marching on Rome—he returned to the attack. This time his objective was not Norman-held Sicily, but the towns and villages along the Calabrian coast. Nicotera suffered particularly severely at his hands as did the suburbs of Reggio, where the Saracens desecrated and despoiled two churches before making their getaway. But the worst atrocity of all was yet to come; at the beginning of autumn Bernavert's ships descended upon the Convent of the Mother of God at Rocca d'Asino[1] and carried all the nuns back in triumph to the Emiral harem.

These last outrages introduced a new and sinister element into the struggle. Although, largely for reasons of morale, Robert Guiscard and Roger had both stressed the crusading aspect of the Sicilian

[1] The village can no longer be identified.

conquest during its early years, from the moment that Roger began building up a multiracial society and administration he had been careful to show respect and, later, his genuine admiration for the traditions of Islam. No one knew better than he that a viable Sicilian state could be constructed only on a basis of complete religious toleration, and he was always at pains to emphasise to his Saracen subjects that such military measures as might still be necessary were being undertaken—often with Muslim contingents fighting on the Norman side—for the sole purpose of political unification. Freedom of religion would always be granted to the conquered. As time went on, the majority of Saracens in Norman-held territory had grown to accept these assurances and, mellowed by the return of an ordered and efficient government and the promise of further prosperity to come, had been ready to give Roger their loyalty. Now, suddenly, there came a deliberate attempt by the Emir of Syracuse to reawaken religious animosities. Already in Calabria Christian opinion had hardened once more against the Muslims; if Bernavert were not quickly eliminated, confessional strife would flare up again throughout Sicily also, and all Roger's work would come crashing down in ruins.[1]

Immediately Roger began to prepare for a major campaign, on a scale unequalled since that which he had led against Taormina five years before. Throughout the winter and spring he worked, until in mid-May 1085 all was ready. On Wednesday the 20th his fleet set sail from Messina.[2] That night it reached Taormina; on Thursday it was near Catania; and on Friday evening the ships anchored off Cape S. Croce, some fifteen miles north of Syracuse, where Jordan— now fully restored to his father's favour—was waiting with the cavalry. Before going farther, Roger decided on a reconnaissance.

---

[1] Chalandon infers, from accounts of the religious ceremonies which accompanied the military preparations for the Syracuse expedition, that Roger deliberately set out to inflame the passions of his Christian subjects against the Infidel. He underestimates the Count. It was normal to say masses, give alms and perform sundry special acts of devotion before embarking on any military enterprise; but to stoke confessional fires at such a moment would have been contrary to his whole Sicilian policy and might well have proved disastrous.

[2] Amari, who puts the expedition a year later, in 1086, has got his chronology a little confused. I follow Chalandon, whose reasoning (vol. I, p. 338) seems incontrovertible.

The Tiber Island, Rome. The tower by the bridge is the Torre della Contessa, part of the Countess Matilda's fortress in which Popes Victor III and Urban II both took refuge

Canosa di Puglia:
Bohemund's Tomb

The Sarcophagus
of Count Roger I
(Archaeological
Museum, Naples)

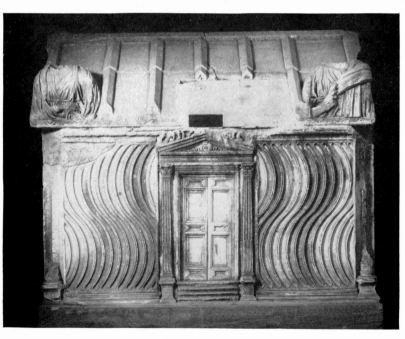

A certain Philip was sent forward in a light pinnace manned by twelve Arabic-speaking Sicilians—the greater part presumably Saracens themselves—and managed, under cover of darkness, not only to enter the enemy harbour but by passing his ship off as a local vessel to sail right through the middle of Bernavert's fleet. By Sunday he was back with full information about its size and strength. The Count laid his plans accordingly. On a lonely stretch of coast the army and navy assembled together to hear mass; then at nightfall, confessed and newly shriven, they set off on the last stage of their journey.

The battle was fought at daybreak the following morning, in those same waters outside the harbour where the ships of Syracuse had destroyed the Athenian fleet almost exactly fifteen centuries before. Now they were not so fortunate. The Norman crossbowmen, lining the decks and perched at the mastheads, could shoot accurately from a far greater range than Bernavert's archers could hope to command; and the Emir soon saw that his only chance was to move in close and come to grips with his attackers. Giving the order for a general advance and directing his own helmsman to head straight for Roger's flagship, he led his fleet through a hail of arrows into the thick of the Norman line; then, as he came alongside, without waiting for grappling-irons, he leaped for the enemy deck. It was an act of immense courage, but it failed. Whether through miscalculation or exhaustion—for he had already been seriously wounded by a Norman javelin—he jumped short. Into the sea he fell; the weight of his armour did the rest.

Seeing their leader drowned, the Syracusan sailors quickly lost heart. Most of the ships were captured then and there; others fled back into harbour, only to find Jordan and his men already entrenching themselves along the land-walls of the city. The ensuing siege lasted all through the heat of the summer. In vain the defenders tried to appease the Normans by setting free all their Christian prisoners—including, presumably, the luckless nuns of Rocca d'Asino; Roger would accept nothing but unconditional surrender. At last, in October, Bernavert's chief widow, with her son and the leading notables of the town, secretly took ship and, slipping unperceived through the Norman blockade, escaped south to Noto. Their departure settled the issue. Deserted now by their own leaders, the Syracusans gave in.

With the death of Bernavert on 25 May 1085—the very day on which Pope Gregory finally turned his face to the wall at Salerno—Saracen resistance to the Normans was broken. The Emir, even though he possessed little real authority beyond the immediate neighbourhood of Syracuse, had had sufficient force of personality to capture the imagination and fire the enthusiasm of all those of his co-religionists who felt as he did; after him there was no one. The Saracens lost hope: their spirit was gone. Syracuse, as we have seen, held out for a few more months, but only in the hope of gaining more favourable terms. Such other pockets as remained unpacified were to last only for as long as Roger, after his brother's death once again temporally preoccupied with mainland affairs, allowed them to do so.

Some time in September 1085, a week or two after he had laid what was left of his father in his tomb at Venosa, Roger Borsa called a meeting of his chief vassals to receive their formal recognition and homage as Duke of Apulia. Their acclaim was, if anything, even more half-hearted than that of the army in Greece two months before. The rise of the Hautevilles was still resented by nearly all the Norman barons of South Italy. They had given a certain amount of reluctant loyalty to Robert Guiscard, first because they had had little choice and secondly because they had grudgingly recognised his courage and his superb gifts of leadership; even then they had never hesitated to take up arms against him when they got the chance. For his son, who possessed none of Robert's genius and whose very blood was tainted with that of the subject Lombard race, they had little affection and less respect.

But Sichelgaita had done her work well. Key vassals had been approached in advance and bribed as necessary. Out for themselves as always, they were probably only too pleased to give their assent; if they must acknowledge an overlord, then surely the weaker the better. One only remained implacably opposed to Roger Borsa's succession—Bohemund, as impetuous and consumed with ambition as the Guiscard had been before him, knowing himself more justly entitled in law and infinitely better qualified in character and ability to inherit his father's dominions. Unable to find any adherents among his fellow-vassals, Bohemund had looked farther afield and had acquired the support of Jordan of Capua, who naturally leaped at the chance of encouraging dissension among his greatest rivals. Backed by the Capuan army, fresh and well-equipped—in contrast to the debilitated skeletons who had limped home from Greece with Roger Borsa—these two together constituted a formidable opposition; but Sichelgaita had gained for her son what she knew would be the decisive advantage—the championship of his uncle, unquestionably the most powerful figure in South Italy since the Guiscard's death.

Roger's support for his nephew and namesake was no more altruistic than that of the Apulian vassals. Although in recent years he had been the effective ruler of all Sicily, his brother had always retained direct tenure of the Val Demone in the north-east, of the city of Palermo and of half Messina, as well as general suzerainty over the whole island. These possessions would be passed to his successor, and Roger had no wish to find himself hamstrung by a new overlord who would try to take an active part in Sicilian affairs. On the other hand he had his lines of communication to consider. The future of Calabria must be assured and, with Bohemund and the Prince of Capua both out for his blood, it hardly looked as though Roger Borsa would be the best man to assure it. And so the Count too had asked his price. In return for his support, he had demanded from his nephew the immediate cession to him of all the Calabrian castles that had in the past been held jointly by Robert Guiscard and himself. It was the first of many agreements by which, while remaining a loyal vassal, a wise counsellor and an indispensable ally, Roger would over the next fifteen years steadily increase his own power, on both sides of the straits, at his nephew's expense.

The Count had left the siege of Syracuse for Salerno, to pay homage to Roger Borsa after his installation. The ceremony was concluded without incident, but no sooner had the vassals dispersed than Bohemund launched his attack. He struck at the farthest and, probably, the most inadequately defended corner of his half-brother's domains—the heel of Apulia. Sweeping southward from his own castle at Taranto, he had seized Oria and Otranto almost before Roger Borsa knew what was happening. Now he was in a position to dictate his own terms, and the new Duke had little alternative but to accept them. Peace was not restored until he had ceded to Bohemund not only the conquered cities but also Gallipoli, Taranto and Brindisi and most of the territories between Brindisi and Conversano, with the title of Prince of Taranto. Thus, within a few months of the Guiscard's death, the first and greatest of his dukedoms had been irreparably split. Roger Borsa had not started well.

His uncle, on the other hand, was rapidly building up his strength. By the spring of 1086, with Calabria at last under his effective control and an uneasy peace patched up between his nephews, Count Roger felt ready to devote his attention again to Sicily. On 1 April his army laid siege to Agrigento. The town fell on 25 July, and among those taken prisoner were the wife and children of a certain Ibn Hamud, who had succeeded old Ibn al-Hawas as Emir of Enna. Ibn Hamud was the last of the leading Saracens to remain unsubdued—largely because the Normans had never until now made any effort to subdue him; and Roger, remembering the towering impregnability of his citadel and the fruitless siege of a quarter of a century before, was anxious at all costs to bring him to terms. He therefore gave orders that his distinguished captives should be treated with honour and due deference, and began forthwith to plan his approach to the Emir.

The rest of the year was taken up with entertaining Roger Borsa —now making his first visit to Sicily as its Duke—rebuilding the fortifications of Agrigento, and generally consolidating Norman control over the newly-won territory. Meanwhile, Roger felt, he could profitably leave Ibn Hamud to reflect on his situation. Apart from Enna, only two small pockets of resistance now remained in all Sicily—Butera and Noto, neither of which was equipped to withstand a concerted attack. Final pacification of the island was, therefore, imminent and inevitable. The Emir could no longer expect aid from outside; with his wife and family already in Norman hands, he would be well-advised to come to terms.

Early in 1087, with a hundred lancers as his escort, Roger rode from Agrigento to the foot of the great pinnacle on which Enna stands and invited Ibn Hamud, under a promise of safe-conduct, down for a parley. He found the Emir in entire agreement with everything he had to say, perfectly prepared to capitulate and exercised only by the problem of how best to do so without losing face. By now the Count had lived too long among the Muslims to underestimate the importance of such a question; he too wanted the surrender to pass off as smoothly as possible, and was more than willing to co-operate in whatever way Ibn Hamud might suggest. A solution was soon found, and it was with a good deal of quiet satisfaction that Roger rode back with his men to Agrigento. Some days later Ibn Hamud descended again from his castle, this time at the head of his troops and accompanied by a number of his principal advisers. Their route took them through a narrow defile; just as they entered it they were set upon by a vastly superior Norman force and surrounded. In such circumstances resistance was out of the question. Their captors then moved on to Enna itself which, deprived of Emir, army and notables, also gave in at once. Ibn Hamud, his family restored to him, had himself baptised—the fact that his wife now fell within the prohibited degrees of kinship was discreetly overlooked—and retired to Calabria where Roger, in accordance with his usual practice, had provided him with an extensive estate. There he lived out his remaining years, far removed from his old spheres of influence, but happily and in the style to which he was accustomed, like any other Christian gentleman.

Meanwhile, on the mainland, a new and pressing problem had arisen. It was now more than a year since Pope Gregory had died, and the perennial difficulties over the succession were looming larger than ever. The anti-Pope Clement, having failed to ingratiate himself with the Romans, had been expelled from the city, and the throne of St Peter lay once again untenanted. Not that there was any dearth of candidates; Gregory himself had named four on his deathbed—Archbishop Hugh of Lyons, Bishops Odo of Ostia and Anselm of Lucca, and Desiderius of Monte Cassino. Of these the majority of the Cardinals—as well as the people of Rome—favoured Desiderius. As abbot of one of the greatest and most venerable monasteries of Europe, he had influence and the control of enormous wealth; his talents as a diplomat were well known; he had long enjoyed the respect and trust of the Normans, having successfully mediated between Robert Guiscard and Richard of Capua in 1075 and having also been largely responsible for Robert's reconciliation with Pope Gregory at Ceprano five years later. Admittedly, by acting as broker between Richard's son Jordan and Henry IV in 1082, and in that same year himself coming to a separate agreement with the Emperor-to-be, Desiderius has been considered by many good churchmen to be carrying his peace-making activities too far, and had suffered a twelve-month papal ban for his pains; but Gregory had later forgiven him and, in the now more moderate climate of political opinion, it was thought that the abbot's excellent personal relations with the Emperor would prove, if anything, an advantage. Desiderius thus seemed to be in all respects an admirable candidate for the Papacy. There was only one drawback: he categorically refused to accept it.

His attitude is easy enough to understand. He was a natural recluse, a scholar and a contemplative. Forty years before, with considerable difficulty, he had succeeded in renouncing the palace of a Lombard prince in favour of a monk's cell; having eventually found his way to Monte Cassino, he had shown himself a great abbot, bringing the monastery the peace and tranquillity it needed after many years as a battleground, and securing for himself the way of life for which, he believed, God had intended him. All his political exertions, all his celebrated diplomacy, had been directed towards these two objects. As a result his abbey had grown and flourished, and with its ever-increasing wealth Desiderius had transformed it from a ramshackle collection of buildings, strife-torn and long-neglected, into the most magnificent architectural and artistic achievement in the South. He had done more; by bringing from centres as far afield as Constantinople skilled craftsmen in mosaics, fresco and *opus Alexandrinum*—that ornamental marble pavement-work which still glorifies so many churches in South Italy—he had become a patron and cultural influence unique in his country and his age.[1]

[1] Desiderius's basilica at Monte Cassino, dedicated in 1071 by Pope Alexander in the presence of Hildebrand, St Peter Damian and all the principal Norman and Lombard

Monte Cassino, then, was Desiderius's life, its adornment his pleasure, its greatness his ultimate ambition. He had no desire to exchange that most comfortable of cloisters for the intrigues and passions, the danger and heat and violence of papal Rome. He knew, too, that he was without the force of character or driving determination that was the most necessary qualification for the Papacy. A man of gentleness and peace, he possessed none of the Hildebrandine steel. Besides, his health was beginning to give way. He was only fifty-eight, but he may well have already suspected that he had not much longer to live. As soon as the anti-Pope had fled, he had therefore hastened to Rome in an effort to ensure the rapid election of some other suitable candidate, and he did his best to persuade Jordan of Capua and the Countess Matilda to support his efforts; but when he saw that they too were determined on his own succession he could only repeat his refusal and return hurriedly to his beloved monastery.

His champions, however, proved just as stubborn; they would not even consider an alternative candidate, and so the stalemate dragged on for nearly a year until, at Easter 1086, a body of cardinals and leading bishops assembled in Rome and sent Desiderius a formal summons to join them in their deliberations. Reluctantly he obeyed —and once again found himself deluged with entreaties to change his mind. Still he stood firm. At last, in desperation, the assembly agreed to accept whatever candidate he chose to name. Desiderius immediately proposed Odo of Ostia, adding with characteristic diffidence that if this choice did not meet with immediate approval in Rome he would willingly give the new Pope shelter at Monte Cassino for as long as was necessary. But it was no use. The more he spoke, the greater grew the determination to have him and no other. Odo's candidature was rejected on the grounds that it would

leaders in South Italy—excepting only Robert Guiscard and Roger, busy besieging Palermo—has, alas, been destroyed; his hand can, however, be clearly seen in the exterior of Robert Guiscard's cathedral of Salerno, built in the form of a Roman basilica with an atrium adorned with antique columns from Paestum, and mosaics of Byzantine style but Italian workmanship. More remarkable still, and one of the treasures of Italy, is the little church of S. Angelo in Formis, just outside Capua, whose frescoes still seem as brilliant as on the day they were painted, and show just how fresh and vigorous Italian romanesque painting could be.

contravene Canon Law, which everybody knew was nonsense; the Roman populace, doubtless well-briefed in advance and anyway trained to this sort of thing since the election of Hildebrand thirteen years before, clamoured louder than ever for Desiderius; and the reluctant abbot was carried, struggling, off to the nearby church of S. Lucia where, to his despair, he heard himself joyously proclaimed as Pope Victor III. The red cope was cast about his shoulders before he could prevent it; but no amount of cajolery could persuade him to don the rest of the papal insignia.

Four days later, riots broke out in the city. Roger Borsa had chosen this moment to liberate the Imperial Prefect of Rome, whom his father had taken prisoner two years before. Whether in doing so he was deliberately spiking the guns of Jordan of Capua and the papal Curia (who had recently refused ratification for his new Archbishop of Salerno) or whether he was simply acting with his usual cluelessness is not certain; at any rate it was a foolish move. Desiderius, well-disposed and malleable, was the best possible choice of Pope from the Norman point of view; but now the Prefect went straight to Rome where, stirring up the old imperialist faction, he successfully prevented the formal consecration in St Peter's. For the new Pope this was confirmation of his worst fears. He seemed almost to welcome the opportunity to prove that he was not of papal calibre. Making no attempt at resistance, he left the city at once and took ship to Terracina whence, having made a full and formal renunciation of his throne, he returned with all speed to Monte Cassino.

Now the situation was worse than ever. Now, too, the first voices hostile to Desiderius began to be heard. Hugh of Lyons and Odo of Ostia, both nominees of the dying Gregory and both considering themselves eminently suitable candidates for the papal tiara, naturally resented the manner in which it had been thrust on to the head of a colleague who was at once unwilling and manifestly incapable. In October these two disgruntled prelates, accompanied by several others who had by now come round to their way of thinking, arrived at Salerno; Roger Borsa, still thwarted over his Archbishop, gave them a ready welcome; and though we cannot be sure just what took place during their deliberations, from that time the abbot's popularity began to wane. Had he not made a separate treaty with Henry

IV when Henry was openly threatening not only the city of Rome but even the person of the Pope himself? Had he not, indeed, suffered a year's excommunication in consequence? Was such a man truly the best that could be found to assume the Vicariate of Christ?

It was inevitable, sooner or later, that these rumblings from Salerno should reach the ears of Desiderius, safely back in his abbey. What was more surprising was the effect they had on him. For the first time since Gregory's death he began to show signs of determination. Perhaps it was the thought of seeing one of his opponents on the throne that goaded him into action. He had never liked Hugh of Lyons, who had publicly expressed disapproval at his dealings with the imperialists; while Odo, whom he himself had nominated only a few months before, had chosen an odd way to express his gratitude. But Desiderius was by nature neither jealous nor vindictive. For more than thirty years his actions had been motivated by two considerations only—the good of his monastery and the peaceful continuance of his own life within its walls—and it is here that we must seek an explanation for the steps he now took. It may be that Jordan, still his determined champion, suddenly hit upon the one way to infuse him with a little spirit and suggested to him that the elevation of either of his opponents might have unfavourable effects on his own position as abbot; similar rumours may even have reached him from other, better-placed sources. Whatever the reason, Desiderius pulled himself together and, by virtue of his former authority, summoned a council of the Church at Capua. There, in March 1087, he solemnly announced his resumption of the Papacy. His clerical opponents walked out forthwith, doubtless trusting that their ally Roger Borsa would support them; but the Duke had been summoned secretly by Desiderius the previous night and had come to a very satisfactory arrangement about his Archbishop of Salerno. Unreliable as always, he now proclaimed himself for the Pope. Victor resumed, without further reluctance, the vestments he had so eagerly cast off and started at once for Rome, the combined Norman troops of Apulia and Capua in his train.

The atmosphere in the City had not improved during his absence. The Imperial Prefect, whom his departure had left in undisputed control, had summoned back anti-Pope Clement and reinstalled him in the Vatican; and it was the Vatican, and in particular old St Peter's itself, that now received the full shock of the Norman attack. Its defenders did their best, but St Peter's was no St Angelo's; it could not be held for long. Clement withdrew to the Pantheon and barricaded himself in; and on 9 May the Bishop of Ostia, reconciled at last to the inevitable, consecrated Victor III in the basilica. Even now, however, the Pope's triumph was far from complete. Trastevere was his, but Rome itself remained in imperialist hands and the Normans, their primary purpose achieved, were understandably reluctant to venture once again into the old city, where memories of 1084 were still dangerously fresh. In the circumstances Victor had no difficulty in persuading himself that it was useless to remain in his see; within a fortnight he was back at Monte Cassino.

This time he felt safe from his enemies; but God, who had in other respects treated him with so much consideration, still refused to protect him from his friends. Now it was Countess Matilda of Tuscany who appeared at the gates of Rome, intent on expelling Clement and his supporters, insistent on Victor's presence at her side. Wearily the wretched pontiff dragged himself back to the city where, immured with his unwanted champion in the Pierleoni stronghold on the Tiber Island,[1] he had to face another two months' tribulation through the height of the Roman summer while the tide of battle swung back and forth, ever bloodier but always inconclusive. In July, by now seriously ill, he could bear it no longer and departed, via Benevento, for the monastery he should never have left; and there, on 16 September, he died. He was buried in the chapter-house; but the whole abbey, which he had reconceived and recreated, was his monument. For the monks of Monte Cassino his memory would be imperishable; for the rest of the world he had proved a disappointment and an anticlimax, whose story served only to corroborate two truths which should have been self-evident—that great abbots do not necessarily make great popes, and that, just as in the days of Gregory, the Papacy still depended for its survival on Norman steel.

[1] The mediaeval tower which still rises from the island just south of the Ponte Fabricio is part of the old fortress. It is still known as the Torre della Contessa, in memory of Matilda. The Pierleoni had further guarded the approach by fortifying the theatre of Marcellus, immediately opposite the island on the left bank.

19

THE GREAT COUNT

Lingua facundissimus, consilio callidus, in ordinatione agendarum rerum providens.

(Most ready of tongue, wise in counsel, far-sighted in the ordering of affairs.)

Malaterra on Roger, I, 19

SEVENTY-ONE years had passed since that day when Melus had approached the pilgrims in the Archangel's cave—seventy-one years during which the great tide that had swept across South Italy, carrying the Normans upon its crest and engulfing all others, had never once faltered in its career. It had carried them through Aversa, Melfi, and Civitate, through Messina, Bari and Palermo, and even to Rome itself; it had raised them, with each succeeding decade, to new heights of glory and power; and if occasionally for a year or two the impetus had seemed to diminish, it had always proved merely to be gathering strength for a still grander forward surge. Now, suddenly, in the last dozen years of the century, the pace slackens. The old momentum is lost. It is as if, no longer able to cope with so relentless an onrush of events, time itself has grown tired.

So, at least, it appears to the historian. To those of the Duke's subjects who lived in mainland Italy during those years, life probably continued much the same—except that it was perhaps a little duller since the Guiscard's death, for his energy and ebullience had made themselves felt far beyond the immediate sphere of his vassals, his soldiers and those whose lives were immediately affected by his policies. But dullness, alas, did not mean security. The old quarrel between Roger Borsa and Bohemund broke out again in the autumn

267

of 1087, and during the next nine years few regions of the South were to escape the consequences of their rivalry. Civil wars tend inevitably to be sterile, exhausting a country physically and financially while offering no hope of expansion or conquest or economic gain; that which now spread across the peninsula was even more profitless than most since, though it enabled Bohemund to tighten his grip on his half-brother's dominions, its effects were largely to be nullified when, in 1096, he left on the First Crusade.

But it was not only the local populations that had cause to regret the passing of the old order. There were others, outside the Dukedom, who found themselves increasingly concerned over the anarchy into which it was slipping; and chief among these was Odo, the former Bishop of Ostia who, six months after the death of Pope Victor, had been elected to succeed him on the papal throne under the name of Urban II. This stately, scholarly aristocrat from Champagne, a zealous reformer who had been Prior of Cluny before coming south to join the Curia, had little in common with his pathetic predecessor. He was, instead, a staunch upholder of papal supremacy on the Gregorian model—except that he possessed all the polish and diplomatic finesse that his exemplar had so disastrously lacked. Since his city was now once again firmly in the hands of the anti-Pope Clement and the imperialists he had been elected and consecrated at Terracina, and he well knew that Norman help would be necessary if he were ever to return to Rome. At the beginning of his pontificate, with the Duke of Apulia fully occupied with the Prince of Taranto, such help was obviously out of the question; and it was only after a personal visit by Urban to Sicily that Count Roger was able to patch up another temporary peace between his nephews and so to make possible an armed expedition to Rome by which, in November 1088, the Pope entered the city. Even then he found himself, like Victor before him, confined to the tiny Tiber Island; and by the following autumn he was back in exile. Not until Easter 1094, and then by bribery, was he able to penetrate to the Lateran Palace and, six years after his consecration, to assume his rightful throne.

Most of those six years Urban had spent wandering through South Italy; and the more he wandered the more convinced he must have become that it was on Count Roger rather than his nephew that the mantle of Robert Guiscard had fallen. The new Duke of Apulia was a well-meaning but worthless cypher, despised by Normans and Lombards alike, struggling along as best he could but increasingly dependent on his uncle and more and more inclined to take refuge from his inadequacy in the churches and monasteries where, alone, his open-handedness and undoubted piety made him genuinely popular. Bohemund on the other hand, if he was already showing some of his father's genius, had also inherited his restlessness and irresponsibility. Although in the Pope's eyes he was an outlaw—having taken up arms against a papal vassal—his stength was rapidly increasing: in 1090 he had managed to annex Bari, as well as several towns in Northern Calabria, and he now exercised effective control, not only over the heel of Italy but also over the entire region between Melfi and the Gulf of Taranto. Even if he could be prevented from destroying the South, his influence in the peninsula would never be anything but disruptive. There was equally little hope to be drawn from the principality of Capua; Jordan had died in 1090 and his son Richard, still a minor, had been thrown out by the populace and was now living in exile.

In 1094 Count Roger was sixty-three years old, and at last the undisputed master of Sicily. Butera had yielded to him soon after Urban's visit in 1088 and Noto, the last bastion of Saracen independence, had followed voluntarily in 1091. That same year, as an additional protection against raids from the south, he had led an expedition to Malta, which had also surrendered without a struggle. Of those areas of Sicily which Robert Guiscard had retained for himself, half the cities of Palermo and Messina and much of the Val Demone remained technically the property of Roger Borsa— the other half of Palermo having been acquired by the Count the previous year in return for helping his nephew at the siege of Cosenza. But although he was deprived of their revenues, Roger's authority ran as firm here as everywhere else on the island.

The two decades that had elapsed since the fall of the Sicilian capital had had a deep effect on his character. During his youth he had shown as much hot-blooded impetuosity as any of his Hauteville brothers; but whereas the Guiscard had remained to the end of his life the adventurer and soldier of fortune he had always been, Roger had developed into a mature and responsible statesman. Moreover, despite his conquests, he had proved himself to be fundamentally a man of peace. Never during the slow extension of his authority over the island had he used military force to gain results which might have been achieved by negotiation; never, when war was inevitable, had he embarked on it until he could be confident of victory. The process, from first to last, had taken a long time—most of his adult life—but it had enabled him to consolidate as he went along, and it had eventually secured for him the respect and trust of the large majority of his subjects, whatever their religion or race. It was more than Robert Guiscard had ever been able to boast.

Robert, it must be admitted, had had to contend with one immense and perhaps ultimately insuperable handicap—his vassals. Jealous, insubordinate, ever resentful of his domination, they were the curse of the South, the supreme obstacle to its prosperity and cohesion. They had, however, an undoubted right to be where they were: many of their families had already settled in Italy before the the first of the sons of Tancred had left their father's manor. The Guiscard had been forced to accept them as a necessary evil and to deal with them as best he could. In Sicily, on the other hand, things were different. There the Hautevilles had arrived first in the field with full papal authority behind them; they constituted the only fount of honour; and they had taken care from the outset to prevent the establishment of any large fiefs that might subsequently jeopardise their own position.

Thus it was that Roger of Sicily had become, by the beginning of the last decade of the eleventh century, the greatest prince of the South, more powerful than any ruler on the Italian mainland. To Pope Urban, whose tenure of Rome was still by no means assured— the Castel S. Angelo was to remain in the hands of the anti-Pope's faction till 1098—it was clear that if the Papacy were once again seriously threatened only the Count would be able to provide the necessary southern support. Roger, to be sure, was not the easiest of allies. He knew his worth and, with the Pope just as with his nephew, he drove hard bargains. On the other hand he needed a strong Latin element in Sicily. Without it he would not only have found his present position difficult but would have had no religious backing on which to rely in time of crisis; and he well understood that three potentially opposing factions tend to be safer and easier to handle than two. Thus, while taking care never to offend or frighten the Greek and Islamic communities, he had from the outset given cautious encouragement to the vanguard of Latin churchmen who had arrived in Sicily in the early years of the conquest. By April 1073 a Latin Archbishopric had already been established in Palermo; during the next fifteen years, as the ecclesiastical immigration gathered strength, Frenchmen were installed as bishops in Troina, Mazara, Agrigento, Syracuse and Catania; and before 1085 the first Sicilian Benedictine abbey had been founded, at Roger's own expense, on the island of Lipari.

The Papacy, while obviously gratified to see the influence of the Mother Church so rapidly expanding in a land where it had been unknown only a few years before, at first viewed Roger's actions with some misgiving. Gregory VII, as we have seen, did not take kindly to the appointment of bishops by lay rulers; and though the Great Count never claimed the right of investiture as a matter of principle as Henry IV had done, he plainly had no intention of relinquishing his effective control of Church affairs. Fortunately Gregory had been too fully occupied elsewhere to bother overmuch with Sicily; and Urban, though his views on the subject were avowedly identical,[1] approached the problem with a degree of diplomacy of which his predecessor would never have been capable. It was not only a question of needing Roger as an ally. The Pope, who may have been already pondering the idea of a huge international Crusade to deliver the Holy Land from the Infidel, could hardly come out in active opposition against the one successful crusader in the West, who after two and a half centuries had restored much of Sicily to the Christian fold. Lurking, too, at the back of his mind there was possibly a further uneasy doubt: could he be alto-

---

[1] 'All that he [Gregory] rejected I reject, what he condemned I condemn, what he loved I embrace, what he regarded as Catholic I approve, and to whatever side he was attracted I incline' (from a circular letter written by Urban immediately after his election, March 1088).

gether sure of Roger's own devotion to the True Faith? Admittedly the Count, for purposes of practical administration, had subordinated the Orthodox churches in Sicily to his Latin hierarchy; but he had taken this step more in self-defence against Byzantine influence than in submission to Rome. He was, moreover, setting up Basilian monasteries at an alarming rate, and rumours of a possible important conversion had long been current in Palermo and elsewhere. Urban could not afford to take any chances.

Neither, however, could he allow the Count to claim rights which belonged properly to himself; and whatever may have been the primary reason for his visit to Roger at Troina in 1088—whether it was to seek help for a march on Rome or, as Malaterra suggests, to discuss Byzantine proposals for an end to the schism—it seems clear enough that the two reached a mutually satisfactory agreement on the whole question of the Church in Sicily. Henceforth, in return for his recognition of papal supremacy in ecclesiastical affairs, we find Roger enjoying a large measure of autonomy, making his own decisions in the Pope's name and only in the last resort—as when Urban refused to elevate Lipari to a bishopric in 1091— submitting to papal *force majeure*.

For a decade all went smoothly. In the interim Roger's daughter Constance married Conrad, Henry IV's rebel son who had allied himself with his father's enemies, and soon Sicily became known as one of the leading champions of the papalist cause. Then, in 1097, Urban miscalculated. Without giving the Count any prior warning, he appointed Robert, Bishop of Troina and Messina, as his Apostolic Legate in Sicily. For Roger such interference was unwarranted and intolerable. The unfortunate Robert was seized in his own church and put under instant arrest.

In other circumstances and with other protagonists such a crisis might have spelt serious trouble between Sicily and the Papacy; but Roger and Urban were both consummate diplomats, and, by a lucky chance, an opportunity to settle the matter soon presented itself. Some months before, Jordan of Capua's son Richard, now grown to manhood, had appealed to both the Duke of Apulia and the Count of Sicily for help in regaining his principality, from which he and his family had been expelled soon after his father's death.

They had agreed—Roger Borsa in exchange for suzerainty over all Capuan lands, his uncle in return for the surrender of Capuan claims to Naples. The siege began in the middle of May 1098 and lasted forty days; and it was an easy matter for the Pope, on the pretext of an attempt at mediation, to travel down to the beleaguered city. Roger received him with every courtesy, putting, we are told, six tents at his disposal; and in the talks that followed—which were attended also by Bishop Robert as a proof of the Count's goodwill— he seems to have admitted that he had acted hastily and expressed suitable regret. While these talks were still in progress, Capua surrendered and its Prince was reinstated; Pope and Count accordingly withdrew to Salerno, and it was there that they decided upon a formula which has led to more speculation and heated controversy than any other incident in the whole history of Sicilian relations with Rome. This formula was enshrined in a letter, addressed by Urban on 5 July 1098 to 'his most dear son, Count of Calabria and Sicily', in which he undertook that no papal legate should be appointed in any part of Roger's dominions without the express permission of the Count himself or his immediate heirs, whom Urban now formally invested with legatine powers. The letter further granted Roger complete discretion in the choice of bishops whom he might send to future councils of the Church.

Several distinguished historians of the period[1] have argued that by acquiring the perpetual Apostolic Legation the Great Count was obtaining rights which far exceeded those enjoyed by any other lay potentate in the Christian West. Catholic apologists, on the other hand, anxious to refute the exaggerated claims of later Sicilian rulers down the centuries, have gone to immense pains to show that the Pope in fact gave away very little; and recent research seems to have proved them right. Certainly the legatine office was withdrawn from Bishop Robert; yet it is worth noting that Urban's letter is careful not to confer it formally on Roger but merely authorises him to act *instead* of a Legate ('*Legati vice*'). Moreover, the letter purports to be merely a written confirmation of an earlier verbal promise; and though the Pope may be referring to an undertaking given immedi-

---

[1] Chalandon, *Histoire de la Domination Normande,* and Caspar, *Die Legatengewalt der normannisch-sicilischen Herrscher,* to name but two.

ately beforehand at Capua or Salerno, an examination of Roger's
handling of Church affairs during the previous ten years suggests
that he had in fact considered himself empowered with legatine
rights ever since Urban's visit of 1088. This would also explain his
fury at the appointment of Robert—the only time in his career that
he is known to have laid hands on the clergy.[1]

If, then, we accept this modern interpretation of the Pope's letter,
it emerges simply as the record of a ten-year-old agreement from
which both sides stood to gain. The powers it gave Roger were by
no means absolute, nor were they long to remain unique: a few years
later King Henry I was to acquire almost identical rights over the
Church in England. But they should not be underestimated on
that account. Roger now had written authority from Rome to take
decisions on his own initiative which would have been impossible
if the Pope had possessed full local representation, and which gave
him an effective practical control of the Latin Church in his
dominions such as he already enjoyed over the Orthodox and Muslim communities. It may not have been so brilliant a diplomatic
victory as was previously supposed, but it was no mean achievement.

Pope Urban was not the only distinguished ecclesiastic to appear
below the walls of Capua during those summer days of 1098. St
Anselm, Archbishop of Canterbury, who was a Lombard by birth,
had left England in despair the previous October—William Rufus,
having, not for the first time, made his life intolerable—and was
staying in the neighbourhood when he received a message from
Roger Borsa inviting him on a short visit to the siege. According to
Anselm's friend and biographer, the monk Eadmer (who was also
present), the Archbishop accepted and remained outside Capua
until the fall of the city, 'living in tents set well apart from the noise
and tumult of the army'; and there, soon after his arrival, the Pope
had joined him. The following story is best told in Eadmer's own
words:

The Lord Pope and Anselm were neighbours at the siege . . . so that their
households seemed rather to be one than two, nor did anyone willingly
come to visit the Pope without turning aside to Anselm. . . . Indeed,

---

[1] This whole question is brilliantly discussed by E. Jordan, 'La politique ecclésiastique de Roger I et les origines de la "Légation Sicilienne"'.

many who were afraid to approach the Pope, hurried to come to Anselm, being led by that love which knows no fear. The majesty of the Pope gave access only to the rich: the humanity of Anselm received all without any exceptance of persons. And whom do I mean by *all*? Even pagans as well as Christians. There were indeed pagans, for the Count of Sicily, a vassal of Duke Roger, had brought many thousands of them with him on the expedition. Some of them, I say, were stirred, by the reports of Anselm's goodness which circulated among them, to frequent our lodging. They gratefully accepted offerings of food from Anselm and returned to their own people making known the wonderful kindness which they had experienced at his hands. As a result he was from this time held in such veneration among them, that when we passed through their camp —for they were all encamped together—a huge crowd of them, raising their hands to heaven, would call down blessings on his head; then, kissing their hands as they are wont, they would do him reverence on their bended knees, giving thanks for his kindness and liberality. Many of them even, as we discovered, would willingly have submitted themselves to his instruction and would have allowed the yoke of the Christian faith to be placed by him upon their shoulders, if they had not feared that the cruelty of their Count would have been let loose against them. For in truth he was unwilling to allow any of them to become Christian with impunity. With what policy—if one can use that word—he did this, is no concern of mine: that is between God and himself.   [tr. Southern.]

Eadmer was never the most objective of biographers, and it is difficult to believe that Count Roger's Saracen troops were either as numerous or as adulatory as he suggests. His account is interesting, however, for its reference to their master's refusal to allow their conversion. In years to come, succeeding rulers of Sicily were to incur much odium for the apparent coldbloodedness with which they used Muslim soldiers against their Christian enemies, and for the vigour with which they were wont to oppose all evangelical attempts. Such policies may well have seemed immoral to bigoted mediaeval minds, but they certainly justified themselves in practice. First of all, by establishing a crack force of Saracen troops, commanded by Saracen officers and maintaining their traditional fighting methods, Roger provided a useful outlet for the military instincts and talents of his Muslim subjects, preventing them from feeling second-class citizens and giving them a pride of participation in the new Sicilian state. Secondly, he knew how dangerously religious sanctions could affect the morale of any Christian fighting force. His relations with the Papacy were normally amicable enough, but there was no telling how long they might remain so. Only by preserving a strong Islamic contingent in his army could he be sure that, in the event of a brush with the Pope, he would still retain a body of first-class soldiers whose loyalties would continue undivided. Finally, the addition of the Saracen brigades made the Count's army supreme in the peninsula, stronger than that of Capua or even that of the Duke of Apulia himself.

Roger's growing respect for the Saracens as soldiers had its counterpart in his civil administration. As he slowly won their confidence they began to respond to his leadership; and as their qualities, particularly in commercial and financial affairs, became more apparent, so the governmental posts held by Muslim function-aries increased in number and importance. In Palermo itself the Governor was always a Christian—though even here he retained the Arabic title of Emir, which passed into the Latin language in the form of *ammiratus* and from which, through Norman Sicily, our own word *admiral* is derived; elsewhere, in nearly all regions of the island whose populations were wholly or predominantly Muslim, government was left in the hands of the local Saracen Emirs. And so, with the return of peace and security to the land, the old Arab artistic and intellectual traditions were reawakened; poets, scientists and craftsmen appeared anew and were greeted with admiration and encouragement; and the foundations were laid for the great cultural efflorescence of twelfth-century Sicily, to which the Arab contribution was to be the richest and brightest of all.

In these circumstances it is hardly surprising that when, at Clermont in November 1095, Pope Urban summoned the princes and peoples of Christendom to take up arms against the Saracen and deliver the Holy Places from heathen pollution, his words should have had little appeal for the Count of Sicily. Among the knights and barons of Apulia, in whose hearts the old Norman wanderlust still burned as fiercely as ever, the response had been enthusiastic and immediate—to such an extent that Roger Borsa, who was, as usual with his uncle's help, busy besieging a rebellious Amalfi when the news of the Crusade reached South Italy, suddenly found himself faced with the mass desertion of nearly half his troops and was obliged to raise the siege. A few months later the great Crusading army, marching down the peninsula to its ports of embarcation, was swelled beyond all estimates as Norman warriors in their hundreds joined its ranks, led by the gigantic Bohemund himself, with no fewer than five other grandsons and two great-grandsons of old Tancred de Hauteville in his train.

For the Duke of Apulia, despite the unfortunate depletion of his army, the general exodus must have come as a godsend, delivering him at one stroke of all the most dangerous and disruptive elements in his duchies. But the excitement and commotion of that summer seem to have left his uncle unmoved. Roger had had enough of crusading. The Arab historian Ibn al-Athir tells of how, at about this time, the Count was offered the assistance of a Frankish army if he would lead an expedition to Africa against Temim, the Zirid Sultan of Mahdia, in what is now Tunisia. He continues:

At these tidings Roger assembled his companions and asked their advice. All replied: 'By the Gospel, this is an excellent plan for us and for him; thus will all the country become Christian.' But Roger lifted his foot and made a great fart, saying 'By my faith, here is far better counsel than you have given. . . . When that army is here I shall have to provide a numerous fleet, and much else besides, to transport it across to Africa, it and my own troops too. If we conquer the country, the country will be theirs; meanwhile we shall have to send them provisions from Sicily and I shall lose the money I draw each year from the sale of my produce. If on the contrary the expedition is unsuccessful, they will return to Sicily and I shall have to suffer their presence. Moreover Temim will be able to accuse me of bad faith towards him, claiming that I have broken my word and that I have severed the links of friendship existing between our countries.

Ibn al-Athir was writing some hundred years after Roger's death. His facts are a little confused; the episode in question is most probably connected with Roger's known refusal to join a joint Pisan and Genoese expedition against Temim in 1086. The account is therefore less remarkable for its historical accuracy than for the light it sheds on the Count's reputation in the Arab world. It is also one of the few anecdotes to have come down to us that gives us a picture, however imprecise or fleeting, of Roger the man. About his personality and his private life we know infuriatingly little—save that he certainly seems to have possessed in full measure the

philoprogenitiveness of the Hautevilles. Existing records testify
to at least thirteen and probably seventeen children by various
mothers, to three of whom—his beloved Judith of Evreux having
died young—he was successively married; but the list may not be
exhaustive. The rest of his character can only be deduced from
what we know of his career.

But what a career it was. When Roger died, on 22 June 1101,
in his mainland capital of Mileto, he was seventy years old. Forty-
four of those years had been spent in the South, and forty had been
largely devoted to the island of Sicily. The youngest of the Hautevilles, he had begun with even fewer advantages than his brothers;
but by the time of his death, though still only a Count and remaining
the faithful vassal of his nephew, he was generally reckoned as one
of the foremost princes of Europe, one whom no less than three
Kings—Philip of France, Conrad of Germany[1] (son of Henry IV)
and Coloman of Hungary—had sought as a father-in-law. Sicily he
had transformed. An island once despairing and demoralised, torn
asunder by internecine wars, decaying after two centuries of misrule,
had become a political entity, peaceful and prosperous, in which four
races—since, as a result of Roger's efforts, several thriving Lombard
colonies were now established round Catania—and three religions
were living happily side by side in mutual respect and concord.

Here—with its significance extending in time and space far beyond
the confines of the central Mediterranean—lies the cornerstone of
Roger's achievement. In a feudal Europe almost entirely given over
to bloodshed, loud with the tumult of a thousand petty struggles,
rent by schism, and always overshadowed by the titanic conflict
between Emperor and Pope, he left a land—not yet even a nation—
in which no barons grew over-turbulent, and neither the Greek nor
the Latin Churches strove against the lay authority or against each
other. While the rest of the continent, with a ridiculous combination
of cynical self-interest and woolly-headed idealism, exhausted and
disgraced itself on a Crusade, he—who alone among European
leaders had learnt from his own experience the vanity of the crusading spirit—had created a climate of enlightened political and reli-

---

[1] Conrad died before his father, having revolted against him; but he was acknowledged king in Italy.

gious thinking in which all races, creeds, languages and cultures were equally encouraged and favoured. Such a phenomenon, unparalleled in the Middle Ages, is rare enough at any time; and the example which Count Roger of Sicily set Europe in the eleventh century might still profitably be followed by most nations in the world today.

20

ADELAIDE

While all the other Christian princes of the world have always done their utmost, both personally and by their great generosity, to protect and nurture our kingdom like a tender shoot, this prince and his successors have never to this day addressed us one word of friendship—despite the fact that they are better and more conveniently placed than any other princes to offer us practical assistance or counsel. They seem to have kept this offence always green in their memory, and so do they unjustly visit upon a whole people a fault which should properly be imputed to one man only.

William of Tyre, Bk XI

NOTHING now remains of Count Roger's abbey of the SS. Trinità at Mileto. An earthquake destroyed it, with the rest of the town, in 1783, and all that could be salvaged of its founder's tomb was the antique sarcophagus itself, which now lies in the Archaeological Museum at Naples.[1] Its church was neither large nor particularly grandiose, but on that late June day in 1101 it must have offered the mourners physical as well as spiritual consolation; and it was from its cool shadows that, the funeral service over, a dark-haired young woman stepped out with her two little boys into the sunshine.

Countess Adelaide was the daughter of a certain Marquis Manfred, brother of the great Boniface del Vasto of Savona. She had married Roger as his third wife in 1089, when her husband was approaching sixty and, despite an undoubted virility to which his two sons and a dozen-odd daughters bore more than adequate testimony, still without any suitable male heir. Jordan, whom he loved and who had inherited all the Hauteville qualities, had been born out of wedlock;

[1] See photograph opposite p. 257.

while Geoffrey, his only legitimate son, was a leper who lived secluded in a remote monastery. For a time it had looked as though Adelaide were going to fail in her duty; and when, two years after the marriage and with the young Countess still as slim as ever, the news spread through Sicily that Jordan had died of a fever at Syracuse,[1] Roger's hopes of founding a dynasty seemed bleak indeed. At last, however, his prayers were answered. In 1093 Adelaide was brought to bed of a son, Simon; and two years later, on 22 December 1095, she presented him with another, whom, with justifiable pride —for he was now sixty-four—he called Roger.

The succession no longer gave cause for concern; but the future of Sicily still looked bleak, and many of the congregation that day in the SS. Trinita must have found their minds wandering from the words of the Requiem to dwell on the difficult years ahead. Simon was just eight years old, Roger barely five and a half; a long regency was inevitable. Adelaide was young and inexperienced, and a woman. A North Italian from Liguria, she had no deep hold on the loyalties of any of the peoples whom she was now asked to control —Normans, Greeks, Lombards or Saracens. Her knowledge of languages is unlikely to have stretched further than Italian, Latin and a smattering of Norman French. How could she possibly cope with the government of one of the most complex states of Europe?

The chronicles of this period are so lamentably thin that we have little means of telling how Adelaide overcame her difficulties. Ordericus Vitalis, a mine of misinformation in many respects but often surprisingly well-documented where South Italy and Sicily are concerned, tells us that she sent to Burgundy for a certain Robert, son of Duke Robert I, married him to her daughter—he presumably means one of her eleven step-daughters—and entrusted the government to him for the next ten years, after which she had him poisoned. As we saw in the case of Sichelgaita, Ordericus is all too ready to ascribe perfectly natural deaths to sinister causes, and this part of his account is almost certainly untrue. For the rest, it seems a little

[1] A stone recording Jordan's death and burial is still preserved in the exquisite little Norman Church of S. Maria at Mili S. Pietro, a few miles south of Messina. This was built by Count Roger in 1082 as one of his many Basilian foundations. Though sadly dilapidated and now part of a remarkably ramshackle farm, it is well worth a visit.

strange that Robert's name should not once be mentioned in
contemporary local records, though these are too sketchy to allow
us to draw any firm conclusions. Of the two greatest modern
authorities on the subject, Amari dismisses Ordericus's story as a
complete fabrication; Chalandon, with reservations, accepts it.
We can take our choice.

However she managed, Adelaide was outstandingly successful.
For her ministers she seems to have relied principally on native
Sicilians of Greek or Arab extraction, while such Norman barons—
always more trouble than Greeks and Saracens put together—who
hoped to take advantage of her regency to increase their own rights
and privileges soon discovered their mistake. Thus the Countess
was able to devote much of her time to her chief responsibility, the
bringing up of her two sons as worthy successors to their father.
Here too she did her work well—in so far as fate permitted. But on
28 September 1105 her elder son Simon died; and it was young
Roger, not yet ten years old, who now became Count of Sicily.

Of Roger's childhood we know next to nothing. There is an
undocumented tradition to the effect that at the end of 1096 he was
baptised by St Bruno, founder of the Carthusian Order, who
was then living in a hermitage next to his monastery of La Torre,
near Squillace; apart from this, we can only fall back on the equally
unsatisfactory testimony of a certain Alexander, Abbot of S. Salvatore near Telese, who later produced a tendentious and extremely
patchy account of the earlier part of his reign. Alexander tells of
how, while their father was still alive, the two little princes used to
fight together and how Roger, who always came out on top of his
elder brother, would claim Sicily for himself, offering to compensate
Simon with a bishopric or, if he preferred it, the Papacy. By this
alone, the abbot suggests, he proved himself born to rule—a theory
for which he finds additional confirmation in Roger's somewhat
exaggerated charity; never, we are told, did the boy refuse alms to
beggar or pilgrim, but would always empty his pockets of all that
he had and then ask his mother for more. Unfortunately Alexander
is writing at second-hand and his work, which was commissioned
by Roger's sister Matilda, is often nauseatingly sycophantic. Later
he becomes a useful and even fairly reliable source, but for this

period he is neither informative nor trustworthy; and it is only in default of anything better that these two dreary little contributions to our knowledge—if such they are—have found their way into this book.

There occurred, however, in these cloudy but apparently uneventful years one development of immeasurable significance both for the future of the state and for the shaping of its ruler. When in Sicily and not engaged on campaign, Roger I—as we must now call him—had based himself first at Troina and, latterly, at Messina, whence he could keep a closer eye on his Calabrian domains; but his personal preference was always for his old mainland castle at Mileto. Here it was that he normally kept his family and here, however frequent his absences, that he had made his home. Adelaide changed all that. In Calabria she doubtless felt herself hemmed in by the Norman barons, whom she disliked and distrusted. Messina was better, but it was still a small town and life there must have had little enough to offer. S. Marco d'Alunzio, where Roger also seems to have spent some of his childhood, was smaller still, though perhaps cooler and healthier in the summer months. There was only one real metropolis in Sicily, and that was Palermo—a city with a population now approaching three hundred thousand, and two centuries as a thriving capital already behind it; with flourishing craft centres and industries; with palaces, administrative offices, arsenals and even a mint.[1] The date at which Countess Adelaide finally fixed her capital at Palermo is uncertain. The process was probably a gradual one, but it was certainly complete by early 1112, when, in the old palace of the Emirs, the city witnessed the knighting of its young prince. It was a great day for Roger. Shortly afterwards, in June, when he and his mother together issued a grant of privileges to the Archbishop of Palermo, he could proudly style himself *Rogerius, jam miles, jam comes*.

The move to the metropolis was the last stage in the building-up of Sicilian, and especially Saracen, self-respect. Here was final proof that Sicily was no longer looked upon by her conquerors as a

---

[1] The Sicilian treasury and mint was to remain largely staffed by Muslims (though controlled by Greeks) throughout the Norman period. Many Norman coins continued to bear Arabic inscriptions and even Islamic ones—though they sometimes had a cross added, or the Byzantine legend 'Christ conquers'. The Italian word for mint, *zecca*, is a direct appropriation from the Arabic, dating from this time.

subordinate province. Adelaide and Roger, by coming to live permanently in Palermo, were showing that they not only trusted but depended on their Saracen subjects for the prosperity and smooth running of the state. More important still was the effect which it had on the formation of Roger himself. His father had grown up a Norman knight, and a Norman knight he had essentially remained throughout his life. The son, deprived of paternal influence from the age of five, was first and foremost a Sicilian. Apart from one or two close relations he knew few Normans; his Italian mother, whom he worshipped, infinitely preferred the Greeks, and thus the world in which he grew up was a Mediterranean-cosmopolitan one of Greek and Muslim tutors and secretaries, of studies pursued and state affairs conducted in three languages under cool marble colonnades, while outside the fountains splashed among the lemon-trees and the muezzin interminably summoned the faithful to prayer. It was all a far cry from Hauteville-la-Guichard; and it infused Roger's character with an exotic strain which cannot wholly be ascribed to his mother's Mediterranean blood. This was obvious enough in the darkness of his eyes and hair; but those in later years who came to know him well, and such of his fellow-princes as were to cross swords with him in the diplomatic field, soon learned to their cost that the Count of Sicily was not only a southerner; he was also an oriental.

The First Crusade had been a resounding, if undeserved, success. Its journey across Europe and Asia Minor had taken a heavy toll, and there had been anxious moments at Constantinople when the Emperor Alexius, understandably disturbed at the presence of a huge, heterogeneous and largely undisciplined army at his gates, had insisted that the Crusaders should swear fealty to him before continuing on their march. In the end, however, all the difficulties had been overcome. The Seljuks had been smashed at Dorylaeum in Anatolia; Frankish principalities had been set up at Edessa and Antioch; and on 15 July 1099 amid scenes of hideous atrocity and carnage, the soldiers of Christ had battered their way into Jerusalem, where, in the Church of the Holy Sepulchre, they had clasped together their bloodstained hands in prayer and thanksgiving.

Of all the Crusaders one man stood out head and shoulders above the rest. Bohemund, though no match in rank for such mighty princes as Godfrey of Bouillon or Raymond of Toulouse, had quickly shown his superiority as a soldier and a diplomat. He knew the Balkans well from his earlier campaigns; he spoke fluent Greek; he had been the hero of Dorylaeum and of the siege of Antioch. At Antioch he had stayed, and there he had established himself as the most powerful figure among all the Franks of Outremer. It was a magnificent performance, one that his father might have envied; it set the seal upon his greatness and assured him his place in history. But it did not last. In the summer of 1100 Bohemund had led an expedition against the Danishmends along the upper Euphrates, in the course of which he had been defeated and taken prisoner. Ransomed after three years' captivity, he had regained Antioch only to find that increasing pressures from the Saracens on the one hand and from Alexius and Count Raymond on the other had made its position almost untenable. Only massive reinforcements from Europe could save the situation. The year 1105, therefore, saw him back in Italy. There and in France, where the following year he married King Philip's daughter Constance, he managed to raise a new army; but his ambition led him astray and instead of returning directly to the East, he unwisely decided to march on Constantinople. Once again the Emperor, helped as usual by the Venetians, proved too strong for him, and in September 1108, in the gorges of the river Devol in what is now Albania, Bohemund was forced to seek terms. Alexius let him off lightly enough; he was allowed to remain in Antioch as an imperial vassal, though most of his Cilician and Syrian coastline was to be surrendered to the Emperor's direct control, and the Latin Patriarch of Antioch was to be replaced by a Greek. For Bohemund, however, the humiliation was too great to be borne. He never returned to the East but retired, broken, to Apulia where in 1111 he died. He was buried at Canosa; and visitors to its Cathedral can still see, huddled against the outside of the south wall, his curiously oriental-looking mausoleum—the earliest Norman tomb extant in South Italy.[1] Its beautiful bronze

[1] They should also take care not to miss the superb late eleventh-century Bishop's throne, supported on two marble elephants.

doors, engraved with Arabic designs and a eulogistic inscription, open to reveal an interior bare but for two little columns and the tombstone itself—on which is carved, in letters whose coarse magnificence still catches the breath, one word only: BOAMVNDVS.

But as Bohemund's star had waned, another had been steadily on the ascendant—that of Baldwin of Boulogne, formerly Count of Edessa, who on Christmas Day 1100, in the church of the Nativity at Bethlehem, had been crowned King of Jerusalem. In the first decade of his reign Baldwin, despite a youthful period in Holy Orders, had brilliantly maintained the supremacy of the lay power over that of the Church, and had already gone a long way towards converting the poor and scattered territories of his kingdom into a strong, cohesive state. Matrimonially, however, he had been less successful. He had always had an eye for a pretty girl, and the prevailing atmosphere of his court, though never undignified, could scarcely have been described as monastic; but the Armenian princess whom he had taken as his second wife was generally agreed to have gone too far. Her rumoured reception of certain Muslim pirates into whose clutches she had fallen—not, it was said, with as much reluctance as might have been supposed—on her way from Antioch to assume her throne had not endeared her to her husband; and after a few years in which she had done little to redeem her reputation he had dismissed her—first to a nunnery in Jerusalem and then, at her urgent request, to Constantinople, where she found the permissiveness of the capital a good deal more to her taste. Baldwin had meanwhile resumed with relief his bachelor life; and this he continued to enjoy until, at the end of 1112, he heard that Countess Adelaide of Sicily, having laid aside the cares of the Regency with the coming of age of her son, was looking for a second husband.

In spite of the profitable trade agreements which he had been able to conclude with the Italian mercantile republics, Baldwin's kingdom was chronically short of funds. On the other hand it was common knowledge that Adelaide had amassed enormous wealth during her years in Sicily, which was rapidly becoming one of the chief centres of the entrepôt trade between Europe and the Levant. There were other considerations as well. The Sicilian navy was already a force to be reckoned with; and its support would immeasurably strengthen the position of Jerusalem among her neighbour states, Christian and Saracen. Baldwin made up his mind. An embassy was immediately despatched to Palermo with a formal request for the Countess's hand in marriage.

And Adelaide accepted. She had never liked the Franks as a race, but how could anyone refuse an offer to be Queen of Jerusalem? Moreover she had no delusions about her worth and knew that she could name her own terms. If Baldwin stood to gain from the alliance, she would take good care that her son Roger would not be the loser. Her acceptance, therefore, was given on one condition; that, if the marriage was childless—and she was, after all, no longer in her first youth—the crown of Jerusalem should pass to the Count of Sicily. Baldwin, who had no children living, raised no objection; and so, in the summer of 1113, the Countess Adelaide sailed for the East.

Her journey was not without incident. An attack by pirates was successfully beaten off, but shortly before her arrival there arose so terrible a storm that the three ships sent out by Baldwin to escort her were driven far off course into the Bay of Ascalon, still in Saracen hands, and only with difficulty managed to fight their way out. But when at last the Sicilian galleys glided proudly into the harbour of Acre, the King and all those around him saw that here indeed was a bride worth waiting for. Albert of Aix, one of the most informative of the historians of the First Crusade, was not present on that August morning; but his account of the scene, written some twenty years later, is worth quoting for the picture it gives of a landfall probably unequalled in splendour since the days of Cleopatra.

She had with her two triremes, each with five hundred warriors, and seven ships carrying gold, silver, purple, and great quantities of precious stones and magnificent vestments, to say nothing of weapons, cuirasses, swords, helmets, shields blazing with gold, and all other accoutrements of war such as are employed by mighty princes for the service and defence of their ships. The vessel on which the great lady had elected to travel was ornamented with a mast gilded with the purest gold, which glinted from afar in the sunlight; and the prow and the poop of this vessel, similarly covered with gold and silver and worked by skilful craftsmen, were wonderful to behold. And on one of the seven ships were the Saracen archers, most stalwart men clothed in resplendent garments of great price, all destined as gifts to the King—such men as had no superiors in their art in the whole land of Jerusalem.

The effect of Adelaide's arrival was not lost on the knights of Outremer; few countries of the West would have been capable of such a display. But Baldwin had done his best to arrange a reception worthy of his Queen.

The King, informed of his illustrious lady's arrival, went down to the port with all the princes of his kingdom and the members of his court, magnificently and variously clothed; he was surrounded by all his royal pomp, followed by his horses and his mules covered with purple and gold, and accompanied by his musicians sounding trumpets and playing on all kinds of instruments to delight the ear. So the King received the Princess as she descended from the vessel. The open spaces were strewn with beautiful carpets of many colours, and the streets were swathed with purple in honour of the great lady, herself mistress of such abundance.[1]

A few days later the marriage was solemnised, amid scenes of comparable splendour, in the palace of Acre; and the royal couple proceeded in state, through towns and villages hung with flags, to Jerusalem. All too soon, however, rejoicing gave way to disillusion. Baldwin's army had not been paid for months; Frankish barons and knights had to be compensated and indemnified for lands recaptured by the Saracens; and by the time these and other outstanding debts had been settled there was little left of Adelaide's immense dowry. The Queen, for her part, found the Normans and Franks of Outremer no more congenial than their counterparts in South Italy. More serious still, Baldwin was soon forced to admit that although he had put away his previous wife he had never formally divorced her. Suddenly a great wave of popular feeling arose against Adelaide—and also against the Patriarch Arnulf of Jerusalem, to whose well-known simonies was now added the yet graver charge of conniving at a bigamous marriage.

For some time Baldwin prevaricated. Adelaide bored him and he had spent all her money, but the link with Sicily was still valuable to him and he hesitated to send her away. In the spring of 1117, however, he fell dangerously ill; and Arnulf, who had been deposed from his Patriarchate and then reinstated by the Pope in return for a

[1] Albert of Aix, Bk. XII.

promise to work for the Queen's dismissal, managed to persuade him that only by taking such a step could he avoid the pains of eternal damnation. The Patriarch's further injunction—that Baldwin should also summon his former, legitimate, wife back to Jerusalem—went unfulfilled; she was still living it up in Constantinople and enjoying herself far too much to contemplate a return. But as far as Adelaide was concerned, this was the end. Baldwin, restored to health, held firm to his decision; and the unhappy queen, despoiled and humiliated, was packed off home to Sicily with the minimum of ceremony or consideration. She had never particularly liked Baldwin, and she cannot have altogether regretted leaving the rigours of Palestine for the sophistication and comfort of Palermo; but she had sustained an insult which neither she nor her son ever forgave. She herself died the following year and was buried in the cathedral of Patti, where her tomb—not, alas, contemporary—may still be seen.[1] As for Roger, another historian of the Crusade—William of Tyre—was to report in about 1170 that this treatment of his mother 'imbued him for ever with a violent hatred of the Kingdom of Jerusalem and its people'. The humiliation of Adelaide, grave as it was, was not the only offence of which Baldwin had been guilty; by renouncing her he also broke the promise he had given in their marriage contract—that, in default of further children, the Crown of Jerusalem should pass on his death to Roger. Thus when, a decade or so later, the King of Sicily was to show his strength for the first time in the Eastern Mediterranean, he was acting not just as an aggrieved son avenging his mother's honour, but as a defrauded and ambitious monarch, in arms against the usurpers of his realm.

[1] The tomb itself is obviously Renaissance, though the recumbent effigy above it may be original. It will be found in the south transept of the Cathedral, set into the east wall. The inscription describes Adelaide as Roger's mother, but makes no mention of her period as Queen of Jerusalem—a chapter of her life which she, and Roger, doubtless preferred to forget.

21

THE FLEDGLING YEARS

O young son of Ali, O little lion of the holy garden of the Faith, for whom
the lances form a living hedge! Thou didst show thy bared teeth, and the
blue points of thy lances! Those blue-eyed Franks, surely they shall receive
none of thy kisses!

Ibn Hamdis of Syracuse

THE good fortune that had attended the Countess Adelaide throughout her regency—only to desert her so shatteringly thereafter—
remained true to her son during the first few crucial years of his
personal rule. Roger was barely sixteen and a half when he assumed
effective power, the untried ruler of a heterogeneous state which,
though prosperous, was still potentially explosive. He desperately
needed a period of peace in which to flex his muscles, to feel his own
authority within him, not as a mere tool of government, but as an
integral part of his being.

And it was granted to him. The great exodus to Outremer had
drained off many of the most obstreperous of his mainland vassals
and lowered the political temperature throughout South Italy.
To Sicily, meanwhile, it had brought only increased affluence, and
the island was now richer than at any time in its history. Even before
the Crusade the volume of Levantine commerce—with cities like
Tripoli, Alexandria and Antioch, as well as with Constantinople
itself—had been steadily growing; and the Norman conquest of
the South had now made the straits of Messina safe, for the first time
in centuries, to Christian shipping. To the Italian mercantile republics of the west coast such a development was of enormous significance; we know, for example, that in September 1116 Roger
granted a plot of land at Messina to the Genoese consul for the

building of a hospital there, and it is safe to assume that Pisa, Naples, Amalfi and others had also staked their claims. In such conditions the Greeks and Arabs of Sicily—two races in which the commercial sense was, then as now, particularly highly developed—were in no mind to make trouble; they were far too busy making money instead. And so the young Count was able to settle himself comfortably on his throne, thanking God for the priceless gift of a Crusade, of which he himself, though not even a participant, was ultimately to prove the greatest beneficiary of all.

This new outburst of military and commercial activity in the Mediterranean fired Roger's imagination and awoke his ambition. He did not, he knew, possess his father's—still less his uncle's—military gifts. The warlike pursuits which played so large a part in the education of other young Norman knights had been largely absent from his own woman-dominated upbringing, a fact which reinforced that natural preference for diplomatic rather than military methods which he was to keep throughout his life. But Sicily was no longer the geographical backwater it had been when the conquest was launched half a century before. Its economic explosion had been meteoric and spectacular; Palermo, long a thriving metropolis, was now busier than ever in the past; Messina and Syracuse were boom-towns; the island had suddenly become the hub of a newly-expanded and fast-developing Latin world. Roger was determined that his own political influence should grow in due proportion; and that he himself, like Robert Guiscard before him, should make his presence and power felt among the princes of Europe—and of Africa and Asia too.

As a first step, wealth must be converted into strength; and strength for an island realm could mean only one thing—an invincible navy. The Sicilian fleet had been an important force ever since the Guiscard's day; Roger I had kept it up, enlarged it, and put it to good use at Syracuse, Malta and elsewhere; but only Roger II was to make it supreme. From his day until the extinction of Norman power in the island, nation and navy were one and inseparable; it is hardly possible to conceive of either without the other. The navy meant Sicily's prosperity in peace, her sword and her shield in time of war; and in the years to come the promise of its support or the threat of its opposition was to cause many a foreign power to think again.

Just as the navy was more than a navy, so was its admiral more than an admiral. At first, as we have seen, the word *ammiratus* had no nautical implications; it was merely a latinisation of the Arabic title of Emir which, after the change of capital, came to be applied in particular to the Emir of Palermo, since 1072 traditionally a Greek Christian. In the early days of Count Roger I this official had been merely a local governor. His responsibilities had been great, embracing every aspect of the administration of a city which had by now probably surpassed Cordova as the greatest Muslim metropolis of Europe; but his authority had been confined within narrow geographical limits. As time went on, however, and particularly during Adelaide's regency, his position grew in importance until it covered all the Count's dominions in Sicily and Calabria. The fixing of the court in Palermo was the first and most obvious reason for the change, but there was also another—the character and ability of the Emir himself. He was at this time a Greek Christian called Christodulus, known to the Muslim chroniclers as Abdul-Rahman al-Nasrani. These two names seem to be connected—the Greek means *Slave of Christ*, the Arabic *Slave of the All-Merciful, the Christian* —and thus he may well have been an Arab convert, or perhaps even, as Amari suggests, a member of one of those originally Christian but long apostatised families which had now returned to their original faith. At all events he seems to have been the outstanding figure of his time, who received in succession the titles of *proto-nobilissimus* and *protonotary*—innovations which reveal how the Norman court was consciously basing itself on Byzantine models— and before long found himself President of the Council of State. As such he was made responsible for the building-up of the fleet— of which, as a natural extension of his duties, he soon assumed the overall command. It may be that he was abler as an administrator than as a strategist; certainly, as we shall shortly see, he fails to emerge with any particular distinction from the one naval operation of which a full account has come down to us, and this probably explains why, from about 1123, he was gradually to fall under the shadow of his still more brilliant and dashing successor, George of

Antioch. But for some fifteen years before that, saving only the Count himself, Christodulus was supreme in Sicily—the first of that coruscating line of Sicilian Admirals who contributed so much to the glory of their country and bequeathed their title to the world.

For the historian these first years of Roger's reign are unutterably frustrating. The sources are so few, so barren of any significant or revealing information, that we cannot hope to build up an accurate picture. Just occasionally, as in the Jerusalem episode, when the external affairs of Sicily bring her into contact with other, better-documented societies, some narrow shaft of light manages to filter through the mist and allows us a glimpse of a prosperous and fast-developing state; for the rest of the time, until her local chroniclers resume a coherent tale, we can see this period of her history only in the light of one of those opaque but luminous summer mornings in which the early haze is finally dispelled to reveal a blazing, crystalline noon-day.

For the young Count, on the other hand, it must have been a happy and exhilarating time as he watched his power and wealth increase, learned how to wield and enjoy them, and gradually became aware of his own remarkable gifts. Inevitably there were problems; equally inevitably the Pope ranked high among them. Urban had died in 1099, a fortnight after the Crusaders entered Jerusalem, but—ironically enough—just before news of the victory reached Rome. He had been succeeded by a good-natured Tuscan monk, Paschal II. It is said that when William Rufus of England was told that the character of the new Pope was not unlike that of Archbishop Anselm, the King exclaimed: 'God's Face! Then he isn't much good'—a remark which, though quietly memorable in its way, is hardly fair to either ecclesiastic. Paschal may have been of gentle disposition; he may have lacked that last ounce of moral fibre which would have enabled him to stand firm after his two months' imprisonment, with sixteen of his cardinals, by the Western Emperor Henry V in 1111;[1] but he was no weakling, and he

[1] Ordericus Vitalis's bland statement that two thousand Normans from Apulia hurried to his rescue and drove Henry from Rome is without any kind of foundation. Prince Robert of Capua tried to send three hundred, but they were turned back half-way by the Count of Tusculum. Ordericus is probably confusing 1111 with 1084.

was certainly not prepared to remain silent while the young Count of Sicily arrogated to himself privileges which properly belonged to the See of St Peter.

Roger for his part had taken a high-handed line from the start. Already in 1114 he had deposed the Archbishop of Cosenza, and there is other evidence to suggest that he had largely forgotten his father's undertaking, made in return for the legatine privileges of 1098, that henceforth the Latin clergy of Sicily should be subject only to Canon Law. By 1117 his relations with the Pope had deteriorated still further, for it was Paschal who had insisted on his mother's removal from Jerusalem, and whom he therefore held to be equally responsible, with Baldwin, for her humiliation. There was certainly some acrimonious correspondence at this time between Palermo and Rome, in the course of which the Pope seems to have tried still further to limit the terms of the 1098 agreement. The letter which he wrote Roger on this occasion is however couched in language so deliberately ambiguous as to raise more problems than it solves, and to have inspired more learned speculation, even, than Urban's original. A detailed discussion of it falls mercifully outside the scope of a general history;[1] suffice it to say that there is no evidence, over the remaining twenty-seven years of his reign, to suggest that Roger took the slightest notice.

All too soon, however, the young Count found himself beset by a graver and more immediate problem, this time of his own making. Conscious of his growing strength, confident of his naval supremacy, he soon began to cast covetous eyes southward across the sea to the African coast. Sicilian relations with the Zirids of Africa had been excellent ever since his father's day; Roger I had been bound by treaty with Temim, Prince of Mahdia, and had refused on at least one occasion—that of the Pisan-Genoese expedition of 1086—to attack him. More recently, internal strife between the Zirids and the Berber tribe of the Beni-Hammad had led to the devastation of much of the fertile North African coastal strip, and Sicily had been able to export all her surplus grain to the famine-stricken areas on highly profitable terms. In return she had begun to accept increasing

[1] Such a discussion will be found in E. Jordan's article referred to above (p. 274 n).

quantities of Arab merchandise; and by the time Temim's son Yahya
died in 1116 a Sicilian commercial mission was permanently established at Mahdia and there was a frequent, friendly traffic of Sicilian
and Saracen ships in both directions across the narrow sea.

But trade was not enough for Roger; his thoughts were on
conquest, for how else could he prove himself a ruler worthy of his
father, his uncle and his Hauteville name? All he needed was a suitable excuse, and in 1118 it was offered. A certain Rafi ibn Makkan
ibn Kamil, described by Amari as half-governor, half-usurper of the
African city of Gabes, had recently built and equipped a great
merchant galley with which he proposed to carry on a profitable
trading business on his own account. Prince Yahya, during his lifetime, had raised no objection and had even gone so far as to provide
Rafi with iron and timber for the work; but his son and successor
Ali proved less easy-going. Claiming that the right to engage in
merchant shipping was a prerogative of the Prince alone, he warned
Rafi that his ship would be confiscated the moment it put out of
harbour, and lent additional force to his threat by sending ten of his
own vessels to Gabes. Rafi, outraged, appealed to Roger. He had
intended, he wrote, that his ship's maiden voyage should take her
to Palermo, with a cargo of gifts which would reflect the high esteem
in which he had always held the Count of Sicily. Ali's attitude was
thus not only an injustice to himself but an insult to Roger. Surely
it would have to be avenged.

Roger doubtless treated the bit about his presents with the
scepticism it deserved. He had lived too long among the Arabs to
be taken in by that sort of thing. Anyway, he needed no such
additional persuasions. Shortly afterwards some twenty-four of his
best warships appeared off Gabes. Ali was ready for them and
watched as they drew nearer. His timorous advisers urged him at all
costs to preserve the Sicilian alliance, but he ignored them. This
was a matter of principle and he had no intention of backing down.
That night the Normans landed. Rafi received them well and held a
great banquet in their honour; but no sooner had they settled down
at the table than the doors were flung open and Ali's men burst,
sword in hand, into the room. The Sicilians were taken completely
by surprise; they could offer little resistance. They barely managed

to regain their ships and, confused and humiliated, to beat their way home to Palermo. Ali had won the first round.[1]

Relations now quickly deteriorated on both sides. Ali first imprisoned all Sicilian commercial agents in his territories, confiscating their property, Soon after, in a rare gesture of conciliation, he released them again; but Roger immediately demanded further concessions which he probably knew to be unacceptable, and on Ali's refusal threatened a full-scale naval attack on Mahdia. Ali replied with dark hints about a combined onslaught against Sicily by himself and his Almoravid neighbours, who by this time controlled Southern Spain and Portugal, the Balearic Islands and all North Africa west of Algiers. War seemed inevitable, and preparations began in earnest. They were still continuing when, in July 1121, Ali suddenly died. His son Hassan was a boy of twelve; the cares of government were entrusted to his chief eunuch; and the resulting unrest—for Saracen Emirs tended to be no more amenable than Norman barons—led to general confusion on the lines already familiar in South Italy and elsewhere. Had Roger struck now, North Africa might have been his for the taking; but he missed his chance. For reasons which need not concern us at present, he had chosen this moment to make his first major foray into Apulia; and by the time he had regrouped his forces the situation in Mahdia had changed.

Roger's Apulian adventure was, as we shall see in the next chapter, by no means unsuccessful; and it would probably have distracted him for some years from the North African question but for a new and unexpected development which brought him abruptly down to earth. In the summer of 1122 a Saracen fleet commanded by a privateer named Abu Abdullah ibn Maimun, in service with the Almoravids, descended in force on the town of Nicotera and its neighbouring villages along the Calabrian coast. It was the first attack Roger had sustained on his own territory—the first from

[1] Such, at least, is the version of the story told by the Tunisian writer at-Tigani two hundred years later. Ibn al-Athir makes no mention of any engagement; according to him, the Sicilians simply saw that the opposition was too strong for them, and sailed away again without disembarking. The truth will never be known—though it seems unlikely that Roger's navy, outnumbering as it did Ali's ships by more than two to one, should have behaved quite so cravenly as either of the two chroniclers suggests.

Africa since his father's pact with Sultan Temim some forty years before. There must have been many in Nicotera who still remembered that fearful raid by Bernavert of Syracuse in 1084; but this was infinitely worse. The entire town was sacked; women and children were raped and carried off into slavery; and every object of value that could not be carted down to the waiting ships was burnt or otherwise destroyed.

Roger had paid little attention at the time to Ali's threats of an alliance with the Almoravids; but now, rightly or wrongly, he decided that this outrage had been inspired from Mahdia and he held young Hassan responsible. His military preparations, in suspense since Ali's death, were resumed with a new intensity and determination. This would no longer be a war of national aggrandisement; it would be a war of revenge. Additional ships and men were summoned from Italy; a security embargo was placed on all vessels bound for Arab ports in Africa or Spain; and by midsummer 1123 the fleet was ready. According to the official Saracen account subsequently compiled on Hassan's orders, it consisted of three hundred ships, carrying a total of a thousand and one mounted knights and thirty thousand footsoldiers. As usual, the numbers are probably exaggerated; but the expedition was almost certainly larger than anything seen in Sicily since the early days of the conquest.

The very scale on which it was conceived and launched makes it all the more surprising that Roger should not have led it in person. He was now twenty-seven, an age by which the average Norman knight usually had a good ten years of hard campaigning behind him. He had been married five years—to Elvira, daughter of King Alfonso VI of Castile—and had already at least two sons to succeed him. And this was the first important military undertaking of his career. There is no record of any major crisis elsewhere that might have retained him at home or even drawn him to Apulia; indeed, he seems to have spent most of the late summer and autumn of 1123 rather desultorily in Eastern Sicily and his Calabrian domains. And so, in the absence of any evidence to the contrary, we can only conclude that he did not accompany the expedition because, quite simply, he preferred not to. All his life he was more an intellectual than a soldier; war was the one art in which he never excelled. Though he did not recoil from it as an instrument of policy, he always saw himself primarily as a statesman and administrator and tended, when he could, to leave the fighting to others more suited by aptitude and inclination for the job. There would, to be sure, be periods of his life during which, like any other ruler of his time, he would be obliged to take the field in person. On these occasions he would normally acquit himself well enough. But there would also be times when it was clear that physical courage was never, as it was with his father or uncles, an inherent part of his character—that it could be summoned, when required, only by dint of a deliberate and conscious effort.

It was, therefore, under the command of Admiral Christodulus that the expedition set sail from Marsala in July 1123. Almost at once a storm arose—the Normans were always very unlucky with their weather—and the ships were forced ashore on Pantelleria, where the troops lost no time in practising all the things that they intended to do to the Arabs of Mahdia. But they were soon able to put to sea again, and on 21 July the fleet hove to off some little islets then known simply as the *Ahasi* (the sandy ones) some ten miles north of the town.[1] They seemed adequately protected from enemy attack by the narrow strait which separated them from the mainland; but this strait was itself dominated by a castle, known locally as ad-Dimas, which accordingly became the first Sicilian objective. Before moving to the attack, Christodulus needed more information about Saracen strength in Mahdia itself. A detachment of cavalry was put ashore under cover of darkness and headed south towards the town; and the following morning the admiral personally led twenty-three ships on a similar sortie to brief himself on the maritime defences.

He was not gone for long; the most cursory inspection was enough to convince him that, from the sea at any rate, Mahdia was virtually impregnable. To a commander who thought largely in

[1] There is some doubt as to which precisely these islands were. My own inclination is to identify them with the Kuria group; but the area is full of shallows and shoals, and the whole conformation may well have changed significantly in eight centuries.

terms of naval power, this was a serious blow; but worse was to come, for he returned to the islands to find the Sicilian camp in desolation. Somehow an Arab raiding party had managed to cross the straits, liquidated such opposition as it had encountered, sacked the commissariat and returned with a rich plunder of arms and equipment. Suddenly Christodulus saw his whole expedition threatened with failure. That night, in what was left of the camp, Sicilian morale was at a very low ebb indeed.

Meanwhile, however, the admiral's young lieutenant George of Antioch had not been wasting his time. This extraordinary man, whose imagination and initiative were soon to make him famous throughout the Mediterranean, had been born in Antioch of Greek parents; but at an early age he had accompanied his father to North Africa where they had both taken service with Sultan Temim. On Temim's death, George found himself on bad terms with his successor, Yahya; he probably also recognised that it was Palermo, and not Mahdia, that held the key to future power in the Mediterranean. One Friday morning in 1108, while his Muslim superiors were all at prayer, he accordingly disguised himself as a sailor and slipped on to a Sicilian ship that was lying in the harbour. It took him to Palermo, where he went straight to the palace and presented himself for government service. Within a few years, first in the revenue department and later on an official trade mission to Egypt, George established himself as one of the ablest and most devoted servants of the Sicilian state, and won the favour of Christodulus and of the Count himself. It was not surprising; his qualifications alone made him unique. Here was a skilled administrator, a Christian bilingual in Greek and Arabic and a fine seaman whose knowledge of North Africa's coastal waters matched his understanding of her political, economic and diplomatic affairs. Thus, when Christodulus had begun to plan his expedition against Mahdia, he had had no hesitation in appointing the brilliant young Levantine as his second-in-command.

And George, for his part, had not been slow in justifying the appointment. By means unknown he quickly succeeded in suborning the garrison commanders of ad-Dimas, and on the third day after their arrival the Sicilians gained possession of the fort without a

struggle and installed their own garrison—estimated by at-Tigani
at a hundred men. Here was victory of a kind; but even this was to
be turned, all too soon, to defeat. In the two years that had passed
since the death of Ali, his son Hassan, though still only fourteen,
had managed to assert his authority over most of the country; and
this unprovoked invasion—for he appears to have had nothing to
do with the Nicotera raid—was just what he needed to rally the
waverers to his banner. At the first approach of the Sicilian fleet
he had proclaimed a *jihad*—holy war on the infidel—and on 26 July,
the fourth night after the landing, he struck. His army advanced
quietly from the south, under cover of darkness; and then suddenly, with a great shout of '*Akbar Allah!*' which, the chroniclers
tell us, caused the very earth to tremble, flung itself against
ad-Dimas.

Once more we are forced to rely on later Arab sources for the
story of the battle that followed, though at-Tigani reproduces the
text of the official report circulated by Hassan immediately after
his victory. We may therefore suspect, even though we cannot
entirely discount, tales of the blind panic that seized the invading
army, of the headlong rush to the ships, of the terrified cavalry
pausing only to cut the throats of their horses rather than see them
fall into Saracen hands. What seems certain is that Roger and his
advisers had again miscalculated. Pride in their fleet had led them
to neglect the land army and to underestimate the strength of the
African opposition. It was their second humiliation in five years;
and on this occasion, trounced by a child of fourteen, they had lost
their honour and a good deal more besides.

Safely aboard their ships and out of range of Hassan's archers, the
Sicilians regained a little of their morale—enough, at least, to enable
them to assess the situation. Their main concern now was for the
garrison still holding out at ad-Dimas. Christodulus was unwilling
to leave them to their fate without making an attempt at rescue. For
a week his galleys hovered off the coast awaiting their opportunity;
but they waited in vain. The Muslims, well aware of Sicilian intentions, maintained ceaseless vigilance over the castle; and at last,
with his own supplies beginning to run short, the admiral saw that
the situation was hopeless. He gave the order to depart; and his

fleet spread its sails to the wind and vanished over the northern horizon. In the whole unedifying campaign, it was now left to the garrison to show the first—and last—flicker of Sicilian spirit. All attempts to buy their lives from the Saracens having failed, they resolved to sell them dearly. They held out as long as they could; then on 10 August, their supplies of food and water alike exhausted, they burst out from ad-Dimas, sword in hand. They were slaughtered to a man. Meanwhile their returning comrades had once again run into bad weather; many ships were lost; and of the three hundred that had sailed so confidently from Marsala a month before, only a hundred—according to Hassan's claim—returned to Sicily.

Virtually overnight, young Hassan—whose appreciation of the value of publicity and whose technique in its handling marks him out as a ruler far in advance of his time—had become the hero of Islam, to be celebrated by poets from Cordova to Baghdad. Roger, on the other hand, had suffered a loss of prestige from which he would take long to recover. The first important military enterprise of his reign, his first venture into the international field to prove himself a major power in Europe, had ended in fiasco. He does not seem to have looked for scapegoats. Christodulus, who must be held largely responsible for the disaster, was to decline in influence from this time, but he was neither disgraced nor dismissed; while George of Antioch, whose initial capture of ad-Dimas was the only triumph —however shortlived—of the whole campaign, emerged with his reputation untarnished. But for all the Christians in Sicily it was a bitter blow; and a contemporary Arab historian[1] reports an eye-witness account of a 'Frankish knight' in Roger's audience-chamber, tearing at his beard until the blood streamed down his face and swearing revenge. The Count himself, though less demonstrative, must have felt much the same. There was a strong streak of vindictive-ness in his character, and he never forgot an injury. But he was also a patient man, and he had no intention of risking his reputation still further with a third attack—not, at least, for the moment. Hostilities with Hassan continued for some years, but only in a desultory way; an alliance which Roger was to form in 1128 with Count Raymond of Barcelona was directed principally against the Almoravids of Spain,

---

[1] Abu es-Salt, quoted by Amari, *Storia dei Musulmani di Sicilia*, vol. III, p. 387.

rather than the Zirids, and anyway it came to nothing. By then, however, he had preoccupations elsewhere. He was to experience many more triumphs and disasters before that day, just a quarter of a century later, when George of Antioch would carry his banner proudly into Mahdia and set the record straight at last.

22

REUNIFICATION

The ducal towns like Salerno, Troia, Melfi, Venosa, and others which
were left without protection of their lord, were seized with tyrant force
by this man or by that. And each man did that which seemed good in his
own eyes, for there was no one to say him nay. And since none feared
punishment in this life, so did men deliver themselves up more and more
freely to evil deeds. Thus it was not only travellers who journeyed in
fear of their lives, but the very peasants themselves, who could not even
till their own fields in safety. What more can I say? If God had not kept
alive a scion of the Guiscard's line to preserve the ducal power, the whole
land would surely have perished of its own wickedness and cruelty.

Alexander of Telese, Bk I, ch. 1

DURING the forty-odd years that had elapsed since Robert Guiscard's death, the fortunes of the Duchy of Apulia had suffered a
steep and steady decline. Roger Borsa, plodding miserably in his
father's footsteps, had done his pathetic best to hold it together,
and indeed after the submission of Capua in 1098 [1] could even boast
technical dominion over all South Italy—more than Robert had
ever been able to achieve. But Capua, like most of his other successes,
had been won only by courtesy of his uncle, the Count of Sicily,
who always demanded territorial concessions in return; and when,
after the Count's death, the poor Duke of Apulia found himself
largely deprived of Sicilian help, his patrimony began to disintegrate faster than ever into anarchy. Roger Borsa died in February
1111, a week or so before his old enemy Bohemund and ten days
after Pope Paschal had been carted off by an implacable Henry V
into captivity, still pleading in vain for Norman assistance. He
was laid to rest in his father's cathedral of Salerno, where his tomb
—a somewhat unsuitable fourth-century sarcophagus carved with

[1] See p. 273.

figures of Dionysus and Ariadne, but covered with a contemporary representation of its present occupant in high relief—stands in the south aisle. For all his inadequacies as a ruler, he had been a good and upright man in his way; but his death was not widely mourned outside his immediate family and the churches and monasteries he had so loved to endow—as, in particular, the Abbey of La Cava near Salerno where prayers are still offered every evening after compline for the repose of his soul.[1]

He was succeeded by a child—William, the youngest and sole survivor of his three sons, whose mother, Alaine of Flanders, now assumed the regency. It was an unfortunate state of affairs to arise at such a moment, when a strong hand was more than ever needed; and it was made more unfortunate still by the death of Bohemund. If he had lived, he might have seized control and saved the dukedom; as things turned out, he left his widow, Constance of France, on the throne of Taranto, governing on behalf of their infant son Bohemund II. Thus, with the country in chaos, the Pope in prison and a strong-willed and determined Emperor encamped only a few miles from Rome, South Italy found itself under the titular authority of three women—Adelaide, Alaine and Constance—all of them foreigners and two without the slightest experience of politics or government. It was small wonder that, particularly among the Lombard populations, the general atmosphere of demoralisation and hopelessness should have developed into a great resurgent wave of anti-Norman feeling. What advantage, men asked, had these brigands ever brought to Italy? In the century since their arrival, hardly a year had passed without its quota of ravaged towns and devastated harvests, without its addition of further pages to the South's sad history of bloodshed and violence. Here were the destroyers of the old Lombard heritage; yet they had proved incapable of setting up anything lasting in its place. The country had only one chance of salvation—Henry the Emperor who, having just dealt so successfully with the Pope, would now doubtless turn his attention to the Normans themselves.

---

[1] In a letter dated St Valentine's Day 1966, the keeper of the monastic Archive, Dom Angelo Mifsud, O.S.B., writes that 'the gratitude of the monks of La Cava towards their illustrious benefactor has not ceased, nor has it ever been interrupted'.

But Henry did nothing of the sort. He marched his army north instead of south, leaving Paschal—by now free again and growing in confidence with every step the Emperor took away from Rome—more closely linked than ever to the Normans, his only southern allies. His dependence on them was to increase still further after the death, in 1115, of the seventy-year-old Matilda of Tuscany; and meanwhile the Duchy of Apulia continued on its mouldering course. The Regent Alaine, too, died in 1115. Her son William was described by Romuald, Archbishop of Salerno, as 'generous, kind, humble and patient, pious and merciful and much beloved by his people'; he also, it seems, was a great respecter of Church and clergy. Unfortunately the good archbishop had used almost exactly the same words when speaking of Roger Borsa; and William was soon revealed as being even more disastrously incompetent than his father had been before him. Whereas Roger Borsa had at least tried to make his presence felt—and, with his uncle's assistance, had occasionally even succeeded—William hardly seemed capable of making the effort. He never lifted a finger, when Henry V descended once again on Rome in 1117, to assist his papal suzerain who had confirmed him in his rank and titles only three years before; it was to Capua, not to Salerno, that the wretched Pope had to turn in his hour of need. Nor was he any more effectual within his own dominions. Throughout South Italy his vassals had taken the law into their own hands; all were perpetually at loggerheads; and even a long-drawn-out civil war in Bari, culminating in the murder of its Archbishop, the imprisonment of Princess Constance and the enthronement of a usurper, Grimoald, elicited only a token protest from the Guiscard's grandson.

Such was the chaos which prevailed when, in 1121, Roger of Sicily decided that the moment had come to intervene. The reasons for his timing are not altogether clear; nor do we have any certain knowledge of his area of operations, though these were presumably first directed against those regions of Calabria which had not already been acquired by his father in return for services rendered. But whatever the details, the expedition proved even more successful than Roger could have hoped. Ignoring the entreaties of the new Pope, Calixtus II, who was anxious to do all he could to buttress his ineffectual neighbour against the growing threat of Sicily, he manoeuvred his cousin during the next twelve months to no less than three separate treaties. It was not a difficult task. William was not only weak militarily; he was also desperately short of money, so that even when he could assemble an army in the field he usually found himself quite unable to pay it. Roger, for his part, always preferred to make his purchases with gold rather than blood; and thus it was that all three sets of negotiations seem to have been conducted on a largely financial basis. The last of them actually came about through an appeal from William for help; and the account by a local chronicler[1] of the incident reveals as much about the character of the Duke himself as it does about the state of his Dukedom.

And when [William] was come to the Count of Sicily, he wept, saying, 'Noble Count, I appeal to you now in the name of our kinship and because of your great riches and power. I come to bear witness against Count Jordan [of Ariano], and to seek your aid in avenging myself upon him. For recently, when I was entering the city of Nusco, Count Jordan rode out before the gates with a troop of knights, and showered threats and insults upon me crying, "I will cut your coat short for you"; after which he plundered all my territory of Nusco. Since I have not sufficient strength to prevail against him, I had perforce to endure his offences, but now I eagerly await my revenge.'

Roger, as usual, had asked his price; and by the summer of 1122 he had gained possession not only of all Calabria that was not already his—first pledged for a consideration of sixty thousand bezants, and subsequently surrendered to him outright—but of those halves of Palermo and Messina which had heretofore technically remained ducal property. Even now he kept up the pressure against his cousin—particularly around the territory of Montescaglioso in the instep, as it were, of the peninsula—but his initial object had been achieved. For the rest, he could afford to bide his time.

He had not very long to wait. The next two or three years made it plain that Duke William and his Lombard wife could expect no children, and William himself may have had intimations of an early death. At all events he accepted, in 1125, an invitation to meet the Count at Messina to discuss the future of his Duchy, and there it

---

[1] Falco of Benevento.

306

was that, in return for another heavy subsidy, he formally recognised
Roger as his heir.

On 25 July 1127, at the age of thirty, Duke William of Apulia
died in his turn at Salerno. His wife Gaitelgrima, who loved him,
cut off her hair to cover his corpse; it was then laid, as his father's
had been, in an antique sarcophagus and placed in the Cathedral.[1]
Like Roger Borsa, William seems to have been popular enough as a
man; Falco, the Lombard chronicler of Benevento who hated the
Normans and all they stood for, has left us a moving account of how
the people of Salerno flocked to the palace to look for the last time
on a ruler 'who was lamented more than any duke or emperor,
before him'. But William had shown himself unworthy of his name
and of his throne, and with his death the once-great Duchy of Apulia
flickered ingloriously to its end.

He died as incompetently as he had lived; for, while occupied to
his last breath in making bequests to Monte Cassino, La Cava and
other favoured foundations, he seems to have forgotten, deliberately
or otherwise, to ratify his promise to Roger over the succession.
Certainly no mention of the matter appeared in his will; worse,
his disastrous anxiety to please everybody had apparently led him
to make similar promises elsewhere. According to one report[2]
the dying duke, in an access of piety, had crowned his other endowments by leaving his entire estate to the Holy See; while William of
Tyre, the great historian of Outremer, speaks of an arrangement he
had made with Bohemund II before his departure to the Holy Land
in 1126, according to which the first to die, if he left no issue, should
bequeath his dominions to the other. Thus, on his cousin's death,
Roger found himself not, as he had expected, the sole and unquestioned heir to South Italy, but merely one of a number of rival
claimants.

By this time young Bohemund was too far away to cause trouble,

---

[1] The sarcophagus, which is adorned with a frontal relief of Meleager and the boar, is
Roman, and of the third century. It now stands beneath the arcade just outside the main
entrance.

[2] Walter of Thérouanne in his life of Charles, Count of Flanders, to whose account
Ordericus Vitalis, Bk XII, ch. 44, lends additional strength.

but Pope Honorius II[1] was very much harder to ignore. For more than sixty years, ever since Alexander II had discovered the advantages of playing Robert Guiscard and Richard of Capua off against each other, it had been papal policy to keep the Normans divided; Honorius, a man of humble origins but considerable ability, was well aware of the danger of allowing the Count of Sicily to seize his cousin's realm and thus bringing an influential, self-willed and ambitious ruler to the very threshold of the Papal States. Moreover, as suzerain of all South Italy, he had no need to assert his own claims to Duke William's inheritance; if he could merely show Roger's to be invalid, the Duchy of Apulia would revert to him by default. He believed, too, that he could count on the support of the Norman baronage. Several of its members had already taken advantage of Duke William's death to make formal declaration of the independence they had long enjoyed in practice, and many others were determined to prevent the Duchy from reconstituting itself in the firm, authoritative hands of the Count of Sicily.

Against such opposition, Roger knew that his best hope lay in being able to present the Pope and his allies with a *fait accompli*; and in the first days of August he sailed, with a hastily-gathered fleet of seven ships, to Salerno. His reception was frigid. The widespread grief at William's death had not apparently prevented an anti-Norman faction from immediately seizing control of the city; the gates were closed against him; and, to the protestations of his spokesmen that their Lord had come in peace, to take possession of his Duchy by a hereditary right confirmed in person by the late Duke, the Salernitans replied simply that they had suffered too much and too long from Norman occupation and that they could tolerate it no more. But the Count would not take no for an answer. Day after day, with quiet determination, he urged his claim. Tension gradually mounted; the city elders, courteous at first, grew hostile; but even after one of his chief negotiators was murdered by a Salernitan mob, Roger preserved his calm. And all the time his ships remained in full view, firmly anchored in the bay.

[1] Not to be confused with the anti-Pope, also styled Honorius II, who had so complicated the life of Alexander II some sixty years before.

At last his patience was rewarded. He soon managed to make secret contact with the pro-Norman party in the city led by Archbishop Romuald, and it was they who finally persuaded their recalcitrant fellow-citizens to submit to the inevitable. In existing circumstances Salerno would not in any case be able to maintain its independence; surely it was wiser to negotiate while the Count was still prepared to offer favourable conditions than to risk the sort of siege by which his uncle had captured the city half a century before. And so, on the tenth day, the Salernitans came to terms. They would accept Roger, they promised, as their Duke, on three conditions: first, that the fortifications and castle should remain in their hands; second, that they should never be conscripted into military service more than two days' march from Salerno; and thirdly, that no Salernitan should be imprisoned without proper trial. Roger had no time to waste; he accepted. The gates were opened, and he made his ceremonial entry into the city, where the Bishop of Cappaccio, traditional enthroner of Salernitan princes, anointed him Duke of Apulia. It was a near-bloodless victory, a victory of patience and diplomacy—the kind Roger liked best; and it was followed at once by the submission of Amalfi on similar lines.

Meanwhile Count Rainulf of Alife, husband of Roger's half-sister Matilda, had hurried south to greet his brother-in-law and pledge his support. All he asked in return was that the new Duke should grant him suzerainty over his neighbour the Count of Ariano. The request was well-timed; Count Jordan of Ariano, Duke William's persecutor, had been killed the previous week, and his son was hardly in a strong position to object. Roger had no wish to see Rainulf, whom with good reason he heartily mistrusted, any more powerful than he was already; but he needed his help. Once again he agreed. It was a decision he would live to regret.

The news of Roger's success reached Pope Honorius at Benevento, where he had gone to keep a closer watch on developments. It caught him largely unprepared; but now he too acted with decision, and sent a message to Roger at Salerno, formally forbidding him on pain of anathema to assume the ducal title. He might have saved himself the trouble; only two days after his own arrival a troop of four hundred cavalry appeared outside the walls of Benevento with Roger at their head. It was the second time in a week that he had taken the Pope by surprise, but on this occasion he may well have been equally surprised himself. His journey to Benevento seems to have been made in response to a message he had received from certain supporters in the city, congratulating him on his succession and assuring him of their good will. It had probably encouraged him to think that even this outpost of papal power in the South might be his for the taking—in which case the presence of Honorius in his palace must have come as something of a shock.

Roger was anxious not to antagonise the Pope unnecessarily while there still remained a chance of obtaining his recognition; but Honorius was not like the men of Salerno—arguments, promises and bribes alike left him cold. In such circumstances to delay in Benevento was pointless. Instructing the local barons, whom he knew to be on his side, to keep the papal troops occupied by harrying the city and its surroundings till further notice, the Count accordingly left with his own army for Troia. From here, the gateway to Apulia and the scene of one of the earliest Norman triumphs in Italy, he passed to Melfi, where his new dukedom had had its first uncertain beginnings almost a century before; and, as he rode, he must have gazed over the plain of Apulia to where the dark massif of the Gargano crouched on the horizon—sheltering, somewhere in its depths, the cave of the Archangel. Roger would have been brought up on Malaterra's history, and the first sight of a land he knew so well by repute may have added still further to his conviction that he and he alone was born to rule it. The people of the towns and villages through which he passed seemed to share this view; as he continued south-east along the foot of the mountains, he was everywhere acclaimed with apparent rejoicing. The end of August found him, with a great gathering of bishops, barons and notables, including his Emirs Christodulus and George of Antioch, at Montescaglioso; thence, moving slowly through loyal Calabria, he at last reached Reggio where he received solemn recognition of his Calabrian claims; and before the onset of winter he was back in Sicily.

The unexpected warmth of his reception throughout the duke-

dom from the moment he had left Salerno had persuaded Roger
that his position was already secure. Only the Pope was still holding
out against him, but sooner or later even the Pope was bound to see
reason. And if he did not, what harm could he do without a single
powerful ally in the South? So at least Roger must have reckoned;
never otherwise would he have taken the huge risk of returning at
such a moment to Sicily and leaving the field free for his enemies.

Roger's lightning progress had certainly given him the advantage
of surprise, but its very speed carried its own dangers. The towns
at which he had stopped, the barons through whose fiefs he had
passed, had had no opportunity to take stock of the situation or to
consult one another. Thus, unprepared and undecided, they were
virtually forced to pay lip-service to his claims—an obligation which
they performed the more readily in the knowledge that these claims
had no validity until they were recognised by the Pope. And Roger,
in the exhilaration of his success, had believed them.

Honorius had been slower off the mark, and had been further
obstructed by the gadfly tactics of Roger's partisans round Benevento. But he had lost no time in raising support, and by the end of
October had rallied to his cause most of the leading barons of the
South—Grimoald of Bari, Robert, Tancred, and Alexander of
Conversano, Geoffrey of Andria, Roger of Ariano and, the moment
his brother-in-law's back was turned, Rainulf of Alife, who had
pledged his allegiance to the new Duke only two months before.
Meanwhile the citizens of Troia, under the guidance of their
bishop, William,[1] had also revised their opinions; and it was at
Troia that Honorius's villainous crowd—all of whom had long his-
tories of faithlessness and rebellion behind them—assembled in November and, in the presence of the Pope himself, bound themselves in
solemn league against the usurper. A few weeks later they received
a further addition to their strength—Prince Robert II of Capua, who
had just succeeded his father and was crowned on 30 December.

---

[1] Bishop William's portrait can still be made out on the bronze doors of Troia Cathedral, which date from 1119. Near it is an adulatory inscription, describing him as
'*Liberator Patriae*' and adding that 'in the year of the death of Duke William of Salerno
the people of Troia destroyed their citadel and fortified the city, in the cause of liberty,
with walls and a palisade'.

He was, we are told by Falco, a puny creature; 'of delicate constitution, he could endure neither labour nor hardship'. But Honorius, overjoyed by this opportunity of reviving the old Apulia–Capua counterpoise, determined to take full advantage of the occasion. Having failed, Falco tersely points out, to achieve anything good or useful in Benevento, he rode to Capua to attend the ceremony in person; and there, before the assembled congregation of Robert's vassals, he delivered himself of a passionate oration in which, after dwelling at length on the atrocities committed by Roger's men against the Beneventans, he confirmed the Count as excommunicate and granted indulgences to all those who should take up arms against him. The movement was beginning to assume all the trappings of a Crusade.

Away in Palermo, Roger had recognised his mistake. Once again, just as in the North African affair three years before, he had underestimated the opposition. But this time he was less concerned. It was typical of him that even now, with the papal league already massing its forces, he should have tried to buy Honorius off with the surrender of two towns—Troia and Montefusco—and a substantial sum of money. Only when these attempts failed did he begin serious preparations for war, and still he seemed to be in no particular hurry. It was not until May 1128 that he returned, with an army estimated at two thousand knights and fifteen hundred archers, to the mainland. His plan of campaign was to assure himself of the southern half of the dukedom, where the forces of the league were at their weakest, before pitting himself against the main body of the opposition in the north. Hastening through Calabria, to which his title was unquestioned, he therefore struck straight across to those regions around the heel of Italy which his cousin Bohemund, before departing for the Holy Land, had left in the joint care of the Pope and Alexander of Conversano. It was a wise decision. Taranto, Otranto and Brindisi surrendered without demur, and by mid-June Roger was in undisputed control of all Italy south of the Brindisi-Salerno line.

The Pope, meanwhile, had been in serious difficulties. Rainulf of Alife and Robert of Capua—the first through self-interest, the second through pusillanimity—were threatening to withdraw from the league, while Roger's supporters had increased their pressure on

Benevento. It was already midsummer before Honorius made sure of his allies and led them to the relief of his city; only then could he concentrate his full attention on Roger in Apulia. Early July found him and his forces in the region of Bari, still having encountered neither sight nor sound of the enemy; then, turning towards the south-west, he advanced to a point on the Bradano, no longer identifiable, where the shallow, stony river-bed provided an easy ford; and it was here that he saw the Sicilians waiting for him, strongly entrenched among the hills on the farther bank.

Roger had the advantage of position; his army was fresh and rested, and his Saracen shocktroops were probably eager for the fray. Yet, typically, he refused to attack. Alexander of Telese sycophantically suggests that veneration for the Pope restrained him; this seems highly improbable. Far likelier is it that the size of the papal army, together with his own instinctive aversion from unnecessary bloodshed, convinced the Count that there were other, better ways of gaining his objective. He was right. For more than a month the two armies faced each other, as one attempt after another failed to lure the Sicilians down from their vantage-point. Meanwhile Honorius's feudal levies, who could be conscripted only for a limited period in any one year, grew increasingly restive; quarrelling broke out, as it always did, among the various league members; and the fierce July sun beat remorselessly down on the unprotected papal camp. From his shady retreat on the opposite hillside Roger could imagine the Pope's discomfiture; and he was not surprised to receive a message one night informing him that His Holiness might, after all, be prepared to negotiate.

And indeed Honorius had no choice. He was now beginning to understand what Roger had perhaps known all along—that his league was too fissile to last, its individual members too long accustomed to independence and lawlessness to be able to sink their differences in a common cause. Already they were at each other's throats; soon they might well be at his; and Robert of Capua, who had, predictably, fallen ill and was now lying groaning in his tent, was not the only one to be speaking of giving up the struggle. The Pope also saw that he was faced with an adversary too powerful to be crushed, and with too much moral right on his side to be dismissed out of hand. South Italy needed peace—so much was certain—and although the Count of Sicily could be trusted to disrupt that peace for as long as the dukedom were denied him, he might also be the one man capable of imposing it if he were given the chance. The danger of accepting so formidable a figure as a neighbour was still undeniable, but it was a risk which would have to be taken.

The negotiations, which were conducted on the papal side by the Papal Chancellor, Cardinal Aimeri of S. Maria Novella, and by Cencius Frangipani, took place at night in conditions of the utmost secrecy; for Honorius was understandably anxious that his allies should not hear of their betrayal until his dispositions were made. He was a proud man and now thought only of saving his own face; he seems to have made no effort to obtain terms for anyone else. Roger too knew just what he wanted—investiture as Duke of Apulia, under papal suzerainty as always but with no other strings attached. Granted this, and provided only that his own dignity were preserved, he was prepared to fall in with Honorius's wishes; he had no desire to humiliate him unnecessarily. And so it was agreed. Nothing would be done on the spot, but if Roger would come himself to Benevento and formally seek investiture, it would no longer be denied him. The barons of the league, informed of the cessation of hostilities and somehow dissuaded from taking their vengeance on the papal person, dispersed in fury; and Honorius set off for Benevento to await his distinguished visitor.

Roger arrived early on 20 August and set up his camp on Monte S. Felice, just outside the city. Three more days of negotiation followed on points of detail. There could, he explained, be no further question of surrendering to the Pope the towns of Troia and Montefusco which he had offered him some months before; but he would willingly swear to respect the papal status of Benevento and even— if His Holiness insisted—guarantee the continued independence of Capua. This last concession—a final, pathetic attempt on the part of Honorius to preserve that traditional balance of power by which he had always set so much store—must inwardly have irked him; certainly Robert of Capua had done little enough to deserve such consideration. For the moment, however, the matter was unimportant—it could always be renegotiated later if necessary.

By the evening of 22 August everything was settled. On one point, however, the Count had remained adamant: he refused to allow the ceremony to take place on papal territory. It had therefore been agreed that he should meet Honorius outside the walls of Benevento, on the bridge spanning the Sabato river. There, soon after sunset, by the light of countless flaming torches and in the presence, according to Falco, of twenty thousand spectators, the Pope invested Roger with lance and gonfalon, just as Pope Nicholas had invested Robert Guiscard nearly seventy years before; while the Duke of Apulia, secure at last in his title, placed his hands within those of his suzerain and swore him fealty. Once again, as in Robert's day, Apulia, Calabria and Sicily were united under the same ruler. And he was still only thirty-two. Only one more step remained to be taken.

23

CORONATION

And so, when the Duke was led in royal state to the Cathedral, and was there anointed with the holy oil and invested with the dignity of kingship, the splendour of his majesty and the magnificence of his apparel were beyond the power of words to express or imagination to conceive. Truly it seemed to those who saw him as if all the riches and honours of the world were there assembled.

Alexander of Telese, ch. IV

By granting Roger the investiture of all the territories previously held by Robert Guiscard, Pope Honorius had admitted himself beaten; but not all the southern barons were prepared to surrender so easily. The new Duke was clever—anyone could see that—and more cunning even than his uncle had been before him. His military reputation, on the other hand, was still extremely questionable. Ever since his first intrusion into mainland affairs he had displayed a suspicious reluctance to do any real fighting. His successive triumphs had all been won by bribery, diplomacy, speed of movement or slow attrition; it still remained for him to prove himself as a soldier against a determined enemy. Besides, even the Guiscard had failed to establish any permanent peace in his domains; and the Guiscard had not had Sicily to look after as well. With so large and so remote a dukedom under his direct control in addition to the mainland territories—and one, moreover, in which he apparently intended to retain his capital—the new Duke would find it still more difficult to impose his authority. Militarily his investiture was of little significance. Henceforth he might enjoy papal support, but recent events had shown just how little that was worth in terms of effective power. And though South Italy was full of fair-weather friends who would bow before him as he passed, there was still not one town or village throughout the peninsula on whose loyalty he could wholly rely in time of crisis. And so, once again, the barons and the cities of Apulia rose up against their lord; and Roger's new dominions, on that historic evening when Pope Honorius entrusted them to his care, were already in a state of armed and open rebellion.

Roger was beginning to grow accustomed to this state of affairs. Characteristically, he looked upon his dukedom with the eye of an administrator rather than that of a soldier; and he had always known that Apulia, with its enormous fiefs and its traditional hatred of centralised authority, would present a far greater administrative problem than he would ever encounter in Sicily. His task would be to succeed where his uncle had failed and to set up, for the first time in centuries, a strong and enforceable government all through the South, firmly based on the rule of law. Such a task would not be accomplished overnight. But Roger also knew that the very same spirit of independence which had created the problem would also make possible its solution, since it would ensure that his enemies remained divided. Even under the leadership of the Pope they had been unable to act together; now that they were deprived of it they would be more ineffectual still. The few weeks of summer that remained he spent trying to consolidate his position in the north; then, as winter approached, he returned via Salerno to Sicily.

In the spring of 1129 he was back, with an army of three thousand knights and twice that number of infantry, including archers and his regiment of Saracens. The ensuing campaign went much as he had planned. Brindisi, admittedly, under the able command of his own cousin, young Geoffrey of Conversano,[1] withstood his on-slaught until the besiegers were forced by hunger to retire; but few other towns seemed disposed to offer much resistance. While Roger's army moved along the coast, mopping up the opposition as it went, sixty of his ships under George of Antioch blockaded Bari. Its self-styled prince, Grimoald, had been one of the most determined and

---

[1] This Geoffrey, described by the Abbot of Telese simply as the 'son of Count Alexander', may possibly have been of the family of Clermont rather than that of Conversano; but the latter is more likely.

powerful of the rebels; but early in August he too had to give in. His surrender led to the capitulation of Alexander, Tancred and Geoffrey of Conversano; and the revolt was over.

Or very nearly. One important city alone remained unsubdued. The people of Troia to whom, less than two years before, the Pope had granted a commune in return for their support, were reluctant to renounce so soon their newly-acquired privileges. Now that Honorius had betrayed them, they looked desperately round for other protectors. First they turned to Capua; but Prince Robert, as might have been expected, was unwilling to antagonise the new Duke of Apulia. Understandably most other barons felt much the same, and the Troians had given up hope of ever finding a champion when there suddenly appeared at their gates the one man who could never resist the chance of adding to his fiefs, whatever the attendant disadvantages—Roger's renegade brother-in-law, Rainulf of Alife. Eagerly they accepted his terms—protection in return for possession —and Rainulf moved in with his followers. But within a few days his new subjects saw how rash they had been. Roger was already on the march. He did not head straight for Troia—that was no longer necessary. An attack on one of the outlying castles was quite enough, as he knew it would be, to bring Rainulf hurrying to him with peace proposals, and a pact was quickly concluded. The Count of Alife might retain possession of Troia on condition that he held it in fief from his brother-in-law. It was an arrangement eminently satisfactory to both parties. Only the citizens of Troia, who now found themselves landed with two liege-lords instead of one, had any cause to complain. They had nobody but themselves to blame. Had they known Rainulf a little better they might have guessed that he never intended to hold out against the Duke, and that his one idea was to improve his own bargaining position. But it was too late now. Troia, twice betrayed, resisted a few days longer; then, inevitably, it too surrendered.

It may seem surprising that Roger should have allowed Rainulf to get away with so barefaced a *coup*—particularly after his record over the past two years. The truth is that the Count of Alife, slippery as he was, was no less trustworthy than most of his fellow-vassals— indeed, he may have been slightly more so, if family ties counted for

anything—and those vassals had somehow to be persuaded to accept
the ducal dominion. Roger's task was to win their support, not to
antagonise them. His attitude towards his brother-in-law was, in
fact, typical of that which he showed in his dealings with the defeated
rebels. Outwardly at least—for no one ever knew what he was
thinking—he bore them no malice. Once or twice, as at Brindisi or
in the following year at Salerno, he manned the local citadel with a
Sicilian garrison to prevent further outbreaks against his authority;
but there as elsewhere the rebel lords were granted his full
pardon and confirmed—even Grimoald of Bari—in their former
possessions.

Only among deserters from his own ranks did the Duke show
unyielding firmness. Some weeks previously another of his cousins,
Robert of Grantmesnil,[1] had withdrawn with his men from the
siege of Montalto, ostensibly on the grounds that his fief was too
small and he himself too poor to support a long campaign. The
length of the obligatory period of a vassal's service to his lord was
a common ground for complaint and often a genuine cause of
hardship; but it was also one of the cornerstones of the feudal
system and could not be modified. Roger was not unsympathetic;
he even went so far as to promise to increase his cousin's holding
as soon as the revolt was crushed. But he was powerless to prevent
Robert's defection. The moment peace was restored, he pursued
him to his castle at Lagopesole and forced his submission. There,
before the assembled knights, Robert was obliged to accept a public
reprimand; Roger then granted his request for leave to return to
Normandy, provided that he renounced all his southern fiefs. It took
another year, and another campaign, before the troublesome count
was finally banished from Italy; but he had served as a useful example
to his fellows. A vassal, once he had sworn fealty to his lord, was
bound to him by certain obligations. For as long as Roger II was
Duke of Apulia, no refusal to acknowledge these obligations would
be tolerated.

In September 1129 Duke Roger, his authority at last firmly

---

[1] The son of William de Grantmesnil and the Guiscard's daughter Mabilla. He is not
to be confused with his namesake, the guardian of Roger I's first wife, Judith.

established, summoned all the bishops, abbots and counts of Apulia and Calabria to a solemn Court at Melfi. It was the first of a series of such Courts that would mark his reign; and its purpose was to lay the foundations of his future government in South Italy. Each of his vassals in turn was now required, in the presence of his assembled fellows, to swear a great oath not only confirming his feudal obligations but, in the interests of pacification, carrying them a stage further. The precise wording of this oath is, alas, lost to us, but it seems to have fallen into three main parts. It began with the normal swearing of fealty and obedience, first to the Duke himself and then to each of his two eldest sons who had accompanied him— young Roger, now about eleven years old, and Tancred, a year or two younger. There followed a specific undertaking to observe a ducal edict now promulgated forbidding all private war—that favourite pursuit among members of the knightly class, with which so much of their time and energy was normally occupied. Finally the counts were made to swear to uphold order and justice by with-holding their aid from thieves, robbers and all who sought to despoil the land, by surrendering them to the Duke's Courts wherever they might be established, and by promising their pro-tection to all feudal inferiors, clerical or lay, as well as to all pilgrims, travellers and merchants.

It was a compendious oath, and even more far-reaching than appears at first sight. The swearing of fealty was usual enough; though even here it is interesting that Roger should have specifically involved the two young princes, thereby strengthening their claims to the eventual succession—and, perhaps, giving a first hint of his future policy of setting up his sons as viceroys over the mainland. He also made it abundantly clear that what he was demanding of his vassals was something more than a formality. In the years to come we find him imposing this oath, time and time again, not only on the barons and knights but on all free classes of his subjects, as a constant reminder of their duty. Was he, by this continued insistence, already moving towards that exalted, semi-mystical concept of kingship on the Byzantine model, which so appealed to his oriental spirit and which, in his later years, he was so successfully to realise? It is possible. What is certain is that he was, deliberately or not, 'preparing the way for the extended theory of treason which was peculiar, in the twelfth century, to the Sicilian monarchy'.[1]

But the real significance of the Court of Melfi is to be found not in the first but in the second section of the vassals' oath. It had occasionally happened in the past that the South Italian barons had sworn—usually for a strictly limited period—to respect the rights and property of the non-knightly classes; but they had always preserved the right of feud, by which they could—and did—make war on each other to their hearts' content. Only when a Pope promulgated the so-called *Treuga Dei*, the Truce of God, could they sometimes be persuaded to suspend these activities. In recent years at least three Popes—Urban, Paschal and Calixtus—had tried by this means to halt the decline of Apulia into anarchy; but none of them had been conspicuously successful, if only because the maintenance of such a truce depended entirely on voluntary oaths sworn by the various parties concerned. This time it was different. The right of feud was abolished from above, at one stroke and for ever —an achievement at that time unparalleled in Europe outside England and Normandy. The oath accepting this abolition was sworn to Roger personally; and thus was brought into being the Duke's Peace, for which he himself assumed the ultimate responsibility, both in its maintenance and in the punishment of those by whom it should be disturbed—for the third part of the oath, with its reference to the surrender of malefactors to the Duke's Courts, made it clear that Roger had no intention, even now, of relying solely on the honour of his feudatories. This was the beginning of his penal code, and he intended to give it teeth.

The first great assembly of Melfi, at which in 1043 the pioneer generation of Norman barons, with Roger's uncle William the Iron-Arm at their head and Gaimar of Salerno as their suzerain, had divided their conquered territories into the twelve counties of Apulia, had long since passed into history. There may, however, have been a few old men in the little hill-town who still dimly remembered that August day just seventy years before when Robert Guiscard, colossal in his prime, had received his three duchies from Pope Nicholas II. Both of these occasions had marked

[1] Evelyn Jamison, 'The Norman Administration of Apulia and Capua'.

new chapters in the epic of the Norman domination of South Italy. Here, now, was a third. This time there were no investitures, no allocations of fiefs; but there was, for every Norman knight and baron present, the same unmistakable intimation that one era was past and another just beginning. It cannot have been an altogether welcome sensation. The old ways, the chaotic legacy of Roger Borsa and his son, might have proved disastrous for the security and prosperity of the land as a whole, but for the privileged classes they had often been agreeable—and profitable—enough. Now, for the first time in forty-five years, the South found at its head a strong man, able and determined to rule. Things would be different in future.

The year 1129, already an *annus mirabilis* for Roger, was to end with a further triumph. The position of Capua had been ambiguous ever since the death of its prince, Richard II, in 1106. Now Richard had, eight years before, recognised the suzerainty of the Duke of Apulia in return for help in his reinstatement; but his successors do not seem to have followed his example, and neither Roger Borsa nor Duke William was of the calibre to assert their claims. Thus, by default, Capua had once again become an independent state—the sovereignty of which Roger, by the terms of his Benevento investiture, had bound himself to respect. How long he would in fact have done so is an open question; Capua, though now but a poor shadow of its former self and constituting no conceivable military threat, remained an irritation and an obstacle to the complete unification of the South which sooner or later he would surely have found intolerable. Fortunately the matter was decided for him. The gutless young Robert, finding himself now entirely bereft of allies, decided to come to terms with his neighbour before it was too late, and voluntarily recognised the Duke as his lawful suzerain.

This unsolicited submission, which effectively reunited Capua with the Duchy of Apulia and so left Roger the undisputed master of the Norman South, marked the final frustration of all Honorius II's efforts to maintain the tenuous balance of power; and it might well have been expected to provoke angry reactions from Rome. But by the time the news of Prince Robert's capitulation reached the Lateran, Honorius was lying desperately ill; and in the months that

followed—months that would bring the Duke of Apulia the greatest
prize of his career—the Papal Curia would find itself saddled with
other more urgent preoccupations.

The Jewish colony has existed in Rome uninterruptedly since the
days of Pompey. Having first settled in Trastevere, by the Middle
Ages it had already crossed the river and now occupied that same
quarter on the left bank, just opposite the island, which Pope Paul
IV was later to enclose as a ghetto and in which its synagogue still
stands. Nowadays, as it slowly recovers from its recent sufferings, it
presents little enough evidence of prosperity; but in the early
twelfth century Roman Jewry enjoyed, by reason of its enormous
wealth, both influence and prestige within the papal city. Pre-eminent
among its leading families was that of the Pierleoni, whose close
connexions with succeeding Popes had led them, the better part of
a century before, to embrace the Christian faith; and since that time
the continuance of the papal favour, assisted by the panoply and
splendour with which they surrounded themselves, had raised them
to a social and financial position at which they admitted no superiors
among the most illustrious princely houses of Rome.

One distinction only was still lacking—but that the most important
distinction of all. The Pierleonis had not yet themselves produced a
Pope. The omission was understandable in the circumstances, but
it would have to be rectified. For some years, therefore, their eyes
had been hopefully fixed on the most brilliant of their scions, a
certain Peter di Pierleoni who was rising rapidly in the hierarchy.
His qualifications were excellent. His father had been a trusted
lieutenant of Gregory VII, and he himself, after a period of study
in Paris under the great Abelard himself, had become a monk at
Cluny. Recalled to Rome in 1120, he had been appointed Cardinal
by Paschal II at his father's request and had subsequently served as
Papal Legate first in France and then in England, where he had
appeared with a particularly splendid retinue at the Court of King
Henry I. Henry seems to have been impressed: if we are to believe
William of Malmesbury, the Cardinal returned to Rome so laden
with rich presents as to cause raised eyebrows at the Curia.
There is in fact no evidence to suggest that Pierleoni was more

venal or corrupt than any other of the contemporary princes of the
Church; on the contrary, his genuine piety and irreproachable
Cluniac background had made him a staunch upholder of many
aspects of Reform.[1] But he was capable, strong-willed and intensely
ambitious; and, like every potential candidate for the throne of
St Peter, he had enemies. Of these the most dangerous were the
Hildebrandine party—what might be called the left wing of the
Curia—who feared that a Pierleoni Pope would lead the Papacy
back into its bad old ways until it became once again the tool—or
even the plaything—of the Roman aristocracy; and his family's
most implacable rivals, that other formidable brood of fellow-
upstarts—the Frangipani.

By the beginning of February 1130 it was clear that Pope Honorius
was near his end; and Cardinal Pierleoni, who enjoyed the support
of many of the Sacred College, most of the nobility and practically
all the lower orders in Rome, among whom his carefully dispensed
generosity had become proverbial, was the obvious successor. But
the opposition was taking no chances. Led by the Chancellor of the
Curia, Cardinal Aimeri[2]—whom we last met, with Cencius Frangipani, negotiating with Roger II on the banks of the Bradano—they
seized the dying Pontiff and carried him off to the monastery of St
Andrew, safe in the centre of the Frangipani quarter, where they
would be able to conceal his death until suitable dispositions had
been made for the future.[3] Next, on 11 February, Aimeri summoned
to the monastery such cardinals as he felt he could trust and began
preparations for the new election. Now such a proceeding, apart
from being manifestly dishonest, was also a flagrant breach of Pope
Nicholas's decree of 1059, and it provoked an immediate reaction

---

[1] Other more outspoken accusations, by such robust prelates as Manfred of Mantua
or Arnulf of Lisieux (who actually wrote a book called *Invectives*) to the effect that the
cardinal seduced nuns, slept with his sister, etc., can be discounted as being simply
the normal, healthy Church polemic of the kind to be expected at times of schism.

[2] Aimeri was a Frenchman, and I have therefore preferred the French version of his
name. He is often called Almeric, or Haimeric, in the German fashion.

[3] This monastery was founded by Gregory the Great. The site is now part of the
Church of S. Gregorio Magno, to the left of which there stands among the cypresses a
chapel still dedicated to St Andrew, traditionally on the site of Gregory's original oratory. Opposite, at the end of the Circus Maximus, a ruined tower marks the site
of the old Frangipani fortress.

from the rest of the Curia. Hurling anathemas against 'all those who would proceed to the election before the funeral of Honorius', they thereupon nominated a commission of eight electors of all parties who, they decreed, should meet in the Church of St Adrian—not St Andrew—when, and only when, the Pope had been safely laid in his grave.

This refusal to countenance an election at St Andrew's was clearly due to the unwillingness of Cardinal Pierleoni and his adherents to put themselves at the mercy of the Frangipani, but when they arrived at St Adrian's they found the situation no better there. Aimeri's men had already taken possession of the whole place and had fortified it against them. Furious, they turned away and—accompanied now by several other cardinals who had no particular love for Pierleoni but were outraged by the conduct of the Chancellor—gathered instead at the old Church of S. Marco, where they settled down to await developments.

On 13 February the rumour swept through Rome that the Pope was dead at last, and that the news was being deliberately suppressed. An angry crowd gathered outside St Andrew's, and was dispersed only after poor Honorius had shown himself, trembling and haggard, on his balcony. It was his last public appearance. The strain had been too much for him, and by nightfall he was dead. In theory his body should have been allowed to lie for three days in state; but since the election of a new Pope could not take place before the burial of the old, Aimeri had no time for such niceties. Almost before the corpse was cold it was flung into a temporary grave in the courtyard of the monastery, and early the following morning the Chancellor and those who shared his views elected to the Papacy Gregory, Cardinal-deacon of S. Angelo. He was rushed to the Lateran and formally, if somewhat hastily, installed under the title of Innocent II; he then retreated to S. Maria in Palladio—now S. Sebastiano in Pallaria—where, thanks to the Frangipani, he could keep out of harm's way.

The lovely ninth-century basilica of S. Marco in Rome has suffered as grievously as most of it fellows from the indignities of baroque restoration; but its great apse mosaic still glows as glorious as ever, and the church itself offers a haven of silence and peace after the tumult of the Piazza Venezia outside. The atmosphere must have been very different on the morning of St Valentine's Day 1130, when the news of Honorius's death and Innocent's succession was brought to those assembled within its walls. Their numbers had been steadily growing, and they now comprised virtually all the high dignitaries of the Church—apart from those who had sided with Aimeri—including some two dozen Cardinals, together with most of the nobility and as many of the populace as could squeeze their way through the doors. With one accord the Cardinals declared the proceedings at St Andrew's and the Lateran uncanonical, and acclaimed Cardinal Pierleoni as their rightful Pope. He accepted at once, taking the name of Anacletus II. At dawn that morning there had been no Pope in Rome. By midday there were two.

Innocent or Anacletus—it is hard to say which candidate possessed the stronger claim to the Papacy. Anacletus, certainly, could boast more overall support, both among the Cardinals and within the Church as a whole. On the other hand those who had voted for Innocent, though fewer in number, had included the majority of the electoral commission of eight which had been set up by the Sacred College. The manner in which they had performed their duties was to say the least questionable, but then Anacletus's own election could scarcely have been described as orthodox. It had, moreover, taken place at a time when another Pope had already been elected and installed.

One thing was certain. In Rome itself, sweetened by years of bribery, the popularity of Anacletus was overwhelming. By 15 February he and his party were in control of the Lateran, and on the 16th they took St Peter's itself. Here, a week later, he received his formal consecration—while his rival, whose place of refuge had already been the object of armed attacks by Anacletus's partisans, had to be content with a similar but more modest ceremony at S. Maria Novella. Day by day Anacletus entrenched himself more firmly, while his agents dispensed subsidies with an ever more generous hand, until at last his gold—supplemented, according to his enemies, by the wholesale pillage of the principal churches of Rome —found its way into the Frangipani fortress itself. Deserted by his last remaining champions, Innocent had no choice but to flee.

Already by the beginning of April we find him dating his letters from Trastevere; a month later he had secretly hired two galleys, on which, accompanied by all his loyal cardinals except one, he escaped down the Tiber.

His flight proved his salvation. Anacletus might have bought Rome, but elsewhere in Italy popular feeling was firmly behind Innocent. In Pisa he was cheered to the echo, in Genoa the same; and while his rival lorded it in the Lateran he himself was now free to canvas support where it most mattered—beyond the Alps. From Genoa he took ship for France, and by the time he sailed into the little harbour of St Gilles in Provence much of his old confidence had returned. It was well justified. When he found, awaiting him at St Gilles, a deputation from Cluny with sixty horses and mules in its train ready to escort him the two hundred odd miles to the monastery he must have felt that, at least so far as France was concerned, his battle was as good as won. If the most influential of all French abbeys was prepared to give him its support in preference to one of its own sons, he had little to fear from other quarters; and when the Council of Etampes, summoned in the late summer to give a final ruling, formally declared in his favour, it did little more than confirm a foregone conclusion.

France then was sound; but what of the Empire? Here lay the key to Innocent's ultimate success; and here Lothair the Saxon, King of Germany, showed no particular eagerness to make up his mind. His inclinations and background should have predisposed him favourably enough; he had long upheld the ecclesiastical and papalist party among the German princes, and had received in return the support of Honorius II and Chancellor Aimeri. On the other hand, he was still engaged in a desperate struggle for power with Conrad of Hohenstaufen, who had been elected King in opposition to him three years before, and he had to weigh his actions with care. Besides, he had not yet been crowned Emperor in Rome. To antagonise the Pope who actually held the City was a step that might have dangerous implications.

Innocent, however, was not unduly worried; for his case was by now safely in the hands of the most powerful of all advocates and the outstanding spiritual force of the twelfth century—St Bernard of

Clairvaux. Later in this story we shall have to take a closer look at St Bernard, whose influence on European affairs in the next quarter-century was to be so immense and, in many respects, so disastrous. For the moment let it suffice to say that he had thrown all his formidable energies, all the weight of his moral and political prestige, into the scales on Innocent's behalf. With such a champion the Pope could afford to be patient and allow events to take their course.

The same, however, could not be said for Anacletus. He too was conscious of the need for international recognition, particularly in Northern Europe; but whereas Innocent was able to whip up support in person, he had had to rely on correspondence, and he had so far been singularly unsuccessful. In an effort to reassure King Lothair he had even gone so far as to excommunicate his rival Conrad, but the King had been unimpressed and had not even had the courtesy to answer his subsequent letters. In France, too, his Legates were snubbed; and now, as reports reached him of more and more declarations for Innocent, he began to grow seriously alarmed. The weight of the opposition was far greater than he had expected; and, more disturbing still, it was not only the ruling princes who appeared to favour his antagonist, but the Church itself. During the past fifty years, thanks largely to the Cluniac reforms and to the influence of Hildebrand, the Church had shaken off the shackles imposed on it by Roman aristocrats and German princelings, and had suddenly developed into a strong and cohesive international authority. Simultaneously the mushroom growth of the religious orders had given it a new efficiency and impetus. Cluny under Abbot Peter the Venerable, Prémontré under Norbert of Magdeburg (he who had persuaded Lothair to leave Anacletus's letters unanswered), Cîteaux under St Bernard—all were vital, positive forces. All three were united in favour of Innocent, and they carried the body of the Church with them.

And so Anacletus took the only course open to him: like many another desperate Pope in the past, he turned to the Normans. In September 1130, just about the time when the Council of Etampes was deciding in Innocent's favour, he left Rome via Benevento for Avellino, where Roger was waiting to receive him. The negotiations were soon completed. They may have been carefully prepared

in advance; on the other hand the main issues were simple enough
and can have called for little discussion. The Duke of Apulia would
give Anacletus his support; in return, he demanded one thing only
—a royal crown.

The request was prompted by something far deeper than personal
vanity. Roger's task was to weld together all the Norman dominions
of the South into one nation. The resulting state could be nothing
less than a Kingdom; to maintain the identities of three separate
duchies would be to invite disintegration. Moreover, if he were not
a King, how would he be able to treat on equal terms with the other
rulers of Europe and the East? Domestic considerations pointed in
the same direction. He must have a title that would set him above
his senior vassals, the Princes of Capua and Bari, one that would
bind all his feudatories to him with a loyalty deeper than that which
a mere Duke could command. Briefly, he needed kingship not just
for its own sake but for the sake of the mystique surrounding it.
But the Pope remained and would remain his suzerain, and he knew
that if he were to assume a crown without the papal blessing, his
prestige, far from being enhanced, would be gravely endangered.

Anacletus was sympathetic. If, as now seemed likely, the Duke of
Apulia was to be his only ally, it was plainly desirable that his
position should be strengthened to the utmost. And his claims were
incontrovertible. There was no reason for delay. On 27 September,
back at Benevento, he issued a Bull granting to Roger and his heirs
the Crown of Sicily, Calabria and Apulia, comprising all those
regions which the Dukes of Apulia had ever held of the Holy See,
together with the Principality of Capua, the 'honour' of Naples—a
deliberately ambiguous phrase, since Naples, still technically
independent and with vague Byzantine affiliations, was not the
Pope's to endow—and the assistance of the papal city of Benevento
in time of war. The seat of the Kingdom would be in Sicily, and the
coronation ceremony might be performed by the Sicilian archbishops. In return Roger pledged his homage and fealty to Anacletus
as Pope, together with an annual tribute of six hundred *schifati*—a
sum equivalent to about 160 ounces of gold.

It remained only for Roger to make similar dispositions with his
own vassals. He was determined that no one should be able, now or

in the future, to charge him with usurpation. Returning to Salerno, he therefore called another assembly, on an only slightly smaller scale than that which had met at Melfi the previous year, still comprising all the senior and most trustworthy nobles and clerics and probably including representatives of the chief cities and towns. To them he submitted proposals for his elevation, which they unanimously accepted. It may have been a formality, but similar formalities had been traditional preliminaries to coronations in England,[1] France and Germany for two centuries, and to Roger it was vital. However much his personal sympathies and upbringing might have inclined him towards the Byzantine concept of absolute rule, he knew that he could win the support of his Norman barons only by presenting them with an unexceptionable, legally-constituted monarchy as it was understood in the West. Now that he had been acclaimed at Salerno his legal and moral position was, he knew, as secure as he could possibly make it. He had the approval of both Church and State, of his suzerain and of his vassals. He was free to go ahead.

'It was,' wrote the Abbot of Telese, who was there, 'as if the whole city was being crowned.' The streets were spread with carpets, the balconies and terraces were festooned in every colour. Palermo was thronged with the King's vassals, great and small, from Apulia and Calabria, all of whom had received a royal summons to the capital for the great day, each trying to outdo his rivals in the magnificence of his train and the splendour of his entourage; with wealthy merchants, who saw in this huge concourse possibilities of gain that might never be paralleled in their lifetime; with craftsmen and artisans, townsmen and peasants from every corner of the Kingdom, drawn by curiosity and excitement and wonder; Italians, Germans, Normans, Greeks, Lombards, Spaniards, Saracens, all adding to the clamour and colour of what was already the most exotic and cosmopolitan city of Europe.

Through such crowds as these, on Christmas Day 1130, King Roger II of Sicily rode to his coronation. In the Cathedral there

---

[1] Acclamation of the monarch is still, eight hundred years later, an integral part of the English coronation service.

awaited him the Archbishop of Palermo and all the Latin hierarchy of his realm, together with representatives of the Greek Church to which he had always shown such favour. Anacletus's special envoy, the Cardinal of S. Sabina, first anointed him with the holy oil; then Prince Robert of Capua, his vassal-in-chief, laid the crown upon his head. Finally the great doors of the Cathedral were flung open and, for the first time in history, the people of Sicily gazed upon their King.

The crisp winter air was loud with the cheering of the populace, the pealing of the bells and the jangle of the gold and silver trappings on the seemingly endless cavalcade which escorted the King back to the Palace. Thither his guests followed him; and there, in a great hall that glowed red with scarlet and purple hangings, he presided at a banquet the like of which had never before been seen in Palermo. The abbot records with amazement how there was not one dish for the meats, not one cup for the wines, that was not of the purest gold or silver; while the servants, 'even those who waited at the tables', were resplendent in garments of silk. Now that Roger was at last a King, he found it both agreeable and politic to live like one.

Coronations are normally less likely to mark the ends of stories than their beginnings; that of King Roger does both. He was to reign for another twenty-three years, during the greater part of which his life would continue in much the same way as before—in building up his own position and that of his country, in playing off successive Popes and Emperors against one another, and in ceaselessly struggling, as his father and uncle had struggled before him, to keep his vassals under adequate control. But 25 December 1130 nevertheless represents something more than a convenient point at which to pause. On that day the object for which the Hautevilles had so long striven—subconsciously perhaps, but striven none the less—was achieved; henceforth Sicily seems to radiate a new confidence, a new awareness of her place in Europe and of the mission she has to fulfil. The chronicles become fuller and more informative; the characters recover their flesh and blood; and the cultural genius that was Norman Sicily's chief legacy to the world bursts at last into the fullness of its flower. The years of attainment are ended; the years of greatness begin.

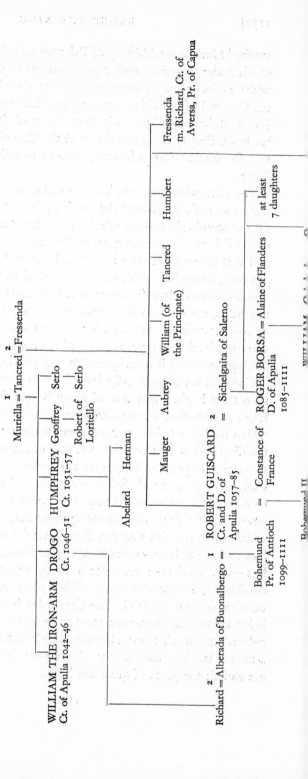

THE HOUSE OF HAUTEVILLE

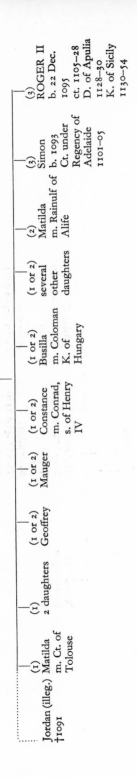

ROGER I
Great Count of Sicily

= 1. Judith of Grantmesnil
2. Eremberga, d. of William of Mortain
3. Adelaide, d. of Manfred of Savona

Jordan (illeg.) †1091

(1) Matilda m. Ct. of Tolouse

(1) 2 daughters

(1 or 2) Geoffrey

(1 or 2) Mauger

(1 or 2) Constance m. Conrad, s. of Henry IV

(1 or 2) Busilla m. Coloman K. of Hungary

(1 or 2) several other daughters

(2) Matilda m. Rainulf of Alife

(3) Simon b. 1093 Ct. under Regency of Adelaide 1101–05

(3) ROGER II b. 22 Dec. 1095 ct. 1105–28 D. of Apulia 1128–30 K. of Sicily 1130–54

THE NORMAN DYNASTY OF AVERSA AND CAPUA

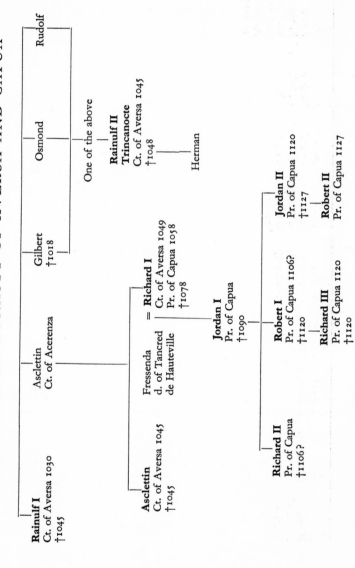

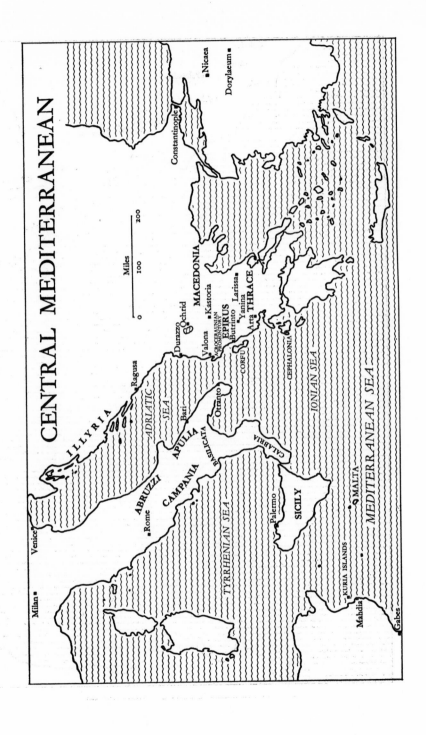

CENTRAL MEDITERRANEAN

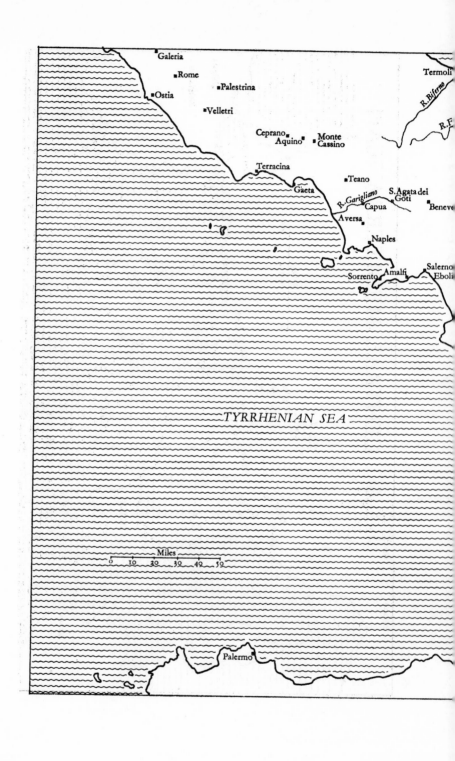

Galeria

Rome

Ostia

Palestrina

Velletri

Ceprano
Aquino

Monte
Cassino

Terracina

Gaeta

R. Garigliano

Teano

S. Agata dei
Goti

Capua

Aversa

Naples

Sorrento

Amalfi

Salerno
Eboli

Termoli

R. Biferno

R. F

Benev

TYRRHENIAN SEA

Miles

0   10   20   30   40   50

Palermo

SOUTHERN ITALY

TREMITI

MONTE GARGANO
Paolo di   Monte
vitate   S.Angelo
         Siponto

Foggia

ADRIATIC SEA

Troia
Bovino
         Barletta
         Cannae✗ Trani Bisceglie
         Canosa   Andria Giovinazzo
Ofanto✗ Montemaggiore Corato
         Minervino   Bari
Melfi   Venosa
                        Monopoli
Lagopesole
Montepeloso   Acerenza
                    Cisternino
                                    Brindisi
              Matera
              Montescaglioso
                    Taranto Oria
                                  Lecce
         S.Martino d'Agri
                                  Nardo
                                  Otranto
                                  Gallipoli

Scalea

R.Crati
         Rossano
    S.Marco
    Argentano   Cariati
    Scribla

              Nicastro
              (Leucastro)
              Squillace

CAPE VATICANO   Mileto
              Nicotera

IONIAN SEA

         Gerace

         ASPROMONTE
Messina   Reggio

YNS

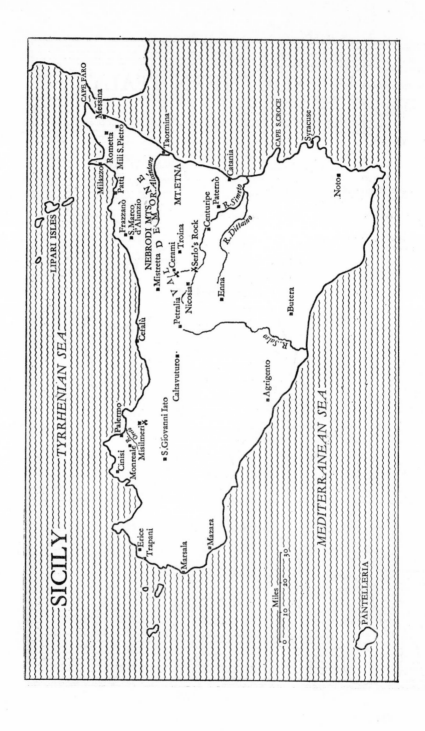

SICILY

TYRRHENIAN SEA

LIPARI ISLES

CAPE FARO

Messina

Milazzo
Rometta
Patti Mili S.Pietro

Taormina

Frazzanò
S.Marco
d'Alunzio

NEBRODI MTS
OR
N.Alcantara
M.OR

MT.ETNA

Catania

Mistretta D E
A L Cerami

Petralia V
X Serlo's Rock
Centuripe
Paternò
R.Simeto

CAPE S.CROCE

Syracuse

Troina

Nicosia

R.Dittaino

Noto

Cefalù

Caltavuturo

Palermo

Cinisi
Monreale S.Ciro
Misilmeri

S.Giovanni Iato

Enna

Butera

R.Salso

Agrigento

Erice
Trapani

Marsala

Mazara

MEDITERRANEAN SEA

Miles
0   10   20   30

PANTELLERIA

BIBLIOGRAPHY

NOTES ON THE PRINCIPAL SOURCES

Amatus (Aimé) of Monte Cassino

Amatus lived as a monk at the monastery of Monte Cassino during the second half of the eleventh century. He was thus presumably an eye-witness of many of the events he chronicles, and is consequently the best source for the early history of the Norman conquest of Italy, covering the period from its beginnings to 1080. His main object is avowedly to tell of the glories of Robert Guiscard and Richard of Capua, but his facts seem to be generally accurate.

The original Latin text of Amatus's work has been lost, but there exist at the Bibliothèque Nationale two early fourteenth-century copies of a translation into an Italianate Old French. A page from one of these (No. 688, *fonds français*) is reproduced opposite p. 49. The work has never to my knowledge been translated into English.

Geoffrey Malaterra

A Benedictine monk of Norman origin, Malaterra seems to have come to Apulia as a young man and later to have settled at Robert Guiscard's foundation of S. Eufemia, from which he eventually moved to its daughter house, S. Agata at Catania. At the outset he makes it clear that he is writing on the instructions of Count Roger I, and that his chronicle is based not on documents but on oral tradition and hearsay; it is therefore not surprising that the first part should be rather vague. After 1060, however, his narrative tightens. Apart from one longish digression about Robert Guiscard's Byzantine expedition, he is now dealing with Roger in Sicily to the exclusion of all else, and may well be recording on occasion the Count's own reminiscences; at any rate he is the best—indeed, practically the only—source for Roger's Sicilian wars and, in view of his semi-official standing, he is presumably fairly trustworthy. His chronicle stops in 1099. No English or French translations exist.

William of Apulia

William's epic poem was written at the instigation of Pope Urban II and is dedicated to Roger Borsa. It can be dated fairly accurately to the last few years of the eleventh century—probably between 1095 and 1099. It tells the story from the beginning until the death of Robert Guiscard in 1085, and the return of Roger Borsa and the army to Italy. Unlike other pro-Norman chroniclers of the period, William was an Italian; Chalandon suggests that he came from Giovinazzo, which certainly seems to get more than its share of favourable mentions. Relying largely on local sources, he is particularly useful where events in Apulia are concerned; he is less good on western Italy and Sicily. His work has two main themes—the providential succession of the Byzantines by the Normans, and the glorification of the House of Hauteville. There is a French translation by Marguérite Matthieu (see below).

Leo of Ostia

Leo Marsicanus came from a noble family of the Marsi and entered Monte Cassino in about 1061. Forty years later Paschal II created him Cardinal-Bishop of Ostia. He was a personal friend of Abbot Desiderius, at whose request he wrote his chronicle of the monastery and to whom it is dedicated. Although the work was begun only after 1098, Leo's first draft takes no note of Amatus and is based on archives and oral traditions; later, however, he seems to have come across his predecessor's work and rewrote much of his own in consequence, bringing his account up to the year 1075. It was subsequently continued by Peter the Deacon who, though he was to become librarian of the monastery and to play an important part in its affairs, proved an unscrupulous and untrustworthy chronicler: Chalandon, in a rare burst of feeling, speaks of his '*détestable réputation*'. Leo's own work, however, is well-informed and of considerable value. There is no English or French translation.

Falco of Benevento

Member of one of the leading families of Benevento, a Palace notary and scribe, Falco wrote a retrospective history of his own city and South Italy as a whole between 1102 and 1139. It is of interest not only for its own qualities—it is reliable, methodical, vivid, and contains much of which its author was an eyewitness—but also because it reflects the opinions of a Lombard patriot, for whom the Normans were little better than a bunch of uncivilised brigands. An Italian translation exists and is listed below.

Alexander of Telese

Alexander, Abbot of the monastery of S. Salvatore near Telese, wrote his chronicle at the request of the Countess Matilda, sister of Roger II. Though ostensibly a biography of Roger, the first part is sketchy in the extreme; we are told nothing about Adelaide's regency and the account becomes interesting only from 1127, with the events leading up to the establishment of the Sicilian Kingdom. From that point until 1136, when Alexander abruptly breaks off, he becomes a valuable source—though allowance must be made for his extreme tendentiousness. For him Roger was divinely appointed to bring peace and order to the South, after meting

340

out just punishment for earlier iniquities. Despite his cloth, the Abbot has little respect for the Pope, and even chides Honorius II for his 'insolence'. There is an Italian translation listed below.

I. ORIGINAL SOURCES

1. Collections of Sources
(The abbreviations used elsewhere in this bibliography and in the footnotes follow each entry in parentheses.)
AMARI, M. *Biblioteca Arabo-Sicula*. Versione Italiana, 2 vols. Turin and Rome, 1880–81. (*B.A.S.*)
ARCHIVIO STORICO SICILIANO. (*A.S.S.*)
BOUQUET, M. *et al*. *Recueil des Historiens des Gaules et de la France*. 23 vols. Paris, 1738–1876. New Series, Paris 1899– (in progress). (*R.H.F.*)
Corpus Scriptorum Historiae Byzantinae. Bonn, 1828–97. (*C.S.H.B.*)
GUIZOT, F. *Collection des Mémoires Relatifs à l'Histoire de France*. 29 vols. Paris, 1823–27. (*G.M.H.F.*)
JAFFE, P. *Bibliotheca Rerum Germanicarum*. 6 vols. Berlin, 1864–73. (*J.B.R.G.*)
MIGNE, J. P. *Patrologia Latina*. 221 vols. Paris, 1844–55. (*M.P.L.*)
Monumenta Germaniae Historica, ed. G. H. Pertz, T. Mommsen *et al*. Hanover, 1826– (in progress). (*M.G.H.*)
Monumenta Gregoriana, ed. Jaffé. *J.B.R.G.*, vol. II.
MURATORI, L. A. *Rerum Italicarum Scriptores*. 25 vols. Milan, 1723–51. (*R.I.S.*)
RE, G. DEL. *Cronisti e Scrittori Sincroni della Dominazione Normanna nel Regno di Puglia e Sicilia*. 2 vols. Naples, 1845, 1868. (*R.C.S.S.*)
Recueil des Historiens des Croisades. Publ. Académie des Inscriptions et Belles Lettres, Paris, 1841–1906. *Historiens Occidentaux*, 5 vols (*R.H.C.Occ.*)
WATTERICH, J. M. *Pontificum Romanorum qui fuerunt inde ab exeunte saeculo IX usque finem saeculi XIII vitae ab aequalibus conscriptae*. Leipzig, 1862. 2 vols. (*W.P.R.*)

2. Individual Sources
ALBERT OF AIX. *Liber Christianae Expeditionis pro Ereptione, Emundatione et Restitutione Sanctae Hierosolymitanae Ecclesiae*. In R.H.C.Occ., vol. IV.
ALEXANDER OF TELESE. *Rogerii Regis Siciliae Rerum Gestarum Libri IV*. In R.C.S.S., vol. II (with Italian translation).
AMATUS OF MONTE CASSINO. *Ystoire de li Normant*, ed. V. de Bartholomaeis, Fonti per la Storia d'Italia, Scrittori, Rome, 1935.
ANNA COMNENA. *The Alexiad*, tr. E. Dawes, London 1928.
Annales Barenses. In *M.G.H. Scriptores*, vol. V.

341

ANNALES BENEVENTANI. In *M.G.H. Scriptores*, vol. III.

AN-NUWAYRI, ed. Amari, with Italian translation. *B.A.S.*, vol. II.

ANONYMUS VATICANUS. *Historia Sicula*. In *R.I.S.*, vol. VIII.

AT-TIGANI, ed. Amari, with Italian translation. *B.A.S.*, vol. II.

BERNARD OF CLAIRVAUX, ST. *Vita Prima*. In *M.P.L.*, vol. 185.

BRUNO. *Vita Sancti Leonis IX*. In *W.P.R.*, vol. II.

CEDRENUS, GEORGIUS. *Synopsis Historiarum*, ed. Bekker. In *C.S.H.B.* Bonn, 1839. 2 vols.

EADMER. *Historia Novarum in Anglia et de Vita Anselmi*, tr. R. W. Southern. London, 1962.

FALCO OF BENEVENTO. *Chronicon*. In *R.C.S.S.*, vol. II (with Italian translation).

GLABER, RADULF. *Historiarum Sui Temporis, Libri V*. In *R.H.F.*, vol. X.

IBN AL-ATHIR. *Kamel al Tawarikh*, ed. Amari, with Italian translation. *B.A.S.*, vol. I.

IBN HAMDIS OF SYRACUSE. Ed. Amari, with Italian translation. *B.A.S.*, vol. II.

IBN JUBAIR. *Account of a visit to Sicily*. French translation, with notes by M. Amari, *Journal Asiatique*, Series IV, vols 6 and 7, December. 1845, January/March 1846; Italian translation in *B.A.S.*, vol. I.

JOHN OF SALISBURY. *Historia Pontificalis*, ed. with translation by M. Chibnall. London, 1956.

LEO OF OSTIA (MARSICANUS). *Chronicon Monasterii Casinensis*. In *M.G.H. Scriptores*, vol. VII, and *M.P.L.*, vol. 173.

MALATERRA, GEOFFREY. *Historia Sicula*. In *M.P.L.*, vol. 149 and *R.I.S.*, vol. V.

ORDERICUS VITALIS. *The Ecclesiastical History of England and Normandy*, tr. with notes by T. Forester. London 1854. 4 vols.

PSELLUS, MICHAEL. *Chronographia*, tr. E. R. A. Sewter. London, 1953.

ROMUALD OF SALERNO. *Chronicon*. In *R.C.S.S.*, vol. I with Italian translation; also in *M.G.H., Scriptores*, vol. XIX or *R.I.S.*, vol. VII.

SKYLITZES, JOHN. ’Επιτομή ἱστοριῶν, ed. Bekker (Cedrenus's Copy of main section). In *C.S.H.B.*, vol. II.

WIBERT. *Vita Leonis IX*. In *W.P.R.*, Vol. I.

WILLIAM OF APULIA. *Gesta Roberti Wiscardi*. In *M.G.H., Scriptores*, vol. IX. For French translation see M. Mathieu, *Guillaume de Pouille: La Geste de Robert Guiscard*. (Istituto Siciliano di Studi Bizantini e Neoellenici. Palermo, 1961.)

WILLIAM OF MALMESBURY. *Gesta Regum Anglorum*. In *M.P.L.*, vol. 179 and *M.G.H., Scriptores*, vols X, XIII. English translation with notes by J. A. Giles, London, 1895.

WILLIAM OF TYRE. *Belli Sacri Historia and Historia Rerum in Partibus Transmarinis Gestarum*. *R.H.C.Occ.*, Vol. I. Also with French translation in *G.M.H.F.*, vols. 16–18.

II. MODERN WORKS

AMARI, M. *Storia dei Musulmani di Sicilia.* 3 vols. Florence, 1854–72.

Atti del Convegno Internazionale di Studi Ruggeriani (21–25 Aprile, 1945). Società Siciliana di Storia Patria, Palermo, 1954.

BARLOW, J. W. *A Short History of the Normans in South Europe.* London, 1886.

BIBICOU, H. 'Une page d'histoire diplomatique de Byzance au XIe. siècle: Michel VII Doukas, Robert Guiscard et la pension des dignitaires', *Byzantion*, 29–30, 1959/60.

Biblioteca Storica Principato, vol. XVI, *Il Regno Normanno.* Istituto Nazionale Fascista di Cultura, 1930.

BLOCH, H. 'The Schism of Anacletus II and the Glanfeuil Forgeries of Peter the Deacon of Monte Cassino', *Traditio,* VIII, 1952 (Fordham University).

BORDENACHE, R. 'La SS. Trinità di Venosa, Scambi ed Influssi architettonici ai tempi dei primi Normanni in Italia', *Ephemeris Dacoromana, Annuario della Scuola Romena di Roma,* VII, 1938.

BUCKLER, G. *Anna Comnena.* London, 1929.

BURY, J. B. *History of the Later Roman Empire.* London, 1889. 2 vols.

— *History of the Eastern Roman Empire.* London, 1912.

— 'The Roman Emperors from Basil II to Isaac Komnenos', *English Historical Review,* IV, 1889.

CAHEN, C. *Le Régime Féodal de l'Italie Normande.* Paris, 1940.

— 'Notes sur l'histoire des croisades et de l'orient latin', *Bulletin de la Faculté des Lettres de l'Université de Strasbourg,* XXIX, 1950–51.

Cambridge Medieval History. 8 vols. Cambridge, 1911–36.

CASPAR, E. *Roger II und die Gründung der normannisch-sicilischen Monarchie.* Innsbruck, 1904.

— *Die Legatengewalt der normannisch-sicilischen Herrscher im 12. Jahrhundert.* Rome, 1904.

Catholic Encyclopaedia, The, ed. C. G. Herbermann. 15 vols. London and New York, 1907–12.

CHALANDON, F. *Essai sur le Règne d'Alexis I Comnène.* Paris, 1900.

— *Histoire de la Domination Normande en Italie et en Sicile.* Paris, 1907. 2 vols.

COHN, W. *Die Geschichte der normannisch-sicilischen Flotte unter der Regierung Rogers I und Rogers II, 1060–1154.* Breslau, 1910.

CRONIN, V. *The Golden Honeycomb.* London, 1954.

CURTIS, E. *Roger of Sicily.* New York, 1912.

DELARC, O. *Les Normands en Italie.* Paris, 1883.

Dictionary of National Biography.

Dictionnaire de Théologie Catholique, ed. Vacant and Mangenot. 9 vols in 15. Paris, 1926–50.

Dictionnaire d'Histoire et de Géographie Ecclésiastiques, ed. Baudrillart. Paris, (in progress).

DIEHL, C. *Etudes Byzantines*. Paris, 1905. 2 vols.

— *L'Art byzantin dans l'Italie Méridionale*. Paris, 1894.

DOUGLAS, N. *Old Calabria*. London, 1920.

Enciclopedia Italiana.

Encyclopaedia Britannica. 11th edn.

FASOLI, G. 'Problemi di Storia medievale siciliana', *Siculorum Gymnasium* N.S.4. 1951.

FOORD, E. *The Byzantine Empire*. London, 1911.

FREEMAN, E. A. *A History of Sicily*. 4 vols. London, 1891–94.

FUAINO, M. 'La Battaglia di Civitate (1053)' in *Archivio Storico Pugliese*, II, fasc. 1–2, 1949.

GAUTTIER DU LYS D'ARC. *Histoire des Conquêtes des Normands en Italie, en Sicile et en Grèce*. Paris, 1830.

GAY, J. *L'Italie Méridionale et l'Empire Byzantin*. Paris, 1904.

GIBBON, E. *The Decline and Fall of the Roman Empire*, ed. J. B. Bury. London, 1896. 7 vols. (See especially Chap. LVI.)

GREGOIRE, H., and DE KEYSER, R. 'Le Chanson de Roland et Byzance', *Byzantion*, XIV, 1939.

GREGOROVIUS, F. *History of the City of Rome in the Middle Ages*, tr. A. Hamilton. 8 vols. in 13, London, 1894–1902.

HASKINS, C. H. *The Normans in European History*. London, 1916.

— 'England and Sicily in the twelfth century', *English Historical Review*, July and October, 1911.

— *Studies in the History of Mediaeval Science*. Cambridge, Mass., 1924.

JAMISON, E. 'The Sicilian Norman Kingdom in the Mind of Anglo-Norman Contemporaries', *Papers of the British Academy*, XXIV, 1938.

— 'The Norman Administration of Apulia and Capua, especially under Roger II and William I, 1127–66', *Papers of the British School at Rome*, VI, 1913.

JORANSON, E. 'The Inception of the Career of the Normans in Italy', *Speculum*, XXIII, July 1948.

JORDAN, E. 'La politique ecclésiastique de Roger I et les origines de la "Légation Sicilienne"', *Le Moyen Age*, 33/34, 1922–23.

LENORMANT, A. *La Grande Grèce*. 3 vols. Paris, 1881–84.

LA LUMIA, I. *Studi di storia siciliana*. Palermo, 1870. 2 vols.

MASSON, G. *The Companion Guide to Rome*. London, 1965.

MENAGER, L. R. 'L'Institution Monarchique dans les Etats Normands d'Italie', *Cahiers de Civilisation Médiévale*, II, 1959.

— 'Les Fondations Monastiques de Robert Guiscard, Duc de Pouille et de Calabre', *Quellen und Forschungen aus Italienischen Archiven und Bibliotheken*, 33, 1959.

— 'La "Byzantinisation" réligieuse de l'Italie Méridionale (IX–XIIe.

344

siècles) et la politique monastique des Normands d'Italie', *Revue d'Histoire Ecclésiastique*, 53/4, 1958–59.

MOR, C. G. 'Roger II et les assemblées du royaume normand dans l'Italie méridionale', *Revue historique de droit français et étranger,* Série IV, 36, 1958.

OSBORNE, J. VAN WYCK. *The Greatest Norman Conquest.* New York, 1937,

OSTROGORSKY, G. *History of the Byzantine State,* tr. Joan Hussey. Oxford. 1956.

PACE, B. *I barbari e i bizantini in Sicilia.* In *A.S.S.,* vols 35, 36. Palermo, 1911.

PARDI, G. 'Storia demografica della città di Palermo', *Nuova Rivista Storica,* 3, 1919. (Corrected by J. Beloch, *Bevölkerungsgeschichte Italiens,* I, Berlin, 1937.)

PONTIERI, E. *Tra i Normanni nell' Italia Meridionale.* Naples, 1948.

ROUSSET, P. *Les Origines et les Caractères de la Première Croisade.* Neuchâtel, 1945.

RUNCIMAN, S. *History of the Crusades.* Cambridge, 1954. 3 vols.

— *The Eastern Schism.* Oxford, 1955.

SCHLUMBERGER, G. *L'Epopèe byzantine à la fin du Xe siècle.* Paris, 1896–1905. 3 vols.

STEFANO, G. DI. *Monumenti della Sicilia Normanna.*

STEINBERG, S. I Ritratti dei Re Normanni di Sicilia', *La Bibliofila,* XXXIX, 1937.

SYMONDS, J. A. *Sketches in Italy and Greece.* London, 1874.

WALEY, D. P. '"Combined Operations" in Sicily, 1060–78', *Papers of the British School at Rome,* XXII, 1954.

WHITE, L. T. *Latin Monasticism in Norman Sicily.* Pub. 31 (Monograph 13), Medieval Academy of America. Cambridge, Mass., 1938.

WILL, C. *Die Anfänge der Restauration der Kirche im 12. Jahrhundert.* Marburg, 1859–61.

WILLIAMS, W. *St Bernard of Clairvaux.* Manchester, 1953.

INDEX

NOTE: *The names of countries and peoples occurring constantly in the text, e.g. Italy, Sicily, Lombards, Byzantines, etc., are not included in the index. Nor are those of modern historians listed in the bibliography.*

Ather, Cape, 245
Aubrey de Hauteville, 40
Augsburg, 213
Avellino, 328
Aversa, 37–8, 40, 43, 59, 62, 67–8, 74, 79, 108, 131, 216
Ayub ibn Temim, 155–6, 164, 166–7
Azzo, Marquis of Este, 202, 217

Baldwin, King of Jerusalem, 286–9, 294
Bamberg, 20, 23–6, 32, 80
Bari, 9, 12, 14–15, 25, 60–2, 70, 111, 126, 132, 138, 148, 168–73, 174, 195, 245, 269, 305, 313, 317
Basil I, Byzantine Emperor, 12–13
Basil II, the Bulgar-Slayer, Byzantine Emperor, 19–20, 22–3, 33–5, 45
Basil of Gerace, 149
Beatrice, Marchioness of Tuscany, 121, 202
Belisarius, 51, 229
Benedict, St, 15, 27, 110
Benedict VIII, Pope, 22–9, 33, 73
Benedict IX, Pope, 73–4, 80, 95, 123
Benedict X, Pope, 122–4
Benevento, 10–11, 22, 28, 35, 74–5, 82–5, 89–90, 94–5, 99–100, 111, 127, 129, 199, 203, 214–16, 219, 243, 266, 309–15, 328–9
Bernard of Clairvaux, St, 327–8
Bernavert, Emir of Syracuse, 254–8, 298
Bertha of Turin, Western Empress, 238–9
Bethlehem, 286
Biferno, river, 90
Bisceglie, 194
Bisignano, 78
Bohemund I of Taranto, Prince of Antioch, childhood, 116, 118; passed over in succession, 195–6, 258–9; on Robert Guiscard's Byzantine expeditions, 227–8, 231–2, 235, 243–5; struggle with Roger Borsa, 249–51, 258–60, 267–9; on First Crusade, 277, 285; death, 285–6, 303–4. Other references, 247
Bohemund II, Prince of Antioch, 304, 307, 312
Boioannes, Basil, Catapan, 19, 21, 23, 25–6, 28–31, 33–5, 45
Boioannes, his son, 61–2
Boniface del Vasto, Marquis of Savona, 280
Bovino, 82, 90

Bradano, river, 313, 324
Brindisi, 9, 138, 162, 165, 226–7, 260, 312, 317, 319
Brixen (Bressanone), 219
Bruno, St, 282
Butera, 156, 260, 269
Butrinto, 228, 244
Byzantius of Bari, 170

Calixtus II, Pope, 305, 321
Caltavuturo, 156
Cannae, 19–20, 61, 162
Canosa di Puglia, 194, 236, 247, 285
Canossa, 194n., 213–15, 218, 236
Capua, 11, 26–7, 29–31, 33–6, 38, 40, 74, 88, 95, 108–9, 124–5, 127, 129, 195, 200, 212–13, 215–16, 263n., 265, 269, 272–4, 303, 305, 312, 314, 322, 329
Cariati, 129, 132
Cartomi, Elias, 254
Castel Sant' Angelo, 159n., 236–8, 240, 270
Castello Maniace, Syracuse, 55n.
Castrogiovanni, see Enna
Catania, 133, 135, 141, 176–7, 189, 254–6, 271, 278
Centuripe, 143
Cephalonia, 245, 252
Ceprano, 218–20, 237, 262
Cerami, 156–8 160, 166, 184
Cerularius, Patriarch Michael, 97, 99–105
Chanson de Roland, 246
Charlemagne, Western Emperor, 9–12, 127
Charles III, the Simple, King of France, 6
Christodulus, 292–3, 298–301, 310
Cinisi, 253
Cisternino, 194
Cîteaux, 328
Civitate, 90–6, 97, 100, 107–8, 110, 126, 203, 240
Clement II, Pope, 74–5, 80, 82, 127
Clement III, Anti-Pope, 219, 234–9, 242–3, 261, 265–6, 268
Clermont, 276
Cluny, 268, 323, 327–8
Coloman, King of Hungary, 278
Comnena, Anna, 69, 78, 117, 206n.–207n., 223–6, 231–2, 244–5, 248
Conrad II, the Salic, Western Emperor, 32–3, 35, 41–3, 73, 81
Conrad III of Hohenstaufen, King of Germany, 327–8

348

Geoffrey de Hauteville, son of Tancred, 39, 107, 198–9
Geoffrey de Hauteville, son of Roger I, 281
George of Antioch, 292–3, 299, 301–2, 310, 317
Gerace, 132, 149–51, 254
Giato (S. Giuseppe Iato), 253
Gibbon, Edward, 6, 67, 89, 109n., 117, 119, 247, 248
Gilbert, 20
Giovinazzo, 62, 64, 180, 194, 339
Girard of Buonalbergo, 68n., 78, 92
Gisulf II, Prince of Salerno, 87–8, 107–8, 116–17, 129, 180, 201, 203, 210–14
Glaber, Radulph, 29
Godfrey IV, the Bearded, Duke of Lorraine, 111n., 121–3
Godfrey V, the Hunchback, Duke of Lorraine, 202
Godfrey of Bouillon, 285
Gregory the Great, St, 5, 243, 324n.
Gregory VI, Pope, 73–4
Gregory VII, Pope, 81, 189; election, 196; character, 196–7; relations with Robert Guiscard, 198–204, 214–18; quarrel with Henry IV, 205–10, 213–14; invests Robert Guiscard at Ceprano, 218–19; havers over Byzantine expedition, 225–6; recalls Robert Guiscard from the Balkans, 233; besieged in Rome by Henry IV, 234–42; dies at Salerno, 243, 245; names successors, 261; his policy followed by Urban II, 271. *See also* Hildebrand
Gregory, Bishop of Vercelli, 207–8
Grimoald, Prince of Bari, 305, 311, 317, 319, 329
Guiscard, Robert, *see* Robert Guiscard
Guy de Hauteville, son of Robert Guiscard, 244
Guy of Salerno, 183
Guy, Duke of Sorrento, 66, 87–8, 108

Hassan ibn Ali, 290, 296–7, 300–1
Hastings, 96, 163, 231
Hauteville, *see Christian names*
Hauteville, family, 38–40
Hauteville-la-Guichard, 39, 284
Helena, daughter of Robert Guiscard, 223–7, 251
Henry II, the Holy, Western Emperor, 20–2, 23–32

Henry III, Western Emperor, 72–5, 80, 82, 85, 89, 94, 106, 119–20, 123, 127
Henry IV, Western Emperor, 120–1, 125, 129–30, 204–10, 213–15, 218–19, 226, 233–40, 262, 265, 272
Henry V, Western Emperor, 293, 303–5
Henry I, King of England, 274, 323
Henry II, King of England, 7, 8
Herman, son of Rainulf II of Aversa, 79
Herman, son of Humphrey de Hauteville, 180, 194, 235–6
Hildebrand, Archdeacon, secures election of Stephen IX, 119–20; of Nicholas II, 122; appeals to Normans, 123; part in papal election reform, 124–5, 130; supports Alexander II, 159, 195, 262n.; elected Pope, 196. *See also* Gregory VII, Pope
Honorius II, Pope, 308–18, 322, 324–7
Honorius II, Anti-Pope, 159, 341
Hugh of Este, 217
Hugh of Jersey, 253
Hugh, Archbishop of Lyons, 237, 261, 264–5
Humbert de Hauteville, 40
Humbert of Mourmoutiers, Cardinal, 99–105, 119, 122
Humphrey de Hauteville, Count of Apulia, 39–40, 75, 79, 87, 90, 92–3, 95, 107–8, 164, 247

Ibn al-Athir, 135, 277, 296
Ibn Hamdis of Syracuse, 252, 290
Ibn Hamud, Emir of Enna, 260–1
Ibn Haukal, 177
Ibn al-Hawas, 133, 135–8, 141–5, 160, 164, 166, 260
Ibn at-Timnah, Emir of Syracuse, 133, 135–6, 138, 141–2, 144, 145, 148, 151, 155, 160, 176
Innocent II, Pope, 325–8
Isaac I Comnenus, Byzantine Emperor, 229
Ithaca, 245

Jericho (Orikos), 246
Jerusalem, 9, 86, 182, 245, 284, 286–9, 293–4
Jews, 23n., 323
Jocelin of Molfetta, Duke of Corinth, 164, 171–2
John XIX, Pope, 33, 73
John, Abbot of Fécamp, 82

John the Orphanotrophos, 46, 48, 57, 63–4, 99
John, Bishop of Trani, 99–100
Jordan, Count of Ariano, 306, 309
Jordan I, Prince of Capua, 214–18, 224, 235, 237, 259, 262–5, 269
Jordan, natural son of Roger I, 252, 254–7, 280–1
Judith of Evreux, wife of Roger I, 146–7, 151–4, 156, 176, 192, 278
Justinian I, Byzantine Emperor, 11, 51

Kairouan, 47, 133
Kastoria, 233, 235, 254
Kuria islands, 298n.

La Cava, Abbey, 79, 304, 307
Lagopesole, 319
Larissa, 243
Lateran Palace, Rome, 73, 95, 122, 125, 240–1, 268, 325–7
La Torre, Monastery, 282
Laurentius, Bishop of Siponto, 4, 5
Lavello, 60, 75
Lecce, 107
Legatine Powers, 273–4, 294
Leo I, Pope, 242
Leo IV, Pope, 159n.
Leo IX, Pope, 80–96, 97, 99–102, 111, 119–23, 196–7, 215
Leo VI, the Wise, Byzantine Emperor, 12
Leo di Benedicto Christiano, 122
Leo, Bishop of Ochrid, 97, 99–100, 102
Leo, Bishop of Ostia, 76, 340
Lipari, 271–2
Lothair I, Western Emperor, 124
Lothair III, the Saxon, King of Germany, 327–8

Mabilla de Grantmesnil, 319n.
Mahdia, 277, 294–302
Malaterra, Geoffrey, 39, 60, 106, 113–14, 117n., 140, 144, 149, 151, 153–4, 156–8, 161–3, 166–7, 169, 172, 183–4, 229, 233, 254n., 267, 273, 311, 339
Malta, 176, 269
Malvito, 77
Manfred of Hohenstaufen, King of Sicily, xiii
Manfred, Marquis, 280
Manfred, Bishop of Mantua, 324n.

Maniakes, George, 47, 54–6, 58–9, 64–5, 67, 137, 142
Mantzikert, 200, 230, 232
Margaret of Navarre, Queen of Sicily, 54n.
Marsala, 298
Matera, 62, 64
Matilda, Countess of Alife, 282, 309, 340
Matilda, Countess of Tuscany, 202–3, 207, 213, 235, 237, 263, 266, 305
Mauger de Hauteville, Count of the Capitanata, 40, 107, 134
Mazara, 133, 183, 271
Melfi, 57–62, 66–7, 70, 79, 107–8, 113, 116n., 126–8, 131, 135, 138, 148, 194, 216, 303, 310, 320–1
Melus, 9–10, 14–15, 17, 19–20, 23–4, 56
Messina, 52–3, 134, 136–44, 146, 148, 158, 160, 175–6, 183, 254, 256, 259, 269, 283, 290–1, 306
Michael IV, the Paphlagonian, Byzantine Emperor, 46–7, 57, 63
Michael V, Calaphates, Byzantine Emperor, 63–4, 70
Michael VII Dukas, Byzantine Emperor, 200, 220, 222–7
Milan, 206
Milazzo, 136
Mileto, 135, 146, 149, 151, 278, 280, 283
Mili S. Pietro, 281n.
Minervino, 107
Misilmeri, 166–7
Mistretta, 255
Monopoli, 62, 64, 170
Montalto, 319
Mont-St-Michel, 9
Monte Cassino, 15, 22–3, 25–6, 27, 29, 40–3, 71–2, 110, 111, 121, 124, 126, 242–3, 251, 262–6, 307, 339–40
Montefusco, 312, 314
Monte Gargano, 3, 9, 67, 75, 81, 83, 90, 232, 310
Montella (Monte Ilaro), 84
Montemaggiore, 61, 66
Montepeloso, 61, 66, 165–6, 174
Monte S. Angelo, 4, 5, 9
Monte S. Felice, 314
Montescaglioso, 306, 310
Monte Siricolo, 61
Muriella de Hauteville, 39

Naples, 11, 21, 29–30, 34–6, 38, 43, 213–15, 273, 280, 291, 329

351